ENGLISH
BATTLEFIELDS
AN ILLUSTRATED ENCYCLOPAEDIA

ENGLISH
BATTLEFIELDS

AN ILLUSTRATED ENCYCLOPAEDIA

MICHAEL RAYNER
FOREWORD BY RICHARD HOLMES

TEMPUS

For Su

First published 2004

Tempus Publishing Limited
The Mill, Brimscombe Port,
Stroud, Gloucestershire, GL5 2QG
www.tempus-publishing.com

© Michael Rayner, 2004

British Library Cataloguing in Publication Data.
A catalogue record for this book is available from the British Library.

ISBN 0 7524 2978 7

Typesetting and origination by Tempus Publishing Limited
Printed in Great Britain

CONTENTS

FOREWORD
by Richard Holmes

It is always dangerous to describe any book as definitive, but I believe that this one comes as close to deserving that rare description as any reasonably can. Michael Rayner is certainly not the first scholar to address this topic: I think particularly of my old boss Brigadier Peter Young and his collaborator Lieutenant Colonel Alfred Burne, and, more recently, of the careful work of David Smurthwaite. Yet as Michael Rayner observes in his introduction, many English battlefields remain very poorly described in print, and are often badly interpreted on the ground, if, indeed, they are interpreted at all. The foundation of the Battlefields Trust has, I believe, made a real difference, but even its best efforts, and those of English Heritage, still do not prevent local authorities from granting planning permission to sites on registered battlefields. We may have restricted, but we have not yet definitively checked, the intrusion of brick, concrete or tarmac onto ground where history was made.

To understand a battle fully we need to know something of the men who clashed there and the weapons they used, the leaders who commanded them and the purpose of their action. Yet we must also have a sense of the ground they fought on, and one of the great strengths of Michael Rayner's work is its feel for the field. His entry on Bosworth, for instance, reflects the current disagreements over the site of the battle, concludes that with the current state of research we cannot take a definitive view, and rightly commends Leicestershire County Council for its fine visitor centre. I regularly ride my

sturdy grey horse Thatch over the 1644 battlefield of Cheriton, and agree with
the author that the battle monument is actually to the north of the field itself;
this is one of the many examples of the simple commemoration of a battle not
necessarily helping the casual visitor. His use of the best modern scholarly
assessment, flagged up as a key reference for each battle, provides the serious
student with further reading, but the format and liberal use of maps will not
deter the less committed.

   This is understandably strong in the major key, with important actions like
Towton, Naseby and Sedgemoor described at length. Yet I particularly like its
inclusion of minor key, which is often so hard to hear. For instance, the action
at Winwick Pass on 19 August 1648 was effectively the last act of the Scots-
Royalist invasion, and deserves the mention that it gets here. The battle sticks
in my mind because I recall a Parliamentarian officer writing of how 'a little
spark in a blue bonnet' in the Scottish ranks gallantly held his men together
until he was eventually killed. This brings us to the heart of the matter.
Battlefields, as Churchill put it, are indeed the punctuation marks of history.
Michael Rayner has done us a great service in helping us to make sense of
them, and to begin to understand how men, doing their duty as they saw it,
left their mark on these haunted acres.

                                                                Richard Holmes

ACKNOWLEDGEMENTS

In writing this volume I have been assisted by many individuals and organisations to whom I am most grateful: without their help, selflessly given, this work would be all the poorer. In particular I would like to thank all members of the Battlefields Trust, past and present, for their support, advice and good company over the last ten years or more. Without them I would never have been in the position to write this work. To name just a few of these who have aided my thoughts on various battlefields in sun, wind and (too often) rain: Frank Baldwin, Alastair Bantock, Andrew Boardman, Matthew Bennett, David Buxton, David Chandler, David Cooke, Alastair Cowan, David Delaney, Iain Dickie, Steve Goodchild, Paddy Griffith, Philip Haigh, Ann Hannon, Michael Hannon, Martin Marix Evans, Peter Marren, James Parker, Peter Norton, Christopher Scott, Jonathan Smith, Frances Sparrow, Tony Spicer, Ken Taylor, Paul Taylor, Kelvin van Hasselt, Harvey Watson, Charles Wesencraft. Glenn Foard, the Battlefield Trust's Project Officer, has been most generous with advice and practical help, while Dr Paul Stamper of English Heritage has provided further assistance. My sincere thanks go to Richard Holmes for agreeing to write a foreword for this, my first book, especially as he has so many demands on his time. Stephen Beck has been more than generous in granting permission to reproduce some of his splendidly atmospheric 'picture-maps' of Civil War sieges. Writing a book while pursuing a busy career is certainly not easy and I would like to thank my last three successive headmasters for being so understanding in enabling me to juggle commitments, in particular Michael

Hepworth who gave me permission to attend the inaugural Battlefields Trust conference, and Jim Malcolm of Langley School, Norfolk, where I am currently employed as Deputy Headteacher. Colleagues have also been patient, while various students have shown a great deal of interest in this project, although sometimes I suspect this is an effort to avoid more serious work! In particular I must thank Adam Ainley, Joshua Hirst, Howard Lloyd, Helen Mann, William Nokes, Emma Tills, Jake Titterington, Jason Williams, Jolyon Wright, my Year Eleven History GCSE set and Year Eight class of 2002–2003. Jonathan Reeve at Tempus has been the driving force behind this project from the start, for which I thank him. Most of all I owe a huge debt of gratitude to my mother, father and brother, David, for instilling in me a love of all things historical. My thanks go to my eldest daughter Emily for being my fieldworker and companion on many expeditions, and to Holly, my youngest, for allowing me to monopolise the home computer. Finally, gratitude goes to my wife Su, for her never-failing support, patience and encouragement, without which this book would most certainly not have been written.

INTRODUCTION

This volume is designed to be a reference work for all English battles and battlefields, explaining not only the events of these actions but also the ground upon which they were fought. To aid the reader the work is organised as an encyclopedia or dictionary, alphabetically and with each entry appearing in a similar format. An effort has been made to identify a key work of reference for further reading for at least the major actions. Forty-two registered battlefields, as well as several others, are provided with a map, while many have illustrations to accompany them.

Since the late 1980s, battlefields in England have increasingly come under the spotlight, due initially to part of the battlefield of Naseby coming under threat from the then new A14 dual carriageway. Opposition to that scheme was largely uncoordinated and confused, and the road-building went ahead. However, what that episode showed was just how poorly researched were many of England's most famous battlefields, with historians disagreeing about the extent and area of the fighting at Naseby. It also made many sit up and realise that battlefields were and are an important part of the historic environment, not least English Heritage, who started to compile the *Register of Historic Battlefields*, which was published in 1995. The Naseby road also led directly to the formation of the Battlefields Trust, which resulted from a conference organised to look at the case for battlefield preservation. The Battlefields Trust, a charity dedicated to the preservation and better interpretation and presentation of battlefields, has worked with English Heritage and other interested parties to raise the profile of battlefields with noted successes over the last ten years, in particular at Blore Heath and Tewkesbury, where developments detrimental to the battlefields have been halted. In addition, the Trust has funded various interpretation projects, most notably at Roundway Down and towards a battlefield trail from Edgehill to Edgcote via Cropredy Bridge. It continues to grow, with a branch network, quarterly journal and programme of events, along with the work of Glenn Foard as its largely Heritage Lottery-funded Project Officer, working towards the creation of an impressive Battlefield Resource Centre. This is available at the Trust's website at www.battlefieldstrust.com along with membership details and further information. If you enjoy visiting battlefields and share the sentiments expressed here I would urge you to consider joining this extremely worthwhile organisation.

In researching this work it has become clear just how poorly interpreted are many of our battlefields, both in print and, more obviously, on the ground. At the same time this volume can only hope to be an up-to-date survey of current knowledge and opinion, with both likely to change in the coming years. Indeed, this would be welcomed, as there is much further research to be undertaken in order to help locate many of the battlefields with certainty and to explain more clearly the actions which took place. To do this the terrain itself is a hugely important source of evidence and this should be reason enough to preserve it. Although the landscape will have changed since the time of any given battle, it is still a source which can be 'read' like any other, so long as these post-battle changes are taken into account and understood. By looking at and walking the landscape, one becomes aware of a range of factors which otherwise would probably be missed. The folds in the ground, lines of sight, and whether there were leaves on the trees are among these factors which can best be understood on the battlefield. Further work in association with archaeology and landscape studies would add to the arsenal of the battlefield researcher. Although the written records are essential to understanding certain aspects of a battle, it is to these other branches of study that one must turn to gain a complete picture. Landscape study can help to interpret the evolution of the battlefield from the time of the battle, in particular to see how its land-use has changed. Here it is essential to know whether the ground at the time of the battle was open or enclosed, or to what extent the land was wooded. The work of archaeologists, especially in regard to carefully recorded artefact-recovery programmes, is also essential to improving our knowledge and refining interpretations. Hopefully this combined approach will lead to a multi-disciplinary school of study, which will greatly improve our understanding of battlefields over the coming years.

In this work I have attempted to follow this approach where possible, including archaeological and landscape details to help formulate my interpretation in addition to using written sources. With the latter, primary sources have been consulted where possible, although inevitably work of scholars past and present has also been utilised. Naturally, any mistakes and errors which do appear in the work are entirely due to my fallibility. The maps, which are drawn by the author, may lack the style of professionally drawn plans, but hopefully do reflect exactly what has been intended. Where possible, frontages of units have been shown as occupying the correct amount of ground, although unit depths are nigh on impossible to show to scale. This approach has served to illustrate the problems experienced when using numbers of participants from the contemporary sources, particularly for pre-seventeenth-century battles. Nearly always the figures are inflated, something which is clear when attempting to fit the chroniclers' numbers onto the landscape. On the other hand there are occasions, for example at Cheriton (1644), when the numbers employed seem barely adequate to occupy the ground. Again, the terrain serves to provide the most useful clues and insights for the historian. All the maps are drawn from one-inch Ordnance Survey maps from the first half of the twentieth century. This means that contour heights were in feet, so although these have been converted into metres, the numbers are not regular multiples of 10m as found on modern OS maps. The maps generally show the positions of the armies at the beginning of the battles, with some further details being provided, such as the location of monuments etc. On occasion, the road pattern has changed since the time of the battles and, where known, the original roads have been shown in addition to the later pattern to enable the visitor to orientate himself, as well as to allow the armchair reader to appreciate the importance of the contemporary routes.

It is hoped that this will be a standard work of reference to be updated where and when appropriate as new editions are published. The author invites suggested additions and, dare he say it, amendments. The aim was to produce a one-volume work with every battle fought in England, together with every major siege and skirmish. With the sieges and skirmishes, discretion had to be employed and I can only apologise if a particular 'favourite' has been omitted. Within the definition of 'battle', naval and air actions have also been included where these have been fought close to the land of England. Only major actions have been included, so that single-ship actions, for example, have not been given an entry. Certainly there is scope for more air actions, although by their nature these are hard to locate. Bombing raids have not been included, even though these could be argued to be 'battles', although the military losses were usually relatively small. Some actions which could best be described as incidents of civil disturbance have been included where there was significant loss of life and a military force was involved on one side, although even here my subjectivity has occasionally been employed, for example in including the curious engagement of Bossenden Wood. Naturally, any selection such as this comes down to one's opinion, but hopefully more has been unexpectedly included than not included.

Hopefully this work will encourage more to visit these important features of England's historic environment and will help to promote their further study. There is no better way to study and enjoy these 'haunted acres' than to visit them oneself, preferably in good company and with the reward of a good pint at the conclusion, over which the merits of the various interpretations can be debated. I can only hope that my own musings, interpretations and conclusions will provoke and promote future debate, encourage more visits to these battlefields and go some small way towards further putting them on the map and thus aiding their preservation. The men who fought and often died at these sites at least deserve their endeavours, triumphs and suffering to be remembered and honoured.

MAPS

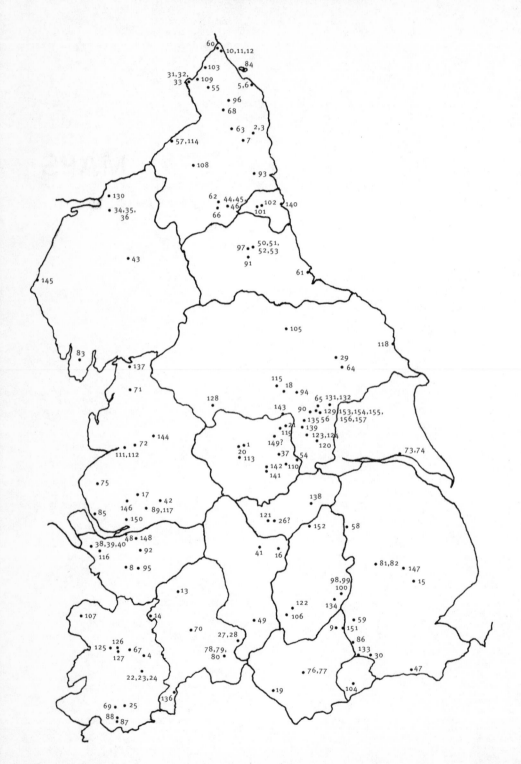

ENGLISH BATTLEFIELDS – THE NORTH

KEY TO MAP

Approximate locations shown where known or most likely

1 Adwalton Moor, battle of, 1643
2 Alnwick, battle of, 1092
3 Alnwick, siege and battle of, 1174
4 Apley Castle, siege of, 1644
5 Bamburgh, siege of, 993
6 Bamburgh Castle, siege of, 1464
7 Battle Bridge, battle of, 875
8 Beeston Castle, siege of 1644-1645
9 Belvoir Castle, siege of, 1645-1646
10 Berwick-on-Tweed, siege of, 1296
11 Berwick-on-Tweed, siege of, 1311
12 Berwick-on-Tweed, siege of, 1318
13 Biddulph, siege of, 1644
14 Blore Heath, battle of, 1459
15 Bolinbroke Castle, siege of, 1643
16 Bolsover, siege of, 1644
17 Bolton, storming of, 1644
18 Boroughbridge, battle of, 1322
19 Bosworth, battle of, 1485
20 Bradford, siege of, 1644
21 Bramham Moor, battle of, 1408
22 Bridgnorth, siege of, 1102
23 Bridgnorth, siege of, 1155
24 Bridgnorth, siege of, 1646
25 Broncroft Castle, siege of, 1645
26 Brunanburgh, battle of, 937
27 Burton Bridge, skirmish of, 1643
28 Burton Bridge, stand-off of, 1322
29 Byland (Abbey), battle of, 1322
30 Bytham Castle, siege of, 1220
31 Carham, battle of, 1018
32 Carham, battle of, 1370
33 Carham, siege of, 1138
34 Carlisle, sieges of, 1136 and 1157
35 Carlisle, siege of, 1315
36 Carlisle, siege of, 1644-1645
37 Castleford, battle of, 948
38 Chester (Cair Legion), battle of, 605, 606 or probably between 613-616
39 Chester, battle of, 893
40 Chester, siege of, 1643-1646
41 Chesterfield, battle of, 1266
42 Chowbent, skirmish of, 1642
43 Clifton Moor, battle of, 1745
44 Corbridge, battle of, 913-915?
45 Corbridge, battle of, 918?
46 Corbridge, battle of, 1312
47 Crowland, siege of, 1643
48 Davenport, battle of, 920
49 Derby, battle of, 917
50 Durham, battle of, 1006

51 Durham, battle of, 1069
52 Durham, siege of, 1088
53 Durham, raid of, 1312
54 Ferrybridge, battle of, 1461
55 Flodden, battle of, 1513
56 Fulford Gate, battle of, 1066
57 Fulhope Law, battle of, 1400
58 Gainsborough, skirmish of, 1643
59 Grantham, skirmish of, 1643
60 Halidon Hill, battle of, 1333
61 Hartlepool, raid of, 1153
62 Heavenfield, battle of, 635
63 Hedgeley Moor, battle of, 1464
64 Helmsley Castle, siege of, 1644
65 Heworth Moor, battle of, 1453
66 Hexham, battle of, 1464
67 High Ercall, sieges of, 1645; 1645; 1646
68 Homildon Hill, battle of, 1402
69 Hopton Castle, siege of, 1644
70 Hopton Heath, battle of, 1643
71 Hornby Castle, siege of, 1643
72 Ho(u)ghton Tower, siege of, 1643
73 Hull, siege of, 1642
74 Hull, siege of, 1643
75 Lathom House, siege of, 1644-1645
76 Leicester, siege of, 943
77 Leicester, siege of, 1645
78 Lichfield, siege of, 1643
79 Lichfield, siege of, 1643
80 Lichfield, siege of, 1646
81 Lincoln, battle of, 1141
82 Lincoln, battle of, 1217
83 Lindal-in-Furness, skirmish of, 1643
84 Lindisfarne, raid of, 793
85 Liverpool, siege of, 1644
86 Losecote Field, battle of, 1470
87 Ludford Bridge, battle of, 1459
88 Ludlow, siege of, 1646
89 Manchester, siege of, 1642
90 Marston Moor, battle of, 1644
91 Merrington, skirmish of, 1346
92 Middlewich, skirmish of, 1643
93 Morpeth Castle, siege of, 1644
94 Myton, battle of, 1319
95 Nantwich, battle of, 1644
96 Nesbit Moor, battle of, 1402
97 Neville's Cross, battle of, 1346
98 Newark, siege of, 1643
99 Newark, siege of, 1644
100 Newark, siege of, 1645-1646
101 Newburn Ford, battle of, 1640
102 Newcastle (upon Tyne), siege of, 1644
103 Norham Castle, siege of, 1513
104 North Luffenham, siege of, 1643
105 Northallerton, battle of, 1138
106 Nottingham Castle, siege of, 1194

107 Oswestry, siege of, 1644
108 Otterburn, battle of, 1388
109 Piper Dene, battle of, 1435
110 Pontefract, siege of, 1648-1649
111 Preston, battle of, 1648
112 Preston, battle of, 1715
113 Rawfolds Mill, attack on, 1812
114 Reidswire, raid of the, 1575
115 Ripon, raid to, 948
116 Rowton Heath, battle of, 1645
117 St. Peter's Fields, encounter of, 1819
118 Scarborough Castle, siege of, 1645
119 Seacroft Moor, battle of, 1643
120 Selby, battle of, 1644
121 Sheffield Castle, siege of, 1644
122 Shelford House, siege of, 1645
123 Sherburn-in-Elmet, skirmish of, 1642
124 Sherburn-in-Elmet, skirmish of, 1645
125 Shrawardine Castle, siege of, 1644-1645
126 Shrewsbury, battle of, 1403
127 Shrewsbury, siege of, 1645
128 Skipton Castle, siege of, 1644-45
129 Skipton Moor, battle of, 1405
130 Solway Moss, battle of, 1542
131 Stamford Bridge, battle of, 1066
132 Stamford Bridge, battle of, 1454
133 Stamford castle, siege of, 1153
134 Stoke, battle of, 1487
135 Tadcaster, battle of, 1642
136 Tettenhall, battle of, 909 or 910
137 Thurland Castle, sieges of, 1643
138 Tickhill Castle, siege of, 1193-1194
139 Towton, battle of, 1461
140 Tynemouth, siege of, 1648
141 Wakefield, battle of, 1460
142 Wakefield, storming of, 1643
143 Wetherby, skirmish of, 1642
144 Whalley, battle of, 798
145 Whitehaven, skirmish of, 1778
146 Wigan, skirmish of, 1651
147 Winceby, battle of, 1643
148 Winnington Bridge, skirmish of, 1659
149 Winwedfeld or Winwaed, battle of, 654
150 Winwick Pass, battle of, 1648
151 Woolsthorpe, siege of, 1646
152 Worksop, battle of, 1460
153 York, battles at, 866 and 867
154 York, battle of, 919 or 923
155 York, battle of, 1069
156 York, battle of, 1069
157 York, siege of, 1644

ENGLISH BATTLEFIELDS – CENTRAL

KEY TO MAP

Approximate locations shown where known or most likely

ENGLISH BATTLEFIELDS – THE SOUTH-EAST

KEY TO MAP

Approximate locations shown where known or most likely

ENGLISH BATTLEFIELDS – THE SOUTH-WEST

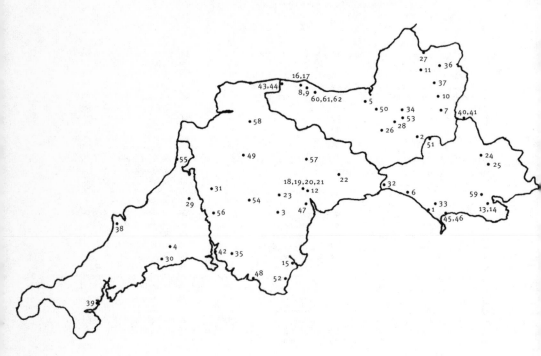

KEY TO MAP

Approximate locations shown where known or most likely

A

Abbotsbury, siege of, early November 1644

Dramatic, if minor, siege of the First Civil War.

Abbotsbury in Dorset had a Royalist garrison from early 1643 commanded by Sir John Strangeways. In early November 1644, Sir Anthony Ashley Cooper led a force of Parliamentarians against them, first driving a force of thirteen musketeers from the church, before moving against the main house. The garrison resisted, but the house was then set on fire after an artillery bombardment followed by burning faggots being thrown through the windows. As the Parliamentarians rushed forward to attack while the defenders were choking from the thick smoke, the Royalist gunpowder magazine exploded, taking many from both sides and much of the house with it. Understandably, nothing remains of the original house, although there are two shot holes in the church's pulpit.

Abingdon, storming of, 11 January 1645

Royalist attempt to capture this important Parliamentarian base towards the end of the First Civil War.

Abingdon had been a Royalist base from 1642 until May 1644, when the troops of the garrison were needed elsewhere. Parliament then occupied the town during their siege of Oxford. King Charles I's nephew, Prince Rupert, attempted to storm the town on 11 January 1645 in a surprise attack with some 1,800 men. After some initial success, the attack was driven back by Major-General Browne, commander of the garrison. The noted Royalist Sir Henry Gage (who was the Governor of Oxford and had led the storming of Boarstall House in 1644) was killed leading an attack near Culham Bridge a little downstream of Abingdon, to be buried in Christ Church Cathedral, Oxford, two days later. His memorial consists of a wall tablet in the Lucy Chapel (it had originally been in the North Transept) near to seven other Royalist memorials.

Adwalton Moor, battle of, 30 June 1643

Important battle which temporarily wrested control of West Yorkshire from the Fairfaxes for King Charles I.

KEY REFERENCES: Cooke, D. *The Forgotten Battle: the Battle of Adwalton Moor 30 June 1643* (Battlefield Press, 1996) and Foard, G. 'The Forgotten Battle: Adwalton Moor – 1643' in *Battlefields Review* (issue 23).

During the early summer of 1643 the Royalists under the Earl of Newcastle made what they hoped would be a decisive move against Lord Fairfax, the Parliamentarian commander. Wakefield changed hands twice, and after the Royalist storming on 22 June, Newcastle decided to march upon Bradford. Fairfax took the bold step of fighting to protect this town, and marched out to meet the larger Royalist force on the morning of 30 June. Fairfax had an army of nearly 4,000 fully-armed men, with a further number of local 'club-men', who were poorly armed. The Royalists had far superior cavalry, perhaps as many as 4,000, with probably as many infantry, although the musketeers were short of supplies. This was a typical encounter battle, with neither side apparently fully prepared to fight and therefore choose the ground for battle. As was the norm, both sides had an advance guard or 'forlorn hope' of musketeers who contested a series of enclosed fields and houses between two hills, with the Parliamentarians having the upper hand due to them possessing a large proportion of musketeers to pikemen among their foot. These musketeers initially contested the imposing Westgate (Wyket, Wiskeard or Wiskett in contemporary sources) Hill. It seems likely, especially with the discovery by Glenn Foard of a detailed map of the immediate area drawn by Christopher Saxton in 1599, that the Royalists were driven from Westgate Hill and then to a lesser hill just short of modern Drighlington, now partially covered by a plantation, but in 1643 probably forming the western edge of

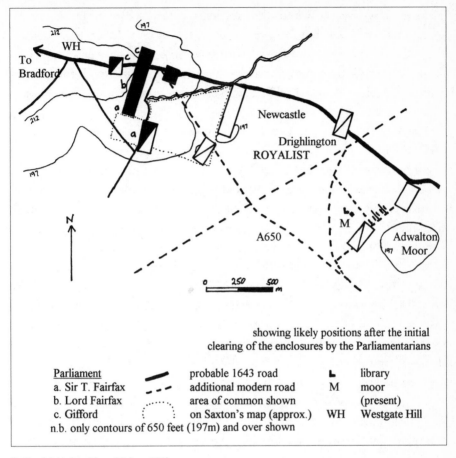

Battle of Adwalton Moor, 30 June 1643.

Adwalton Moor. Unfortunately, Saxton's map, which shows part of Tong and Drighlington Common on its eastern edge, goes no further, so it is not clear whether there were further enclosures before Adwalton Moor, or whether this common land extended directly into the Moor. Only further landscape research will clear this matter up. In the meantime one can see how the latter interpretation fits in with Thomas Fairfax's account, which informs us that

> our Forlorn Hope gained [a hill] by beating theirs into their own body, which was drawn up half a mile further up, on a place called Adderton [Adwalton] Moor.

This suggests that the Parliamentarians advanced down Westgate Hill having formed into order of battle once the Royalist 'forlorn hope' had been driven off. They must have had difficulty crossing the barrier formed by the stream called 'Inmoor Dyke', but managed to reach the edge of the enclosed fields at the edge of the Moor. Lord Fairfax then sent out his son Thomas to the right, with 1,000 musketeers and 300 cavalry, himself in the centre with the infantry reserve and Major-General Gifford with a similar number and type to Thomas Fairfax on the left.

The Parliamentarians forced the Royalists onto and across Adwalton Moor but were then charged on their right (Thomas Fairfax) by a strong force of cavalry, who had struggled to deploy due to old coal pits on that side of the Moor. As Fairfax's men were still behind hedges and a large ditch, the Royalists made no headway, as they tried to fight through a small opening wide enough for only five or six abreast. Having defeated this attack, the Parliamentarians debouched onto the Moor and pressed on towards the Royalists along the crest to their front. By early afternoon it looked as if Parliament was about to win an impressive victory, as the troops neared the top of the Moor and the Royalist guns. This position may well have been back on that part of the Moor which now consists of recreation fields in the village of Drighlington and is marked by a battlefield trail. It is easy to imagine part of the Royalist force being deployed on the first hill at the foot of Westgate Hill, while the slower-moving artillery had to deploy further back on what is today called Adwalton Moor, especially as this was fought as an encounter battle, with the Royalists in particular unable to form up before entering the action. Indeed, this interpretation fits in well with the accounts which tell of Thomas Fairfax ending up out of sight of the main Parliamentarian force. Meanwhile the cavalry on the Royalist right had success against Gifford's wing, possibly due to half-heartedness or worse on Gifford's part. Then, a crucial counter-attack was put in by a 'stand of pikes' led by a Colonel Kirton and helped by the fire of the Royalist gun battery, one of whose likely cannon balls can be viewed in nearby Bolling Hall. This turned the tide and pushed the remaining attacking Parliamentarians back. Lord Fairfax does not appear to have committed his reserve, possibly because they were still beyond the north-west side of the Moor, in the enclosures, or on the intermediate ridge by the modern plantation. The success of the Royalist right and their subsequent advance had in turn almost cut off Thomas Fairfax's command, which had to quit the battlefield via a lane (probably Warren Lane) to Halifax.

The Parliamentarian gamble had failed and Bradford soon fell to Newcastle. Control of West Yorkshire had gone to the Royalists, but Thomas Fairfax was to gain revenge in October when, having linked up with the Eastern Association, a victory was gained at Winceby to the east. The battlefield of

Adwalton Moor has a short trail around the remaining rearward open moorland part of the action, with four stones with panels marking the route. In addition, there is an interpretation board on the outside wall of Drighlington library, which stands on the north-eastern side of the current open land on Moorland Road. The hill where the main first clash took place is beyond this area to the west and is not crossed by public rights of way, while only the eastern lower slopes of Westgate Hill are free from later development.

Aethelingadene, battle of, 1001

Danish victory against the men of Hampshire at Alton, with the English losing five named casualties and having eighty-one others killed, with the Vikings losing more, indicating that this was a hard-fought if relatively minor action.

Aldbourne Chase, skirmish of, 18 September 1643

Skirmish fought two days before the first Battle of Newbury, which helped the Royalists to reach the town of Newbury before their opponents.

The Parliamentarian commander, the Earl of Essex, was closing in on Newbury, an important town securing the passage to London. However, on 18 September 1643, Prince Rupert (nephew of King Charles I) led a surprise attack on Essex's column. His 5,000 cavalry caught Essex's army in order of march, with gaps between units and heavy drizzle making firing muskets very difficult. Rupert's men certainly damaged Essex's rearguard before order was restored. This had the desired result of slowing up the Parliamentarian march, which in turn enabled the Royalists to reach Newbury first, forcing Essex to attempt to fight his way through on 20 September.

Alnwick, battle of, 13 November 1093

Defeat of a Scottish invasion, resulting in the death of King Malcolm III.

King Malcolm III of Scotland invaded northern England in 1093, camping his army just north of Alnwick. Robert de Mowbray led a smaller Anglo-Norman force from Bamburgh Castle, where he was Governor, to attack the Scots. They managed to launch a surprise attack on Malcolm's force, killing the King and his son. It is claimed that he was wounded at the site where there is now a

Alnwick, 1093. An eleventh-century manuscript showing warriors in battle. The round convex shields are clear, as are the large, straight swords and spears. Long-sleeved mail shirts may be shown under short-sleeved tunics.

memorial cross to the east of the B6341, just to the north of Alnwick, and that he died at the site nearby where a hospital was established a hundred years after the battle.

Alnwick, siege and battle of, 1174 (battle on 13 July)

Siege of this important stronghold by the Scots, leading to a battle fought for its relief.

William the Lion of Scotland invaded the north of England in April 1174, capturing Burgh and Appleby, although he failed to take Prudhoe. At that point he crossed the Tyne and moved back into Northumberland, beginning a siege of Alnwick. The English responded and gathered an army together under the leadership of Robert of Estouteville, Rannulf de Glanville, Bernard de Balliol and William de Vesci. Their rapid march took the besieging Scots by surprise, with this being compounded by a heavy mist at Alnwick. After a twenty-four-mile march in five hours, the English force arrived as the mist cleared, revealing William and a group of sixty horsemen nearby in the open. At first it seems that William assumed the force looming out of the mist was that of his own men, and by the time he realised his mistake the only option was to try and fight his way out. This he bravely tried to do, but his horse was killed, leading to his capture. The English took him back to Newcastle in triumph.

Alresford, battle of, *see* Cheriton

Alton, battle of, 13 December 1643

Battle which displayed the tactical skill of Sir William Waller while providing a memorable end-piece with its fighting inside Alton Church.

KEY REFERENCE: Morris, R. *The Storming of Alton and Arundel*, 1643 (Stuart Press, 1993).

The Parliamentarian commander Sir William Waller sensed an opportunity to cut off and destroy a Royalist garrison at Alton in Hampshire in December 1643. Waller conducted a night march with some 5,000 men – an operation which went surprisingly smoothly, with this force appearing to the north, north-west and west of Alton on the morning of 13 December, after a march from Farnham to the north-east. The Royalist commander Lord Crawford had less than 1,000 cavalry and 1,000 infantry, the latter under Colonel Bolle.

Waller positioned his own regiment of foot, along with parts of two others, probably about 1,000 men in total, to the north of Alton, where they waited for the London militia regiments to reach their positions further to the west. The Royalists, realising that they were close to being surrounded, escaped with most of their horse, leaving the foot to defend themselves in the houses and church of Alton, as well as in defensive works they had constructed. The first Parliamentarian force, supported by artillery, forced the Royalists from a large brick house near the church, while the London regiments stormed the enemy trenches and a 'half-moon' earthwork under cover of a fired thatched cottage. This forced the remaining defenders back into the church, churchyard and a large defensive earthwork to the north of the church. After two hours' fighting the remaining Royalists were forced back inside the church, which they proceeded to barricade with dead horses. The Parliamentarians surrounded the church, throwing hand-grenades through the windows before rushing the door. Fighting continued inside the church, as the still visible bullet marks testify. Colonel Bolle died in the hand-to-hand fighting, urging his men to carry on the fight with the threat that he would 'run his sword through the heart of him which first called for quarter'. However, the game was up and the fighting petered out soon after Bolle's death. The victory at Alton enabled Waller to strengthen his hold of eastern Hampshire in the following weeks, while Hopton, the overall local Royalist commander, was forced onto the defensive. As well as the various bullet marks, the church has a plaque commemorating Colonel Bolle.

Anderitum, siege of, 491

Early Anglo-Saxon siege of British forces using a Roman fort for protection.

Anderitum was the Roman Saxon shore fort at Pevensey. Aelle and his son Cissa led the invaders against the Britons. The latter had no escape and were killed to a man.

Apley Castle, siege of, March 1644

Minor castle which changed hands twice during the First Civil War, typifying the fate of many such properties of the period.

Apley Castle in Shropshire was garrisoned by the Royalists during the First Civil War. A Parliamentarian force from Wem captured the castle in March 1644, but the castle was soon retaken by Royalists led by Sir William Vaughan. Following this, the Royalists seemingly slighted the castle to prevent it falling into Parliamentarian hands again.

Archenfield, battle of, 914

Fought by the men of Herefordshire and Gloucestershire against the invading Danes, beating them off in a battle where the Danes were driven back into a park in Archenfield after they had raided up the River Severn and taken the local bishop prisoner.

Arundel, siege of, 17 December 1643–6 January 1644

Parliamentarian siege made possible by William Waller's victory at Alton earlier in December 1643.

KEY REFERENCE: Morris, R. *The Storming of Alton and Arundel*, 1643 (Stuart Press, 1993).

As soon as Alton had been secured after his victory there on 13 December 1643, the Parliamentarian William Waller marched towards the Royalist garrison at Arundel. By dawn on 17 December, skirmishing had begun in advance of the artillery opening up on the earthwork defences from the west side of 'the Great Fishpond'. The Parliamentarian attack came from the north, with some 1,400 men under the immediate command of Potley moving against the defences on either side of 'the Great Fishpond'. They fought their way across the main rampart, but were then thrown back by a counter-attack of Royalist horse. The Parliamentarians managed to remain on the town side of the earthwork rampart, enabling their own horse to cross. A fierce fight ensued in the space between the outer rampart and the town wall, with heavy casualties on both sides, including the serious wounding of the Parliamentarian Lieutenant-Colonel Birch of Hazelrige's regiment of foot. The Lieutenant-Colonel has left us a detailed account through the words of his secretary, who tells us that Birch, wounded in the belly, stopped the hole with his finger and carried on for some minutes before collapsing. The determined assault forced the Royalists back into the castle by late afternoon, leading to the more formal siege which continued until 6 January 1644. The Royalist General Hopton considered attempting a relief of the garrison, but the castle fell before he could organise a large enough force to fight Waller. Many of the garrison had died of fever, with possibly only 200 surviving out of nearly 1,000, although this figure may not take account of those who changed sides.

Ashby-de-la-Zouch, siege of, October 1645–February 1646

Midlands castle in the care of English Heritage, which was not besieged in the First Civil War until late 1645 but fell after a winter siege, leading to the slighting of the castle after the war.

Ashdown, battle of, 8 January 871

Victory of Wessex against the Danes, although this was unable to prevent further Danish advances westwards.

KEY REFERENCE: Burne, A.H. *The Battlefields of England* (Greenhill Books, 1996).

As with the majority of Anglo-Saxon battlefields, that of Ashdown cannot be located with one hundred per cent certainty. However, modern interpretations since Burne's *The Battlefields of England*, which was first published in 1950, have tended to favour a site astride the Ridgeway to the north-east of the village of Compton and north-west of Aldworth. The Danish Vikings had moved into Wessex in 870 and had taken Reading at the end of the year, beating off a Saxon attack on 4 January 871. The Saxons were led by the King of Wessex, Aethelred, with his younger brother Alfred in support. From the *Anglo-Saxon Chronicle* and from Bishop Asser's slightly later account we discover that the Battle of Ashdown was fought four days after the action at Reading, which has led some to place

Part of the *Anglo-Saxon Chronicle* dealing with the build-up to the Battle of Ashdown, 871. The chronicle in its various versions remains the most useful historical source for battles in the Anglo-Saxon period, with other sources such as Asser's *Life of King Alfred* adding further details.

the fighting further to the west, for example above the White Horse at Uffington. However, there is no reason to suppose that the two armies marched hard after Reading and the battle is more likely to have taken place at the site above Compton and Aldworth. Lowbury Hill on the Ridgeway would have made a good rallying and meeting place for the Saxons, just to the north of the Ridgeway, enabling them to block the advance of the Danes from Reading.

The Danes moved forward at first light on 8 January, with one division commanded by Kings Bagsecg and Halfdan and the other by a group of earls. The former were met by King Aethelred while the earls faced Alfred. Alfred thought that force should be met with force and so moved his men forward to attack, himself 'acting courageously, like a wild boar', meeting the Danes at a solitary thorn tree. Aethelred's division joined the mêlée a little later, whether by accident (Asser tells us that he was still at his devotions when the fighting began) or design. These fresh men tilted the balance in the Saxons' favour, probably because they then outnumbered the Danes. King Bagsecg and five earls were among the fatalities leading to the breaking of the Danish army. Many more were cut down in the rout, which went on until the short winter day ended, mercifully drawing proceedings to a close. The Danes regrouped at Reading, from where they launched a renewed assault on Wessex less than a month later.

Ashingdon, battle of, 18 October 1016

Battle which resulted in the partition of England between Edmund 'Ironside' and Cnut (Canute).

KEY REFERENCE: Rodwell, W. 'The Battle of Assandun and its Memorial Church: A Reappraisal' in Cooper, J. (ed.) *The Battle of Maldon: Fiction and Fact* (Hambledon Press, 1993).

The Danes had raided England throughout the 990s, sometimes in conjunction with the Norwegian Olaf Tryggvason. By 1016 the Danes, led by Cnut (Canute) were strong enough, with a fleet of 160 ships according to the *Anglo-Saxon Chronicle,* to besiege London twice and raid across the country to Wiltshire, fighting two battles at Penselwood and Sherston. The Vikings of Cnut were forced away from London by the English King Edmund 'Ironside', but were still able to mount another far-reaching raid, taking their fleet up the River Orwell and then setting off across country into Mercia, although part of the Viking force appears to have been based in Kent, on the Isle of Sheppey (it is possible that Cnut had gone to the Orwell and then to Sheppey, and was forced from there back to Essex from where his raid of Mercia was re-

Ashingdon, 1016. Mounted infantry from an eleventh-century manuscript. It was standard practice among Anglo-Saxon armies and Viking raiding armies to ride to battle before dismounting to fight. The headgear in this picture is a little curious, but probably shows the soft 'Phrygian' hats.

launched.) It is likely that Edmund gathered his army together and mopped up Danish resistance in Kent before turning back across the Thames to track Cnut with the main force. Edmund was joined by Earl Eadric, who, earlier in the year, had taken men and ships over to Cnut's side. Together they overtook Cnut at Ashingdon Hill in Essex, bringing him to battle. The exact sequence of these events is not clear, as Cnut may have been caught on his way to Mercia, or more likely on his way back, being overtaken on his way to the fleet.

The battlefield's location is disputed, with Ashingdon near Southend-on-Sea being the most favoured site. However, a strong case has been put forward by Warwick Rodwell for a site at Ashdon in north-west Essex. Certainly this location fits in better with a route to or from Mercia from the River Orwell, but the key to the correct location lies with the identification of a memorial church or minster, built on the orders of Cnut after the battle. Here, field-name and boundary evidence suggest that the now ruined building may lie beneath or near 'Old Church' field on a hill above Ashdon, especially as the church at Ashingdon and known post-battle land-holdings there do not entirely fit the interpretation of a minster church. Archaeology, led by a resistivity survey, would help to solve this dispute one way or another.

The details of the battle are equally vague, with Edmund forming up on a hill with Cnut below him. The battle was fiercely fought, but Edmund was let down or, worse, betrayed by Eadric, who fled with his men. Cnut won the battle, killing several English earls, while Edmund was able to escape to Deerhurst on the River Severn in Gloucestershire. Cnut followed him and a treaty was arranged whereby Edmund was allowed to retain Wessex, while Cnut was king over the remainder. The issue was finally settled even more conclusively with the death of Edmund on 30 November, which left Cnut to become undisputed king over the whole country.

Assandun, battle of, *see* Ashingdon

Assundun, battle of, *see* Ashingdon

Aston Hall, siege of, 26 December 1642

Occupied by a Royalist garrison, this hall just to the north of Birmingham (still standing and open to the public) was attacked by 1,200 men with artillery, who quickly captured and took over the house for use by Parliament for the rest of the First Civil War.

Aylesbury, battle of, 1 November 1642

Skirmish following the battle of Edgehill, when the Royalists were forced out of Aylesbury.

KEY REFERENCE: Griffin, S. *The Battle of Aylesbury 1642* (Stuart Press, 1998).

There is some doubt over whether this battle took place, and if so, exactly where. This is due to there being only one contemporary account of the engagement which contains several inaccuracies and is heavily biased towards Parliament. Unfortunately, no precise details of the battle's location are given, although it is likely that it took place at Holman's Bridge, just to the north of the town of Aylesbury. Bones of apparently some 247 people were discovered nearby in 1818 but it is not certain whether these date from the battle, especially as this would appear to be too large a number of casualties. According to the Parliamentarian account of the battle, Prince Rupert (who may not have been at Aylesbury at this time) entered the town at 6.00 a.m. with 10,000 horse and foot. They were soon aware of a smaller Parliamentarian force under Balfour approaching the town. Accordingly, Rupert arrayed his cavalry on a narrow front and charged. He was met by a counter-charge, including one to his right flank. The fighting continued until Lord Wilmot, another Royalist commander, was shot in the shoulder, leading to a fall in morale and retreat. This 'good and joyful news' certainly exaggerates the numbers involved and the number of casualties, although it would appear that Balfour did win a small victory over the Royalists at Aylesbury.

Aylesford, battle of, 455

First recorded battle of the Anglo-Saxons in England.

Although impossible to separate fact from myth, this battle, recorded in the *Anglo-Saxon Chronicle,* marks the beginning of the recorded tradition of Anglo-Saxon battles in the fifth century. Aylesford is on the Medway, upstream from the Roman bridge at Rochester. It was here that the Anglo-Saxons, invited into Britain by King Vortigern and led by Hengest and Horsa, turned against their employers, resulting in the death of Horsa. The result of the battle is not recorded.

Babylon Hill, battle of, 7 September 1642

Early skirmish of the first English Civil War, fought outside Yeovil.

KEY REFERENCE: Morris, R. *The Battle of Babylon Hill, Yeovil 1642* (Stuart Press, 2000).

The Marquis of Hertford and Sir Ralph Hopton moved against the largely Parliamentarian or neutral counties of Somerset and Dorset in August and September 1642, using Sherborne Castle as their main base. They were soon besieged there by the Earl of Bedford, but the Royalists put up a vigorous defence which persuaded Bedford to retreat to Yeovil in south Somerset on 2 September. On 5 September at 2.00 p.m. Hopton moved towards Yeovil with probably 400 horse, 100 dragoons and 140 foot. They positioned themselves on Babylon Hill overlooking the town, close to where the modern A30 now sweeps down into Yeovil. In 1642 there were only two lanes giving access down to the bridge at the foot of the hill, with the road to Sherborne going directly up Babylon Hill from what is now a light industrial estate, before climbing the hill through a spectacular rock-cut route, which is now a footpath. The road then follows what is now a minor road via Bradford Abbas to Sherborne. Muskets were fired down at the bridge's guard, but with no effect. After an hour of this firing, Hopton decided to withdraw, but before this was carried out, a Parliamentarian force was seen climbing the hill. With sunset only an hour away, the Royalist horse charged into their Parliamentarian counterparts. Confusion soon reigned, with both sides making gains but then becoming disordered. Any coordinated action must have been impossible down the steep and narrow tracks. With darkness falling, Hopton carried out his retreat to Sherborne, while the Parliamentarians went back into Yeovil, which they abandoned the next day.

Badon, battle of Mount, 490-518?

The most likely named and recorded battle to have taken place involving King Arthur.
KEY REFERENCE: Alcock, L. *Arthur's Britain* (Pelican Books, 1982).

Three central and probably unanswerable questions pertain to this battle: firstly, did it took place at all? secondly, if it did take place, then where did it occur? and thirdly, did Arthur command the Britons? Each of these questions has been the subject of much debate and it is impossible to do justice to them within the scope of this entry. However, it seems safe to say that there was indeed a Battle of Mount Badon, or Mons Badonicus, which took place at the turn of the fifth and sixth centuries, in which the Saxon invaders were heavily defeated, gaining respite for the western Britons for some years. We have the twelfth-century account by Geoffrey of Monmouth, but this is so far removed from the time of the battle and is so riddled with inaccuracies and fabrications that it is impossible to know what is reliable in his account, if anything, despite the weight given to it in many accounts of the battle, notably by Burne. Much closer to AD 500 is the account by the monk Gildas, which, although unreliable in some respects and lacking in detail, does at least give sufficient grounds for accepting that the battle did take place. Gildas probably wrote his account in the 530s and is supported by entries in the margin of the *Easter Annals*, although doubts persist about the dates of these entries and therefore the details contained in them. In particular the reference in these annals to the presence of Arthur at the Battle of Badon may well be a later addition, made once the personality cult of the long lost, and by then largely mythical, king had developed. Further information comes from the *Historia Brittonum*, which provides us with a list of twelve Arthurian battles with Badon being the last, although again the reliability is questionable. Further clues come from the *Welsh Annals*, which talk of a second battle of Badon in the second half of the seventh century, adding weight to the likelihood of there being a first battle.

As to where it took place, the most popular choice is at Liddington Castle above the village of Badbury in Wiltshire, although other Badburys, such as Badbury Rings in Dorset, also have a claim. There is certainly no clue from the sources, other than that the seventh of the twelve listed battles took place in Scotland and the ninth took place at either Caerleon or Chester. Later Welsh sources equate Badon with Bath, providing the possibility that the battle was fought on one of the hills surrounding the town. A hilltop location with fortifications is likely, as Gildas refers to the action as being the Siege of Mons Badonicus, while the entry in the *Easter Annals* speaks of a three-day battle which would also qualify as a siege. To give any further details would be more an act of faith than historical fact, although when one stands on Liddington Hill it is difficult not to be persuaded that Arthur did indeed emerge from the ancient defences with his heavy cavalry to carry all before him.

Bamburgh, siege of, 993

A Viking raiding army besieged, took and looted this important Northumbrian stronghold before moving on to the Humber estuary.

Bamburgh Castle, siege of, late June 1464

Fall of the last Lancastrian stronghold in the North, following defeat at the Battle of Hexham.

With the defeat, capture and execution of many Lancastrian lords following the Battle of Hexham in May 1464, the Yorkists turned to the mopping up of the remaining Lancastrian castles in Northumberland. Alnwick and Dunstanburgh surrendered on terms, but Bamburgh, held by Sir Ralph Grey, refused to do likewise, no doubt because Grey realised that he would receive no mercy as he had swapped sides. The Earl of Warwick, rather than the newly created Earl of Northumberland, led the Yorkists, bringing up three large guns named 'London', 'Newcastle' and 'Dijon'. Grey was knocked unconscious from one of the shots of the latter. While he was 'out cold', his second-in-command negotiated terms for surrender, which unfortunately for Grey led to his own arrest, trial and execution.

Banbury, siege of, August–26 October 1644 and January–8 May 1646

Important Royalist stronghold which held out until nearly the end of the First Civil War.

Banbury in Oxfordshire was initially held for Parliament, but the Earl of Northampton secured the town and its castle for King Charles I on 29 October 1642. The town was taken by Parliament in August 1644, but attempts to capture the castle failed, despite having a battery of guns in St Mary's churchyard. By 1646 the situation had changed, with little chance of relief for the beleaguered garrison under Sir William Compton. Accordingly, the 3,000 besiegers forced the 400 strong garrison to surrender after a five-month siege. Very little survives of the castle, although Banbury Museum (relaunched in 2002) does have a display dedicated to the Civil War.

Barnet, battle of, 14 April (Easter Sunday) 1471

Confused battle of the Wars of the Roses fought in heavy mist, ending with the death of Warwick 'the Kingmaker'.

KEY REFERENCE: Hammond, P.W. *The Battles of Barnet and Tewkesbury* (Alan Sutton, 1990).

Following a brief exile, Edward of York (Edward IV) returned to reclaim the throne from Henry VI of Lancaster, who owed his position to the support of the Earl of Warwick, 'the Kingmaker'. Edward landed at the mouth of the Humber on 4 March 1471 and marched into London on Maundy Thursday, 11 April, taking not just the capital but Henry VI with it. His march had been detected by Warwick, who had hoped that Edward would be refused entry into London, but this was not the case and Edward was able to make use of the military supplies in the Tower of London. The boot was now on the other foot and it was Warwick who ended up on the defensive. He chose a ridge across the Great North Road, just to the north of High Barnet. The written sources are not clear about the exact location of the battlefield and various interpretations have been suggested. However, there is enough on close inspection to be fairly confident that the battle was fought on the plateau-like ridge running perpendicular to the Great North Road through Hadley Green, just to the north of Barnet. Indeed, some iron shot, typical of that fired from hand-guns of the period, has recently been found on Hadley Green to the west of the Great North Road as part of the work for the BBC television series *Two Men in a Trench*. Although the area has a lot of modern development, there is still much open ground to be appreciated. We are told that the Lancastrians under Warwick were camped between half a mile to a mile north of Barnet. The Yorkist scouts discovered this after chasing some of their opponents back to their lines beside a hedge on 13 April. It is likely that part of this hedge still survives, as first identified by Colonel Burne, with its bank and ditch partly intact across the Old Fold Manor golf course. In a letter from a Hanseatic merchant, von Wesel, we find out that Warwick had 'pitched camp a mile beyond the said village [High Barnet], right beside the St Albans high road, on

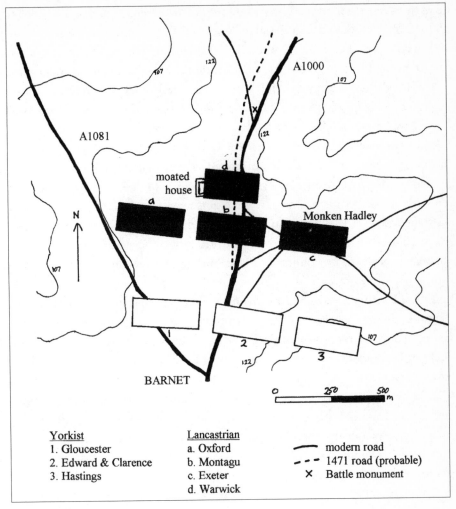

The Battle of Barnet, 14 April 1471.

a broad green'. Not only does this suggest the Great North Road, but the description of the 'broad green' admirably fits the landscape at Hadley Green. Von Wesel goes on to say that Edward's men camped the other side of the road from the Lancastrians, 'right opposite Warwick', which could be taken to support some interpretations of the battle, notably that of Sir James Ramsay (1892.) This places the two armies facing each other, formed up from north to south, rather than west to east. However, the *Arrivall* mentions a west and east end of the lines, while the landscape and strategic situation make Ramsay's interpretation untenable. Von Wesel's quote, if reliable, can be explained simply by accepting that at least most of the Yorkists were on the opposite side of the road from those Lancastrians from whom they had recoiled and sought shelter in the hollows to the east of the main road. Once there, they were still opposite the main force of Warwick to the north. The major remaining concern about the accepted location of the battlefield is that none of the sources mention it being fought at or next to Old Fold House or Hadley Church, or among enclosures which are likely to have existed close to the latter in particular. Given this, along with the possibility that the settlement of Barnet in 1471 could have extended into Monken Hadley (certainly later maps suggest this), making the half a mile to a mile north of Barnet actually meaning this distance to the north of Monken Hadley, the battlefield could be placed on the next cross-ridge to the north. This interpretation is backed up by Taylor placing a battlefield sign at this point on his map of 1759, just to the east of the main road. Clearly further research, especially regarding the nature of the historic landscape, needs to be conducted before one can be certain about this battle's precise location.

Edward seems determined not to let Warwick escape, and so advanced his army as close as possible to the Lancastrians, despite the fact that night was falling. The terrain has several deep folds and valleys, cutting into the plateau, and it is likely that the Yorkists made their camp there, as well as across the high road. This inadvertently benefited them during the night, as Warwick ordered gunfire which overshot its targets, due in part to the closeness of the Yorkists and because many of them would have been out of sight in the hollows. The other consequence of the late evening advance, together with a heavy mist the following morning, was a misalignment of the two armies, with both right wings overlapping the opposing left wings.

Numbers vary considerably from source to source, although 12,000 Yorkists against 15,000 Lancastrians is generally accepted. Each army was divided, as was usual, into three divisions or 'battles', probably along with a reserve, although who commanded which 'battle' varies from account to account. We know that Richard, Duke of Gloucester (later Richard III) commanded the Yorkist van. By custom, this would place them on the right of the line. However, the *Great Chronicle* tells us that the Earl of Oxford was on the Lancastrian right and that his men defeated those of Gloucester, placing the latter on the Yorkist left. In the absence of other clear evidence, this would seem to be the correct interpretation, especially as it is clear that Gloucester commanded the van which took its place on the Yorkist left at Tewkesbury less than a month later. This then gives us, on the Lancastrian side from west to east: Oxford, Montagu and Exeter plus Warwick with a central reserve. On the Yorkist side were, respectively: Gloucester, Edward and Clarence in the centre, and Hastings.

Edward attacked at dawn on Easter Day, eager to keep the initiative. Due to the overlapping of each wing and the heavy mist or fog, the fighting quickly became confused. In the east, the Yorkist advance was hampered by the difficult ground, leaving Edward in the centre to bear the brunt of the fighting for some time. In the west, most of Oxford's Lancastrian 'battle' found themselves unopposed and so advanced from behind their hedge. They soon found Richard of Gloucester's men, who had little hope against greater numbers and a flank attack. The Yorkist left crumbled, but luckily for the rest of the army, Oxford's men streamed down towards High Barnet and the enemy's baggage rather than turning in to attack Edward's centre. Due to the fog, it is likely that the Yorkist centre were unaware of the rout of their left wing, which meant that they were still happy to fight on. Edward and Hastings carried on the fight against Montagu, Exeter and Warwick until Oxford's men started to return to the main fray. Due to their unexpected line of advance, which must have made them appear more like Yorkist reinforcements than their own men, the Lancastrians started to fire at Oxford's troops, leading to cries of treason and much confusion. This mistake was easily made, due not just to the line of their advance, but also to the heavy mist and the fact that their badge was very similar to that of the sun in splendour of Edward of York. In the chaos which resulted, the Yorkists gained the upper hand as the Lancastrian lines started to dissolve amidst the suspicions of treachery.

The Lancastrian line broke and in the ensuing mêlée the heaviest casualties were caused, possibly in the region of 'Dead Man's Bottom' just to the north, including Warwick as he attempted to escape through a wood, probably close to the memorial obelisk on Hadley Green, if the traditional interpretation of the battle is followed. A seal ring, said to have been taken from Warwick's body, is now in Liverpool City Museum. Losses were heavy on both sides, with the Lancastrians' probably in the region of 1,000. That one of these was the Earl of Warwick makes the battle of Barnet highly significant. It also led, along with Tewkesbury, to the throne being secured for Edward IV, and heralded a period of peace after so much bloodshed.

Basing, battle of, 23? January 871

After their success at the battle of Ashdown, King Aethelred of Wessex and his brother Alfred pursued the Vikings to Reading. Marching on to Basing, a battle was fought in which the Saxons were defeated and forced to retreat.

Basing House, sieges of, 6–14 November 1643; 4 June–15 November 1644; 20 August–14 October 1645

Three sieges of the First Civil War of what was probably the finest privately owned house in England.

KEY REFERENCE: Adair, J. (ed.) *They Saw It Happen: Contemporary Accounts of the Siege of Basing House* (Hampshire County Council, 1981).

Basing House was owned by John Paulet, the Marquis of Winchester, who had declared for King Charles I in July 1643. Given the house's size, strength and strategically important position on the road from the West Country to London, it was inevitable that attempts would be made by Parliament to capture it. During the First Civil War, Basing House consisted of three main parts. Firstly, there was the Old House within a massive brick-lined earth ring-work. Secondly, the New House had been built during the sixteenth century as what can best be described as a palace. Thirdly, outside the main defences was the Grange, with its main feature being the Great Barn. The buildings, particularly the Old and New Houses, were strengthened further by a strong loop-holed curtain wall and earthworks which had evolved during the wars. The site is the most rewarding siege site of the Civil Wars to visit, being in the care of Hampshire County Council and open to the public during the spring and summer months. Although largely destroyed during and after the last siege in 1645, the remains still survive, including the Great Barn, the foundations of the Old House and traces of the earthworks.

The Parliamentarian Sir William Waller moved against Basing House in November 1643 after an attempted *coup de main* against the house in July of the same year had failed. He had a mixed force of probably 8,000 men including a variety of ordnance. The Royalist garrison consisted of about 400. The house was invested by noon on 6 November, with Waller siting his artillery to the north on Cowdray's Down. The outlying Grange was assaulted and taken on 7 November, although some of the garrison prevented any further advance by sallying out and setting fire to a number of buildings in the area. The fighting lasted all day, with the Parliamentarians withdrawing to regroup. They returned to make a further attempt on 12 November using ladders and at least one petard. The defenders resisted staunchly, with the women of the house throwing 'down stone and brickes, which hurt some of our men' according to Elias Archer. The attack again lasted all day, but was again driven off, despite assaults from both the north and across the Park from the south-west. The weather worsened on 13 November with 'a very tempestuous morning of wind, raine and snow', leading Waller to abandon the siege and move to Farnham amidst rumours that the Royalist Hopton was approaching with his army.

The second siege began on 4 June 1644 when the Parliamentarian Colonel Norton moved a small force of horse and dragoons towards the house, with perhaps 2,000 more foot and horse arriving on 11 June. At the beginning there was some skirmishing between Basing House and Basingstoke during foraging and intelligence-gathering expeditions by both sides. By the end of June the Parliamentarians had established artillery behind gabions in the Park as well as on Cowdray's Down, and by 3 July a trench had been dug to within about 60m of the defences. Throughout July the attackers' emplacements increased the stranglehold on the house, with heavy mortars making life for the defenders even more unpleasant. This continued during August despite sallies from the garrison, with supplies starting to run out. A summons to surrender on

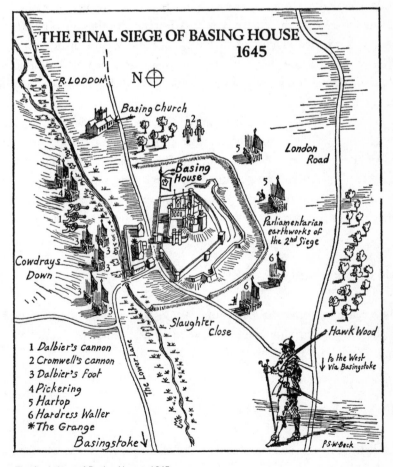

The final siege of Basing House, 1645.

2 September was rejected by the Marquis of Winchester, as relief from Oxford was expected. This did arrive, although a few days late, in the form of Colonel Henry Gage who managed to cross through Parliamentarian territory partly through the wearing of 'orange tawny scarfs and ribbands in our hats' according to his own account. Fighting their way through to Basing House on 11 September, Gage's men brought in vital supplies, which were further added to when he was able to open the way to nearby Basingstoke on its market day. Gage returned to Oxford while the siege continued. Parliamentarian forces marched past the house on their way to the second Battle of Newbury, but they did not add to the besieging force. Instead, in mid-November Norton abandoned the siege, as sickness and the worsening conditions wore down his men. At the same time, Gage arrived again with a renewed relief force.

The third and final siege came in 1645 after the King's defeat at Naseby. This time the attackers were led at first by Colonel Dalbier, a Dutch engineer, who carefully planned the siting of his batteries, the main one being by the church to the north-east of the house. Cromwell arrived at Basing on 8 October, adding further men and guns to the besieging force. A large breach was opened on the east side of the New House, which was stormed at 6.00 a.m. on 14 October. Colonel Pickering stormed the New House, while Montagu's regiment and Sir Hardress Waller attacked the defences to the south-west. The attack lasted only forty-five minutes according to one of the Parliamentarian soldiers, although the search for plunder carried on for many hours. In the chaos of the attack, the New House caught fire and was totally destroyed, leaving the Old House to be pillaged for stone and other building materials. After such stout and prolonged resistance throughout the war the end came quickly and with notable decisiveness.

Battle Bridge, battle of, 875

Possible battle between the Danes and Anglo-Saxons, fought to the north of Edlingham in Northumberland, where a hamlet bears the name of Battle Bridge, by a stream which feeds into the River Aln.

Battle Wood, battle of, 584

At this battle, possibly at Stoke Lyne in Oxfordshire, the West Saxon Cutha was killed, but the army still won under Ceawlin, defeating the Britons.

Commemorative medals became increasingly common during the seventeenth century. This one depicts one of Admiral Blake's victories such as that at Beachy Head in 1653 during the first Anglo-Dutch war.

Beachy Head, battle of, 20 February 1653

End of a prolonged action moving along the English Channel during the first Anglo-Dutch War.

Admiral Blake intercepted a Dutch squadron under Admiral van Tromp escorting a convoy off Portland in Dorset on 18 February 1653. Blake's fleet of about eighty-five ships destroyed five of van Tromp's ships, as well as capturing several ships of the convoy. The action continued along the Channel, being fought off the Isle of Wight on 19 February and culminating off Beachy Head on 20 February.

Beachy Head, battle of, 30 June 1690

French naval defeat of a combined British and Dutch fleet as part of the attempt to oust William III from the British throne.

Following William's accession in 1688, the French supported attempts by the deposed James II to regain his throne, leading most notably to the Battle of the Boyne in Ireland in 1690. A fleet of eighty-two French ships led by Admiral de Tourville met an Anglo-Dutch force of fifty-six ships off the Isle of Wight, moving to the sea off Beachy Head. The Earl of Torrington in command of the Allies left a gap in the middle of his line, to avoid the French overlapping him at either end. However, the Dutch and the British Squadron of the Blue at the rear of the line were defeated and five ships sunk. The French retired without destroying the fleet, but this defeat led to unease in London.

Bea's Mount, battle of, 614

Victory of the West Saxon Cynegils at this unidentified site, killing according to the Anglo-Saxon Chronicles a precise, if possibly confused, total of 2,065.

Beacon Hill, battle of, 21 August 1644, *see* Lostwithiel, battle of, 21 August–2 September 1644

Beda's Head, battle of, 675

Battle at an unidentified site between Aescwine of Wessex and Wulfhere of Mercia, with the latter dying later in the year.

Bedcanford, battle of, 571

Victory for the Saxon Cutha or Cuthwulf (possibly the same person) at an unidentified site, which led to further Saxon expansion in the Chilterns area.

Bedford, battle of, 917

The Vikings had lost Bedford to Edward of Wessex in 915 and so they tried to recapture it in 917, but were driven off in a battle outside the settlement.

Bedford, siege of, 915 (just before 11 November)

King Edward of Wessex captured the Viking stronghold of Bedford, strengthening its defences by building a fort on the south side of the river after his victory.

Bedford, siege of, 1137–1138

Early siege in the Civil War of King Stephen's reign.

Fought over the Christmas season, this siege saw Stephen move to take Bedford Castle from Miles Beauchamp. The castle was surrounded, with archers suppressing any defenders. In the meantime, siege engines were built and then used against the defences. After five weeks the castle surrendered.

Bedford Castle, siege of, June–14 August 1224

The castle was besieged, captured and destroyed by Hubert de Burgh on the orders of King Henry III, after the defeat of a rebellion by Fawkes de Breauté – a grassy mound still marks its site.

Beeston Castle, siege of, November 1644–16 November 1645

Parliamentarian siege of this Royalist stronghold.

Cheshire and Staffordshire were keenly contested between the Royalists and Parliamentarians during the first English Civil War. Parliament held the castle on the crags at Beeston first from early 1643, but they were displaced after a surprise attack on 13 December 1643.

In November 1644 the Parliamentarians were starting to tighten their grip on these counties, especially after their success at the Battle of Nantwich in January 1644. Beeston Castle and the important city of Chester were besieged by forces under the command of the local Sir William Brereton. The Royalists maintained a vigorous defence, setting fire to a house at the foot of the hill where a group of Parliamentarians were dining, killing twenty-four of the twenty-six men there. The defenders were sustained by two successful attempts to bring in more supplies, which were then countered by the Parliamentarians digging a trench around the foot of the hill. In the end, starvation defeated the garrison, with their surrender being agreed on 16 November 1645, when only 'a piece of turkey pie, two biscuits, a live peacock and a peahen' remained inside the castle to eat.

The castle is under the protection and management of English Heritage, who supervised excavations which uncovered two possible skeletons of casualties of the Civil War siege.

Belvoir Castle, siege of, October 1645–January 1646

Capture of this impressively sited castle by Parliament during the First Civil War.

Towards the end of the First Civil War, Belvoir Castle was held by the Royalists. It was besieged by Colonel Poyntz over the winter of 1645–1646, falling once the water supply had been cut off. The present castle has little surviving from the building which stood in the seventeenth century, as that was destroyed after the war. The current building is open to the public during the summer months and houses the regimental museum of the Queen's Royal Lancers.

Benfleet, battle of, 893

Benfleet in Essex had been fortified as a large-scale base for various Viking raiding forces. While part of the main Viking force was away, led by Haesten, the English attacked and captured Benfleet, taking prisoners and captured ships to London.

Benson, battle of, 779

Battle between Cynewulf of Wessex and Offa of Mercia, which was won by the latter.

Beorgford, battle of, 752

Battle traditionally located at Burford in Oxfordshire between King Cuthred of Wessex and King Aethelbald of Mercia.

Bera's Stronghold, battle of, 556

The Britons were defeated by the West Saxons, led by Cynric and Ceawlin, at a place which was probably Barbury Castle, an Iron-Age hill fort in Wiltshire.

Berkeley Castle, siege of, September 1645

Capture of this Royalist stronghold during the First Civil War, after a Parliamentarian force established a battery in neighbouring St Mary's churchyard, leading to a successful storming on 25 September 1645.

Above: Unarmoured Scottish soldier with spear and exaggerated sword, *c.*1300. Such soldiers fought at the Siege of Berwick-on-Tweed, 1318.

Left: The armour depicted in this brass is typical of the armour worn by both English and Scottish knights who fought one another at Berwick, 1296.

Berwick (-on-Tweed), siege of, 30 March 1296

Decisive storming of this northern town, which at that time was in Scottish hands, by King Edward I, leading to a savage sacking and many civilian deaths.

King Edward I had played a large part in securing the Scottish throne for John Baliol after the death of the Scottish King Alexander III. However, Baliol decided to exert some independence from Edward, leading to a rapid and deliberately heavy-handed reaction from the English king, determined to quell what he saw as a revolt. To that end he moved first against Berwick, which at that time was one of Scotland's major ports. Arriving outside the town, he immediately ordered an attempt to storm the defences. This was carried out and, once inside the town, Edward's soldiers went on the rampage, looting, murdering and burning. Chronicles claim that between a possible 7,000 and a shocking but unfeasible 60,000 were put to the sword.

Berwick (-on-Tweed), siege of, 6 December 1311

Failed attempt by Robert Bruce to seize the town and castle of Berwick, when a barking dog alerted the defenders to an attempt to scale the walls.

Berwick (-on-Tweed), siege of, ending on 28 March 1318

Successful Scottish capture of the town of Berwick, followed by the surrender of the starving castle garrison, gaining some revenge for the loss of the town in 1296.

Biddulph, siege of, 20–22 February 1644

Siege of an Elizabethan hall in Staffordshire by the Parliamentarian Sir William Brereton against his Royalist nephew Lord Brereton, who surrendered after heavy artillery was brought up during a three-day siege.

Bigbury, siege of, *see* Caesar's second expedition

Blackheath, battle of, 17 June 1497

Defeat of the Cornish rebellion against King Henry VII.

Blackheath in 1497 was open ground overlooking London from south of the River Thames. An army of perhaps 15,000 rebels, led by a blacksmith called Michael Joseph and the Bodmin lawyer Thomas Flamank, had marched from the south-west in an attempt to persuade King Henry VII to change his advisors, who were blamed for tax increases. The force was made up largely of Cornishmen, who would have been armed with a mixture of weapons and agricultural implements. As they marched east, their numbers increased and they were even joined by Lord Audley. They arrived at Blackheath on 16 June where they made their camp. It became clear that Henry was not going to listen to their pleas, leading to many of the rebels disappearing overnight, leaving perhaps 10,000 to face the king's forces on 17 June. Henry's trained soldiers made short work of the rebels as they attacked their camp in the early morning. Those who were not killed were scattered, while Flamank and Joseph were captured to be hung, drawn and quartered on 27 June. Lord Audley was also captured and executed, although in his case by the more gentlemanly axe, on 28 June.

Bleamfleote, battle of, *see* Benfleet

Blore Heath, battle of, 23 September 1459

First set-piece battle of the Wars of the Roses.

KEY REFERENCE: Griffith, P. (ed.) *The Battle of Blore Heath, 1459* (Paddy Griffith Associates, 1995).

By September 1459, a Yorkist faction led by Richard Duke of York had emerged seeking to control the Lancastrian King Henry VI, after initial problems had resulted in fighting at St Albans in 1455. In 1459 the Yorkist Earl of Salisbury began to move from Yorkshire towards the Duke of York who was at Ludlow on the Welsh border. However, a Lancastrian force under Lord Audley moved to intercept Salisbury before he could join York.

Audley outnumbered Salisbury by about three to one, with some 12,000 men against 4,000. Moreover, he placed his army in a strong defensive position, behind a thick hedge on the top of a slope, within easy bowshot of a steep-sided stream, the Hempmill Brook. Salisbury approached from the north along the road which in 1459 crossed the Hempmill Brook about one kilometre to the east of the current road. This sunken road can be easily traced on the south side of the stream, where it partially follows a modern footpath, just to the west of Blore Farm. In addition it should be noted that the brook now flows in one channel, but that even sixty years ago it ran in two or three rivulets, suggesting that the ground would have been boggier in 1459 than it is today. Given that Salisbury was outnumbered and facing a difficult attack to break through the Lancastrians to reach Ludlow, it is surprising to read the sources for the battle which agree that it was Audley who attacked, although his superior numbers must have boosted confidence. Certainly, at the outset, both sides would have been unwilling to join in battle, for it was clear to all involved that full-scale Civil War was likely to follow. Our two main sources, Jean de Waurin and Edward Hall, agree that Salisbury also prepared a defensive position with an encampment. This, according to Waurin, was strengthened further by a line of stakes and a wagon laager on one flank. The other flank rested upon a wood – Rowney Wood according to the historian Twemlow, meaning that the laager was on Salisbury's right. Both sides faced each other through the night and into the morning of 23 September, neither willing to assault the other's position. It would appear that Salisbury then, still in the early morning, started to make the appearance that he was about to retreat, and also ordered his archers to send arrows towards the Lancastrians to goad them into an attack. Audley, not wanting Salisbury to escape and trusting in his greater numbers, many of whom no doubt urged him to move forward, launched an assault.

As soon as his mounted men reached the stream, the Yorkist archers sent a stream of arrows into their ranks, forcing them to retire out of bowshot. A second mounted attack was attempted, but met the same fate, with the banks difficult to negotiate and archers shooting down from less than 100 metres away. Some of Audley's men managed, despite the odds stacked against them, to cross the stream and move up the slope towards the main Yorkist position, Lord Audley included. It was probably during this second attack that Audley was struck down at the spot still marked by his cross (sadly not accessible by a public right of way.) The Lancastrians still outnumbered their opponents and so Lord Dudley attempted a dismounted attack, with around 4,000 men. This had limited success, as it appears that his men did manage to reach the Yorkist line. However, they received no support and, according to Waurin, part of Dudley's force changed sides during the mêlée, causing the remainder to flee.

The battle could possibly have gone the other way if Queen Margaret (Henry VI's wife) had managed to bring further forces to bear on Salisbury's rear, as it

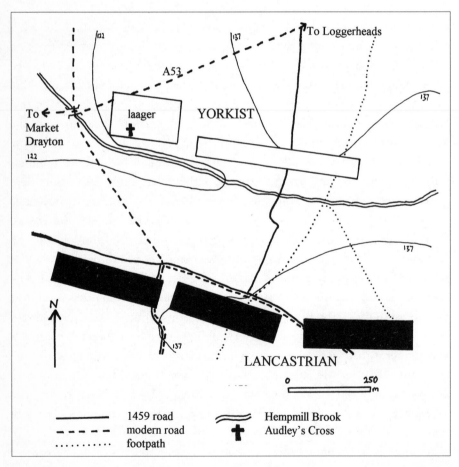

Battle of Blore Heath, 23 September 1459.

seems likely that she watched the battle from nearby Mucklestone Church. Moreover, the Stanleys, who were to prevaricate again at Bosworth in 1485, were in the vicinity and could have made a large difference to either side. However, they were assumed to be supporting the Yorkists and were included in the act of attainder passed shortly after the battle against the Yorkist leadership. The Lancastrians had suffered perhaps 2,000 casualties, losing many men in the pursuit which followed, while the Yorkists may have lost less than 100. The Lancastrians soon recovered from their defeat, as in October Richard of York's army was trapped at Ludford Bridge, leading to York deserting his forces to flee into exile.

The battlefield can be seen just to the east of the A53 where a lane runs along the front of the Lancastrian position to Blore Farm. The footpath already mentioned gives excellent access to the Hempmill Brook, from where the difficulties facing the Lancastrian attackers can be appreciated.

Boarstall House, siege of, 10–24 June 1644 and 9–10 June 1645

Typical example of a garrisoned house which changed hands on several occasions during the First Civil War.

Boarstall House to the east of Oxford was held for King Charles I until April 1644, when it was decided to use fewer men dispersed in garrisons, thus abandoning Boarstall to Parliament. However, the new garrison soon started to cause problems for the Royalist supply lines running into Oxford, leading to the Royalist Sir Henry Gage being dispatched with a force of 1,000 men to retake it on 10 June 1644. He first took the nearby church and outer works, before setting up artillery to fire on the house, which led to its surrender. Gage died attacking Aylesbury in January 1645, and then, in May 1645, the Parliamentarian General Skippon attacked Boarstall House, but failed to take it. Thomas Fairfax finally captured Boarstall at his second attempt after a short siege, with the house surrendering to him on 10 June under the governor, Sir Charles Campion. Only the gatehouse still survives, which is under the care of the National Trust, with the site of the main house being clear apart from the remaining moat.

Bolingbroke Castle, siege of, September–October 1643

Birthplace of Henry IV, which fell to Parliament during the First Civil War.

Held by the Royalists, Bolingbroke Castle was besieged by the Earl of Manchester's Army of the Eastern Association by the end of summer 1643.

Edward Montagu, 2nd Earl of
Manchester, was, and is often
criticised for being over-
cautious to the point of
treachery. In 1643 his army
captured Bolingbroke Castle
after defeating a Royalist
attempt to relieve the castle at
the Battle of Winceby, which
was won by Cromwell and
Fairfax. He is depicted in a
silver medal he issued as a
military reward to his soldiers.

Although the castle was strong, it could be shot at from a hill towards Winceby. Accordingly, Manchester took the hill and mounted cannon there: it is likely that the still-visible earthworks on the hill relate to his siegeworks. Although most of the besiegers were drawn off temporarily for the Battle of Winceby on 11 October 1643, they returned after their victory to take the castle in the same month. It was then slighted and abandoned shortly afterwards.

Bolsover Castle, siege of, 12 August 1644

The Royalist garrison under Colonel Muschamp surrendered to the Parliamentarian Major Molanus and his 500 men, despite attempts to improve the defences as suggested by an excavated re-cut and faced medieval ditch.

Bolton, storming of, 28 May 1644

Storming of this Lancashire town by Prince Rupert *en route* to Marston Moor.

After earlier Royalist attempts to take Bolton on 18 February and 28 March 1643 had failed, Prince Rupert and the Earl of Derby with a much larger force moved against the town in this wide-ranging march from Oxford to York in 1644. Although Bolton was defended by a mud wall and some 3,000 men under Colonel Rigby, these were insufficient to hold up Rupert's forces, who broke in and sacked the town, killing many civilians in the slaughter which accompanied the looting. Much of this is recorded on the tomb of John Okley, a townsman of Bolton who lived through the Civil Wars, which can be found in the churchyard of St Peter's. The Earl of Derby was captured in 1651 some time after a skirmish at Wigan during the third Civil War. He was taken to Bolton and executed for his part in the massacre after the storming in 1644.

Boroughbridge, battle of, 16 March 1322

Battle fought by rebel barons who were trapped between two royal forces at the river crossing in Boroughbridge.

KEY REFERENCE: English Heritage *Battlefield Report: Boroughbridge 1322* (English Heritage, London, 1995).

Thomas, Earl of Lancaster had fallen out with King Edward II in 1311, when the former had been a key player in the murder of Edward's unpopular favourite Piers Gaveston. Several episodes widened the breach between them, culminating with open rebellion. Unfortunately for them, the rebel barons do not appear to have fully trusted one another and their plans were poorly coordinated, allowing Edward to defeat each group in turn.

Lancaster mustered the largest force at Doncaster and pushed south, but was persuaded to withdraw once Edward advanced and threatened to cut off his line of retreat after the stand-off at Burton Bridge on 10 March. This retreat quickly became demoralising, with supporters probably falling away as they moved further and further north, heading for Dunstanburgh Castle on the Northumbrian coast. At Boroughbridge on the Great North Road their passage was blocked at the River Ure by a Royalist force led by Sir Andrew de Harcla. With Edward moving towards them from the south, the rebels had little option but to try and force their way across the river before they were completely trapped.

Although biased in favour of the local Harcla, the *Lanercost Chronicle* provides seemingly reliable information about the battle, as well as being the most detailed source.

Harcla spent the night before the battle at Ripon and then pressed on to guard the river crossing on receiving news that Lancaster's army was approaching. He dismounted his forces, sending pikemen and knights to the northern end of the bridge, which was on the same site as the current bridge, although narrower and made of wood. There was also a ford, probably about 700 yards to the east of the bridge, which Sir Andrew guarded with further pikemen, formed up in a Scottish-style schiltron (a many-ranked, usually defensive wedge or shield-shaped formation likened to a hedgehog). His dispositions were completed by stationing archers beside each crossing. In total Sir Andrew had up to 4,000 men at his disposal, although this may well be a rather inflated figure.

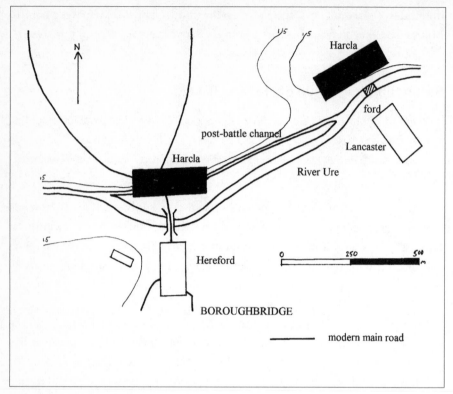

Battle of Boroughbridge, 16 March 1322.

Lancaster arrived with a smaller force, including 800 men-at-arms. A simple attack led by cavalry was planned for both crossings (although it is possible the attack at the bridge was on foot, due to its narrowness) with the Earl of Hereford and Sir Roger de Clifford attacking over the bridge, while Lancaster attacked at the ford. These attacks had little chance of success, however desperate the charge, with the pikes and arrows breaking up the advance and killing the Earl of Hereford. At the ford, Lancaster's men did not even come to blows, with the archers defeating their attempts to cross. Lancaster must have realised that the game was up and negotiated a truce until the morning. However, during the night many of his men slipped away, leaving Lancaster and his remaining followers little option but to surrender. Thomas was taken away to Pontefract Castle and executed, a fate which befell many of his followers and other rebel leaders. However, despite removing so many opponents, Edward II continued to be unpopular with many surviving barons and was never secure on the throne up to his unpleasant death in 1327.

The old monument to the battle, a column, was moved from Boroughbridge to neighbouring Aldborough in 1852. The river and the town of

Boroughbridge have changed greatly since the fourteenth century, with the latter spreading right up to and across the former. The exact location of the ford is not known, but access to its probable site is possible via a riverside footpath. There is a small commemorative plaque to the battle on the southern face of the bridge. If a visit is made, one should also make the short trip to the nearby and near-contemporary battlefield at Myton.

Bossenden Wood, skirmish of, 30 May 1838

Small engagement which included the death of the first officer to die in action during the reign of Queen Victoria.

John Thom (sometimes Tom), or, as he preferred to be called, Sir William Courtenay, proclaimed himself the Messiah come to save the agricultural labourers of Kent from poverty. Most others saw him as 'Mad Tom' and by 1838 he had already spent several years in a local lunatic asylum. Things got out of hand when he gathered a number of followers together, leading to an attempt to arrest him. However, he killed one of the three arresting officers at Bossenden Farm, resulting in reinforcements being called for in the form of 100 regulars of the 45th Foot from nearby Canterbury. Led by Major Armstrong, the 45th split into two groups, with one under Lieutenant Bennett moving into Bossenden Wood where they encountered Courtenay. Bennett called on Courtenay to surrender, but instead Courtenay shot the Lieutenant dead with a pistol. The soldiers fired a volley and moved in against the labourers, killing Courtenay and seven others, while losing a constable who had gone with them. Courtenay's body was taken to the Red Lion public house in what is now the village of Dunkirk, ending this bizarre and tragic episode.

Bosworth (Field), battle of, 22 August 1485

Decisive battle which saw the last death of a King of England in battle and the establishment of the Tudor dynasty.

KEY REFERENCES: Bennett, M. *The Battle of Bosworth* (Gloucester, 1985); Foss, P. *The Field of Redemore: The Battle of Bosworth, 1485* (Newtown Linford, 1998); Jones, M. K. *Bosworth 1485: Psychology of a Battle* (Tempus, 2002).

Richard III had taken the throne from his nephew Edward V after the death of Richard's brother Edward IV, possibly because he felt he had the strongest claim to the throne, or simply because he could. The strongest Lancastrian threat to

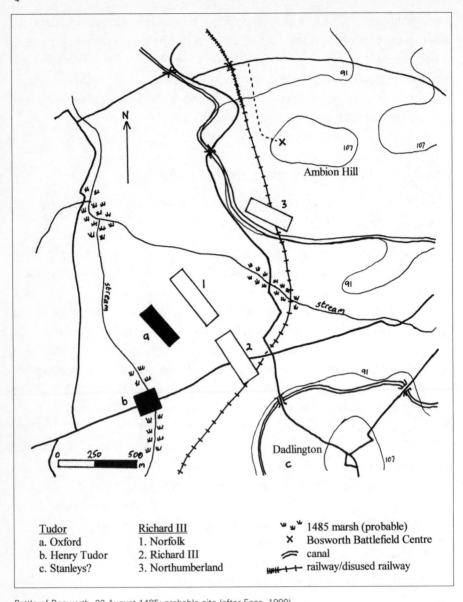

Battle of Bosworth, 22 August 1485: probable site (after Foss, 1990).

Richard emerged from Henry Tudor, who had lived in exile in Brittany since 1471. By 1485 Tudor felt strong enough to mount an invasion through his family's land in Wales, setting sail on 1 August and landing at Milford Haven. It was apparent that the issue could only be decided in battle, as the two leaders organised their forces and then converged on one another, Tudor marching towards the Midlands via Shrewsbury and Richard III moving to Leicester from Nottingham. The king had up to 15,000 troops with him, while Henry's invasion force had only some 5,000 although a core of 2,000 of these were professional French mercenaries, the majority of which were probably armed with the pike and trained to fight in the new Swiss method. In addition, the Stanley family had a further 3,000–8,000 retainers to add to one side or the other if they so chose.

Bosworth is unique among important English battles for having a large amount of controversy surrounding its location, with at least three plausible and well-argued sites being put forward, no doubt in part because of the importance of the battle, the ease with which the winners were able to construct their version of events and because of the desire to stake a claim to the battlefield by later generations. The two main near-contemporary sources for the battle are the *Crowland Chronicle* and Polydore Vergil's account, with the latter being the most thorough, if written from very much a pro-Tudor perspective some twenty years after the battle. In addition there are several more minor, but possibly very telling written sources, as well as the landscape and the as yet untapped battlefield archaeology. The main interpretations are summarised below.

What could be called the traditional interpretation is strengthened by the excellent Bosworth Battlefield Centre, which at present takes the visitor around a battlefield trail and exhibition. It places King Richard's army at the top of Ambion Hill, facing west to meet the advancing army of Henry Tudor, which had camped on Whitemoors, a mile or so to the west of Ambion Hill. The Earl of Oxford, commanding Henry's vanguard, clashed with the Duke of Norfolk, while the Duke of Northumberland, with Richard's rear 'battle' or division, played no part in the battle. Richard, seeing Henry Tudor below, and possibly even while Henry was riding to or from the Stanleys' detachment which was lying to one side of the main battlefield in an effort to persuade them to enter the battle on his side, launched a desperate mounted charge to kill his rival. This charge came very close to success, with Richard cutting down Henry's standard bearer, but at the crucial moment the Stanleys entered the fray and killed Richard by a stream which crosses the current Shenton–Sutton Cheney road, at a place allegedly called Sandeford in 1485. This interpretation can be detected in Shakespeare's *Richard III,* where the king is rushed into battle and is subsequently deserted by many of those he felt had supported him until, isolated and alone, he is cut down.

The main revisionist theory has been advanced by Peter Foss, who places the fighting to the south and south-west of Ambion Hill. Two very early sources refer to the battle as being fought on 'Redemore' or 'Redesmore', which Foss has convincingly located as being to the south of Ambion Hill towards Dadlington. This also fits the claim of several sources which mention the battle as having been fought on a plain, not a hill. In addition, Polydore Vergil writes that:

> There was a marsh betwixt both hosts, which Henry of purpose left on the right hand, that it might serve his men instead of a fortress, by the doing thereof also he left the sun upon his back.

This marsh could be placed to the south-west of Ambion Hill, so that Henry (or to be more precise, Oxford) moved round it to approach across Redesmore from the south-east, thus having the sun at his back in mid-morning.

A third interpretation claims that the current Ambion Hill was only so named relatively recently, and that the 1485 Ambion Hill was to the south-east, bringing the fighting into the same general area, although on a different alignment to Foss' interpretation.

A new interpretation was published by Michael K. Jones in 2002. This re-located the battlefield some five miles to the west, on the flat ground between Atherstone, Mancetter, Witherley, Fenny Drayton and Atterton. This is largely on the grounds where Henry, once king, made compensation grants to these villages for damaged crops 'at our late victorious field'. Jones also focuses on the location given to the battle by the *Crowland Chronicle*, when it relates that 'this battle, which was fought near Merevale...'. Merevale Abbey just to the west of Atherstone is claimed by Jones to be the place where Henry stayed the night before the battle, with further evidence to support this. Of equal significance in this interpretation is that Richard had a pre-arranged battle plan, in which a large-scale cavalry charge along the lines of that favoured by the Spanish at the Battle of Toro in 1476 would be used, partly thanks to the presence of the Spaniard Juan de Salacar with Richard's army, but also due to Richard's superiority in numbers. To do this, flat ground was essential, not a crowded hilltop. Accordingly, Richard camped the night before the battle to the north of Witherley by 'King Dick's Hole'. Henry advanced, swinging round to attack from the south-east after the two vanguards clashed on the plain. Richard, according to this theory, came close to success, but his charge was thwarted by the French mercenaries, who made a defensive pike formation around Tudor, as is suggested by a fragmentary source recorded in 1897 from a letter written by one of the mercenaries after the battle. The Stanleys then entered the fray and the action ended up at the feature now known as Derby Spinney. (Thomas Lord Stanley was created Earl of Derby by Henry VII, and he became associated with the crowning of Henry Tudor on the field, after his brother Sir William Stanley, who actually performed this task, was executed for treason.)

How can one choose between these interpretations? The simple answer is that, at present, one probably cannot decide with full confidence. However, with a thorough study of the landscape history and with future archaeological discoveries, it should be possible to get closer to the real battle and battlefield. There has been a long-standing association of the battle with Ambion Hill in some way, and yet the first mention of this feature dates to Holinshed's *Chronicle*, published in 1577, nearly a hundred years after the battle. Even the name Bosworth became popular only after 1500, after the nearest town. Although, as outlined above, any interpretation of this battle can still at present be contested, there are elements of all the above interpretations which can be fused together to give one theory which admittedly leans more to the work of Foss for the location and to Jones for the course of the battle than to other writers: the night before the battle Richard's army camped on and around Ambion Hill, while Henry Tudor was at Merevale Abbey. The tradition connected to Ambion Hill is too strong to ignore, but it seems logical, apart from further supporting evidence, that Henry would have stayed in the relative comfort and security of the Abbey and its park rather than camping extremely close to Richard's camp on ground which may well have been too wet for practicalities. Ambion Hill may be suitable for an overnight camp, but is certainly too small to form up an army of around 15,000 men, particularly if the commander wanted to attack with cavalry. The location of Richard's overnight camp put forward by Michael Jones would certainly have been a long march from Leicester. More to the point, even more so than Henry's often suggested camp on Whitemoors, it would have been too difficult to access and move from, being at the confluence of the Rivers Anker and Sence. On the morning of 22 August, Richard moved down to block the advance of Tudor along the old Roman road, while at the same time finding the flatter ground of Redemore to suit his planned use of cavalry. Northumberland probably remained in reserve, or possibly moved forward into line, but his troops did not engage due to the presence of marsh to their front. On seeing the king's army deployed in line, the Earl of Oxford commanding Tudor's vanguard swung to the left using the marsh to protect his flank from attack. Just as at Stoke two years later, Oxford pinned the enemy, leaving Tudor some way behind. Despite being outnumbered, Oxford's men bettered those of Norfolk after a hard fight. Richard, seeing that Henry's 'battle' was isolated, charged with his cavalry, but they were prevented from reaching Henry in part by the French pikemen. The Stanleys, who had been observing the battle from a nearby hill, joined the fighting on Tudor's side and won him the victory. The pursuit moved across the Roman road back towards Dadlington and Stoke Golding, where at the latter, on Crown Hill, Tudor was crowned.

While the location of the battlefield may be in doubt, we can be more sure about the events of the battle itself. The sources agree on the clash between Oxford on Henry's side and Norfolk on Richard's, both including many archers. Northumberland's 'battle' played no active role in the fighting. Henry, probably leaving some distance between his 'battle' and that of Oxford, manoeuvred to approach Richard from the south-east, passing marshy ground. After a relatively short time, Richard launched a cavalry charge on Tudor's division. This nearly succeeded, with Richard killing Henry's standard bearer and only being prevented from reaching Tudor by the intervention of John Cheney. Then the arrival of Sir William Stanley and his force of 3,000 cut Richard down and won the battle for Henry Tudor. At some point Richard was urged to flee the battlefield and was offered a horse by his supporters, but he refused this and fought on.

Certainly there is still much to be learned about the Battle of Bosworth, and the best starting point is most definitely the Bosworth Battlefield Centre, so long as one enters with an open mind. It is perhaps ironic that the most impressive visitor centre on an English battlefield is attempting to interpret one of the most confused and contested battles in English history, but Leicestershire County Council should be heartily applauded for their initiative in setting up this superb facility, which hopefully will be mirrored at other important battlefields. In the near future it is expected that the Bosworth Battlefield Centre will be re-designed, along with the displayed interpretation of the battle and its trail, to reflect the largely accepted changes in the location of the battlefield.

Boudicca's defeat, AD 61

The largest battle to be fought on English soil, with as yet an unidentified location.

KEY REFERENCE: Marix-Evans, M. 'Boudicca's Last Battle' in *Battlefield* (vol. 8 issue 1).

Queen Boudicca (or Boudica or Boadicea) of the Iceni tribe had risen in revolt against the Romans after her Norfolk-centred kingdom had been ordered to be incorporated into the Roman province of Britannia, following the death of her husband Prasutagas. Roman heavy-handedness, either deliberately provocative or merely insensitive, led to the Iceni resisting. In turn, Boudicca and her two daughters were beaten and raped, which turned resistance into full-scale revolt. Linking up with the Trinovantes to the south, Boudicca swept through East Anglia, burning the province's capital of Colchester. This was possible with the main Roman army being away on the shores of the Menai Straits under the command of the Governor, Suetonius Paullinus. On hearing of the revolt, he ordered part of IX legion to intercept Boudicca, while II Augusta legion was ordered to march up from Exeter. The detachment of IX Hispana was defeated by the Britons, while II Augusta remained in Exeter. Suetonius marched back from Wales, pushing ahead with his cavalry, while the two legions (XIV and XX) and auxiliary infantry followed on behind. He reached London before Boudicca, but realised he had no chance of stopping her advance. Therefore, he retreated back up the Watling Street (now roughly on the line of the A5), abandoning London and Verulamium (at the foot of the hill where St Albans now stands) to Boudicca, fire and the sword.

Suetonius selected a position in a defile, with woods to his flanks and rear to prevent ambush. He assembled his legions in the centre, with auxiliaries to their sides and cavalry on the flanks, a force of about 10,000. Facing them were several times their number, including wagons piled high with booty and entire families. Their numbers are impossible to calculate, but 50,000 combatants is certainly possible, while some estimates of 80,000 British casualties suggests an even larger force. The exact location of the battlefield is not known, although archaeology may yet provide an answer. Some writers prefer a site near Mancetter, but a site to the south-east of Towcester seems more likely, on the slope above Cuttle Mill. The topography certainly fits, although the woods have long since receded. More persuasive is the evidence provided by a number of artefacts from the immediate vicinity, including numbers of human bone fragments. Unfortunately, precise dating of these finds has not been carried out, but it seems unlikely that they came from carefully dug graves. Detailed survey and field-walking of the area could provide more definitive evidence. Whether this was the exact site or not, the result of the battle was conclusive. The Britons were cut to pieces by the Roman formations, with their numbers being a handicap as they were unable to deploy properly or later flee. Boudicca killed herself amidst the chaos of defeat, leaving Suetonius to complete his victory and restore order to the province, which had survived its most serious threat before the fourth century.

Bovey Heath or Tracey, skirmish of, 9 January 1646

Small-scale but bold and decisive action of the latter stages of the First Civil War.

The Royalist Lord Wentworth stationed his three understrength regiments of horse to the south-east of Bovey Tracey on Bovey Heath, protecting them with a built-up embankment. However, this did not extend to protection against an attack from the north, which is the direction from where Cromwell's Parliamentarians came, consisting of two regiments of foot and one of horse, sweeping through the town and then up Old Newton Road onto the Heath, capturing or routing Wentworth's men as night came at about 6.00 p.m. A Civil War breastplate was found in the grounds of the local primary school and is now in the collection of the Bovey Tracey Heritage Trust.

Braddock Down, battle of, 19 January 1643

Battle which helped to establish the reputation of the Royalist Hopton's Cornish infantry for the remainder of the First Civil War.

KEY REFERENCE: Wilton, R. 'Some Notes on the Battle of Braddock Down' in *Devon and Cornwall Notes and Queries* (vol. XXXV, part VII, Spring 1985).

Despite securing Cornwall for King Charles I by the end of autumn 1642, the situation for the Royalist General Sir Ralph Hopton was looking bleak by January 1643, as he had been forced to retreat from his attempted advance into Devon. Moreover, two Parliamentarian armies were moving towards him, one under the Scot Colonel Ruthin and the other led by the Earl of Stamford. Hopton's best chance lay in defeating each of his enemies in turn before they were able to combine their forces. Therefore, Hopton advanced towards Ruthin's force which was in the Liskeard area, with the former camping in Boconnoc Park near Lostwithiel, which was owned by the Royalist Lord Mohun, on the night of 18–19 January.

Early on the morning of 19 January, the Royalists moved out to find their enemy already debouching onto the eastern part of Braddock (or Broad Oak) Down, where the road from Liskeard started to cross it, probably between East Taphouse and Middle Taphouse. There are serious problems with the definite location of the battlefield, as it seems that Braddock Down consisted of at least two distinct parts in 1643, separated by enclosures, as early maps indicate. The same division is attested by Richard Symonds, a Royalist cavalryman, who has left a diary account of the 1644 Lostwithiel campaign, in which he mentions Braddock Down being in at least two parts separated from one another by enclosures with a lane joining the two parts. However, the battle has traditionally been located a little to the south-west of this area, due to the clear statement by the Royalist Grenville which informs us that they 'came in full view of the Enimies whole Army, upon a faire heath between Bocon: and Braddock Church.' This has been explained by Wilton, who suggests that

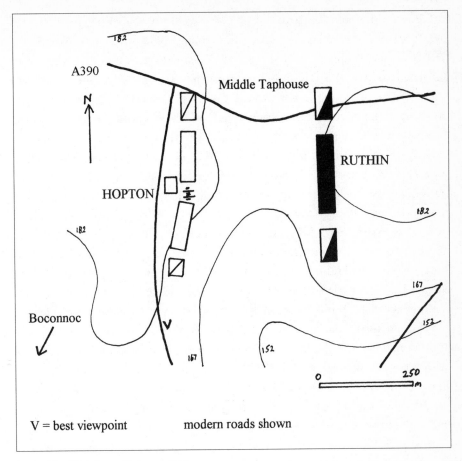

Battle of Braddock Down, 19 January 1643.

Grenville confused Braddock Church with St Pinnock Church, possibly due in part to an inaccuracy in John Speed's map of Cornwall. This, together with other arguments, has persuaded both the Ordnance Survey and English Heritage to place the battlefield just to the south of Middle Taphouse. Certainly, it is hard to imagine how it took Hopton until noon to march to the battlefield from Boconnoc Park, only a mile from the traditional site of the battle. Part of the problem with the location is that the Boconnoc Estate has changed its land-use since 1643, in particular with the growth of large plantations once the parkland was expanded in the eighteenth century, which has obscured the traditional site of the battle. In 1643 the deer-park in which the Royalists almost certainly camped was in the south-western portion of the current estate. With careful landscape research and archaeology the situation may yet be resolved.

Despite this confusion as to the precise location of the battle, the course of events is more straightforward, thanks in particular to clear accounts by Hopton and Grenville. It appears that the 4,000 Parliamentarians under Ruthin were surprised to find the Royalists marching out for battle. Despite this, some Parliamentarian horse, in which arm they were superior despite an overall equality in numbers, pushed back the Royalist vanguard or forlorn hope. Hopton drew up his army with foot in the centre and dragoons and horse on each wing, with two small iron cannons from Boconnoc House being placed on an ancient barrow. To his front a small forlorn hope of musketeers took up station in small enclosures, possibly by Middle Taphouse. Both main forces were drawn up on commanding hills with a valley, probably with some boggy ground between them. As a consequence, neither side was willing to risk an advance, so they remained in position, exchanging fire for two hours. After that time, seeing that Ruthin's guns were not yet on the field, and perhaps fearing further Parliamentarian reinforcements, Hopton ordered his guns to fire and his men, other than a small central reserve, to advance. Led by Grenville, the Cornish infantry attacked down and then up the slopes, soon covering the 100–150m between the armies. It seems that the Parliamentarian foot fled without much of a fight, with the Royalists soon attacking Ruthin's reserves lining hedges to the east of the Down. The pursuit carried on to Liskeard, with the Royalists capturing five guns, large quantities of supplies and between 800 and 1,250 prisoners.

Braddock Down secured Cornwall with its resources of tin and manpower for King Charles I until the next Parliamentarian invasion later in 1643. If the battle had gone the other way the Royalist cause would have suffered a severe blow, as the Parliamentarian forces would probably have taken the county, severely damaging the king's revenue collection and supplies.

Bradford, siege of, 25 March 1644

Third Royalist attack on Bradford of the First Civil War, involving serious fighting as the town fell.

KEY REFERENCE: Newman, P.R. 'The Civil War and Bradford' in *The Siege of Bradford* (Bradford Libraries and Information Service, 1989).

Following a failed attempt to take Bradford in December 1642, and a short successful siege after the Royalist victory at nearby Adwalton Moor in mid-1643, the Royalists returned on 25 March 1644 as part of an attempt to secure West Yorkshire for King Charles I. The Parliamentarian garrison under Lambert faced an attack by a sizeable force of probably over 8,000 led by Belasyse. The Royalist attack was held off for some time, until Lambert's men ran short of powder, at which point they began to move out of the town. However, some Royalist horse were surprised by this movement and they retreated, enabling Lambert to re-secure the town, persuading Belasyse to withdraw. Belasyse retreated to Leeds and then to his base at Selby, where a battle was fought on 10 April.

Bradford on Avon, battle of, 652

Cenwalh fought here, in what was probably a battle of Saxon versus Saxon.

Bramham Moor, battle of, 20 February 1408

Final battle in the Percys' rebellion against Henry IV.

Following Henry Bolingbroke's usurpation of the crown in 1399 to become King Henry IV, a number of risings were attempted against the new king, most notably that of the Percys culminating with the battle of Shrewsbury in 1403. The Earl of Northumberland fled to Scotland after the death and defeat of his son Henry 'Hotspur' at Shrewsbury. He returned in 1408 with a force of Scots and some northern retainers, reaching as far south as Bramham Moor to the south of Wetherby. They were met there, beside the Great North Road (now the A1), by Henry IV's supporter, Sir Thomas Rokeby, the Sheriff of Yorkshire. Few details of the ensuing battle survive, although we know that it started at 2.00 p.m., with Northumberland taking up position to be met by Rokeby. The latter gained the victory, with one of the rebel leaders, Lord Bardolph, being mortally wounded. Northumberland was also killed, either executed in York or in the rout after the battle. The latter is perhaps more likely, as there is a monument, allegedly marking the spot of his death, just to the east of the village of Bramham, along York Lane.

Brampton Bryan, siege of, 1643–17 April 1644

Held for Parliament by Lady Brilliana Harley, this castle held out for a long time during the First Civil War until large cannons were brought to bear in March 1644, leading to its surrender then destruction.

Braydon, raid of, 903

Raid at an unidentified location, probably south of the River Thames near Cricklade, where a Viking army from East Anglia pillaged the area before returning home.

Brentford, battle of, 1016

After two attempts to capture London in 1016, the Danes under Cnut (Canute) were driven away and defeated in a battle at Brentford in Middlesex. In their eagerness to secure plunder, some of the victorious English ended up in the river and drowned.

Brentford, skirmish of, 12 November 1642

Thrust by the Royalist Prince Rupert, associated with King Charles I's advance to Turnham Green.

Prince Rupert swept into Brentford early on the morning of 12 November 1642, surprising the two regiments in the town. Many were captured as Rupert pressed them against the River Thames and occupied Syon House. However, after the face-off at Turnham Green the next day, the Royalist position became untenable and Rupert retreated towards Reading.

Bridgnorth, siege of, 1102

Capture of the castle of Robert de Bellême by King Henry I after construction of a siege castle across the River Severn in which Henry positioned catapults.

Bridgnorth, siege of, 1155

Early in his reign, Henry II conducted a siege against Hugh Mortimer, who had taken this royal castle. The siege lasted a few days until the castle's surrender was secured through re-use of Henry I's earlier siege castle across the river from Bridgnorth.

Bridgnorth, siege of, 31 March–26 April 1646

Dramatic siege of this Shropshire town by Parliamentarians during the First
Civil War.

Held for King Charles I during the First Civil War, Bridgnorth was finally
besieged by Parliament in 1646. A force of Parliamentarian foot forced their
way into the town through the north gate at the end of March, driving the
Royalists back into the castle. Fire broke out and spread to St Leonard's
Church, which housed the Royalist powder. This exploded, destroying the
church (although it was later rebuilt on the same site). Nearly a month of close
siege followed, with the castle being undermined and seriously damaged before
its surrender at the end of April. The keep was left standing, but only just, as it
still does today with a lean of fifteen degrees. Some more of the castle's plan
was re-discovered by a *Time Team* excavation in 2001, although little could be
directly related to the Civil War.

Bridgwater, siege of, 13–23 July 1645

Siege by the New Model Army after their success at the Battle of
Langport.

The Royalists held Bridgwater in Somerset from June 1643, but by the summer
of 1645 Parliament's New Model Army under Sir Thomas Fairfax was moving
through the West Country, following its initial success at the battle of Naseby.
Despite its water-filled defences, the town was not garrisoned strongly enough
to resist for long. During the night of 20 July, after the Royalists refused to
surrender, a Parliamentarian assault was launched against the East Gate. A
foothold was gained, although the garrison under Wyndham continued to resist
for three days until their surrender on 23 July following destructive
Parliamentarian artillery fire.

Bridport, skirmish of, 14 June 1685

Fought after the Duke of Monmouth landed at Lyme on 11 June 1685, as his
men sought supplies, recruits and intelligence in a raid in the early morning of
14 June. Most of Bridport was taken, but the Duke's men were driven off by
the local Dorset militia, with the rebel Lieutenant Colonel Venner of
Monmouth's Red Regiment being wounded.

Bristol, siege of, 23–27 July 1643

Successful storming of England's second city, providing the Royalists with a very important base for the following two years.

KEY REFERENCE: Peachey, S. *The Storming of Bristol 1643* (Stuart Press, 1993).

Bristol was garrisoned for Parliament under Colonel Nathaniel Fiennes with about 1,500 foot and 300 horse, not enough for such a large city with five major forts and around five miles of earthwork ramparts with further small forts, batteries and redoubts to defend. After victory at Roundway Down on 13 July 1643, the Royalists under Prince Maurice, who had perhaps 3,000 foot and 2,000 horse with support from the king at Oxford in the form of Maurice's elder brother Prince Rupert with at least 14,000 men and siege

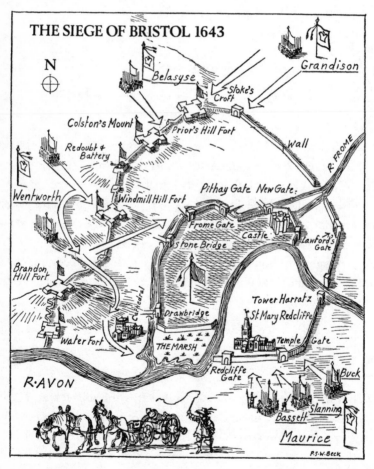

Siege of Bristol, 1643.

artillery, moved against Bristol, arriving on 23 July and investing it the next day after Fiennes refused to surrender. Various probing attacks were launched on 24 and 25 July, while batteries were constructed and a plan for storming the city agreed. This consisted of the western army of Prince Maurice attacking from the south against Temple Gate on the Bath Road, while the larger Oxford forces would assault the defences in the north and west.

Before dawn on 26 July the largely Cornish Regiments in the south attacked, with Slanning leading the central force, Bassett to his left and Buck to the right, but after prolonged and fierce fighting they were driven off. In the north, Grandison met with a similar fate, while in the west Wentworth's forces also struggled to make headway against the Windmill Hill Fort. The defences were overcome between this fort and the next to the south, Brandon Hill, as Wentworth's men, led by Colonel Washington (presumably with his dragoons), found themselves in dead ground once they reached the rampart. Throwing grenades to keep the defenders back, men clambered over, helping more of their comrades to do the same. Once over this first line of defences, at about 4.00 a.m. the Royalists poured into the city's suburbs and took the cathedral before threatening the inner wall. Fighting continued throughout the morning, but with more and more Royalists arriving as Maurice's men found their way round, further resistance would have been futile and extremely costly to the defenders if terms had been refused. A parley was agreed at 2.00 p.m., with talks continuing throughout the afternoon and evening until the terms of surrender were finally agreed at 10.00 p.m. The defenders marched out in the morning of 27 July. Parliament felt that the city had been surrendered too easily, with Fiennes being sentenced to death, although this was not carried out.

Bristol, siege of, 22 August–11 September 1645

Re-taking of England's second city after the Royalists had captured it after a successful storming in 1643.

KEY REFERENCE: Young, P. & Emberton, W. *Sieges of the Great Civil War* (Bell & Hyman, 1978).

By August 1645, Bristol remained one of King Charles I's most important garrisons along with Oxford, Chester, Basing House and Newark, after its capture from Fiennes in 1643. Prince Rupert, Charles I's nephew, had been in command of the besiegers at the first siege, but found himself the besieged in 1645 as roles were reversed. Parliamentarian forces commanded by Sir Thomas Fairfax arrived outside the city on 22 August, aided by their control of the sea

Built, Anno 1110
Demolished 1656

The south prospect of part
of the Castle of Bristoll
Avon flu

Bristol, 1645. Engraving showing Bristol Castle before it was demolished in 1656. Prince Rupert hoped to use the castle as a final stronghold in 1645, but damage to the wall meant that surrender was inevitable.

as ships were used to ensure a complete blockade was maintained. After a major sally led by Rupert himself was driven back into the city on 1 September, the Parliamentarian command decided to attempt a storm of the city, especially as rumours abounded of a major relief attempt by the Royalists. The assault went in on 10 September, with the initial success being in the east, against Lawford's Gate between the rivers Frome and Avon. A further breach was made by Prior's Hill Fort in the north-west, leading to large numbers of Parliamentarians pouring towards the second line of defences, while others continued to assault Prior's Hill Fort, taking it after two hours' fighting. With the fort gone and the New Model Army far outnumbering Rupert's 1,000 foot and 500 horse, a parley was made and terms of surrender agreed. The Royalists marched out on the morning of 11 September, leaving King Charles I with no real hope left in stopping the New Model Army. He blamed Rupert for the early surrender of the city, as the Prince had promised to hold it for four months. Rupert was dismissed from the king's service and sent into exile as a result.

Britain, battle of, 10 July–31 October 1940

Decisive battle which saved Britain from invasion during the Second World War.

KEY REFERENCE: Hough, R. & Richards, D. *The Battle of Britain* (Coronet Books, 1990).

During the course of the Second World War there were countless aerial skirmishes in the skies above Britain, with the series of actions during the late summer and early autumn of 1940 being collectively known as the Battle of Britain. As this is one of the most recent entries in this volume, it is difficult to be entirely subjective, as the battle has become part of the national myth as well as the nation's history, with Churchill's famous words of 'never in the field of human conflict was so much owed by so many to so few' helping to cocoon the actual events from close inspection. However, it is safe to say that success in the battle was vital to Britain as she stood alone (along with her Empire and Dominions) after the fall of France. If events had gone the other way, it is easy to imagine a successful German invasion of mainland Britain, even if Hitler's gaze was already starting to shift east to the USSR. To secure a Channel crossing for his troops, Hitler had to clear the skies in advance, with the attempt to do this commencing on 10 July 1940. German planes largely from Kesselring's Luftflotte (Airfleet) 2 attacked shipping in the Channel and British planes largely from the south-eastern 11 Group of Fighter Command under Park, supported by Leigh Mallory's 12 Group. In overall charge of the German effort was Reichsmarschall Hermann Goering, while at the head of Britain's Fighter Command was Sir Hugh Dowding. The main German attack came in mid-August with the Eagle Attack as efforts turned to hit radar installations and airfields. German pilots at this stage of the war had on average greater experience in action than their RAF counterparts. In addition, the German fighters flew in the tactically adaptable formation of mutually supporting pairs. Against this the RAF generally flew in less flexible V formations of three, while disputes occurred between the grand tactics of the two main fighter wings. Park favoured fighting by single squadrons, while Leigh Mallory preferred to group squadrons together to form a 'big wing'. While such a formation could be effective against large German units, it did take valuable time to assemble. The RAF were helped by the advance warning given by radar and by the Observer Corps, which enabled their fighters more often than not to be in the air in the right place and at the right time, while the German fighters were struggling to conserve fuel supplies, especially if combat was heavy. At the start of the battle the German Luftwaffe outnumbered the RAF by approximately 900 fighters to 600, along with around 1,500 bombers of various types.

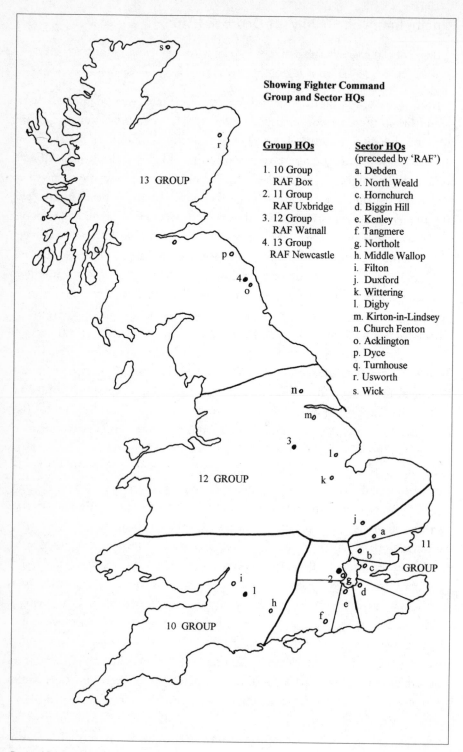

**Showing Fighter Command
Group and Sector HQs**

Group HQs	**Sector HQs**
	(preceded by 'RAF')
1. 10 Group	a. Debden
RAF Box	b. North Weald
2. 11 Group	c. Hornchurch
RAF Uxbridge	d. Biggin Hill
3. 12 Group	e. Kenley
RAF Watnall	f. Tangmere
4. 13 Group	g. Northolt
RAF Newcastle	h. Middle Wallop
	i. Filton
	j. Duxford
	k. Wittering
	l. Digby
	m. Kirton-in-Lindsey
	n. Church Fenton
	o. Acklington
	p. Dyce
	q. Turnhouse
	r. Usworth
	s. Wick

13 GROUP

12 GROUP

11 GROUP

10 GROUP

Battle of Britain, 10 July–31 October 1940.

By late August the Luftwaffe was on the brink of victory as the RAF began to run out of pilots and the damage to airfields came close to crisis point. Night raids by that time were hitting industrial targets hard, although British aircraft production still soared. In a final attempt to destroy the RAF's resistance, large-scale daytime raids of London were ordered from 7 September. After being initially surprised by this change of target, the RAF met subsequent raids on the capital, although heavy damage resulted, particularly at night. A key massive raid came on 15 September, with every available RAF fighter in the air. This proved to be the turning point, as the Luftwaffe sustained proportionately heavier losses continuing through the rest of September. After 30 September daylight raids stopped, although night attacks continued, giving rise to the Blitz, which continued into May 1941. The Battle of Britain ended at the end of October, although Hitler postponed the intended invasion codenamed Operation Sealion on 12 October. During the battle, estimates of enemy planes shot down varied tremendously according to which side's statistics were used. The modern tally gives 1,733 German losses with 915 RAF planes being destroyed. Churchill's famous 'Few' amounted officially to 2,945 aircrew with 507 being killed. About ten per cent of Fighter Command's pilots during the battle came from overseas.

There are many sites to visit connected with the Battle of Britain across the South-East, with impressive displays at the RAF Museum Hendon and the Imperial War Museum Duxford, which was home to Douglas Bader's squadron and others during the battle. Smaller museums with displays on the battle can be visited at Shoreham, Hawkinge (the Kent Battle of Britain Museum) and Lashenden in Kent, while there are impressive memorials at Manston, Croydon in Surrey and on the white cliffs between Folkestone and Dover. A new memorial naming 'the Few' is planned for central London on the Embankment.

Broncroft Castle, siege of, 4 July 1645

Parliamentarian forces moved into this Shropshire castle in June 1645, although the Royalists had slighted much of the original defences earlier in the year. An attack by the latter was attempted on 4 July, but the Parliamentarian defenders fought off the assault.

Brunanburh, battle of, 937

Important victory for the English King Athelstan against a combined force of Scots, Irish and Northumbrian Vikings.

KEY REFERENCE: Wood, M. *In Search of England* (Viking, 1999).

Athelstan had invaded Scotland in 933 or 934, but in 937 the boot was on the other foot, as a coalition force led by the new Norse King of Dublin, Olaf, attacked from the north. The site of the battle has been much debated, with some forty sites being put forward from Devon to Scotland. Modern scholarship has tended to point to a site now largely covered by railway sidings next to Tinsley, between the M1 motorway and Sheffield, not least due to place-name evidence. The nearby village of Brinsworth is the same as the Brynesford in Domesday Book. However, Brunanburh suggests Bruna's hill or fort rather than a ford, so this may not be as convincing as first thought. Certainly though, this area has to be a strong contender for the battle site. It lies at the extremity of Northumbrian territory of the period, making it a natural place for Athelstan to advance to in an attempt to stop the invasion. It is also on one of the few main routes for any invader moving south, with a gap through the ancient forest, which has now shrunk to the few surviving trees of Tinsley Wood.

Wherever the battle was fought, rather more of the details of the action are known, with the *Anglo-Saxon Chronicle* turning to verse. We hear that the English under Athelstan and his brother Edmund put their enemies to flight with spear and sword, after attacking at dawn. The *Chronicle* also mentions the use of elite cavalry by the men from Wessex, which raises the possibility that part of the Saxon armies of this period did have the capability of fighting on horseback, a suggestion normally dismissed. Five kings were 'put to sleep by swords' by Athelstan's men, along with seven of Olaf's Irish Norse earls, forcing him to return to Dublin. The battle certainly helped Athelstan to consolidate his kingdom and to help create a more unified England.

Burton Bridge, skirmish of, 2 July 1643

Gallant charge by the Royalist Thomas Tyldesley and his regiment of horse across the 500m-long Burton Bridge to gain entry into the town of Burton-on-Trent, gaining him his knighthood from King Charles I.

Burton Bridge, stand-off of, 10 March 1322

Preliminary to the defeat of Thomas of Lancaster at the battle of Boroughbridge.

Thomas of Lancaster rose in rebellion against King Edward II and moved against him from his muster-point at Doncaster. The two armies met on either side of the River Trent, at Burton-on-Trent, where the 500m-long Burton Bridge still spans the river, although the structure has been modified from the bridge of 1322. With the king outnumbering him and with the difficulty of crossing the long, narrow bridge, Lancaster sat and waited for three days after the initial skirmishes. The skirmishes had involved Edward sending a force of cavalry and infantry to cross, but they being prevented from doing so by archers and men-at-arms. With Lancaster being reinforced by the Earl of Hereford, Edward made a decisive move by fording the Trent upstream, probably at Walton, despite it running high and fast. This outflanking move made Lancaster's position untenable and his army retreated north, leading to his final stand and defeat at Boroughbridge.

Burwell, attack on, September 1143

Attack by the rebel baron Geoffrey de Mandeville against King Stephen, resulting in Geoffrey's death.

KEY REFERENCE: Bradbury, J. *Stephen and Matilda, the Civil War of 1139–53* (Alan Sutton, 1996).

In 1139 Ely had been a base for rebellion against King Stephen. He moved to counter any future threat by ordering the construction of a number of castles, including one at Burwell. This was still incomplete at the time of this attack by Geoffrey de Mandeville, who hoped to ferment further rebellion in the east. He moved up to survey the castle and to decide upon the direction of his impending attack. This was done without a helmet, an oversight noticed by a crossbowman inside the castle. Sure enough, his quarrel hit Geoffrey in the head, leading to his death a week later. This nipped the eastern rebellion in the bud, allowing Stephen to concentrate his forces in the west.

Byland (Abbey), battle of, 14 October 1322

Last battle of Edward II's Scottish Wars.

Despite the importance of this battle, its exact location is not known, as the two contemporary sources for the action are imprecise or disagree. One, the English

Lanercost Chronicle, has King Edward II at Rievaulx Abbey, with an advance force under the Earl of Richmond on the heights (possibly Scawton Moor) between Rievaulx Abbey and Byland Abbey. This force was defeated by the Scots under King Robert the Bruce, after the Scots climbed up a steep valley cut into the hillside. The English were caught by surprise, and attempted to repel the Scots by flinging stones at them as they climbed. When Edward realised what had happened, he retreated with the rest of his army, 'chicken-hearted and luckless in war' as the *Lanercost Chronicle* informs us, while the Scots raided the abbey and returned north with the Earl of Richmond a prisoner. From the Scottish source of John Barbour, known as *the Bruce,* we learn that Edward II was at Byland Abbey, while the Scots attacked the English force on the high ground to the north (as local legend has it, by Scotch Corner) just to the north of Oldstead. Again Edward is said to have fled, leaving Byland Abbey and his crown jewels to be looted. From this, one can see that the exact site of the battlefield is at present impossible to locate, although the moors between Byland and Rievaulx abbeys (both in the care of English Heritage) provide a likely location, as well as being a beautiful place to visit.

Bytham Castle, siege of, February 1220

Capture of this castle in Lincolnshire after its owner the Baron Albemarle rebelled against King Henry III.

C

Cadbury Castle, siege of, *c.* AD 43

Probable site of a Roman assault during the Claudian invasion of AD 43.

It is from the classical author Suetonius that we discover that the later Emperor Vespasian 'fought thirty battles, subjugated two warlike tribes, and captured more than twenty towns (*oppida*), besides the entire Isle of Wight', while serving as commander of the II Augusta legion in the invasion of AD 43. Archaeology has been able to supply us with the flesh to put on these bare bones, as well as sometimes the bones themselves.

Cadbury Castle in Somerset was excavated by Leslie Alcock and it surrendered a number of finds relating to the early Roman period, although the evidence was not as conclusive as for the other hill forts of Maiden Castle and Hod Hill. A large quantity of human bones were found, possibly victims of a massacre, while there were also several items of Roman military equipment.

The dating tests on these gave two main groupings, which could suggest that the hill fort fell during the initial invasion or, perhaps more likely, that it was stormed as a result of a local revolt connected with the later Boudiccan revolt.

Caesar's first expedition, 25 August–mid-September 55 BC

Earliest entry in this dictionary of known historical actions.

Julius Caesar planned an expedition in strength to Britain because some of the British tribes had provided assistance to the Gauls in France, which had been a nuisance to Rome. There was also the potential of economic gain, but perhaps most importantly of all, a successful expedition across the ocean would add greatly to Caesar's prestige as he strove for greater political power. With an invasion in mind, Caesar built up his forces in 56 BC, but he was forced to delay his expedition until late August 55 BC due to problems with tribes in Gaul and from across the Rhine.

From Caesar's own account of the campaign we learn that his invasion force consisted of two legions (the 7th and the 10th) in about eighty transports, with a number of warships as escorts and to transport the headquarters' staff. He also tells us that the officers of the auxiliary troops were carried on these ships, suggesting that auxiliary infantry could also have been part of the invasion force, as would be expected. Certainly eighty transports seems to be a high number for just two legions (carrying about 100–120 men plus their equipment each). We know that auxiliary cavalry were planned to be part of the invasion, as eighteen transports had been set aside for them, although they sailed from a different port to the north of the main fleet. The latter sailed at midnight on 25 August, appearing off the British coast, probably near Dover, at about 9.00 a.m. on 26 August. The cliffs were already lined with enemy tribesmen, and Caesar waited until 3.00 p.m. for the whole of the main fleet to arrive. He then sailed about seven miles up the coast before attempting to land on the beach in the Walmer area (a commemorative plaque on Walmer Green marks the possible site). Due to the steeply shelving nature of the beach, the transports ran aground while there was still some water to their front, making a landing very difficult as the British had followed the Romans along the coast.

At first the Roman infantry failed to gain a foothold, as the British cavalry and chariots repelled them with javelins. Caesar then ordered his warships to move against the enemy's flank, running aground slightly higher up the beach as they had a shallower draught. Employing missile fire, these ships provided cover for a renewed attempt. At first there was hesitation, but finally the eagle-bearer of the 10th legion jumped into the water and urged his comrades to follow him or else lose their standard. A hard-fought and confused action followed, but eventually the Romans secured a foothold and then a bridgehead on the beach.

Some tribes sued for peace and handed over hostages, while Caesar prepared for a thrust inland. Four or five days later the cavalry transports appeared off the coast, but they were immediately scattered by a storm, which also wrecked many of the beached ships from the main fleet. This made Caesar's situation precarious, as he was without cavalry, supplies or enough ships to take his men back to Gaul. The British responded quickly, gathering a force together to attack the stranded Romans. A large part of (or possibly the entire) 7th legion was caught while foraging for grain by a large native force in a hit-and-run attack with cavalry and chariots, which was beaten off as Caesar arrived with reinforcements. A further battle followed, when a large force of infantry and cavalry attacked the Romans, who were in battle formation outside their camp. The Romans soon won and the Britons again sued for peace. Caesar took more hostages and then returned to Gaul with his army, presumably in repaired transports. He had learned much about the British way of fighting and was determined to return with a larger force to gain greater success. It is possible that a future archaeological discovery will determine where his main camp was, although erosion and coastal changes make this unlikely.

Caesar's second expedition, early July–mid-September 54 BC

Large-scale expedition in which Caesar revealed Britain to Rome.

Following his first expedition to Britain the previous year, Caesar returned with a larger force, determined to gain greater success. For this new attempt Caesar had five legions and 2,000 cavalry, possibly as well as more auxiliary infantry, in a fleet of over 800 ships, many of which were specially designed transports of shallow draught to make beaching easier. Understandably, they landed unopposed, probably near Sandwich, before setting off inland having left the beached fleet guarded by a mixed force under Quintus Atrius.

Caesar pressed inland in a bold night march of about twelve miles, which brought him to a defended river crossing – probably the Stour. The Romans fought their way across, largely thanks to their cavalry, which drove off the British chariots and horsemen. Once across, they found themselves up against a defended hill fort – probably Bigbury, just to the west of Canterbury – which the 7th legion stormed in *testudo* with shields locked over their heads. The next day Caesar sent out three pursuing columns, but news then reached him of a storm and resulting damage to his fleet, much as had happened in 55 BC. He returned to supervise the repairs, giving the British time to regroup under one of their leaders, Cassivellaunus. As Caesar crossed Kent, his forces were attacked on several occasions by raiding-parties, including one more major attack while the Romans were foraging. However, all these were beaten off, leaving Caesar able to cross the Thames into Cassivellaunus's territory.

The Thames was forded, although not without difficulty, as the crossing was defended by sharpened stakes and enemy forces. It seems that Cassivellaunus had realised he stood little chance against the Romans in open battle and so adopted the guerrilla tactics of hit-and-run, with 4,000 charioteers moving quickly against the enemy in largely wooded terrain. However, Cassivellaunus still relied on his bases, such as the large *oppidum* at Wheathampstead in Hertfordshire, which was probably the site of the last major action of the campaign. This was taken when the Romans attacked it from two sides, breaking in and capturing men and cattle, despite it being heavily fortified. Cassivellaunus made a final attempt to defeat Caesar by ordering four allied kings in Kent to attack the defended bridgehead. However, the Romans made a sortie from their camp and defeated the Britons. A peace treaty was drawn up, with Caesar taking hostages back to Gaul to ensure its terms were met. No doubt he intended to return and possibly to bring Britain under the rule of the Republic, but future events dictated that this was not to be. Instead it would be nearly 100 years before Britain fell to Rome.

Camlann, battle of, 511–539?

Possibly mythical battle which saw the death of Arthur.

KEY REFERENCE: Alcock, L. *Arthur's Britain* (Pelican Books, 1982).

Details of this battle are historically more vague than those for Badon. However, it seems likely that such a battle did take place, based on an entry in the *Welsh Easter Annals*, which tells us that Arthur and Medraut (presumably Mordred) perished in the 'strife of Camlann'. That this battle still excites interest cannot be doubted, as there is a visitor centre near Slaughterbridge in Cornwall dedicated to Arthur and the battle, although the battle in question has only a very tenuous link to that area, with the place-name of the nearby River Camel not having a clear and valid connection to Camlann in early Welsh. The later associations of the area with Arthur only came in the twelfth century. A much more likely location is the fort of Birdoswald on Hadrian's Wall, which has the earlier name of Camboglanna. However, it would seem reasonable to suggest that the battle was instead fought in Wales at Camlan, to the south-east of Dolgellau, and therefore has no place in a volume about English battlefields!

Canon Frome, siege of, 22 June 1645

Storming and capture of this fortified manor house in Herefordshire by a force of Scots under Lord Leven, ending with the slaughter of many of the Royalist defenders.

Canterbury, battle of, 851

Having over-wintered in England for the first time, a Viking force of 350 ships stormed London and Canterbury, routing Beorhtwulf of Mercia.

Carham, battle of, 1018

Battle fought between King Malcolm of Scotland and Earl Uchtred of Northumbria, resulting in victory for the Scots and the establishment of the River Tweed as the border in that area. The site of the battle is traditionally placed between Wark and Cornhill, just to the south of the Tweed, rather than at Carham, a little to the west.

Carham, battle of, 1370

Minor battle in which the Scottish Sir John Gordon defeated the English Sir John Lilburn, just to the south of the River Tweed between Carham and Wark.

Carham, siege of, 10 January–February 1138

Siege fought in the build-up to the battle of the Standard at Northallerton later in the year.

William, the nephew of King David of Scotland, made a night attack on the castle at Carham on 10 January 1138. This surprise storming failed, so the Scots waited for a larger force so that a regular siege could be conducted. King David and his son Henry arrived and began a three-week siege with 'battering machines and other implements', according to Richard of Hexham. This still did not succeed, so David gave up the siege and devastated Northumberland instead.

Carhampton, battle of, 836

A Danish raid consisting of twenty-five or thirty-five ships attacked and beat a Saxon force under King Egbert on the shores of the Bristol Channel in Somerset.

Carhampton, battle of, 843

Following their earlier raid in 836, the Vikings returned to this estate in Somerset with a force of thirty-five ships, winning another victory.

Carlisle, sieges of, 1136 and 1157

Capture of this important border town and castle by King David I of Scotland, despite new defences ordered by King Henry I. The town was retaken by King Henry II of England in 1157.

Carlisle, siege of, 22 July–1 August 1315

Siege by King Robert Bruce of Scotland, which was called off after the arrival of a relieving force.

The Scots attacked all three gates into Carlisle, but were driven off by the fire of the defenders. A number of siege engines were used on both sides, with the Scots employing a large 'machine for casting stones' against the Caldew Gate on 26 July as the *Lanercost Chronicle* tells us. However, this did little damage, with just one man being killed. A 'sow' was then used, which was a covered, wheeled machine sheltering a number of men who could then attempt to bring down the wall. This too failed, leading to a major assault from a number of catapults and other engines on 30 and 31 July. This was followed up by a large attack on the eastern defences to draw away defenders from the western side, which was then stormed by James Douglas, although even his attack was driven

Carlisle, 1315. Initial letter of Edward II's charter to Carlisle in 1316. The Scots are shown attacking the city with a 'machine for casting stones', while a miner with a pick works at the foot of a wall.

off. On 1 August the siege was called off with the Scots retiring north on the arrival of a relief force.

Carlisle, siege of, October 1644–25 June 1645

Parliamentarian siege of this important northern town.

Once York had fallen to Parliament after the Battle of Marston Moor , Carlisle became the main Royalist stronghold in the North. Accordingly, Parliament and the Scottish Covenanters moved to capture it, laying siege to the town in October 1644. They occupied the surrounding villages and settled down to a long siege, with the defenders led by Sir Thomas Glemham (who went on to command the garrison at Oxford) surrendering under terms in June 1645 to the Scottish General Leslie.

Castle Cary, siege of, 1138

Early siege during the Civil War of King Stephen's reign.

Similar to the siege of Bedford in the same year, Stephen surrounded and used siege engines against the castle. The garrison soon came to terms and surrendered.

Castle Dore, battle of, 31 August–1 September 1644,
see Lostwithiel, battle of, 21 August–2 September 1644

Castleford, battle of, 948

King Eadred of England returning from the burning of Ripon Minster was caught crossing the River Aire at Castleford by a largely Viking army from York led by Eric 'Bloodaxe' and was defeated.

Cerdic's Ford, battle of, 519

Battle which established the West Saxon Kings.

This was probably fought at Charford in Hampshire, with the Saxons led by Cerdic and his son Cynric fighting against, and presumably beating, a British army.

Cerdic's Shore, battle of, 495 and 514

Two battles fought at the same unknown location.

Cerdic and his son Cynric fought and defeated a British force as they landed at this unknown location in AD 495. Nineteen years later, three ships of West Saxons led by Stuf and Wihtgar defeated another British army.

Cerdic's Wood, battle of, 527

Battle between West Saxons Cerdic and Cynric against the Britons, at an unknown location.

Chalgrove, skirmish of, 18 June 1643

Typical cavalry skirmish of the First Civil War, which would pass largely unnoticed were it not for the leadership displayed by Prince Rupert and the mortal wounding of John Hampden.

KEY REFERENCE: English Heritage: *Battlefield Report, Chalgrove 1643* (English Heritage, London, 1995).

When is a skirmish not a skirmish? A reasonable answer would seem to be 'when it is at a registered battlefield', for Chalgrove in terms of its size and the nature of the action should certainly rank as a skirmish, although it has quite properly been registered as a battlefield by English Heritage, due to the involvement and in particular the mortal wounding of John Hampden, who was one of the five members King Charles I attempted to arrest in the House of Commons in 1642.

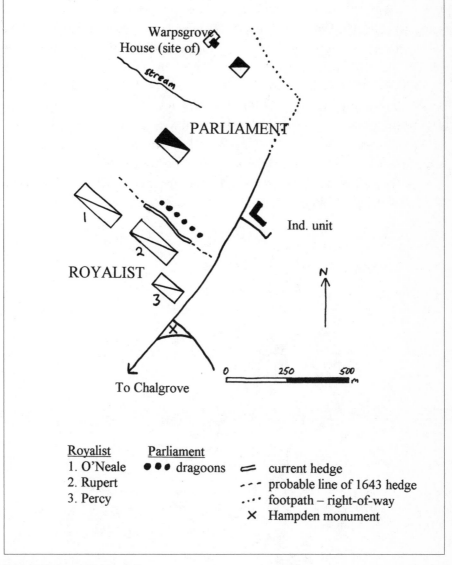

Battle of Chalgrove, 18 June 1643.

Prince Rupert (nephew of King Charles I) had moved out of Oxford with a force of 2,000 foot, horse and dragoons, in an attempt to capture a baggage train carrying the pay chest for the Parliamentarian Earl of Essex's army. He failed to do this, although he did surprise a Parliamentarian force at Chinnor which raised the alarm, forcing him to head back for his uncle's base at Oxford, which involved crossing the River Thame at Chislehampton. In wishing to ensure his men crossed safely, Rupert decided to turn and attempt to surprise his Parliamentarian pursuers, who had picked up the trail and threatened to cut him off. He sent his foot on their way to enable them to cross the bridge, while his dragoons were posted along the hedges lining the road between the bridge and Chalgrove, where he waited with his 1,200 horse. The latter took up position in one of Chalgrove's large, open fields, then with standing growing corn in it, to the north/north-east of Chalgrove village. The road pattern has been altered due to the construction of Chalgrove Airfield in the Second World War, but the location and boundaries of the field, known from a map of 1679 as Sand Field, can be traced. Remnants of the hedged field boundary, then as part of the boundary with Warpsgrove, can be seen from the gate opposite the light industrial unit beyond the Hampden Monument, although sadly there is no public access to this key part of the battlefield.

The Parliamentarians approached over the ridge to the east, sweeping down to approach Sand Field from the north-east from the direction of Warpsgrove.

Drawing from the statue of Sir John Hampden in St Stephen's Hall, Westminster. His nickname, 'the Patriot', explains his lasting popularity. He died as a result of wounds suffered at Chalgrove in 1643.

With perhaps 100 dragoons closely supported by 400 horse in total, the Parliamentarians found themselves outnumbered as they approached the hedge to their front shortly after 9.00 a.m. Prince Rupert, bold or impetuous as ever, put his horse to the hedge and got among the Parliamentarian dragoons on the other side once fifteen or so of his comrades had joined him. The dragoons fled and the main action developed to the left of Rupert where Lieutenant-Colonel O'Neale with a regiment of Royalist horse worked his way round the end of (or possibly at a break in) the hedge to outflank the Parliamentarians. The latter had seen O'Neale move to their right and eight of their eleven troops of horse redeployed to face this new threat, leaving nothing to face Rupert once the dragoons had fled. After firing carbines and pistols at the charging Royalists, the Parliamentarians moved forward and put up a good fight before being overwhelmed. Having manoeuvred to fight O'Neale, they had exposed their left flank to Rupert and his reserves, who forced them to flee. It is quite possible that Rupert only jumped the hedge once the Parliamentarian horse had re-deployed, and perhaps this explains their re-deployment, as to do so after Rupert had crossed the hedge would have been tactical suicide. That the Royalist account puts events into the order relayed above can be explained by the author's wish to heighten Rupert's personal role in the action. Following the defeat of the main body of Parliamentarian horse, the Royalists pursued up towards Warpsgrove House (the original burnt down, but the site is marked by a white house), where a reserve of three troops of Parliamentarians waited in an enclosed field of pasture. These were easily routed and the pursuit continued back over the hill from where the Parliamentarians had come. During the battle, Hampden was mortally wounded to die six days later and some forty-five of his comrades died, with perhaps twenty Royalists meeting the same fate. The monument sited just to the south of the battlefield was unveiled 200 years to the day after the action.

Cheriton, battle of, 29 March 1644

An important turning point in the First Civil War in the South, forcing King Charles I to fight a largely defensive war thereafter.

KEY REFERENCE: Adair, J. *Cheriton 1644: The Campaign and the Battle* (The Roundwood Press, Kineton, 1973)

Cheriton has been strangely neglected in several general battlefield works, for it was in many ways the Marston Moor of the South, guaranteeing the

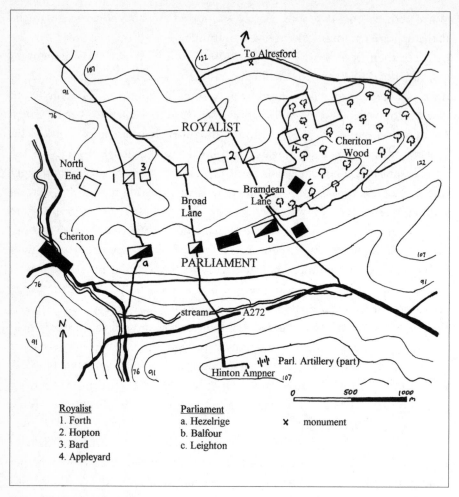

Battle of Cheriton, 29 March 1644.

safety of the southern counties for Parliament just as Marston Moor did for much of the North. Admittedly there were still setbacks to come for Parliament after Cheriton, most notably in the South-West leading to Lostwithiel, but Sir William Waller's victory over his Royalist friend Sir Ralph Hopton was certainly significant. The sources for the battle are varied but at times confusing, which may explain the relative paucity of modern accounts. This has led to much debate as to the precise location of the battle, although the general area is agreed upon, being somewhere between Cheriton Lane to the north towards Alresford and Hinton Ampner to the south of the modern A272 and River Itchen. The most thorough modern work, that of John Adair, places the battle at the southern limits of this area, although this account will argue for a battlefield further north, much as favoured by William Seymour in his *Battles in Britain*, as well as that put forward in the *Register of Historic Battlefields* (English Heritage, 1995.) As is the case with so many battlefields of this period, important new evidence could be discovered by a systematic, professionally overseen metal-detector survey of the area, which may well resolve the still partly unanswered questions about this battle.

The rival forces of Waller and Hopton had manoeuvred and fought against each other during the autumn of 1643 and the subsequent winter. By March 1644 Waller moved against Winchester, giving Hopton the chance to cut Waller's lines of communication with London. To do this Hopton moved towards Alresford, while Waller followed him once he realised what was afoot. The Royalists just won the race to Alresford, camping on the high ground just to the south on 27 March. Waller was not far behind, for there was skirmishing during the next day as the whole of the Parliamentarian army closed up and camped in the valley now followed by the A272 and River Itchen by Hinton Ampner. Immediately to the north of this wet valley was the southern edge of the high ground running north to the Royalists and Alresford. The key to understanding the course of events is to appreciate the nature of the landscape, with a series of three west-to-east ridges, the first overlooking the valley occupied by Waller's army; the second, an 'intermediate' ridge meeting the middle of Cheriton Wood to the east; and the third running to the north of Cheriton Wood. Further north still is Tichborne Down, the site of the Royalist camp and higher than the land further south where the battle was fought. The exact extent of Cheriton Wood in 1644 is not known, although it was certainly substantial, if not spreading quite so far north as it does today. To the west, on a line just north of the first or southernmost ridge, is the village of Cheriton. The high ground is now transected by three lanes running north to south: Bramdean Lane in the east, running beside the western edge of Cheriton Wood; Broad Lane running south to Hinton Ampner; and Dark Lane to the west. These lanes probably all existed in 1644 and were largely hedged, a factor which was to cause problems when deploying during the battle. Hopton had just over 2,000 horse and probably 2,500 foot. In addition, he had a further 800 horse and 1,200 foot under the command of Lord Forth, who was nominally Hopton's superior, although leaving most of the battlefield decisions to Hopton. Opposing these Royalist forces, Waller had 5,000 horse, 5,000 foot and several hundred dragoons, giving them a clear superiority even if 2,000 of Waller's foot consisted of previously untried London regiments.

Hopton informs us that on 28 March, following prolonged but small-scale skirmishing, some of his men reached the top of a hill, which enabled them to look down into the Parliamentarian camp, which must mean they had seized the southernmost crest directly looking down into the valley where the River Itchen flows. Beyond the camp (where there is still a hamlet named Little London, perhaps after the London regiments who camped there), Hopton records Parliamentarian artillery on the high ground by Hinton Ampner. Hopton placed a detachment of 1,000 musketeers under Sir George Lisle in 'a little wood on the top of that hill with a fense [sic] about it', along with 500 horse patrolling a lane. This may mean that Lisle had been placed in the south-western corner of Cheriton Wood, or quite possibly in a smaller, now lost, wood on the crest of the southern ridge, with the horse on Bramdean or possibly Broad Lane. It is hard to imagine Cheriton Wood being described as 'little', nor as having a fence all around it, nor as being on the top of the hill enabling men stationed there to keep watch on the valley floor to the south. Hopton and Forth then pulled back the remainder of their forces to Tichborne Down, leaving Lisle as a forlorn hope, perhaps mindful of Waller's reputation as the 'Night Owl' and not wanting to be caught by any manoeuvres in the dark, which hopefully would be detected by Lisle.

Waller did not disappoint, for towards the end of the night he ordered a force of 1,000 musketeers and artillery led by Leighton into Cheriton Wood: according to Hopton, 'high woody ground that was on the right hand of theire owne [sic] quarters'. From their new position, this force could command the hill where Lisle was, which ties in with the theory that Lisle was in a smaller, separate and slightly lower wood. Forth came forward from Alresford, where he had spent the night, to consult with Hopton, as the force in Cheriton Wood was clearly a threat once their presence was made obvious as the early morning mist cleared at about 9.00 a.m., according to the Parliamentarian Sir Arthur Hezelrige. As the leaves were not yet on the trees, troop movements within the wood, particularly on its edges, could have been detected at some distance. The Royalist forces were brought forward onto the northern of the three ridges and then down into the dead ground between it and the intermediate second ridge before breasting the intermediate crest. Forth's command was on the right towards Cheriton and Hopton's men were in the centre and left, to the north of Cheriton Wood. Hopton ordered 1,000 of his own musketeers under Appleyard into the wood to win it back, as it was the key to dominating both the Parliamentarian right and centre as well as his own left and centre. A fierce fire-fight ensued, to be decided by the arrival of a Royalist flanking party, which drove Leighton's force from the wood. With a decisive move at that point the Royalists may have been able to break Waller's right, but instead Forth dithered, while on the opposite flank Royalist forces became over-committed, giving Waller time to stabilise the situation. Both sides, the Royalists in particular, were stretched with barely enough men to occupy the frontage involved, which may well explain why Forth was unwilling to press forward.

However, it seems that the Royalist right did advance over the intermediate crest and then attacked across East Down towards the Parliamentarian forces, who had climbed the southernmost slope. The forces here were largely horse, as Waller had half of his foot committed on either flank in Cheriton and Cheriton Wood, leaving only about 2,500 for the centre of his position. The Royalist Sir Henry Bard led forward his regiment of foot apparently without orders, to be met by Hezelrige's regiment of armoured horse who cut them off and then killed or captured them to the last man. Fighting spread to the village of Cheriton and its enclosures, where 1,500 Parliamentarian musketeers eventually bettered 1,200 Royalist musketeers. Fighting gradually broke out along the whole line across East Down, between the southern and intermediate ridges. At some point during the afternoon the Royalists attempted to commit their cavalry reserve, but as they filed down one of the hedged lanes (probably Broad Lane) each unit was caught in turn as it tried to deploy. From that point Parliamentarian numbers started to tell, although the fighting continued for perhaps three hours more, until in the late afternoon the Royalists were pushed out of the enclosures by Cheriton on their right and Cheriton Wood on their left. As the Parliamentarians pushed up the slope of the intermediate ridge, the Royalists conducted a fighting retreat back to Tichborne Down. There they gathered themselves and were able to conduct an orderly retreat with most of their forces, first to Basing House and then on to Reading. Lord Forth appears to have commanded the rearguard of horse, which kept turning to face their pursuers. A force of perhaps 1,000 foot held Alresford for a while but they were driven out, killed or captured by Waller's troops. Casualties are hard to assess, particularly as the fighting continued in the retreat after the battle. It would seem that 500 Royalist dead and just over 300 prisoners is a fair estimate, while Waller's losses were not so large.

The battlefield today is a most rewarding site to visit, with the area criss-crossed by public rights of way. There is a battle monument on Cheriton Lane at the foot of Tichborne Down to the north of the battlefield.

Chester, battle of, 605, 606 or probably between 613–616

Victory for the Northumbrians under Aethelfrith.

The *Anglo-Saxon Chronicle* gives the date for this battle as either 605 or 606, although one of the later dates of 613–616 seems more likely. Aethelfrith advanced to Chester and defeated an army of Welshmen, including 200 priests. The *Chronicle* uses the terms 'Britons' and 'Welsh' as one, but as this battle took place so close to modern Wales, it seems appropriate to use the latter term.

Chester, battle of, 893

Leaving their fortification of Benfleet in Essex, a Viking army moved to Chester, slipping into the old Roman city before the English had a chance to catch them, although Viking stragglers were killed and supplies taken.

Chester, siege of, 18 July 1643–3 February 1646

Long-running if intermittent siege of this important Royalist garrison during the First Civil War.

KEY REFERENCE: Barratt, J. *The Great Siege of Chester* (Tempus, 2003).

Chester was held for King Charles I throughout the First Civil War, with the king himself being present during the defeat of his forces at nearby Rowton Heath in 1645. The defences of the city were in good order, with most of the medieval circuit of walls still being visible today. These would have been reinforced by piling earth up against them. Evidence of this was discovered when a ditch 6m inside the wall was found at Abbey Green. It is thought that this was dug to provide the soil for the ramparts. The Parliamentarian commander in the vicinity throughout the war was Sir William Brereton, with him making several attempts against the defences. His first effort came on 18 July 1643 and lasted until 20 July when he withdrew. A more serious attempt came from 7 November 1643 as Brereton conducted a proper siege, blockading the city and capturing some of the outlying garrisons. The situation was becoming serious when a relief force arrived in the form of Charles' Irish army, which landed in North Wales on 18 November and forced Brereton to withdraw a little later. Chester remained safe and not under direct threat until 27 January 1645, when Brereton appeared before its walls once again. An attack was

Chester, 1643–6. Sketch from the 1640s by Randle Holme showing the difficult
approach across the Dee bridge. This was one of the factors which made
bombardment a better option for the attacking Parliamentarians than storming the
town.

mounted against the north gate but this was repelled and soon afterwards on 19
February the city was relieved by a force under Prince Maurice. However, once
Maurice left in March, Brereton returned to resume the siege. He must have
been more confident of success as the garrison had been weakened, leaving only
600 men under the Governor, Lord Byron. During May it looked again as if the
city would fall, although Brereton was also short of troops as he was unable to
press the blockade closely on all sides. On 20 September Brereton moved right
up to the east gate, clearing out the suburbs in that area. However, the king
arrived on 23 September with some 1,500 men, who entered the city while the
2,500 horse under Langdale made to attack the besiegers in their rear, leading
to the battle of Rowton Heath on 24 September. With the Royalist defeat at
Rowton, Charles left Chester for Wales, bringing about the final phase of the
siege. This ran through the winter months, with Brereton's besiegers sealing off
the town and increasing the artillery bombardment. Evidence of the
bombardment during the siege can be found on the east face of the Barnaby
Tower in the south-eastern sector, where twenty cannon-ball marks have been
found on the masonry. The stubborn resistance continued until 3 February,
when the battered and starving defenders finally agreed to terms.

Chesterfield, battle of, 15–16 May 1266

Fought in the aftermath of Simon de Montfort's rebellion against King Henry III.

KEY REFERENCE: Lomax, S. 'The Battle of Chesterfield' in *Battlefield* (vol. 5 issue 4).

Although the barons who fought against Henry III at Evesham had been heavily defeated and their leader Simon de Montfort killed, resistance continued under the banner of 'the Disinherited' until the siege of Ely in 1267. Robert de Ferrers, Earl of Derby, who had been released from prison at the end of 1265, led one group of these barons. He marched from his castle at Duffield to Chesterfield, where reinforcements joined him. However, the king had sent his nephew Henry of Almaine with a group of loyal barons to counter them. Some of the rebels were hunting and it appears that they escaped while Henry's men captured Chesterfield. A rebel counter-attack led by John d'Eyvill seems to have regained control of the town, leading to the king's men setting fire to some houses around midnight. Perhaps aided by this light, the Royalists moved into the town again, securing it despite the efforts of the rebels and some of the townspeople. Ferrers was captured, hiding among wool sacks in the church, then without its famous crooked spire.

Chevy Chase, battle of, *see* Otterburn

Chewton Mendip, skirmish of, 10 June 1643

Vigorous skirmish fought between Prince Maurice for the Royalists and Waller for Parliament.

After their victory at Stratton earlier in the year, Hopton's Royalist Cornish army marched east across Devon and into Somerset, linking up with other Royalist units and coming under the command of Prince Maurice (nephew of King Charles I and younger brother of Prince Rupert). Waller drew some of his army from Bath towards the advancing Royalists, placing his own regiment of horse on Nedge Hill to the south-west of Chewton Mendip. The Royalist horse charged, gaining the upper hand, before Prince Maurice was wounded and disappeared having been captured for a short time. As evening gave way to night the fighting petered out, with the Royalists having had the better of the skirmish, forcing Waller to retreat back towards Bath near where the Battle of Lansdown Hill was fought on 5 July.

Chichester, battle of, 894

A Viking force moved east from Devon, moving against Chichester in Sussex as it went. However, the defenders of the fortified burh forced the attacking Vikings away, killing many and capturing some of their ships.

Chippenham, raid of, 878

A Viking force surprised King Alfred of Wessex towards the end of the Christmas festivities, driving him away from Chippenham and towards Athelney in Somerset.

Chowbent, skirmish of, 24 December 1642

Skirmish fought as part of the Royalist Lord Strange's (later the Earl of Derby) unsuccessful attempts to take Manchester.

Lord Strange was rebuffed by a strong force of perhaps 3,000, made up largely of locals armed with basic weapons and tools, at Chowbent near Oldham. They repulsed the Royalists, but those who were mounted pursued too quickly and suffered a temporary reverse at Lowton Common, before those hurrying along on foot arrived to save the day.

Cirencester, battle of, 628

Penda of Mercia defeated Cynegils and Cwichelm of Wessex.

Cirencester, skirmish of, 5 January 1400

A rebellion against King Henry IV by the Earls of Kent and Salisbury was defeated, with John de Montacute, Earl of Salisbury being beheaded for treason on 7 January 1400 after being overpowered by a group of loyalists in Cirencester on 5 January.

Cirencester, storming of, 2 February 1643

Prince Rupert (nephew of King Charles I) led this successful dawn assault with a coordinated attack of 4,000 men from three directions, capturing 1,000 prisoners.

Clifton Moor, battle of, 18 December, 1745

Traditionally regarded as the last battle fought on English soil, fought on the Jacobites' road from Derby to Culloden.

The Jacobite invasion of 1745 reached as far as Derby before the supporters of Charles Edward Stuart, or 'Bonnie Prince Charlie', decided that they had no real hope of taking the capital and that the best strategy would be to withdraw with their forces intact. The resulting retreat took the western route, with the bulk of the army reaching Penrith on 17 December. The weather was appalling, with strong winds and heavy rain making the going very difficult. The rearguard was commanded by Lord George Murray, who arrived in the village of Clifton just south of Penrith on the afternoon of 18 December, having spent the morning escorting the last of the wagons down from Shap Fell and detaching a small force to keep harrying enemy-mounted militia at bay.

We are fortunate in having a range of sources for the battle, not least a letter from Thomas Savage to a friend. Savage lived in Town End Farm Cottage, which still stands and was garrisoned by Jacobite troops during the engagement. Clifton was a village strung out along the main road (now the A6), with enclosed fields running up the hillside to Clifton Moor in the south. The Jacobites decided to make a stand, probably to give their wagon train more time to make good its escape. The Duke of Cumberland, commanding the Hanoverian force, ordered units of cavalry into the village. They fought past an initial ambush party which was lining the hedged enclosures, but were caught by a second party in the houses at the southern end of the village, although they forced a body of Scots' horse to retreat. The Hanoverians withdrew to formulate a better plan of attack now that they thought they knew the strength of the defenders. They moved forward again at about 4.00 p.m., with the light starting to fail, after Savage had slipped out towards them to issue a warning as to the number of recently reinforced highlanders in the village, attracting their attention by waving his hat.

Three regiments of dismounted dragoons moved forward to attack the reinforced Jacobites, perhaps 500 attacking 1,000. The right-hand Hanoverian regiment, Bland's Dragoons, beat off an advance through the enclosures by the MacPhersons, but Kerr's Dragoons, advancing down the road, took heavy flanking fire and were then charged by the regrouped MacPhersons with their broadswords. In the dark and beset on two sides, the dragoons broke and retreated back up the road to the south.

Lord George Murray then pulled his men back, having ensured that the pursuit would stop for that night. Cumberland occupied the village by 6.00 p.m., sleeping in Savage's cottage. The few Hanoverian casualties (probably ten dragoon troopers) were buried in the churchyard, while the fallen Jacobites were buried in a pit where the 'Battle Oak' now stands, with a memorial stone beside it, down a track just to the south of the George and Dragon public house and opposite Town End Farm. The Jacobites were able to continue their retreat, but were finally brought to battle on Culloden Moor on 16 April 1746.

Clyst St Mary, battle of, early August 1549

Battle of the Western Rebellion against the imposition of the reformed prayer book.

KEY REFERENCE: Gould, M. 'Conflicts of the 1549 Western Rebellion' in *The Battlefields Trust Newsletter* April, 1997.

After their defeat at the Battle of Fenny Bridges the rebels, led by Arundell, regrouped outside Exeter, which they were besieging. The royal forces under Lord Russell followed the rebels and stormed them behind their fortified positions in the village. This attack was successful, but confusion ensued for the royal troops who fell back in disorder. A second attack forced its way into the village, partly thanks to the firing of several houses, although Sir William Francis was killed when a rock hit him on the head. The rebels made a last stand at the bridge over the River Clyst, which is possibly incorporated into the current bridge. Resistance collapsed with the death of a key gunner, one John Hammond, who fell after royal troops forded the river and outflanked the position. With many rebels trapped, much slaughter was done. It was then only a matter of time before the final collapse of the rebellion.

Colchester, battle of, 917

After defeating the East Anglian Danes and killing their king at Tempsford, the English moved further east and stormed Colchester, retiring after their success.

Colchester, siege of, 13 June–28 August 1648

Largest and most dramatic siege of the Second Civil War in England.

KEY REFERENCE: Hodgson, T. *The Siege of Colchester 1648* (Colchester Borough Council and Jarrold Publishing, 1998), Jones, P. *The Siege of Colchester 1648* (Tempus, 2003).

With the outbreak of the Second Civil War in Wales in March 1648, unrest in other areas flared into open insurrection. Royalists in Kent and Essex formed a major part of the uprising, with an army being formed in Kent under the Earl of Norwich (Lord Goring). The majority of this army was defeated at Maidstone on 1 June 1648 by Sir Thomas Fairfax, although the Earl of Norwich was able to extricate himself from Kent, cross the Thames and reach Colchester, where he linked up with the Essex Royalists on 12 June. Fairfax had pursued closely, giving Norwich no chance to escape with his 4,000 Royalist troops. On 13 June Fairfax attempted to storm the town after Norwich refused to surrender. However, this was repulsed and so Fairfax had to resort to a formal siege, laying out trenches and batteries around the town's defences.

The siege began with both sides roughly equal in numbers, but as time went on Fairfax received reinforcements, while the number of Royalists diminished. Fairfax made steady progress throughout the second half of June, constructing his siegeworks, until Royalist horse under Lucas and Lisle attempted a break-out from the east gate on 5 July. They burst through the lines of the Suffolk Trained Bands but were then cut off, and many were killed or captured before the remnants made it back into the town. By 14 July, Fairfax felt strong enough to attack the Royalist outposts, especially St John's Abbey to the south of the town walls, which was the family home of the Royalist leader, Sir Charles Lucas. This was captured after fierce fighting, including an explosion of a Royalist gunpowder magazine in the gatehouse, which took its roof off (this building is ironically the main surviving part of the Abbey today). Following the fighting, many Parliamentarian troops turned to looting, causing the

Siege coinage like this was common throughout the Civil War. This piece was cut from gold plate and then stamped, being used by Royalists during the 1648 Siege of Colchester.

desecration of the tombs of the Lucas family within St Giles' Church, two of which contained only relatively recently buried bodies. One of these, the mother of the besieged Sir Charles Lucas, had hair ripped from her corpse and then worn as a grisly trophy of war in some of the soldiers' hats. The capture of the Abbey grounds provided Fairfax with good artillery positions from which his guns could fire into the town, including the tower of St Mary-at-the-Walls, which housed a Royalist saker (small cannon) and its one-eyed and apparently dead-eyed gunner. On 16 July the Royalists turned down an offer to surrender, still having 3,000 men behind seemingly strong walls.

Conditions by this stage were becoming intolerable, especially for the townspeople who had tried to refuse entry to the Royalists in the first place. Some attempts were made by the Royalists to allow the civilians to leave, but they were driven back into the town, as their presence would only worsen conditions for all concerned inside. On 22 July the Parliamentarians fired arrows into the town with messages attached offering pardons to the Royalists. One of these was returned with a turd attached along with the message, 'an answer from Colchester as you may smell'. The following month became ever more desperate for the defenders and civilians. Hope all but left the Royalists on 24 August when Fairfax flew kites into the town bearing news of Cromwell's victory over the Scots at Preston. After a final attempt at escape collapsed when the ordinary Royalist soldiers suspected their officers of desertion, terms for the surrender were arranged on 27 August. 'Fair quarter' was given to the ordinary soldiers, while the higher officers had to accept the 'mercy' of Parliament, once the Parliamentarians entered the town on 28 August. Of these, four leaders, Lisle, Lucas, Farr and Gascoigne were sentenced to be executed, in part to make an example of them, but also because Lisle and Lucas had been captured during the First Civil War and had been paroled on the condition that they promised not to take up arms against Parliament again. Farr escaped through a window, while Gascoigne was pardoned as he was from Florence, and the Parliamentarians did not want a diplomatic incident on their hands. Sir Charles Lucas and Sir George Lisle were not so fortunate and they faced a firing squad at 7.00 a.m. on 29 August, Lucas being shot first, with Lisle kissing his dead comrade before facing the same fate. The site of their execution behind the castle (which has an exhibition about the Civil Wars, among many other interesting displays) is marked by a small obelisk. Other sites connected with the siege can still be seen, in particular the ruins of St Botolph's Priory, which was badly damaged in the crossfire during the siege. Walking tours of sites connected with the siege can be arranged through the Colchester Visitor Information Centre.

Coleford, skirmish of, 20 February 1643

Action in the Forest of Dean fought as Royalist forces tried to reach the forthcoming Siege of Gloucester.

KEY REFERENCE: Peachey, S. *The Battle of Coleford, 1643* (Stuart Press, 1993).

In early 1643, Lord Herbert recruited an army of about 2,000 from South Wales and started to move east to join the planned siege of Gloucester, which finally commenced on 10 August 1643. The Forest of Dean was garrisoned for Parliament by the regiment of foot of Colonel John Berrow, perhaps 600 men strong. It was this unit which the Royalists decided to clear from their path before moving on Gloucester. Berrow formed his men up in the small town of Coleford, probably with some earthwork defences to strengthen them. The Royalists were urged to the attack by their officers, no doubt making these men clear targets. Certainly, several Royalist officers were killed, including Sir Richard Lawley, commander of the foot. It appears that most of the Parliamentarian defenders fled into the forest after a brief fight, although about forty men were taken prisoner. Following this success, the Royalists proceeded to Highnam House to wait for the start of the Siege of Gloucester. However, they were surrounded there and forced to surrender on 24 March 1643.

Cooling Castle, siege of, 30 January 1554

Cooling Castle, north of Rochester, was taken, along with Lord Cobham, by Sir Thomas Wyatt's rebels as they moved towards London to threaten Queen Mary. This episode lost Wyatt valuable time, giving the queen the chance to make preparations in advance of Wyatt's defeat and capture at Temple Bar on 7 February.

Corbridge, battle of, between 913–915

Victory of the Norse King Raegnald, in which he defeated a combined army of Scots and Bernicians led by Earl Ealdred.

Corbridge, battle of, 918?

Although possibly confused with the earlier battle of Corbridge, it appears that Raegnald won a second victory there, mainly against the Scots, on the banks of the Tyne, with some Englishmen fighting on his side rather than against him.

Corbridge, raid of, 1312

Attack by Robert Bruce of Scotland against northern England, resulting in the burning of Corbridge, where his army then set up camp while raids went further west and south, in particular against Durham and Hexham.

Corfe, attack at, 18 March 978

King Edward of Wessex was killed on the evening of 18 March at Corfe 'passage', probably the gap in the ridge still guarded by the medieval castle. It is likely that this was a small-scale attack rather than a formal battle.

Corfe Castle, siege of, 1 May–4 August 1643 and October 1645–26 February 1646

Two Parliamentarian attempts to capture this impressive castle during the First Civil War, whose defence was inspired by Lady Bankes.

KEY REFERENCE: The National Trust: *Corfe Castle* (1985).

The impressive medieval castle of Corfe in Dorset was garrisoned for King Charles I at the beginning of the First Civil War, while most of the county went to Parliament. At the beginning of May 1643, moves were made to blockade the castle, although it was not put under formal siege until June. During May, attempts were made to intimidate Lady Bankes, the holder of the castle, in the absence of her husband (who was with the king), by threatening the houses of her tenants in the village below the castle. During this phase, the Parliamentarians persuaded Lady Bankes to hand over four small cannon in return for being left more or less to her own devices. She used this breathing space well, by re-provisioning the castle and securing help from nearby Royalist forces at Blandford Forum. Among these reinforcements was Captain Laurence, who took over command of the garrison at Corfe in time for the start of the formal siege in June 1643. The siege lasted for six weeks under the command of the Parliamentarian Sir Walter Erle. It was called off after the loss of at least 100 men to only two casualties among the defenders. During the siege, attempts had been made to bribe the defenders, and when these tactics failed two siege engines were made of wooden boards with bundles of wool for protection, one called 'the sow' and the other 'the boar'. However, these were of little use, with 'the sow' losing nine out of eleven men who were hit in the legs, while 'the boar' didn't advance at all. Later a double assault was launched, but this was beaten back with stones and hot embers preventing ladders being put to the wall. Erle called off the siege at that point, due in part to his losses but also because news of a relief force had reached him.

A second attempt was made against Corfe towards the end of the First Civil War, with a larger besieging force employed under the command of Colonel Bingham. In February 1646, a small party of Royalist horse, led by a Colonel Cromwell, rode from Oxford to attempt a rescue of Lady Bankes. However, even though they reached the castle, the redoubtable Lady chose to stay to the bitter end. This was not long in coming, as one of the defenders, called Pittman, decided to betray the garrison by riding out, then returning with a group of Parliamentarians disguised as 100 reinforcements. They quickly secured the Inner Ward of the castle and after two hours fighting, in which the attackers lost one man and the defenders two, the remainder was taken. Lady Bankes was allowed to retain the keys and seals of the castle in recognition of her bravery, but the castle was slighted on the orders of Parliament in March 1646.

The southern tower of the south-west gatehouse, slumped into the ditch, provides clear evidence of this destruction, while the remains of a small motte (or more correctly, 'ring') and bailey earthwork called 'the Rings' just to the south-west indicates the likely position of a Parliamentarian gun battery. This 'castle' had been built as a siegework for King Stephen during an aborted siege against the Earl of Devon, who was inside Corfe Castle in 1138 and 1139. Corfe Castle is now under the care of the National Trust and is open to the public.

Cornwall, raid of, 815

Egbert of Wessex's first attempt to subdue Cornwall.

The *Anglo-Saxon Chronicle* records this raid through Cornwall, possibly as a reprisal for an earlier Cornish raid. Egbert was successful and able to annex some land, although further Cornish raids were to follow in 825 and 838 before the area was finally brought under English control.

Countisbury Hill, battle of, 878

Morale-boosting victory for the Wessex Saxons when they had been forced onto the defensive by the Danish Vikings.

King Alfred of Wessex had been forced into hiding in Athelney following the surprise attack by the Danes at Chippenham over Christmas. A Viking army from twenty-three ships attacked the Saxon Earl Odda at Countisbury Hill (Cynwit) in north Devon. The Vikings were defeated, with their leader killed, along with 800 men and a further forty of his personal retinue or hearth-troop.

Crayford, battle of, 456 or 457

Battle which secured Kent for the Anglo-Saxons.

After the death of Horsa at the battle of Aylesford, the Anglo-Saxons continued to press for more land. Horsa was replaced by Hengest's son, Aesc. Hengest and Aesc led the invaders in a battle at Crayford, in north-west Kent. A large number of Britons were killed, leading to a withdrawal of British forces from Kent to London.

Cropredy Bridge, battle of, 29 June 1644

Battle in the Oxford Campaign of 1644, which provided Waller's Parliamentarians with a good opportunity to destroy the army led by King Charles I in person.

KEY REFERENCE: Toynbee, M. and Young, P. *Cropredy Bridge, 1644: The Campaign and the Battle* (The Roundwood Press, Kineton, 1970).

The Oxford Campaign had started off brightly for Parliament, with the two armies of Sir William Waller and the Earl of Essex well placed to outnumber, surround and defeat the forces of King Charles I in or near Oxford. However, the two Parliamentarian commanders had little time for one another and after some initial successes for Parliament, such as the taking of Reading, the Royalists had out-manoeuvred their numerically superior opponents. In particular, just as the trap was closing around the king, he slipped between his two enemies with the bulk of his army on the night of 3 June 1644, leaving Oxford with a small guarding force and much artillery. On 6 June Essex and Waller met, probably at Chipping Norton, where they agreed to divide their forces and their aims, with Essex moving south-west to relieve Lyme, while

Waller continued to track and hopefully defeat the king. This was a disastrous decision for Parliament, removing their best chance of defeating the king outright in 1644. Although they could not have known this at the time, it also led to Essex's calamitous Cornish campaign later in the summer, leading to his army's defeat at Lostwithiel, while Waller's reputation was damaged by events at Cropredy Bridge.

The armies of the king and Waller then marched and counter-marched across the Cotswolds and beyond, until finally both were in the Banbury area by 27 June. Their two armies were roughly equal by this time, and both sought to bring the other to battle so long as a tactical advantage could be secured. It seems that the king had about 4,000 horse, divided into four brigades, along with 5,500 foot and ten cannon, while Waller's army was of a similar size and nature, although the exact composition is not as clear as the Royalists'. By the morning of 29 June Waller had taken possession of the commanding Crouch Hill to the north of Banbury, persuading Charles to move away towards Daventry, with the River Cherwell between his forces and those of Waller, who followed him along the river's western bank. The river would probably have been wider and deeper in 1644 than it is today, due in part to the construction of the Oxford Canal, which lies immediately to the west of the Cherwell. When Waller's army reached Bourton Hill, just to the west of the village of Cropredy, the position of the king's army in its column of march to the east was plain to see. Reminiscent of Wellington at Salamanca, except for in that crucial sphere of the battles' comparative outcomes, Waller observed that Charles' army had become too strung out, with the rear separated from the main body and van by well over a mile. Charles, with the van and main body, had already crossed the Cherwell at Hays Bridge to the north of Wardington. He advanced quickly to attempt to cut off a unit of 300 Parliamentarian horse who were trying to reach Waller, while the Royalist rear had not yet reached that village and was continuing to march at a standard speed, with its foremost brigade under Cleveland, followed or flanked by Astley, with Northampton at the back. The road the Royalists were following between Williamscot and Wardington lies along a ridge, although its top is flat and relatively broad, meaning that the road is not visible from Cropredy and its bridge. This perhaps helps to explain how the Parliamentarians were able to cross at Cropredy Bridge (which has a plaque commemorating the battle) only opposed by the small force of Royalist dragoons sent to guard it. It also helps to explain why the Parliamentarians appear to have become somewhat disorientated once over the bridge, as they would have lost sight of the main Royalist formations on the flat-topped ridge to their front.

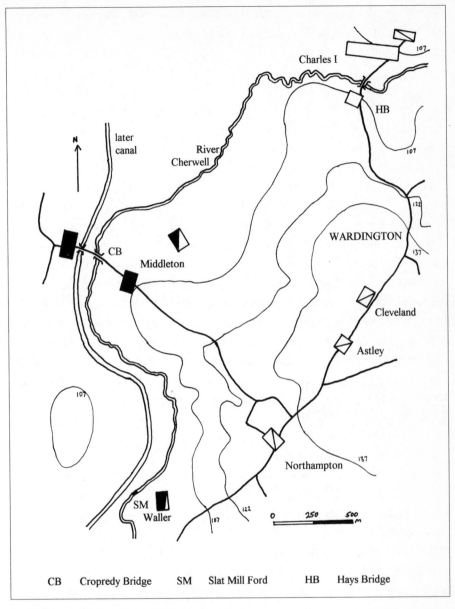

Battle of Cropredy Bridge, 29 June 1644.

Waller ordered forward two bodies of troops at about 1.00 p.m. One of these was under Middleton consisting of nine companies of foot, two regiments of horse and eleven cannon, probably over 2,000 men in total. These were detailed to seize the bridge at Cropredy, which they did with the aid of some dragoons, before scattering the small force of Royalists on the eastern bank. At the same time, Waller led a smaller force of about 1,000 men across the river by a ford at Slat Mill, just over a mile to the south of Cropredy. They were met by the Earl of Northampton's brigade of nearly 1,000 horse, as Waller's men attempted to climb the steep slope leading up to Williamscot. Middleton's force became split as the horse chased the fleeing Royalist dragoons towards Hays Bridge, leaving the foot and artillery behind. This detachment of horse was beaten away by a determined stand of Royalist foot behind an overturned carriage just to the south of Hays Bridge, while the Earl of Cleveland led his horse to the west of the road, from where they could look down to Cropredy Bridge and the flat land leading to Hays Bridge. He saw a large body of Parliamentarian horse, which he charged and routed. By doing so he exposed his own flank to the two original regiments of Middleton's horse. However, this threat was removed when the king ordered forward his own troop, who managed to throw back the Parliamentarians. Cleveland was then confronted by the Parliamentarian foot and further horse to the east of Cropredy Bridge. Having reformed his men, the charge was ordered, probably reinforced by Lord Wilmot's brigade of horse from the Royalist main body. This swept away the opposing horse and foot, enabling the Royalist horse to continue towards Cropredy Bridge, taking the eleven guns of Middleton's command as they advanced. They were halted close to the bridge itself by Parliamentarian dragoons. Meanwhile, Waller's attack had also been thrown back, as Northampton's horse charged down the slope with élan, forcing Waller's men back across the river by Slat Mill.

The Royalists then moved their whole force back towards the crossings at Cropredy and Slat Mill in an attempt to turn their victory into a more decisive one, attacking both crossings at about 3.00 p.m. However, stout defence, particularly by the Tower Hamlets Regiment, prevented a Royalist crossing at Cropredy, although the Slat Mill ford was taken, enabling the Royalists to move some of their force to the west bank. With the bulk of Waller's army on Bourton Hill, no Royalist attack was made, with skirmishing being the order of the remainder of the day. An offer of pardon for those laying down their arms was made by the king, but this was rejected by Waller. The stand-off continued throughout the night and the following day, 30 June, until the Royalists moved off during the next night having heard of the approach of a sizeable Parliamentarian reinforcement.

The battle, although a victory for King Charles, was not a decisive one. It certainly went some way to improving the king's reputation as a general, however, and this would be further enhanced by the Lostwithiel campaign later in the year, while Waller's reputation suffered by the same degree. Waller realised that to avoid further similar defeats and in particular the strategic blunder which led to the losses of Cropredy and Lostwithiel, Parliament should create a more professional force, which came to fruition during the winter of 1644–1645 with the formation of the New Model Army.

The battlefield is still farmland, now enclosed, and has good public access. A battlefield trail linking Cropredy to Edgcote and Edgehill is to be opened in 2004.

Crowland, siege of, early April–28 April 1643

This southern Lincolnshire village was garrisoned for King Charles I, but was besieged by the local Parliamentarians. The latter received reinforcements led by Oliver Cromwell who brought artillery with them, which bombarded the defenders into submission after a further three days.

Crowmarsh Castle, siege of, 1153

One of the three main sieges by Henry of Anjou (later Henry II) in 1153 against the forces of King Stephen.

KEY REFERENCE: Bradbury, J. *Stephen and Matilda, the Civil War of 1139–53* (Alan Sutton, 1996).

Following the Siege of Malmesbury, Henry moved east along the Thames valley and besieged Crowmarsh Castle. This castle was opposing the castle at Wallingford, one each side of the river. Henry put an earthwork around both the castle at Crowmarsh and his own army, in case of an attack by a relieving force. This force duly arrived, but unexpectedly Henry ordered the earthwork to be taken down and moved against Stephen's forces. Probably due to suspicion of treachery among nobles in his own army, Stephen agreed to a truce and treaty at Wallingford. As part of the terms the castle at Crowmarsh was razed to the ground.

Culham Bridge, skirmish of, 11 January 1645

Main action during a failed Royalist attempt to storm Abingdon towards the end of the First Civil War.

The noted royalist Sir Henry Gage (who was the Governor of Oxford and had led the Storming of Boarstall House and been active at the Siege of Basing House) was killed leading an attack near Culham Bridge a little downstream of Abingdon, to be buried in Christ Church Cathedral, Oxford, two days later.

Gage's memorial consists of a wall tablet in the Lucy Chapel (it had originally been in the North Transept) near to seven other Royalist memorials. This attack was made as cover for Prince Rupert's main attempt to storm Abingdon on the same day.

Cymen's Shore, battle of, 477

Early Anglo-Saxon victory against the Britons.

This was probably fought on the Owers' sandbanks near Selsey in West Sussex, when Aelle and his three sons, Cymen, Wlencing and Cissa, landed in Britain for the first time. They won, forcing the Britons to flee back into the Weald.

Cynwit, battle of, *see* Countisbury Hill

Danes Moor, battle of, *see* Edgcote

Dartmouth, siege of, January 1646

Capture of this important Royalist port in the South-West.

Dartmouth had been taken by the Royalists in early October 1643, and then held throughout the First Civil War, until Sir Thomas Fairfax attacked it in early 1646. The town's defences had been strengthened during the war by the construction of an earthwork above Dartmouth, which dominated the river approach, as well as further defences across the river to the east at Kingswear. The former earthwork just to the south-east of the town, known as Gallant's Bower, is still visible. On 18 January Fairfax attacked the town from land and sea, taking the castle as well as the town, and mopping up the remaining Royalist positions, including Kingswear, on 19 January.

Davenport, battle of, 920

Viking raid from Dublin led by Sihtric, which destroyed Davenport in Cheshire. It was probably launched in response to a call for aid from Sihtric's cousin, Raegnald, in York.

Deal Beach, battle of, July 1495

First failed attempt by the Yorkist pretender Perkin Warbeck to land in England.

Warbeck, funded and supplied largely by Margaret, Duchess of Burgundy (the sister of Edward IV), attempted to land on Deal Beach in Kent, having previously concentrated on building up his resources in Ireland. Some of his men got ashore, but were quickly killed, captured or chased back to their ships, thus ending this rather pathetic episode. Warbeck had marginally greater success in 1497 when he managed to land in Cornwall and reach Exeter before his plans fell apart again.

Deal Castle, siege of, 13 July–25 August 1648

Most dramatic siege of the Kentish Rebellion during the Second Civil War.

KEY REFERENCE: Coad, J. *Deal Castle* (English Heritage, 1998).

Kent experienced more fighting during the short Second Civil War than it did in the entire First Civil War, with the battle of Maidstone being Kent's only field action of the Wars. There were also four sieges, of the castles at Dover, Walmer, Deal and Sandown, of which the siege of Deal Castle was the longest and most active. The Royalists conducted a short and failed siege of Dover Castle, while taking over the other three strongholds, largely thanks to the fact that the English fleet stationed in the Downs declared for King Charles I. This meant that once garrisons had been installed, the Royalists could supply the castles by sea and offer them further artillery support. Colonel Rich was sent by Parliament to recapture the three castles. Walmer was taken after a month's siege before Rich moved against Sandown and Deal. However, he had insufficient men to conduct sieges of both castles at once, which made his task very difficult as each garrison could send aid to the other, as well as further problems being caused by the Royalist fleet which could transport men from one sector to another. The Royalists did not have everything their own way, as attempts to land troops were thwarted on 15 July and again after 28 July, although 1,500 Flemish mercenaries were landed at Deal on 16 July. A further landing was made on the night of 13 August, when 800 men moved to attack the rear of the Parliamentarian siege works. However, a deserter warned the besiegers what was afoot and they were able to defeat the raiding party, driving the survivors into Sandown Castle or back to their ships. Once news arrived of Cromwell's Parliamentarian victory at the battle of Preston, further resistance was futile. The garrison were told of this on 23 August, leading to their surrender on 25 August. The Kentish Rebellion ended on 5 September when the garrison of Sandown Castle also surrendered to Colonel Rich.

Degsastan, battle of, 603

Scottish raiding army defeated on English soil.

The site of this battle is disputed, with Dawston in Liddesdale being a possibility. Aedan, King of Scots, probably along with Dal Riadan forces, were defeated by the English led by Aethelfrith, King of Northumbria.

Derby, battle of, July 917

Aethelflaed, sister of King Edward of Wessex, attacked the Danish town of Derby, capturing it and bringing it within the English kingdom.

Devizes, siege of, 9–13 July 1643

Siege by Waller's Parliamentarians against Hopton's Royalists, leading to the Battle of Roundway Down.

KEY REFERENCE: Haycock, L. *Devizes in the Civil War* (Wiltshire Archaeological and Natural History Society, 2000).

After the Battle of Lansdown to the north of Bath on 5 July 1643, Hopton's army retreated to Devizes, largely because supplies were running short. Hopton himself had been temporarily blinded and paralysed when a gunpowder wagon exploded near him after Parliamentarian prisoners on the wagon had been careless while lighting their pipes.

Waller had insufficient men for a close siege but managed to prevent a force of cavalry under Crawford and stop much-needed ammunition from entering the town. To help make up for this, the town was stripped of bedcords to make matches for their muskets and lead from St Mary's Church was taken for shot. On 10 July a break-out by cavalry under Prince Maurice (brother of Prince Rupert and a nephew of King Charles I) went to Oxford to request help. This was vital to the outcome of the siege, as it was the speed of this force and the relief that it brought which led to the battle of Roundway Down on 13 July and the raising of the siege. While the cavalry were away, Hopton had barricades made across the streets, although there was no time to dig earthwork defences. The Parliamentarians bombarded the town from the Downs with seven cannon, the evidence of which can still be seen on the tower of St James' Church. On the afternoon of 12 July, having been delayed by morning rain, Waller sent in an assault, which met with limited success. A truce was negotiated, which was more to the advantage of the Royalists, as they were able to win more time for the relief force, although it is fair to say that Waller hoped for reinforcements as well. A further assault was planned for 13 July, but news came of the approach of the Royalist relief force under Lord Wilmot. This led to Waller withdrawing back onto the Downs above Devizes. At first Hopton kept his men in the town, but once it became clear that there really was a battle and a relief force, rather than Waller's retreat being a ruse, he sent his Cornish infantry up to Roundway Hill, where they played a key part in the destruction of Waller's infantry.

The siege can be traced with some clarity and there are weapons on display in Devizes Museum. The siege played an important role in bringing about the Battle of Roundway Down and the defeat of Waller's army.

Devizes Castle, siege of, 21–23 September 1645

Siege by Cromwell's Parliamentarians against a Royalist force in some ways seen as revenge for their defeats at Devizes in 1643.

KEY REFERENCE: Haycock, L. *Devizes in the Civil War* (Wiltshire Archaeological and Natural History Society, 2000).

After the Battle of Naseby in June 1645, Parliament's New Model Army was sent to mop up Royalist garrisons and to win the West Country. In September Oliver Cromwell commanded a detachment which moved to Devizes, besieging a force of 400 Welsh Royalist troops inside Devizes Castle with 5,000 of his own. The usual pattern of a siege of the period followed, in which terms were offered and then refused, leading to a bombardment. At the first offer of terms, the defenders sent out a dog with a message tied to it in verse rejecting these. Cromwell sent a versed reply ending with the lines, 'Wherein you call us fools – but stay, You'll prove the fools before we go away.' After two days' and two nights' bombardment from artillery in the Market Place, the Royalists surrendered on terms, which allowed them to march to Oxford albeit without weapons. A visit to Devizes Visitor Centre allows one to see and hear an interactive exhibition based on the local experiences of a Civil War soldier, both at the Battle of Roundway Down and in 1645.

Dogger Bank, battle of, 20 May 1665

Action leading up to the Battle of Lowestoft, in which a Dutch squadron led by Admiral van Wassenaer captured nine ships from a British convoy along with one of the escort ships.

Dogger Bank, battle of, 24 January 1915

One of the relatively few ship-to-ship actions of the First World War, fought off the east coast of England.

Thanks to the capture of a German codebook by Britain's Russian allies, the Royal Navy were able to anticipate the moves of a German naval squadron in January 1915. This was fortuitous, as the same squadron under Hipper had shelled several east-coast towns in November and December 1914, including Lowestoft, Great Yarmouth, Hartlepool, Whitby and Scarborough. The Royal Navy's Beatty moved with five battle cruisers against Hipper's three, while both had light cruisers in support. Making contact at 7.14 a.m. on 24 January, Beatty started to chase the German squadron, while the latter tried to escape. One German ship, the *Blücher*, was sunk with heavy loss of life, while both flagships (the *Seydlitz* and *Lion*) were badly damaged. The main action lasted for two hours from 8.52 a.m., when *Lion* opened fire on the *Blücher*, until about 11.00 a.m. Beatty allowed the remainder of Hipper's squadron to retreat, fearing the appearance of a U boat after a false sighting of a periscope was made. The battle, aided by propaganda, boosted British morale, although some felt that Beatty should have achieved a greater victory.

Donnington Castle, siege of, 31 July–9 November 1644 and November 1645–1 April 1646

Key fortress outside Newbury which was held for King Charles I throughout the First Civil War.

From the beginning of the First Civil War in 1642 Donnington Castle was held for the King by Colonel Boys, despite Parliamentarian attempts to take it. In 1644 there were three main attempts: the first by Middleton failed due to lack of artillery; the second under Horton managed to knock down three towers, but when the Earl of Manchester took over command of the besiegers they withdrew to fight the second battle of Newbury on 27 October. There was then a brief third attempt under Waller, but he was forced to pull away in the face of a Royalist relief force. By the end of 1645 Royalist strongholds were falling, due in part to the weakening of garrisons and no doubt demoralisation as men realised their cause was lost. Donnington fell to Colonel Dalbier, leading to the slighting of the castle, which can still be visited today. Inside are the clear remains of an earthwork for artillery, constructed during the Civil War on Boys' orders.

Dover, action of, 18 March 1917

Minor naval action of the First World War in which the British destroyer *Paragon* was sunk by a squadron of German destroyers which were attempting to breach the Dover barrage.

Dover, battle of, 19 May 1652

The inconclusive engagement which precipitated the first Anglo-Dutch War, fought when the Dutch Admiral van Tromp refused to salute the British fleet of Admiral Blake off Dover when Blake attempted to search van Tromp's ships.

Dover Castle, siege of, early June 1216–June 1217

Siege of this important and impressive castle by a French army, which led to the strengthening of the castle by building the Norfolk Towers and an outer earthwork with linking tunnel.

KEY REFERENCE: English Heritage display in the basement of the Keep at Dover.

Seeking to aid the Barons in their Civil War against King John and to profit from this, Prince Louis of France led an army across the Channel to land on the Isle of Thanet in May 1216. John quickly reinforced the garrison of Dover Castle with 140 knights led by Hubert de Burgh. The French moved to begin a siege, concentrating their siege engines on ground overlooking the northern end of the castle, with success coming with undermining work, which led to the collapse of part of the outer defences. This forced the garrison to pull back, but the French continued to mine, bringing down a gate tower, despite a number of sorties and probable counter-mining attempts. With the tower

Missile weapons such as the sling shown on the left would have been crucial in defence at the Siege of Dover in 1217. The larger figure, the socially superior knight, was crucial in the hand-to-hand fighting which developed once the French breached the defences.

down and a breach made, the French stormed through to be met by a determined force of knights. The attack was halted and then turned back in its tracks, with the breach being blocked with logs, so the attempt had ended in failure. The siege was resumed briefly in the spring of 1217 with Henry III on the throne, but the French withdrew after news came of defeat at the Battle of Lincoln.

Dudley Castle, siege of, May–June 1644 and May 1646

Besieged twice by Parliament during the First Civil War, Dudley held out until the summer of 1646.

The first major Parliamentarian siege of this Midlands stronghold came in May 1644, when Lord Denbigh gathered troops from a number of local garrisons to attack Dudley Castle. However, a Royalist relief force arrived under Lord Wilmot, resulting in an action at nearby Tipton Green in mid-June. Although the Royalists were beaten off, the siege fizzled out, as ammunition ran low. The second siege came only in 1646, when the local Parliamentarian commander Sir William Brereton managed to spare some men from the ongoing third siege of Lichfield. This time with no prospect of relief, the Royalists under Thomas Leveson surrendered on 14 May, after a short siege during which several successful sorties were made by the defenders, leaving the castle to be slighted.

Dungeness, battle of, 30 November 1652

Naval battle of the first Anglo-Dutch War in which a Dutch fleet of about eighty ships led by Admiral van Tromp defeated a British fleet half its size commanded by Admiral Blake.

Dunster Castle, siege and battle of, 1139

Result of a West-Country rebellion against King Stephen.

William de Mohun held Dunster Castle in Somerset against King Stephen, using it as a base for raids in the district. Stephen built a counter castle and then moved on, leaving Henry de Tracy to continue the siege. It seems from the *Gesta Stephani* that Henry defeated William in a cavalry battle, although the location and details of this action are not clear. The castle is now under the care of the National Trust, although only the lower parts of two towers and possibly the gatehouse remain from the twelfth century.

Dunster Castle, siege of, November 1645–April 1646

Last major stronghold in Somerset to fall to Parliament during the First Civil War.

Held for King Charles I during the First Civil War by Colonel Wyndham, Dunster fell after a five-month siege when there was no prospect of relief. The castle is now under the care of the National Trust and claims to have a Civil War bullet lodged in one of the wooden gates, as well as Civil War ghosts in the Leather Gallery, which was used by the garrison.

Durham, battle of, 1006

Attempt by Malcolm, King of Scotland to capture Durham, which failed after strong resistance led by Uhtred and culminated in the display of the heads of many of the attackers on the city defences.

Durham, battle of, 28 January 1069

English attempt to turn back the tide of the Norman conquest.

Following the coronation of William I in 1066 some resistance continued, especially in the North. In 1068 Earl Robert de Comines had been given possession of Northumbria and was approaching the stronghold of Durham, where he was attacked in 1069. He was defeated and killed along with 900 of his men in the city. This, along with another Norman defeat at York, helped persuade William to move north himself, which he did with great ferocity, leading to what became known as 'the Harrying of the North'.

Durham, raid of, late 1312

Attack by part of Robert Bruce's Scottish army from their temporary base at Corbridge against Durham on market day, burning part of it and carrying off much loot, while leaving the castle and the cathedral with its abbey alone.

Durham, siege of, 1088

Result of an attempt to wrest the throne from William II for Robert of Normandy.

With the death of William I in 1087 the crown of England passed to William II. However, a group of bishops and barons preferred to put Robert, his older brother, on the throne. The revolt was widespread, starting at Easter 1088 with the rebels taking station at their castles around the country, with Bishop Odo the leader of the rising moving to his castle at Rochester, while Bishop William moved to his castle at Durham. Odo was eventually taken after a siege at Rochester, leaving William to capture the last main stronghold of the revolt, Durham Castle. This was done and Bishop William surrendered his post and went into exile in Normandy.

Dussindale, battle of, 27 August 1549

Bloody culmination of Kett's rebellion.

KEY REFERENCE: Hoare, A. *In search of Robert Kett* (Anne and Adrian Hoare, Wymondham).

Protesting against the local government, enclosure and rent increases in the summer of 1549, during the reign of King Edward VI, Robert Kett led some 20,000 to Norwich. They took the city and then fought off a royal force under the Earl of Northampton in the streets of Norwich on 1 August. A larger royal army was sent under the Earl of Warwick, which arrived on 24 August. He retook the city, but lost much of his artillery in the process. Kett decided to stake everything on a battle, taking his men down from Mousehold Heath to Dussindale, to the north of the city walls. Despite having an advantage in numbers, Kett stood little chance of victory. Against him were professional and some mercenary soldiers, including cavalry, with Warwick's army possibly totalling 10,000. Kett had a number of prisoners chained together in front of his force as 'human shields', with some of them being killed by Warwick's mercenaries in the confusion. The battle opened in the morning with a skilful shot from a rebel cannon bringing down the Royal Standard, although that was the end of the rebels' good fortune. The Royalist pikes and arquebuses advanced and broke into the rebel force. Many ran only to be cut down, while others formed a defensive circle with wagons. Some 3,000 rebels were killed, with their captured leaders being taken back up to Mousehold Heath to be executed in the early evening. Kett had escaped from the battle but was captured the next day. After trial and imprisonment in London he was taken back to Norwich to be hanged from the castle walls in chains on 7 December 1549.

Dyrham, battle of, 577

Important early Saxon victory which led to the capture of Gloucester, Cirencester and Bath.

The Saxon leaders Cuthwine and Ceawlin defeated the Britons to the north of Bath, killing three kings in the process, according to the *Anglo-Saxon Chronicle*. This not only led to the fall of these towns, but also to the opening up of the lower Severn valley to the Saxon invaders, while separating the Britons to the north of that river from those in the South-West.

East Stoke, battle of, *see* Stoke

Edgcote, battle of, 26 July 1469

Result of a rebellion against the Yorkist King Edward IV, leading to his capture and temporary government by the Neville family led by the Earl of Warwick.

KEY REFERENCE: Haigh, P. A. *Where both the hosts fought* (Battlefield Press, 1997).

Edgcote, close by Cropredy Bridge and Edgehill, is evidence of the earlier civil war between the houses of York and Lancaster. Edgcote is a reminder that the Wars of the Roses were not so simple as a conflict between two houses, but something far more complex. By 1469 the Yorkist King Edward IV had ruled relatively peacefully since the Battle of Hexham in 1464, but found his throne threatened by some of his former supporters, especially by the Nevilles, who did not like the way that Edward had become far too independent of their faction, while at the same time favouring the Woodville family. While being a dynamic general on the battlefield, Edward IV had allowed himself to become far too relaxed regarding these threats, with the result that he moved far too slowly once news broke of a rising in Yorkshire led by a certain 'Robin of Redesdale', who was probably Sir John Conyers, related by marriage to the Nevilles. This began in May 1469 and was supported by the most influential members of the Neville faction, the Earl of Warwick, George, Duke of

Clarence (Edward's brother, but who married Isabel Neville on 11 July 1469) and George Neville, Archbishop of York, all of whom landed in Kent from Calais on 16 July.

By that time Edward had called for troops from Wales, largely brought by the Earl of Pembroke, Lord Herbert, so he hoped to defeat Redesdale's force before Warwick could arrive. However, Redesdale's Yorkshire army moved quickly, and unexpectedly caught Pembroke's force before it could join up with Edward at Nottingham. The resulting battle, fought on 26 July, became known as the Battle of Edgcote or later Danes Moor, following preliminary skirmishes over the previous two days.

The Royalist force, led by Pembroke, had the Earl of Devon with them when they moved into Banbury to make camp and take lodgings on the night of 25 July. However, the two men or their retainers argued and fell out over who was to stay where, leading to Devon retiring ten to twelve miles away with his force, which consisted mainly of archers, probably 6,000 strong, leaving Pembroke with perhaps 18,000 but lacking in missile power. Redesdale had a force whose size it is difficult to be certain of given the wildly varying figures from the chroniclers of between 2,000 and 100,000 men. A figure of 20,000 would seem a reasonable estimate.

The site of the battle is also open to question, although most writers agree on the general location if not on the position of the troops. This is largely due to problems with the historical sources, where, although the location is generally given as Edgcote or Hedgecote near Banbury, the details of the fighting vary greatly. The problem with the location is helped by the account within what is known as *Hearne's Fragment* or the *Sprotti Chronica,* written in about 1520, which states that the battle was fought 'upon the ground of a Jentilman namid Clarell'. From an initial study of documents held by the Public Records Office, it appears that a Richard Clarell who died in 1478 owned the manor of Ochecote (Edgcote), which was then disputed between his wife's second husband and his son John Clarell. It would also appear that the manor of Edgcote had been awarded to the Clarells during the reign of Edward IV, indicating that they were Yorkist supporters, which may help to explain why the landowner was recorded by Hearne who was himself a Yorkist sympathiser. With further research it may well be possible to trace the boundaries of the manor as it would have been in 1469; at present it is reasonable to assume that this included the land where Edgcote House now stands, as well as the land up to and surrounding Edgcote Lodge on the hill to the south. This would also include at least part of the largely flat land known as Danes Moor, a traditional site for the battle since the late sixteenth century, although not named as such

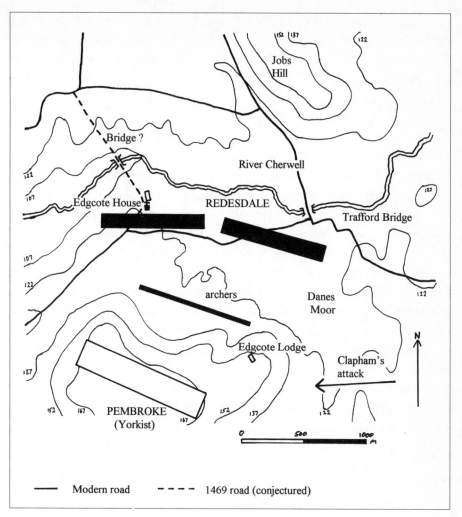

Battle of Edgcote, 26 July 1469.

in the near-contemporary chronicle accounts, which nonetheless tend to claim that the battle was fought on a plain. The most serious problems of interpretation come when trying to locate the troops and their movements. The most comprehensive account of these is Edward Hall's mid-sixteenth-century account, which on the whole is often unreliable although temptingly full of details. In it he describes three hills, one to the west occupied by Pembroke's men, one to the south where Redesdale's force was camped and one to the east, with a valley between. This orientation fits the terrain to the south of the River Cherwell and Edgcote House admirably, although it is very difficult to imagine how Redesdale placed his force to the south of Pembroke, given that Pembroke had marched out of Banbury, a short distance to the south. Therefore, one should probably look away from these details and turn to the other accounts, which tend to say only that the battle was fought on a plain. This is frustrating, but it is difficult to give more information about this engagement unless one is happy to reconstruct events from the terrain and likely avenues of approach.

If this course is taken, it is best to assume that Redesdale camped the night before the battle just to the north of the Cherwell, possibly on Jobs Hill. On the morning of 26 July his force crossed the river, possibly by where Edgcote House now stands rather than at Trafford Bridge slightly to the east, as it seems likely that there would have been a crossing by the church and settlement of Edgcote, in addition to the probably forded crossing at the site of the modern crossing at Trafford Bridge. Pembroke took up position with his inferior force to the south, possibly on the hill where Edgcote Lodge stands. With a serious shortage of archers in Pembroke's army, Redesdale's force started to loose their arrows. This forced Pembroke to charge down the hill into Redesdale's men. A fierce mêlée resulted, which was only decided by the arrival of John Clapham with the mounted vanguard of Warwick's force from Calais, along with various local men collected on his approach march. They crashed into the right flank of Pembroke's force, effectively ending the contest. Pembroke was captured along with his brother, and many men were cut down in the rout. They were both executed the following day, while the Earl of Devon was caught in Somerset and also beheaded. The king had little option but to surrender to the Nevilles, which he did close to Northampton. However, Warwick was unable to rule without Edward and so was forced to release the king in September of the same year.

The battlefield of Edgcote is at the eastern end of a battlefield trail starting at Edgehill and crossing the battlefield of Cropredy Bridge, instigated by the Mid-Anglia branch of the Battlefields Trust.

Edgehill, battle of, 23 October 1642

The opening large-scale battle of the first English Civil War, decisive in that
further conflict became unavoidable but inconclusive on the battlefield itself.

KEY REFERENCE: Young, P. *Edgehill 1642, The Campaign and the Battle* (The Roundwood Press, Kineton 1967).

The Battle of Edgehill was fought at the end of several weeks of manoeuvring by the Parliamentarian army, commanded by the Earl of Essex, and the Royalists, led by King Charles I. After the refusal of Hull to admit the king in

April 1642, both sides started to gather their forces with more urgency, especially following the raising of the Royal Standard at Nottingham on 22 August. Skirmishes followed in the West Country at Marshall's Elm, Sherborne and Babylon Hill, with a more major clash between Essex and Charles' cavalry commander Prince Rupert (his nephew) occurring at Powick Bridge outside Worcester on 23 September. Essex's main task was to prevent the Royalist army reaching London, but although little direct effort appears to have been made towards this aim, the Royalists found themselves slipping past the Parliamentarians on 22 October. The latter were centred on the village of Kineton, while the king was at Edgcote. At that point Prince Rupert discovered the close proximity of Essex and the Royalists prepared quickly for battle the next day. The king received this intelligence shortly after midnight and then ordered a concentration of his army on the impressive scarp of Edgehill at 4.00 a.m. on 23 October. This placed Essex in a difficult situation as the sun rose and he became uncomfortably aware of the presence of large numbers of enemy troops on Edgehill to his front. Short of supplies, with some of his cavalry dispersed and the route to London blocked, Essex had to fight his way through if at all possible. However, with the terrain so much against him, he waited, gathering his army together. The Royalists, seeing that Essex was keeping his forces back around Kineton, decided to descend the hill to draw up their lines of battle in front (i.e. to the north-west) of the village of Radway.

We are fortunate in having several contemporary accounts of this battle, written no doubt in part because of the clearly historic nature of the encounter. Despite these it is still not wholly possible to reconstruct the entire battle and positions of formations with certainty, although the site of the battlefield and much of the action is clear. Musket and cannon balls have frequently turned up on the battlefield, while there are three sites across the centre of the action with a long tradition of being grave-pits. The battlefield today is almost entirely within land owned by the Ministry of Defence and is therefore inaccessible to the public, except on rare occasions when battlefield walks onto this land are permitted. This change of land use has also led to the cutting of the central section of what writers such as Burne refer to as the Kineton to Radway road. The visitor can view a small monument in a lay-by just to the south-east of Kineton on the existing B4086, but views across the largely flat battlefield are impossible due to a high hedge at that point. The best view is to be gained from the top of Edgehill, in particular from the garden of the Castle Inn, the bar of which provides an excellent starting and/or finishing point for a tour. Edgehill is at one end of a battlefield trail running through Cropredy Bridge and on to Edgcote, instigated by the Mid-Anglia branch of the Battlefields Trust.

In 1642 the battlefield was largely open common, although there were a number of hedges running across part of the field on the Royalist right, probably marking a series of small enclosures along the road, now the B4086, and another hedge across the Parliamentarian right-centre. The Parliamentarians waited on the slight ridge running across the battlefield, nearly halfway from Kineton to Radway, now making up part of the Ministry of Defence held land. The Royalists only fully gathered at the top of Edgehill by about 2.00 p.m., so they cannot have been at the foot by Radway until 3.00 p.m. at the earliest, especially as the slope must have been treacherous for the artillery, which had been the last to arrive on the crest.

The battle began with an ineffective artillery bombardment, with Parliament firing the first shots. With Essex occupying the higher ground, and with the confident Prince Rupert advising the king, it was the Royalists who first moved forward to attack. Rupert commanded the right wing with about 1,700 cavalry or horse in five unequally sized regiments. In the centre were five regiments of infantry or foot totalling about 11,000 men, three in the front line and two in the second. On the left led by Lord Wilmot were a further 1,000 horse in five regiments. The only reserve consisted of fifty gentlemen pensioners and a small company of firelocks guarding the baggage. In addition, the artillery, with twenty pieces of various calibres, took station among the infantry if a light piece or to the rear if one of the heavier six pieces, with dragoons to the front of each wing, probably 400 on the right and 600 on the left, acting in a similar way to a forlorn hope. Opposing them, the Parliamentarians deployed an army of very much the same size and proportions, with 12,000 foot, just over 2,000 horse, 700 dragoons and probably thirty, mainly light, artillery pieces. It would appear that their deployment broadly conformed, with horse on each wing and the foot in the centre, although there were also some musketeers stationed behind the hedges on their left.

As the Royalist artillery took up position and began their bombardment, the Royalist dragoons moved forward, clearing the Parliamentarian musketeers from the hedges on the Parliamentarian left, and dragoons from their right. The way was then clear for the horse to move forward. Both wings attacked sword in hand, having been ordered to attack at the charge with cold steel, rather than firing their carbines and pistols as Parliament's horse were trained to do. Rupert's wing swept through Sir James Ramsay's Parliamentarian left and at least one regiment of foot, and pursued on to Kineton, while Wilmot also broke the Parliamentarian horse to his front on the Royalist left, also following onwards to Kineton. The foot then came to blows after they had exchanged musket fire, with the Parliamentarians moving forward just before the point of

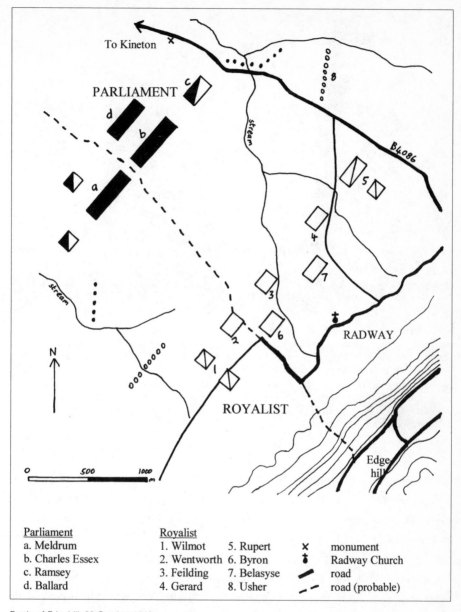

Battle of Edgehill, 23 October 1642.

impact to meet the Royalist charge. The infantry fight was even for a while: 'the foot of both sides stood their ground with great courage' according to Clarendon. With the regiments locked together at 'push of pike', Essex saw his opportunity. Two regiments of horse on his right had not been swept away by Wilmot's charge, probably because they had been deployed just behind their

Left: Robert Devereux, Earl of Essex, from an engraving by W. Hollar. Devereux was the initial field commander of the Parliamentarian army in 1642, who proved to be indecisive and, at times, strategically inept in allowing Royalist forces to interpose themselves between his army and his main supply base, for example at the battle of Edgehill in 1642. *Right:* Musketeer using a rest for his heavy musket, typical of its use in the early Civil War, for example at the battle of Edgehill in 1642. Rests started to be phased out later on the Civil War battlefield. These matchlock muskets were fired by the slow-burning match seen in the print. As the Civil War progressed, the proportion of musketeers to pikemen increased, particularly in the Parliamentarian army.

own infantry. Led by Balfour and Stapleton, these two regiments rode through a gap between two of their regiments of foot and charged into the foot of the Royalist left-centre. Stapleton was forced back, but Balfour broke two Royalist regiments of foot and went on to cut down a number of gunners in a Royalist gun battery, before retiring to their own lines. Meanwhile the infantry battle continued, with the Parliamentarians gaining the upper hand. The Royal Standard was captured with its bearer Sir Edmund Verney being killed in its defence – it was retaken later in the day. Elsewhere, Parliamentarian reinforcements had begun to arrive, largely at Kineton. This persuaded most of the victorious Royalist horse to reform and return to their starting points. By the time they regained their lines, the day had started to turn to night and the Parliamentarian foot were at the brink of breaking the Royalist centre. Their timely arrival, along with the fire of close-range case-shot from the Royalist cannon, prevented collapse. Confusion in the dark led to sensible caution on both sides and the armies drew apart, thus ending the battle.

The battle had ended with no clear result. Parliament had certainly made the most ground by the end of the day, yet the rout of much of their horse provides a good claim for a Royalist victory. The night was bitterly cold and in the morning Essex formed his men up again for a possible renewal of action. However, the king pulled back away from Edgehill, leaving Essex to retire to the safety of Warwick. Certainly both sides were short of supplies and may have been unable to fight on 24 October. Charles I was still blocking Essex's route to London while he could have reached the capital himself, suggesting that Edgehill was more a victory for the Crown than for Parliament, although in the days and weeks following the battle not enough was done to win the war. Indeed, Edgehill served as a bloody lesson for both sides that, while nerves held, the war could not be quickly resolved.

Edington, battle of, *see* Ethandun

Ellandun, battle of, 825

Decisive battle after which the kingdom of Wessex gained supremacy over that of Mercia.

Egbert of Wessex had spent the early part of the campaigning season of 825 in Devon and Cornwall, while Beornwulf of Mercia moved towards the Wiltshire Downs. Egbert met Beornwulf's larger army probably at Wroughton to the south of Swindon (at Lydiard Tregoze to be precise if Burne's case is adopted), as the Saxon estate called Ellandun was in this area. The battle was long and hard-fought, especially due to the intense heat of the summer's day. Egbert secured the victory and Beornwulf fled to East Anglia, where he was killed later in the year. The supremacy of Wessex over Mercia had been confirmed.

Ely, attack on, 1139

Attack by King Stephen against a rebel stronghold.

Ely, as it had been when Hereward led a rebellion against William the Conqueror, was an ideal base for rebellion, surrounded as it was by fenland. However, Stephen built a bridge of boats across the marsh to bring his forces closer to those of the rebel Bishop Nigel. They captured a small castle at Aldreth, which was enough to drive Nigel away from Ely. This brief campaign demonstrates Stephen's energy and determination.

English knight of the late thirteenth-century shown dressed for battle. The English knights who fought the remnants of Simon de Montfort's rebels at the Battle of Ely in 1267 would have been so equipped. His closed helm (or helmet) would have been worn over a chainmail coif for added protection.

Ely, siege of, 1070–1071

Final phase of the Norman Conquest of England, defeating Hereward the Wake's forces.

KEY REFERENCE: Bennett, M. *Campaigns of the Norman Conquest* (Osprey Publishing, Oxford, 2001).

Resistance against King William I continued after the Battle of Hastings for several years, until Hereward the Wake staged a last major rebellion from his captured base of Ely from the summer of 1070. It seems that Hereward hoped for aid from a Viking army and fleet, but they were bought off by William, leaving Hereward and the English stranded on the Isle of Ely, which at that time was surrounded by almost impenetrable fenland. William gathered together an army and a fleet with which to conduct combined operations. His fleet moved in from the Wash to the North, cutting off Ely from any help from the coast. Then, his army moved towards the city, building a causeway to aid their passage as they went. Their first attack failed, but then William ordered two castles to be built, one at each end of the causeway. This second attack came from the direction of Aldreth to the south-west of Ely. This time the attack succeeded and most of the rebels fled before the Normans arrived, with Hereward either disappearing or surrendering.

Ely, siege of, summer 1267

Mopping up of the Barons' Revolt by Henry III in the wake of the defeat of Simon de Montfort at the Battle of Evesham.

Despite the royal victory at Evesham in 1265, various Barons continued to defy the king under the banner of 'the Disinherited'. An important stronghold was at Ely, surrounded by fenland, where the rebels were led by John d'Eyville. However, he left to join forces with the Earl of Gloucester, leaving only a small number of rebels to hold Ely. Largely through conciliation, Prince Edward (later King Edward I) won over these two important Barons, leaving him free to campaign against Ely. Helped by a dry summer and the use of causeways made from wattles, Edward was able to approach the marshland city, putting the defenders under pressure, with them accepting terms in July 1267.

Empingham, battle of, *see* Losecoat Field

Englefield, battle of, 31 December 870

Having taken Reading, a Viking raiding party moved ten miles west to be met by the Saxon Earl Aethelwulf, who defeated them, killing the Viking Earl Sidroc. This encouraged King Aethelred and his brother Alfred to attack Reading four days later.

Ethandun, battle of, May 878

Alfred 'the Great's' victory over the Vikings secured the kingdom of Wessex and enabled Alfred and his successors to forge an English state.

KEY REFERENCE: Peddie J. and Dillon P. *Alfred's defeat of the Vikings* (Castle Camelot Printers, Bristol, 1981).

Following a surprise attack by the Danes on Alfred's Christmas festivities at Chippenham in January 878, Alfred had been forced to retreat into the marshland around Athelney in Somerset. At first he launched guerrilla attacks on Guthrum's Danes and by May had gathered an army together at the meeting point of Egbert's Stone, somewhere near the Wiltshire/Somerset/Dorset border, while Guthrum remained at Chippenham. Between the two forces was high chalk downland, which Alfred started to cross. He was met by Guthrum at an unknown location, but probably above the village of Edington by Bratton Castle hill fort. There are other contenders for the battlefield, including Edington in Somerset, Eddington in Berkshire, Heddington and Yatton in Wiltshire and Minchinhampton in Gloucestershire, while Burne favours a site further to the south of Edington in Wiltshire, nearer Warminster than the site favoured here. This Edington is in the most likely area for a battle being fought between a Wessex army formed from men from all over the south and not just from Somerset on the one hand, and a force marching from Chippenham on the other. Alfred spent the night before the battle at Iley Oak, probably just to the south of Battlesbury Hill, while Guthrum possibly camped at Bratton Castle, having gained intelligence that the Saxons were approaching. The precise events of the battle are not recorded, other than that it was long and hard-fought, with the Vikings fleeing after great slaughter. Alfred followed up his victory by capturing Chippenham, with Guthrum agreeing to be baptized later in the year. Alfred's year had completely turned around, from despair to triumph, with relative peace following which allowed him to embark upon a series of measures to bolster his kingdom.

Evesham, battle of, 4 August 1265

Bloody and decisive battle resulting in the death of Simon de Montfort, who for some is seen as the founder of the English Parliament.

KEY REFERENCES: Carpenter, D.A. *The Battles of Lewes and Evesham* (Mercia Publications Ltd 1987) and Cox, D.C. *The Battle of Evesham: A New Account* (Vale of Evesham Historical Society, 1988).

After the Battle of Lewes in 1264 and the subsequent capture of both King Henry III and his heir Prince Edward (later Edward I), it seems inconceivable that the victorious Simon de Montfort should have faced a renewed Royalist threat one year later. The catalyst for this was the escape of Prince Edward from Hereford in May 1265, who then quickly organised an army to fight against the rebels. Earl Simon was quickly trapped to the west of the Severn by naval patrols and the Royalists taking down the bridges. Simon de Montfort's son Simon had by July 1265 taken one army to the family stronghold at Kenilworth

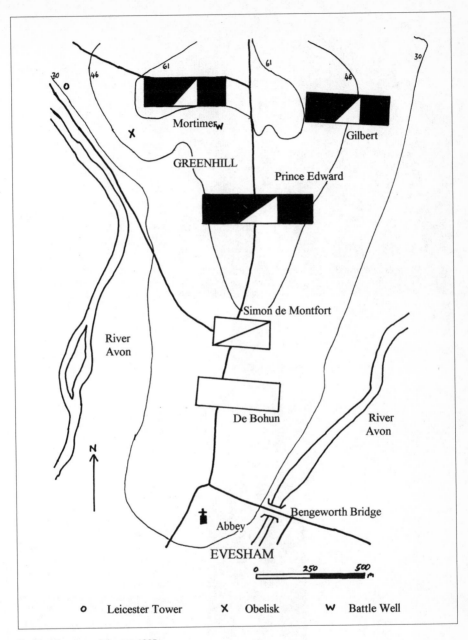

Battle of Evesham, 4 August 1265.

Castle, while the elder Simon was based at Hereford before moving to Evesham, where he arrived on 4 August. They planned to meet up to deal with the threat of various Marcher Lords who, together with Prince Edward, were centred on Ludlow and Worcester, as well as enabling a crossing of the Severn.

Nineteenth-century drawing showing Simon de Montfort's last, desperate fight at the Battle of Evesham in 1265. The artist has used his imagination in showing some of the more ornamental items of armour and equipment.

Very early brass from Stoke d'Abernon Church, Surrey, c.1277. It shows a knight with a small shield with simple heraldic device with a prominent sword and lance to his side. The all-over chainmail is particularly well detailed, covering both hands and feet. This quality of armoured protection made knights formidable opponents in hand-to-hand fighting, such as in the bloody mêlée at Evesham in 1265. Between five and ten per cent of the English army who fought in the battle would have been so equipped; the majority would have had a range of armour from jerkins of mail covering the body to lesser forms of armour such as toughened leather.

Earl Simon must have felt confident, as he and his son were in a position to block any Royalist advance towards London. He was strengthened further by the signing of an alliance with the Welsh Prince Llywelyn ap Gruffydd in June. However, the plans of the de Montforts quickly went awry. Without Earl Simon's knowledge, Edward had fallen upon the younger Simon's army at Kenilworth at dawn on 2 August, catching part of the force outside the castle in their camp. Edward then moved back to Worcester on the same day, before heading towards Earl Simon along the line of the modern A4538.

Simon de Montfort found himself in a very difficult situation as Edward's army was first sighted on Greenhill to the north of the town at about 8.30 a.m. Observed by Earl Simon's barber Nicholas from the abbey tower, they displayed captured banners from young Simon's force, which may have at first deceived de Montfort's men and then dismayed them once the truth was realised. This left them with little choice but to try to fight their way out of Evesham. The town sits inside a meander of the River Avon and Edward's army blocked the northern side without the river. In 1265 there was one bridge leading out of the town to the east. Until the publication of a near-contemporary account of the battle found on the back of a genealogical roll in the possession of the College of Arms in 2000 (*English Historical Review* vol. cxv), it was assumed from other sources and from military common sense that this escape route had been blocked by Edward. However, it is clear from this recent discovery that the option for retreat across the bridge was still there before the battle began. Another option was to stay barricaded within the abbey precinct. Both of these choices would have led to later problems. It was far more in de Montfort's character to gamble on battle, while his army was strong. Moreover, with Edward so close, escape over the bridge would have been extremely difficult if not impossible at such a late stage. Accordingly the army was formed up, probably in one column with the cavalry at least initially in front. Sir Humphrey de Bohun commanded the infantry, with perhaps 4,000 Welsh spearmen contributing to a total force of some 6,000. The Royalists were formed into three divisions, with Edward in the centre, probably Earl Gilbert on his left and Roger Mortimer on the right. Together they certainly outnumbered de Montfort, although probably not by the three to one argued in some accounts.

The battle itself was straightforward. Edward waited for de Montfort at the top of the slope running up Greenhill from the town of Evesham. As de Montfort reached the brow Edward charged, with twelve knights in particular aiming for Earl Simon. The situation deteriorated rapidly, with Earl Simon's foot mainly turning tail and fleeing, possibly once seeing the divisions of Gilbert and Mortimer to the sides. This left a relatively small force with de

Unarmoured Welsh soldiers of the thirteenth century. If this is an accurate depiction, it is interesting to note that the archer is not equipped with a longbow, but with a shorter version. Welsh spearmen made up a sizeable component of Simon de Montfort's army at Evesham in 1265.

Montfort, who had little hope of fighting their way clear. Sure enough, they were surrounded by Edward's and Gilbert's men. Simon's horse was killed and he was finally brought down by a common soldier. Many of his men were drowned trying to cross the Avon, presumably those who had turned away before the fighting proper had begun. Virtually all of the rebel army were killed, drowned or captured. King Henry III, who as a prisoner had been forced to march out with de Montfort, nearly became a casualty, but managed to make himself known to Edward's men. The battle was decisive, but the war still dragged on for two more years, although without Simon de Montfort to lead it the rebellion was doomed to failure.

The battlefield is largely visible, although the main route of de Montfort's advance, Greenhill, has modern housing on either side. However, there are breaks in this as well as footpaths, which enable the visitor to gain access to viewpoints. Battle Well, which allegedly marks the site of de Montfort's death and then became a site associated with de Montfort's miraculous powers, looks rather ordinary today and is on private land. It is in fact probably too far north from the break in the slope and too far from the road to be the spot where Simon was killed. There is an annual commemoration involving a wreath-laying ceremony in the ruins of the abbey at Earl Simon's memorial on the Sunday closest to the anniversary date. On the north-western corner of the battlefield are a memorial obelisk and the Leicester Tower (after de Montfort's title) which form part of the Rudge estate, but are away from where the main fighting took place. The Almonry Museum in Evesham is also well worth a visit, housing a display interpreting the battle.

Exeter, attack on, September 1497

Failed attempt by the Yorkist pretender Perkin Warbeck to take Exeter.

Perkin Warbeck landed at Whitesand Bay in Cornwall with forces supplied by Duchess Margaret of Burgundy, the sister of Edward IV. He then attempted to march towards London to take the throne from Henry VII, proclaiming himself as King Richard IV (pretending to be Richard, Duke of York, the younger brother of Edward V – both of whom were the 'Princes in the Tower'). However, on reaching Exeter he was refused entry into the city, and when Royalist troops confronted his force, he realised that he had no chance of success. Warbeck fled to Hampshire, where he was captured and then put in the Tower of London, until his execution in 1499.

Exeter, siege of, 1001

A Viking raiding army attacked up the River Exe, reaching Exeter, which withstood an attack, and leading to the Vikings moving to fight the battle of Pinhoe.

Exeter, siege of, 1003

Attack by the Danish King Swein 'Forkbeard' aided by a French Count called Hugh, succeeding in capturing and looting Exeter, unlike the earlier attempt in 1001.

Exeter, siege of, 1136

Rebellion against King Stephen before the outbreak of general Civil War.

KEY REFERENCE: Bradbury, J. *Stephen and Matilda, the Civil War of 1139–53* (Alan Sutton, 1996).

A West-Country baron, Baldwin de Redvers, seized Exeter Castle as King Stephen was putting down a more minor revolt at Bampton, also in Devon. Baldwin was to be disappointed, as the citizens of Exeter asked for help from the king. This was sent quickly in the form of 200 cavalry. Baldwin was surprised by their arrival, as they swept into the town. Stephen arrived soon afterwards to direct operations against Baldwin in the castle. The siege continued for some time through the summer, with the castle cut off from the town and Stephen employing siege engines and mining. The hot weather led to the water supplies drying up, which in turn led to the surrender of the garrison on terms. Baldwin escaped to fight again on the Isle of Wight.

Faringdon, siege of, 1145

Major event of 1145 during the Civil War between Stephen and Matilda.

KEY REFERENCE: Bradbury, J. *Stephen and Matilda, the Civil War of 1139–53* (Alan Sutton, 1996).

Faringdon was an important Angevin stronghold, held as it was by Robert of Gloucester. Stephen prepared a determined attack, bringing soldiers from London for the siege. He was also thorough, building a smaller counter-castle to protect his besiegers and siege engines. The pattern of assault used in several other sieges of the period, e.g. Winchcomb, was followed, with archery providing suppressing fire while a storming party was assembled and launched against the defences. This was successful, with surrender terms being agreed.

Farnham, battle of, 893

The raiding army of the Vikings had captured much loot before starting to return to Essex and their fleet. A Wessex army led by Edward, son of King Alfred, intercepted them at Farnham, defeated them and recaptured the booty.

Fenny Bridges, battle of, 26 or 27 July 1549

Largest battle of the 1549 Western Rebellion.

KEY REFERENCE: Gould, M. 'Conflicts of the 1549 Western Rebellion' in *The Battlefields Trust Newsletter* April, 1997.

With the introduction of the new, reformed prayer book there was much dissent and even open rebellion against Edward VI and Lord Protector Somerset. In East Anglia the main local concern had been against land enclosures, while in Devon and Cornwall the objections were mainly of a religious nature. Humphrey Arundell, a Cornish landowner, led the rebel force into Devon, gathering support as he went. He achieved a notable early success by capturing St Michael's Mount and then the town, if not the castle, of Plymouth. Exeter was besieged, but the inevitable royal army approached with reinforcements including German, Spanish and Italian mercenaries from London.

The commander of the royal forces was Lord Russell, who brought his 4,000 men to Honiton and then onwards to the River Otter near Feniton. The 4,000 rebels of whom only 2,000 were properly armed stayed put behind a bridge, forcing Russell to attack, rather than moving out into the open where they could have been dealt with by cavalry. The royal army suffered from longbow fire, but managed to come to close quarters. They then sent in reinforcements which broke the defenders, despite suffering flanking fire from some concealed Cornish archers. After this defeat the rebellion was doomed, as the royal resources could only grow, while rebel support faded away. The battlefield, located by the name 'Blood Meadow', is still largely unspoilt, despite the encroachment on the southern edge by a railway line.

Fens, raid of the, 904

Retaliatory raid by King Edward of Wessex against the Vikings for their raid on Braydon in 903.

The English raided as far as the Cambridgeshire fens, covering the land between the Devil's Dyke, Fleam Dyke and probably the River Ouse. A battle followed where the Kentish contingent of Edward's army appear to have been cut off from their main body. They were attacked by the Danish Vikings, losing several notable casualties while inflicting more losses on their attackers. The Vikings ended the battle at this unidentified location occupying the field.

Ferrybridge, battle of, 28 March 1461

Preliminary to the Battle of Towton, which saw the Yorkists secure a crossing over the River Aire.

KEY REFERENCE: Boardman, A. W. *The Battle of Towton* (Alan Sutton, 1994).

Fought the day before the decisive Battle of Towton, the Battle of Ferrybridge on the road from Pontefract (held by the Yorkists) to York (held by the Lancastrians) usually receives little attention. This is the case with contemporary chronicles as much as with later accounts, leading to confusion about the battle's details. Perhaps the biggest problem is that the most detailed account comes from the chronicle of Edward Hall, written some seventy years after the battle and likely to be full of inaccuracies, exaggeration and embellishments. The current stone bridge is about 200 years old, with the bridge in 1461 being made of wood. Although the site is crossed by the A1 on a raised section, access is still possible to the river and bridge.

Despite this lack of reliable sources, some reconstruction of the events is possible. This key crossing over the River Aire was taken by a Yorkist advance guard, which managed to cross over the bridge by laying down planks where the Lancastrians had removed them. They, in turn, were surprised by a larger Lancastrian force led by Lord Clifford, who recaptured the wooden bridge, killing the Yorkist commander Lord Fitzwalter. This brought out the main Yorkist army from nearby Pontefract Castle, with the first division being led by the Earl of Warwick. They drove the Lancastrians back, although not without suffering losses from archery, including the Earl, who was wounded in the leg. Finally, numbers told and the Lancastrians were forced to flee, possibly as a result of a flanking march by Fauconberg who crossed the Aire at Castleford. Once the Yorkists were across the River Aire, the Lancastrians must have struggled if they attempted to retreat away from the road, as much of the surrounding land was marsh. Indeed, bones and some military artefacts from the period have been found in this area. The pursuit was carried on towards the main Lancastrian force at Towton, with Clifford being killed just to the south of the main army, at Dintingdale. The scene was then set for the massive encounter that became known as the Battle of Towton on the following day of Palm Sunday, 29 March 1461.

Five Boroughs, capture of the, 942

King Edmund led an army against the Danes and captured the five important towns of Leicester, Lincoln, Nottingham, Stamford and Derby.

Flamborough Head, battle of, 23 September 1779

Bloody naval engagement fought as part of the American War of Independence.

John Paul Jones had carried out an audacious raid on behalf of the American Congress at Whitehaven in Cumbria in 1778. On his return to Brest he was given a squadron of seven ships, including his flagship the *Bonhomme Richard* of forty guns, which he used to raid in the North Sea. At 7.00 p.m. on 23 September 1779, he came across HMS *Serapis* (forty-four guns and newly built) and HMS *Countess of Scarborough* (twenty guns) off Flamborough Head, guarding a fleet of merchantmen. In the engagement that followed, Jones' ship lashed itself to HMS *Serapis* to overcome the problem of her superior guns. Unfortunately for Jones, one of his own ships badly damaged the *Bonhomme Richard* while it was alongside HMS *Serapis*. Despite this he was able to capture the *Serapis*, to which he transferred his crew and sailed away, along with the *Countess of Scarborough*, which was also captured and some 500 prisoners.

Flodden, battle of, 9 September 1513

One of the most important and decisive battles to be fought on English soil in which a Scottish army was heavily defeated and King James IV killed by the English.

KEY REFERENCE: Barr, N. *Flodden* (Tempus, 2001).

Henry VIII of England invaded France in May 1513, leading to the French requesting the Scots to launch an invasion of England under the terms of an alliance between them. This King James IV of Scotland was willing to do, especially as financial and material aid was sent by the French. As had been the case in earlier centuries, e.g. at the time of Edward III's Crécy campaign and the resulting Scottish invasion leading to the battle of Neville's Cross, the English expected such an attack. Therefore Henry made arrangements for defence of the North by leaving the old and experienced Earl of Surrey as his Lieutenant-General, with the power to raise an army from these counties. James invaded with a reported, if exaggerated, force of 60,000 on 22 August, while by 4 September Surrey had an army of 26,000 at Alnwick. It seems more likely that by the time of the battle the Scottish army numbered about 30,000, which represents a huge force for the period. Surrey issued a challenge to James on 5 September to accept battle by 9 September, which was accepted, although Surrey did not find out about this acceptance until 7 September. This was issued to ensure that the Scots would not slip back north of the border without a fight, after causing damage in their fortnight's raiding. By the time Surrey

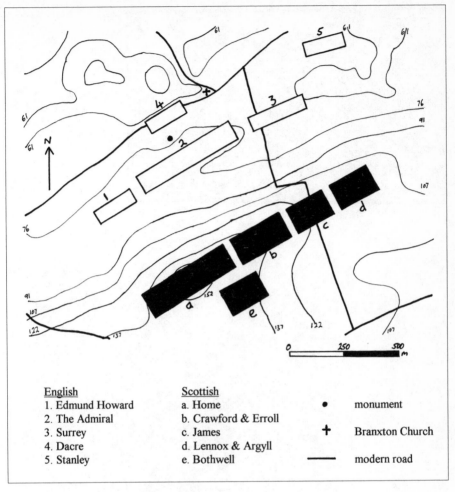

Battle of Flodden, 9 September 1513.

received his reply, James IV had positioned his army on the almost impregnable position of Flodden Edge, which would lead to the English, if attacking from the south, advancing into an impossible situation. Recent archaeological work led by Tony Pollard and Neil Oliver used an earthwork and small finds such as iron nails used to construct gun platforms to confirm the siting of one Scottish gun position looking out to the east/north-east. Perhaps it was in part this prepared strength which persuaded Surrey to commence a flank march with his entire army, around the eastern side of the Scottish position, on 8 September. The English remained safe from being attacked in their flank as they marched, as they kept the River Till between the two armies. This bold move resulted in Surrey's army advancing towards the Scots on the morning of 9

Battle of Flodden, 1513, from Raphael Holinshed's *Chronicles of England, Scotlande and Irelande*, published in 1577, showing the rout of the Scottish army off to the right. There is no town on a nearby hill.

Evocative depiction of the Battle of Flodden of 1513. Many of the soldiers wear armour from later decades, while others have closed helmets more typical of the previous century.

September, as they re-crossed the River Till and marched south. James could still have slipped away if he moved quickly, but instead he decided to fight. Therefore, he ordered his army to about-face and move a mile to the north where they still overlooked the approaching English from the Scots' new position on Branxton Hill. On their new right flank leading off Branxton Hill to the east, the ground was lower but of a more broken nature, which may account for the fact that it took longer for the troops to become engaged on that flank in the ensuing battle. The English were still faced with a very difficult situation, but quickly put their army into line of battle along the lower ridge marked in the right-centre by Piper's Hill, on which there is a monument to the battle and an interpretation panel. The two armies were then close enough for battle to commence at 4.00 p.m. on 9 September.

Surrey's army began in two main formations, each with two wings: the first under the Admiral, Lord Thomas Howard, and the second under the Earl of Surrey. Once on their ridge they assembled into three main 'battles' or divisions, plus a reserve: Edmund Howard on the right with 3,000, the Admiral in the centre with 12,000 and Surrey on the left with 5,000, while Lord Dacre commanded the reserve of 3,000 and Sir Edward Stanley was still marching to the battlefield to join the extreme left with a further 3,000. Opposing them, the Scots were in four main 'battles' with a fifth in reserve: Lord Home on the left with 10,000 (their position on the forward slope of Branxton Hill by modern Branxton Hill Farm being confirmed by artefacts such as a lead cannonball, a metal plate from a jack and buttons found during a recent metal-detector survey for Tony Pollard and Neil Oliver), the Earls of Crawford and Erroll with 6,000 in the left-centre, King James IV in the right-centre, the Earls of Lennox and Argyll on the right and Lord Bothwell with the reserve.

After a short and largely ineffective artillery duel (although *The trewe encounter or batayle lately don between Englande and Scotlande* claimed that the English guns provoked the Scots into making their assault), fighting soon enveloped most of the front line, with Home engaging Edmund Howard, Crawford and Erroll fighting against the Admiral and James IV against Surrey. The exact sequence is not entirely clear, but it seems likely that Edmund Howard edged forward. Seeing such an inferior force to his front, Lord Home charged his men down the slopes of Branxton Hill and crashed into Edmund's battle. It is possible that the Scots planned an attack in echelon, with each pike block fixing their opponents in turn. However, it seems more likely that James, scenting success on seeing Home push Edmund back, ordered the remaining front-line battles down the hill. However, even Home's success was not as it at first appeared, for Lord Dacre moved to Edmund's aid with the reserve. This stabilised the situation on the English right while the other engagements were fought. The Admiral's battle defeated the troops of Erroll and Argyll, while King James' men were beaten back by Surrey's, and, perhaps worst of all, the king himself was killed in the mêlée. It seems that the English archers played only a minor role in this fighting, the engagement being decided by the billmen. To the right of James' battle were the Highlanders of Lennox and Argyll who were the only Scottish infantry not to be armed with the pike and trained by the French in the weeks before the battle. They had stayed on the hilltop while the other three front-line battles fought. They then began to move forwards, but were met by Sir Edward Stanley who had just brought his men onto the field. It would appear that at least some of his force attacked from a gully to the east of the main ridge, into the Highlanders' flank, as one source says that they approached from Sandyford and that they climbed up Branxton Hill 'ere the Scots knew it'. In addition, this source by an author known as 'the unworthy one' tells us that Stanley's men pursued across the ground where Surrey's battle had been engaged, which again suggests an attack on the Scots' right flank, rather than to their front. It would appear that Bothwell's reserve played no significant part in the action.

Scottish casualties were appalling, at perhaps 10,000 including King James IV and many members of the Scottish nobility. English losses were seemingly light in comparison, probably in the region of 1,500. The battle was largely a straightforward slogging match between roughly numerically equal bodies of infantry, suggesting superiority for the bill over the pike, although such a comparison is not quite so clear. This is due to the fact that the Scots had only received a minimal amount of training from the French captains in the use of the pike and its tactics, which, combined with an advance downhill over uneven moorland, must have put the Scottish foot at a disadvantage.

The battle led to a period of instability in Scotland as well as a massive sense of loss, although Surrey made no attempt to follow up his success. The battlefield is open farmland, with the best views being from a minor road leading down Branxton Hill on what would have been the Scottish right-centre, as well as from the Piper's Hill monument. The church in Branxton village just behind the English position has a sign outside saying that it 'received the slain of both nations'. King James' body lay in the chancel of the church on the night after the battle before being taken to Berwick for embalming. Nearby Etal Castle, which had been sacked by the Scots as they raided before the battle, is managed by English Heritage and is open to the public. In the old Presbyterian chapel attached to the site is an impressive exhibition of replica weapons and standards relating to the battle, through which the visitor is conducted with the help of a taped tour.

Standards such as this bloodstained example carried at the Battle of Flodden in 1513 would serve as
mustering and rallying points in battle. They would also invariably become the focus of fierce fighting. The
motto here translates as 'The Truth Prevails' and was the standard of William Keith, the Earl Marischal of
Scotland. A large number of replica standards from the battle are on display at Etal Castle near the
battlefield.

Part of a letter from Thomas Ruthal, Bishop of Durham, to Thomas
Wolsey, written on 20 September 1513, including a full account of the
Battle of Flodden and the death of King James IV, whose body was
found 'having manye wounds and naked'. The first complete paragraph
on this page includes an explanation of the advantage of the English bill
over the long spear favoured by the Scots.

Folkestone, raid of, 991

Large raid probably led by Swein 'Forkbeard', or possibly by the Norwegian Olaf Tryggvason, against Folkestone with a fleet of ninety-three ships, going on to raid other coastal towns and culminating in the Battle of Maldon in August.

Fornham St Genevieve, battle of, 1173

East Anglia's largest recorded pitched battle, fought between the Earl of Leicester's largely mercenary force and a Royalist baronial army.

KEY REFERENCE: Rayner, M. 'The Battle of Fornham St Genevieve' in *Battlefields Review* (issue 4).

In the late summer of 1173 with Henry II in France and his Justiciar Richard de Lucy and Constable Humphrey de Bohun in Scotland, Robert Earl of Leicester took the opportunity to cross over to England from Flanders with an army in order to join up with Hugh Bigod Earl of Norfolk in an attempt to extend their power base. Leicester set off with his army, which consisted largely of Flemings, from Framlingham Castle in Suffolk, heading for Leicester. Meanwhile Lucy and Bohun had rushed back from Scotland on receiving news of Leicester's landing. The Royalist barons gathered at Bury St Edmunds, where they intercepted Leicester on his march next to the church of St Genevieve, to the north of the town on the eastern side of the River Lark.

As well as several contemporary written accounts of the battle there is also some archaeological evidence. A sword, spearhead and arrowhead dated to the twelfth century were found in the 1880s and are now in Moyses Hall Museum in Bury St Edmunds. Also, close to the church of St Genevieve a mass grave has been found. Dealing with Leicester's forces army first, it is clear that many of his men were wool workers rather than soldiers, suggesting a force of about 4,000 armed Flemish mercenary soldiers in addition to a small mounted unit consisting of his own close supporters. The numbers of the Royalist army are not so clear, with no number given for the ordinary fighting men on foot, apart from Ralph de Diceto's estimate that they were a quarter the size of Leicester's force. Certainly the knights, of whom there were many, would have been of very high quality.

It seems most likely that the Royalists left by the east gate of Bury St Edmunds, crossing the Lark knowing that Leicester would be trying to find a crossing further downstream. They were able to catch up with the latter

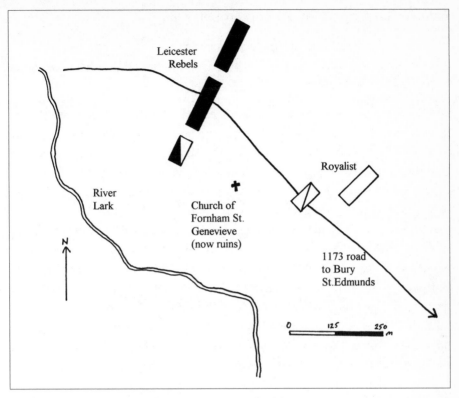

Battle of Fornham St Genevieve, 1173.

quickly and Leicester attempted to make a stand by fighting next to the church of St Genevieve, giving his army the advantage of higher ground. There is little detail among the sources concerning tactics once battle was joined, but it is safe to assume that the battle closed quickly to a large-scale mêlée. The fighting appears to have been over quickly, probably after the first charge of the barons, as their superior cavalry caused havoc with the ill-deployed Flemish infantry. The Earl and his wife were taken prisoner, while the local peasantry went after the defeated Flemings with 'fork and flail'. The majority of the rebel army were killed or captured as they were pinned in marshy ground against the river.

The Battle of Fornham St Genevieve was the most important single event in defeating the 'Leicester Rebellion' of 1173–1174. Sadly, much of the battlefield is already lost, although the land immediately surrounding the ruined church of St Genevieve is still farmland, with the slopes down to the river where most of the fighting occurred being unspoilt. Unfortunately, this land is uncrossed by public rights of way.

Fulford Gate, battle of, 20 September 1066

The 'third' battle of 1066, alongside Hastings and Stamford Bridge, which played
an important part in deciding the course of Harold Godwinson's campaign.

KEY REFERENCE: www.main47.freeserve.co.uk

Although not as well documented or as clearly located as the other two better-
known battles of 1066, Fulford Gate deserves more recognition than it usually
receives. The appearance of a fleet of 300 ships led by Harald Hardrada of
Norway in the North forced King Harold Godwinson to march north to face
the threat, knowing that the armies of the northern earls, Morcar and Edwin,
may not have been strong enough to repel an army of up to 12,000, although
the number of ships and thus the number of men is probably exaggerated. The
situation worsened when Harold's brother Tostig, who had been ousted by
Morcar as Earl of Northumberland in 1065, met Harald Hardrada in Scotland
and became 'his man' according to the *Anglo-Saxon Chronicle*. The combined
fleet sailed down the East Coast, reaching the Humber estuary and then sailing
towards York. They landed at Riccall on the east bank of the Ouse and formed
up ready to march towards York, nine miles away. The brothers Morcar and
Edwin marched out to meet them with a smaller army.

The Norse met the English just outside York at Fulford Gate, probably along
the line of Germany Beck, which admirably fits the contemporary sources.
Despite this and other supporting geological and landscape evidence, the
battlefield was not included on the 'Historic Register of Battlefields' drawn up
by English Heritage in 1995. The battlefield is currently under threat to
development, although it is hoped that recent research will stave off this threat
to the battlefield, which is still surprisingly open, despite its close proximity to
York. Harald drew up his forces along the line of a ditch running down into
the Ouse, with Harald and his banner 'land-ravager' where his line was at its
thickest, next to the river. It seems likely that the English crossed the ditch or
beck, probably upstream against Harald's right flank, and made some headway

Early medieval ship showing the
characteristic pointed prow and stern,
although the height is exaggerated here.
This is shown with a stern rudder rather
than the earlier steering oar. Viking
fleets of the late eleventh century would
have consisted of ships like these.
Hardrada's fleet in 1066 allegedly
contained 300 such vessels, which
disembarked troops to fight at the battle
of Fulford Gate.

until Harald ordered a massive counter-attack. This drove the English back and soon their superior numbers started to tell. The English were pushed back, with many drowning and stumbling in the ditch, while Earl Morcar fell (although he was not killed as he later played a part in the resistance against William the Conqueror). The battle had been hard fought and had lasted most of the day, which perhaps suggests that numbers were more even than the *Anglo-Saxon Chronicle* would have us believe.

Harald's army completed their victory and followed up the defeated English to York, which they captured, although they withdrew to Riccall and Stamford Bridge, where they were met by Harold Godwinson's largely southern army on 25 September. The Battle of Fulford Gate or Gate Fulford is important, not least because, had it gone the other way, Harold Godwinson's army would have been much stronger and fresher when it came to dealing with the army of William the Conqueror at Hastings.

Fulhope Law, battle of, September 1400

Victory for Sir Ralph Umfraville against a Scottish force close to the border near Carter Bar.

Gainsborough, skirmish of, 28 July 1643

Fought by Colonel Cromwell to relieve the town which Parliamentarian forces had taken on 20 July 1643.

Cromwell advanced on 28 July with a force of about 1,200 horse against a much larger Royalist force of nearly 2,000 horse, who were drawn up on a hill just to the east of Gainsborough. As they breasted the slope the Royalists charged, but the Parliamentarians remained steady and broke the Royalists, killing their commander Charles Cavendish. Gainsborough was relieved and Cromwell moved on, but soon the Royalist Earl of Newcastle arrived with a much larger army and took Gainsborough after a short siege.

Galford, battle of, 825

Result of a raid from Cornwall into Devon.

The people of Cornwall, still then known as Britons, were attempting to maintain their independence from Wessex, ruled by Egbert. They raided Devon and fought at the Tax Ford ('Gafol-Ford') or modern Galford. No further details are known, although Egbert's victory in 835 at Hingston Down probably made Cornwall part of England.

Gate Fulford, battle of, *see* Fulford Gate

Gloucester, siege of, 10 August–5 September 1643

Parliamentarian garrison relieved in the nick of time after a hard-fought siege.

KEY REFERENCE: Morris, R. *The Siege of Gloucester 1643* (Stuart Press, 1993).

The important city of Gloucester was held for Parliament by Colonel Massey with a force of about 1,500, mainly consisting of men from two regiments of foot: the Earl of Stamford's and Colonel Henry Stephen's. The defences were largely those of the medieval city, with the stone walls reinforced with earth, although the approaches were cleared through burning the suburbs, with over 240 houses being destroyed, along with new V-shaped ditches being dug in some areas. The Royalists surrounded the city on 10 August, with their forces of at least 8,000 led by King Charles I in person, with an extra 1,500 armed Welshmen and 2,000 armed with clubs, who were about to be given weapons from Bristol. The numbers of those at the siege are difficult to ascertain with certainty, although it is clear that the Royalist forces increased further during the siege, with the arrival of Lord Herbert's command and the reinforcements of Sir Ralph Hopton. After the refusal of the garrison to surrender at the start of the siege, the Royalists started to dig their own siege works, with traces of one of their trenches being excavated in 1988 in front of the South Gate.

As early as 11 August Royalist guns and mortars opened fire from positions to the south, south-east and east of the city. Attempts were made by the garrison to sally out and destroy these, but these failed to make much impact, with much confusion resulting from attempts to attack at night. The most serious threat seems to have been against the defences around Eastgate, where the attackers dug a mine and by 3 September had moved their trenches as close as 100 yards from the gate. To counter this the garrison prepared an inner, second line of defences, with positions for four cannons, as well as digging a counter mine. These precautions proved to be unnecessary, as the Royalists had got wind of the Earl of Essex's approach with a large Parliamentarian relieving army. During the night of 4 September, fires were lit by Parliamentarian scouts on the top of Waynload Hill, giving heart to the defenders, who saw the Royalists destroying their huts and retreating during 5 September. The garrison could not have held out for much longer as they were down to their last three barrels of gunpowder, but providence in the form of the Earl of Essex was at hand. He brought much-needed supplies to Gloucester before marching back towards London, meeting the king on the way at the first Battle of Newbury.

Siege of Gloucester, 1643.

Goodrich Castle, siege of, July 1646

Civil War siege of this impressive red sandstone castle above the River Wye.

Goodrich Castle (now in the care of English Heritage) was held for Parliament at the start of the First Civil War. However, the surrounding area was predominantly Royalist and the castle was given up to King Charles I's forces in 1643. A first attempt to take the fortress in 1645 failed, but Colonel Birch, a local Parliamentarian officer, tried again in July 1646, this time with a large mortar nicknamed 'Roaring Meg'. This time he was successful, bringing down a tower and cutting off the water supply, which forced the garrison to surrender.

Gordon Riots, the, early June 1780

Wave of anti-Catholic violence in London following the repeal of harsh laws against Catholics.

Lord George Gordon drew up a petition demanding a return to the earlier anti-Catholic laws, which he planned to present to Parliament. As the march of an estimated 60,000 in support of this petition got underway it soon turned to violent attacks on the property of known Catholics and those who had brought in the hated Act, such as Rockingham and Devonshire. Attempts were made to stop this, which led to even more violence, with some 12,000 troops eventually being called out, leading to between 300 and 700 deaths by the time order was restored after about a week. The mob even tried to approach King George III but were prevented by the guards. Gordon was tried for treason but was acquitted.

Gosford Bridge, skirmish of, 30 May–1 June 1644

Attempt by the Parliamentarian Earl of Essex to cross the River Cherwell while trying to close on King Charles I and Oxford.

KEY REFERENCE: Toynbee, M. & Young, P. *Cropredy Bridge, 1644: The Campaign and the Battle* (Roundwood Press, Kineton, 1970).

Two Parliamentarian armies converged at Oxford in May/June 1644. One was led by Sir William Waller, the other by the Earl of Essex. It was the latter which, approaching from Reading, crossed the River Thames below Oxford and then skirted the eastern side of Oxford before attempting to cross the River Cherwell from its position at Islip. Gosford Bridge was chosen, but was stoutly defended by Royalist musketeers on 30 May. On 31 May Sir Jacob Astley and two six-pounder guns were there to prevent a renewed attempt. A third assault was made on 1 June along with other attempted crossings at Enslow Bridge and Tackley Ford. Again the Royalists responded by moving musketeers and artillery to the threatened points and a crossing was prevented. It is possible that this was in part due to the river running high because of high rainfall which certainly occurred at this time, which could have stopped any attempts at crossing other than at bridges or low fords.

Grafton Regis, siege of, 22–24 December 1643

Capture of a Royalist stronghold in Northamptonshire, which is one of the few Civil War sites to have been the subject of a modern archaeological survey.

KEY REFERENCE: http://web.ukonline.co.uk/glenn.foard/grafton_siege_paper.htm#

As a minor siege of three days in December 1643, this event would go largely unnoticed were it not for the recent archaeological work at the site, which has included an intensive metal-detector survey. As the house built as a palace for Henry VIII was only stormed once during the period in a short siege, it is ideal for the study of shot distributions. The Parliamentarian Skippon led a force of some 5,000 men with artillery against the settlement and house. It would appear from the collected evidence that a small diversionary attack was launched uphill from the east, while the main attack came from the west, where the main road still passes the village, enabling the attackers to seek cover as they approached. No shot has been found in the open land to the north. This attack went in on Friday 22 December, as soon as Skippon's force arrived, but it was repulsed by the garrison, although it may have succeeded in driving the defenders back to the house from the houses and enclosures along the main road. Two pieces of Parliamentarian artillery were then brought up, with a further two pieces being sent for. This seems to have decided the issue, for as soon as the extra guns opened fire on Sunday afternoon, the defenders under Sir John Digby made a parley, which led to their surrender at 4.00 p.m. Little evidence of the palace exists, as it was burnt at the end of the siege.

Grantham, skirmish of, 13 May 1643

Small cavalry action fought outside Grantham in the early evening of 13 May 1643, when Colonel Cromwell charged a body of Royalist horse led by Charles Cavendish, driving them from the field.

Gravesend, raid of, 24 July 1667

Attack by the Dutch van Nes against a naval squadron under Spragge during the blockade of the Thames at the end of the second Anglo–Dutch War, forcing

Gravesend, 1667. Dutch print of the 1660s showing the first episode of de Ruyter's audacious and successful raid in the Medway, here showing the capture of Sheerness Fort in 1667.

Spragge to retire before the English pushed the Dutch back down the Thames the following day.

Great Fulford, siege of, October 1645

This Royalist garrison in the Teign valley in Devon fell to Fairfax's Parliamentarians after a ten-day siege as they strove to tighten the noose around Exeter, which they were also besieging.

H

Halidon Hill, battle of, 19 July 1333

Failed Scottish attempt to relieve the siege of Berwick from the forces of Edward III.

KEY REFERENCE: Brown, C. *The Second Scottish Wars of Independence, 1332–1363* (Tempus, 2002).

Edward III of England moved north to support the deposed Scottish King Edward Balliol whom Edward III backed. While Edward III contemplated an invasion of Scotland, Balliol and a group of English Lords besieged the border town of Berwick, which was invested in March 1333. By May, Edward III arrived before Berwick, which was suffering due to the siege. Balliol's opponents led by Lord Archibald Douglas sent an army into northern England to carry out raids in an attempt to force the two Edwards to raise their siege. However, this failed and the siege continued, with the commanders in Berwick agreeing to surrender the town if no relief (in the form of at least 200 horsemen) came to them by sunset on 19 July.

Edward III needed to prevent any enemy reaching Berwick, situated on the north bank of the River Tweed. Therefore he positioned his forces on the top of the commanding Halidon Hill to the north-west of the town, forcing the Scottish army of Douglas and the Bruces to attempt a frontal assault or give up Berwick, as the flanks were impassable due to water-courses and boggy ground. Edward's army formed up in three 'battles' or divisions, with Balliol on the left, himself in the centre and the Earl of Norfolk with the Earls of Angus and Atholl on the right, 'nearest the sea' as the Canon of Bridlington (in *English*

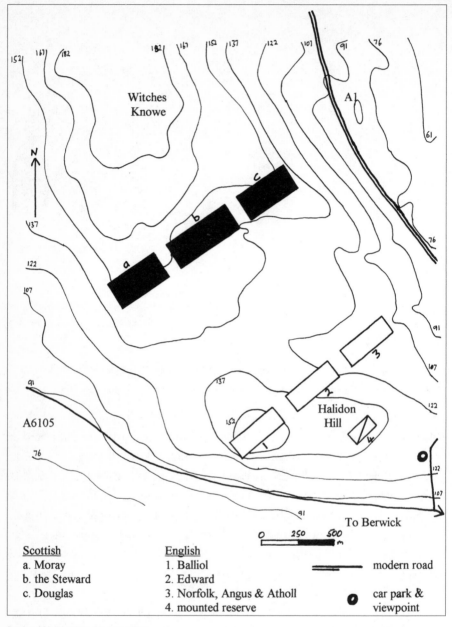

Battle of Halidon Hill, 19 July 1333.

Scottish	English	
a. Moray	1. Balliol	——— modern road
b. the Steward	2. Edward	
c. Douglas	3. Norfolk, Angus & Atholl	⊙ car park &
	4. mounted reserve	viewpoint

Historical Documents vol. IV) tells us. Each of these battles was organised with dismounted men-at-arms in the centre flanked by archers. It is probable that there was also a small mounted reserve, presumably kept behind the front line, roughly where Camphill now stands. The Scots formed up on the opposite hill to the north-west, just forward of the summit at Witches Knowe (the Canon informs us that the Scots were positioned on a hill), rather than attempting to attack up the steeper and higher slopes of Halidon Hill from the west.

Douglas and the Bruces formed up in three (or possibly four) battles facing their opponents and began their advance at 9.00 a.m. The numbers of the two armies are not known, as the figure of 60,000 given to 'the Scots' by the Canon of Bridlington is a wild exaggeration. Armies of 10,000 for Edward and perhaps 15,000 for Douglas would appear to be more realistic. Douglas' army attacked on foot, having left their horses behind in a wood, apart from the 200 horsemen necessary to reach Berwick, no doubt largely due to the unsuitable boggy terrain between the two armies. The best troops were stationed on the left wing under Douglas, closest to Berwick as they attacked, and where the hill was not quite so high. These spent most of the day fighting against the allied right wing of Norfolk, Angus and Atholl. The Earl of Moray on the right attacked Balliol's battle, while Robert the Steward moved against Edward III in the centre. All three attacks made little headway, being beaten by the combination of longbows and men-at-arms, as well as by the difficult uphill slope, after crossing the boggy

Nineteenth-century drawing showing bitter close-quarter fighting at Halidon Hill in 1333, when the Scottish army attacked on foot. Note the accurate preponderance of spears.

ground between the two hills. Eventually the attacking army broke and fled, without breaking through to Berwick. Presumably the 200 horsemen had been shadowed by the larger mounted reserve of Edward III. Losses were horrific in Douglas' army, while Edward's casualties were very light.

Berwick fell on 20 July, but Edward III was unable to secure Balliol upon the Scottish throne, with war continuing until and then beyond 1357 when it became clear that Scotland would remain independent. The battlefield is now open arable farmland rather than moorland and is signposted with brown tourist signs from the A6105 just outside Berwick. There is a car park with viewpoint and interpretation panel, which gives splendid views to the south along the Northumbrian coast to Bamburgh and Lindisfarne. However, this does not give views across the battlefield, which must be confusing to the casual visitor. To obtain these one can walk along the track called Grand Loaning which leads to the right flank of the English position, from where there are excellent views across the battlefield. There is no public access to the top of Halidon Hill, nor to the monument which commemorates the battle.

Hambledon Hill, battle of, 4 August 1645

Major engagement involving the 'Clubmen' during the Civil Wars.

By the summer of 1645 the First Civil War had already dragged on for nearly three years, with many people deciding to take issue with both sides in what was seen as a wasteful and unnecessary conflict. This led to bands of 'Clubmen' being formed to protect their land, homes and crops, especially in the county of Dorset. Between 2,000 and 4,000 of these Clubmen gathered on the huge prehistoric hill fort of Hambledon Hill, armed with a motley collection of weapons and farm implements. Oliver Cromwell moved against them with a 1,000-strong detachment of the New Model Army, launching a two-pronged assault against the hill. His soldiers quickly routed the Clubmen who were led by Revd Bravel, imprisoning some 400 in a local church overnight, before releasing them the next day after a stern lecture to these 'poor silly creatures'. The hill fort is as impressive today as it must have been in 1645.

Hartlepool, raid of, 1153

Norwegian raiders led by King Eystein landed at Hartlepool and looted the town before sailing away.

Hastings, battle of, 14 October 1066

The most famous battle and date in English history, which marked the ending of
Anglo-Saxon England in a decisive victory for Duke William of Normandy.

KEY REFERENCES: Bradbury, J. *The Battle of Hastings* (Sutton Publishing Ltd 1998), Lawson,
M.K. *The Battle of Hastings 1066* (Tempus 2002).

Having fought at Stamford Bridge outside York on 25 September, King Harold
marched back south to face a second threat posed by the landing of Duke
William of Normandy near Pevensey on 28 September. The necessity for
speed to meet William before he had the chance to devastate much of the
country or to capture London was paramount. This meant that Harold hurried
south once he received news of the landing, probably with just those men
who could be mounted, and gathered together men from the South-East as
he passed through London and on into Sussex. Men were still going to join
the army right up to the day of the battle and so it is clear that Harold would
have had a stronger force had he delayed. However, this was not to be the case
and he seems to have wanted to bring William to battle as quickly as possible.
It is impossible to give accurate numbers for Harold's army, although the
numbers in the sources (going up to a fantastic 1,200,000) are clearly

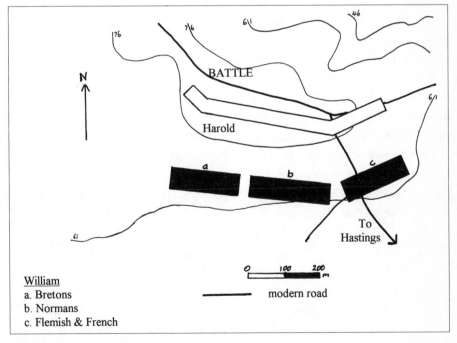

Battle of Hastings, 14 October 1066.

Hastings, 1066. Scene
from the Bayeaux Tapestry
showing Norman horse
transport with ship's crew.

exaggerated. Modern estimates are in the region of 5,000 to 8,000, with
William fielding an army of about 8,000.

The location of the battle is disputed by some, although the majority favour
the site for Harold's line being on Senlac Hill, due to the presence of Battle
Abbey on the top of the hill. William ordered the building of the abbey, with
its high altar at the spot where Harold's standard fell, and this is certainly
convincing. The alternative is Caldbec Hill, slightly to the north, higher and
steeper, due largely to the likelihood that this had the old apple tree mentioned
in a version of the *Anglo-Saxon Chronicle*, which was the place where Harold
'assembled a large army and came against him [William]'. However, the
presence of the abbey is compelling, with Harold possibly gathering his army
together on Caldbec Hill before advancing to Senlac Hill. The building of the
abbey and later landscaping has altered the slope of the hill, although with care
a good view and appreciation of the battlefield can still be had. The slope in
the eastern part of the battlefield below Pyke House is largely unchanged, with
good views to be had from next to the much later ice house to the south of
the site of the high altar. English Heritage manages the site, with some recent
improvements to open up this latter view. There is also a battlefield trail, which,
if the longer route is taken, gives the visitor an excellent appreciation of the
battle, especially from the Norman perspective. It is hoped that in the near
future an improved visitor centre, away from the centre of the battlefield and
hidden from view, will be provided.

Harold deployed his army in a thick line of men about eight men deep, with
his household troops the housecarls in the centre around the standard of the
dragon or wyvern, with possibly his own 'fighting man' standard next to it.
Weapons used by the English and shown on the Bayeux Tapestry consist mainly
of axes (both one-handed and two-handed), spears and javelins, clubs and
swords. It seems that there were very few bows and probably a few more slings.

On William's side there were more missile weapons, with bows, crossbows and slings. The infantry were probably armed principally with spears and the cavalry with what could be termed spears, javelins or lances, as from the Bayeux Tapestry it appears that these could be thrust overarm, thrown or used couched. William had more variety in his troop types and deployed his men to use this flexibility. It was William who seems to have caught Harold unprepared, which may explain why he was able to deploy so close to the English line on Senlac Hill. Marching down from Telham Hill from where he first saw Harold's army in front of him, William ordered his army into three main sections, with each section probably being divided in turn into three. It is generally accepted, although not specifically mentioned in the earlier sources, that William had his Breton contingent on the left, meaning that they would have been in the van, himself with the Normans in the centre behind the standard given to William by the Pope and other French and Flemish troops on

Hastings, 1066. Page from Simeon of Durham's *History of the Kings of England*, describing the Norman conquest. Simeon wrote this chronicle at the beginning of the twelfth century.

Seal of Battle Abbey. William ordered the abbey to be built on the site of the Battle of Hastings fought in 1066, with the high altar traditionally marking the spot where Harold fell. This remains the strongest evidence for the precise location of the battlefield. Other, also circumstantial evidence suggests the battle may have been fought slightly to the north on Caldbec Hill.

the right, bringing up the rear as they marched. Once on the battlefield at the foot of Senlac Hill, the front of each contingent consisted of archers, crossbow and slingers. Behind them were positioned the infantry with close combat weapons and behind them were the cavalry. The tapestry shows the majority of men on both sides wearing chainmail hauberks or byrnies, plus helmets with a nasal guard. It is likely that this is artistic licence, with the embroiderers (probably English ladies living in Canterbury) depicting most of the soldiers as they saw 'their' familiar knights in the 1170s. Certainly on the English side it is likely that many more soldiers, particularly those who were not housecarls, wore more simple or no armour and no doubt carried round shields rather than the more commonly depicted kite shield.

The fighting began at about 9.00 a.m. and was to last until evening. Harold's plan was simple: to form a shield-wall and beat off the Norman attacks. William, on the other hand had to find a way to break through. At first the Norman missile men fired up the hill, causing some casualties, but without making a significant impact on the shield-wall. Next, although largely ignored in the sources, came the infantry, although they were beaten off by the English, who had the advantage of the higher ground and better protection from their dense formation. Then the cavalry moved into action, moving up the hill without too much difficulty but without being able to gather the momentum for a charge. They too were beaten back down the hill, but this success by the English was to sow the seeds of their own defeat. Naturally enough for troops who had just bettered their opponents and who lacked the discipline of the housecarls, the men on the English right started to push on down the slope. At first the Bretons on William's left broke and then the whole line fell back. A rumour spread suggesting that William himself had been killed. The English were on the point of victory. At this point it was William who turned the tide. He must have realised exactly what was happening, so he pushed back his helmet and rallied his men, showing and telling them that he was alive. He urged his horse forward up the slope once more and his men followed him. The majority of the English who had come down the hill from the security of their shield-wall were cut off and killed. What had nearly been a disaster for William had shown him a tactic for success. According to William of Poitiers, Duke William then started to use the tactic of a feigned retreat, moving up the slope and then moving back down as if in retreat, tempting more of the English down to be cut off and killed. Even with this the English shield-wall was still essentially unbroken as the afternoon started to wear on, and the outcome was therefore still in the balance. William then summoned his archers and crossbowmen for another barrage of missiles. Their fire claimed one vital casualty: Harold. Modern scholarship tends to agree that Harold was indeed shot by an arrow in the eye. If the Bayeux Tapestry is read like a cartoon strip, this view can be backed up. On the first frame, a figure with 'Harold' above it is struck in the eye, on the next with the writing 'was killed' above it is a figure being cut down by a mounted swordsman. On close inspection one can see stitch holes for an arrow leading to that figure's eye as well, suggesting that they are both intended to be Harold. Whatever the exact nature of Harold's death, it is clear that he was killed and this marked the end of any hope of victory for the English. Many of the survivors would have fled at that point while others, notably the housecarls, probably fought on.

In the final episode of the battle, the Normans pursued the English from the field but were then met by a group of men in a last stand, fighting in what has become known as the Malfosse incident. This 'evil ditch' is impossible to locate with certainty, although there are several possible sites, with one to the north of Caldbec Hill being the most likely. This last part of the battle continued for some time, with William himself leading the final successful attack. It is even possible that the resistance was so stubborn because the English were relatively fresh, having just arrived at the battle.

This truly decisive battle virtually decided the fate of the kingdom. It is true that there was still the potential for strong resistance, but the defeat and death of Harold along with William's determination meant that he was able to proceed to the throne, being crowned in London on Christmas Day 1066.

The death of King Edwin at Hatfield Chase, 633. The victorious Mercians and Welsh would have been better clothed, and chariots had disappeared from use over 500 years before this battle.

Hatfield Chase, battle of, 633

Probably fought at Hatfield Chase in West Yorkshire and also known as the Battle of Heathfield, with King Edwin and his son Osfrith being killed by the victorious army led by Penda of Mercia and Cadwallon.

Heathfield, battle of, 633, *see* Hatfield Chase

Heavenfield, battle of, 635

Only documented battle to have involved Hadrian's Wall.

This battle was fought between Oswald of Northumbria and King Cadwallon of Wales. The latter had gained supremacy over Northumbria after his victory at Heathfield in 633. Oswald chose his ground just to the north of Hadrian's Wall to the north of Hexham. The Welsh attacked from the north and were defeated, with Cadwallon being killed in the rout. A memorial church was built and then restored in the eighteenth century dedicated to St Oswald. It is assumed that the fields around the chapel mark the battlefield, while it is claimed that many bones and weapon fragments have been dug up nearby. Unfortunately nothing exists of the wall at this point, making visualisation of the battlefield more difficult.

Hedgeley Moor, battle of, 25 April 1464

Minor battle of the Wars of the Roses, fought on open moorland in Northumberland.

Spurning King Edward IV's attempts at reconciliation, the Duke of Somerset openly declared for Henry VI in 1464. After a failed move against Newcastle, the Duke of Somerset moved further north to Bamburgh, where he linked up with other Lancastrians. In an effort to improve the Yorkist bargaining position in Anglo-Scottish talks and to end this northern Lancastrian rebellion, Edward ordered Lord Montagu to Newcastle and beyond. Moving out of Newcastle, Montagu had some 5,000 men. On the moors between Morpeth and Wooler this force encountered a Lancastrian army of similar size under the Duke of Somerset, which included many retainers of the Percys, who held the Earldom of Northumberland.

The site of the battle is by the modern A697 between Wooler and Morpeth, probably on the land between 'Percy's Leap' and 'Percy's Cross', just to the south-east of Wooperton. The two sides formed up opposite each other, with the Lancastrians probably holding the highest part of Hedgeley Moor. This may have forced Montagu to attack, or this may have happened because it was clear to him that part of the Lancastrian force would not fight. Certainly about a third of Somerset's force, that part which was commanded by the Lords Roos and Hungerford, turned away and refused to fight as Montagu's Yorkists advanced. This made the result inevitable, as the remaining Lancastrians were outnumbered and demoralised. Somerset escaped, but Sir Ralph Percy (second son of the Earl of Northumberland and the most senior family member at the battle) died, allegedly after leaping some twelve yards in an attempt to escape, despite having received a mortal wound and presumably being in armour! Although a clear victory for the Yorkists, the Lancastrian cause in Northumberland continued for another month, until the battle of Hexham.

Helmsley Castle, siege of, August–22 November 1644

Siege by Sir Thomas Fairfax following the Parliamentarian victory at Marston Moor.

This impressive castle fell after a three-month siege, due to starvation of the garrison. The castle was then slighted on the orders of Parliament, with the debris from the east tower still being evident today. The castle is under the care of English Heritage.

Hereford, battle of, 1055

Large-scale raid against late-Saxon Herefordshire.

A large army of Irish, Welsh and English led by Earl Aelfgar, who had been outlawed, moved into England to be met by a force led by Earl Ralph. The latter's force fled on horseback with many being cut down. The invaders moved into nearby Hereford, sacking and burning the town. Aelfgar was reinstated later that year.

Hereford, battle of, 1067

Successful raid by the English 'Prince' Eadric with Welsh support against the defenders of the Norman-held castle in Hereford.

Hereford, siege of, 31 July–4 September 1645

Siege by a Scottish army which was driven off by the arrival of King Charles I.

Hereford and its county were largely Royalist during the First Civil War, although Parliamentarian forces held the city briefly on two occasions earlier in the war. The Royalist garrison of about 1,500 men were commanded by Barnabas Scudamore who had repaired and improved the defences. This was just as well, as on 31 July 1645 an army of some 14,000 Scots allied to Parliament and commanded by the Earl of Leven appeared before the city and commenced a siege. The Scottish bombardment destroyed two churches and the bridge over the River Wye was badly damaged. After five weeks of siege King Charles I approached the city, driving off the Scots. Hereford was relieved and Scudamore was knighted for his endeavours.

Hereford, siege of, 18 December 1645

Fall of Hereford to a *ruse de guerre*.

Following its stubborn resistance earlier in the year the Parliamentarians attempted to take Hereford by guile when they returned in December 1645, when there was heavy snow on the ground. At about 6.00 a.m. Colonel John Birch sent forward a few men disguised as workmen, who were admitted into the city, but then proceeded to overpower the guards at Bysters Gate. They signalled to a hidden storming party of 150 men in the nearby ruins of St Guthlag's Abbey to come forward, and the city was quickly taken.

Heworth Moor, encounter of, 24 August 1453

Arguably the first action of the Wars of the Roses.

Predating the first battle of St Albans by two years, this usually overlooked action can be seen as the first encounter of the Wars of the Roses. It was fought as part of a family feud between two very important northern families: the Percys, who became Lancastrian supporters and the Nevilles, who would support the Yorkists. A wedding party of the Nevilles was returning to Sheriff Hutton when they were stopped by the Percys and many townspeople from York on Heworth Moor, then about a mile to the north-east of the city of York, but now part of its built-up suburbs. A contemporary record puts the waiting force at 5,000, but the Nevilles were able to stand up for themselves, and it seems that casualties were light with possibly no deaths. The Nevilles continued on their way, but this incident was followed by a number of raids in the next few months, and probably by the battle of Stamford Bridge in 1454.

Hexham, battle of, 15 May 1464

Decisive follow-up to the Battle of Hedgeley Moor, leading to five years of relatively peaceful rule by the Yorkist King Edward IV.

KEY REFERENCE: Watson, J. 'The Battle of Hexham 1464' in *Hobilar* (issue 36).

After the Yorkist success at Hedgeley Moor in April 1464, the Lancastrians started to re-group, although they were not really strong enough to challenge the local Yorkist commander, Lord Montagu. The exact numbers and positions of the two forces are not known for certain, although it seems likely that the Lancastrians were outnumbered by about 500 men to 4,000, although from the number of executed Lancastrians after the battle (thirty) it could be that 500 is too low a figure for their army under the Duke of Somerset. Somerset had camped about two miles to the south-east of Hexham (on the modern B6306), probably just across the Devil's Water, on the only available level and clear land in the valley, known as Hexham Levels. Somerset was caught by surprise, although he just had time to form up his troops, which included a detachment under the Lords Roos and Hungerford, who had fled from Hedgeley Moor without fighting. Montagu, with help from Lords Greystoke and Willoughby, trapped the Lancastrians against the river to their rear. Roos and Hungerford again fled, probably via a ford, while Somerset was captured. Somerset was executed in Hexham later the same day, while Roos and Hungerford were captured on 16 May and also executed. Montagu had helped to secure the throne for Edward IV for several years, for which he was rewarded with the Earldom of Northumberland. Hexham ended the first bloody chapter of the War of the Roses.

High Ercall House, sieges of, April 1645; July 1645; March (ending 28 March) 1646

Strongly defended Royalist garrison in Shropshire which finally fell to Parliament after three attempts.

KEY REFERENCE: www.channel4.com/history/timeteam/higherc_dig.html

This site is notable not just because it withstood three sieges, but because it is one of the few Civil War siege sites to have had some detailed archaeological work carried out including excavation. Remains of a massive earth bank demonstrate why the house was so difficult to capture, with it having been constructed over an earlier defensive wall to provide protection for the house behind and to provide a firing platform for the defenders. Documentary records provide some details of how the outnumbered defenders fought off the enemy, causing them apparently 500 casualties during the first siege. The second siege followed a similar pattern with some ten per cent of the attackers' 1,000-plus men being killed, as well as the Royalists capturing over a further 300 of their besiegers. By 1646 the situation had changed and, with the failure of a relief force to reach the house, the defenders surrendered.

Highnam House, siege of, 23–24 March 1643

Preliminary to the Siege of Gloucester, where the successful Royalist force from the Battle of Coleford was isolated and caught by a combined Parliamentarian assault.

Following their success at Coleford in February 1643, the army of 2,000 South Welsh Royalists under the command of Lord Herbert marched to Highnam

House to await the siege of the important city of Gloucester, which was held for Parliament by Edward Massey. However, the Parliamentarians were determined not to let the noose close around them without any resistance. Therefore, Massey moved out of Gloucester to attack Herbert's command on 23 March 1643. This did not break through the defences, some of which had been built up in earth on the eastern side of the grounds and church, but the attack was renewed the next day. The second attempt was supported by the arrival of Sir William Waller, who had crossed the River Severn downstream, which enabled him to approach Highnam House from the west with his force of about 2,000 horse and dragoons. The arrival of these men in the middle of the action at their rear broke the Royalist defenders, with about 1,000 surrendering and the remainder attempting to flee. Some of these went north, but were caught at the bridge over the River Leadon near Tibberton, where a stone memorial stands to the Welsh Royalists, some of whose bodies were probably uncovered there in the nineteenth century. The Royalist prisoners were escorted into Gloucester bound together, where they were fed on a diet of bread and turnip tops, until nearly all were released shortly afterwards promising not to fight again, or else enlisted for Parliament, only to desert later.

Hillesden House, siege of, 4–5 March 1644

Fall of one of the Royalist outposts around Oxford to 2,000 men under Oliver Cromwell and Sir Samuel Luke, who drove the defenders from the nearby church, leading to the surrender of the garrison in the main house, which was then destroyed.

Hingston Down, battle of, 838

Final battle of King Egbert which brought Cornwall into the Kingdom of Wessex.

According to the *Anglo-Saxon Chronicle,* a 'great raiding-ship army' of Danes united with the Britons of Cornwall to fight against the men of Wessex under King Egbert. He presumably drove them back, as the final battle was fought at Hingston Down, on the Cornish side of the Tamar. Wessex won, Cornwall was annexed (probably then, but certainly within fifty years) and Egbert died the following year.

Hod Hill, siege of, *c.* 43

One of the hill forts of the South-West to fall to Vespasian in the Claudian
invasion of Britain.

Along with Maiden Castle, also in Dorset and Cadbury Castle in Somerset,
Hod Hill provides clear evidence that it was one of these hill forts or oppida
to have fallen to the thrust of Vespasian's legion in the early part of the invasion.
Hod Hill was excavated by Sir Ian Richmond in the 1950s and the clearest
evidence of the assault came from fifteen ballista bolts which were found
within one large hut, probably belonging to the Chieftain. These may well have
been fired from a raised platform or siege tower overlooking the ramparts,
although some modern interpretations question the possibility of such a
construction and suggest that the bolts come from Roman training after the
fall of the hill fort. After the taking of the hill fort the Romans constructed
their own smaller fort in the north–west corner.

Holm, battle of, 904

Fought somewhere in East Anglia, this battle saw the Danes holding the field
but suffering heavier losses than the English, including their king, Eohric.

Holman's Bridge, battle of, *see* Aylesbury

Homildon Hill, battle of, 14 September 1402

Arguably the greatest victory for the longbow in battle.

KEY REFERENCE: English Heritage: *Battlefield Report: Homildon Hill 1402* (English Heritage,
London, 1995).

Making the most of Henry IV's preoccupation with the Welsh revolt of
Owain Glyndwr, a Scottish army was gathered together by the Duke of
Albany and the Earl of Douglas. This made several raids in June and July 1402
before re-grouping and launching a main invasion in August. This reached
Newcastle before turning back towards Scotland. The Earl of
Northumberland, as chief protector of the region, summoned his forces and
moved to block the Scots at the crossing of the River Glen to the north–west
of Wooler.

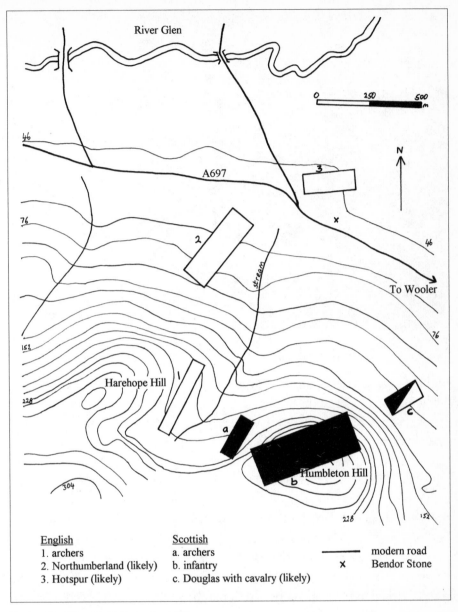

Battle of Homildon Hill, 14 September 1402.

The English took something of a risk by deploying on the south side of the river, which could have been disastrous had they been forced to retreat rather than just blocking the crossing, but this may have been forced upon them by the Scots taking up a defensive position. Moreover, the Earl of Northumberland's son, Sir Henry Percy, was not nicknamed 'Hotspur' for

Imaginative portrayal of Scottish cavalry riding down English longbowmen stationed on Harehope Hill at the Battle of Homildon Hill, 1402. The cavalry are unlikely to have rushed the archers. Elsewhere, Scottish cavalry did attack the main body of English foot soldiers.

nothing, and it is clear that he urged an attack at the earliest opportunity. Allowing for exaggeration in the sources, it is likely that the Scots numbered about 8,000, while the English had perhaps 6,000 foot and men-at-arms and 3,000 archers.

The Scots formed up on top of Homildon (now called Humbleton) Hill, while the English moved towards them from the crossing to the north-west along the road. Rather than launching a frontal charge as suggested by Hotspur from the flat fields at the foot of the slope now known as the Red Riggs, the Earl of March suggested sending forward a sizeable force of archers. Although the Scots had some bows, they had fewer and probably not the powerful longbow. The English archers climbed the slopes of Harehope Hill just to the west of Homildon Hill and separated from it by a valley and steep brook, which ensured the archers were safe from counter-attack. They commenced shooting at the mass of Scottish spearmen, drawn up in a schiltron (see Battle of Boroughbridge entry). In response to this the Scottish archers shot back, but were driven off by the English arrows, 'which fell like a storm of rain' according to Thomas Walsingham's account. The Scots then sent forward cavalry under the Earl of Douglas to drive the archers off. This would have involved them coming down or across Homildon Hill, crossing the stream and then cutting off the archers' route of retreat. On realising this, the archers moved back before

they were cut off, loosing their bows as they went. It is likely that this attack
was driven off too, without the Scots coming to blows, for the Earl of Douglas
was wounded and then captured, while the Scots were smothered 'with arrows
and made…bristly like a hedgehog' (from the *Scotichronicon*). Although the
English account by Walsingham does not mention this, it is likely that a further
force of Scottish cavalry headed by Sir John Swinton charged the main body
of English foot. They did come to blows, but their numbers were too small to
make any real headway and they were driven off after some bloody fighting.
Altogether the battle only lasted about an hour, but in the retreat and rout
which followed many Scots drowned while trying to cross the River Tweed,
making this a heavy defeat.

The battlefield is easy to find two miles to the west of Wooler. Paths allow
access onto Humbleton and Harehope Hills, while there is a prehistoric

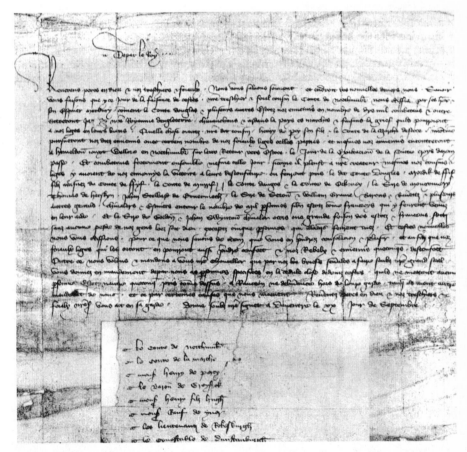

Henry IV's letter to his council after the defeat of the Scots at the Battle of Homildon Hill in 1402. Henry
was not present at the battle, where English forces were commanded by the Earl of Northumberland.

megalith called the Bendor Stone on the Red Riggs just to the north of the modern A697, which has become the battlefield monument. The battle is interesting as, if the English account by Walsingham in his *Historia Anglicana* is taken literally, it was won entirely by the English archers. Certainly their power was ably demonstrated when shooting from a secure position against an enemy who lacked firepower and mobility. The battle also contributed significantly to the Percys' rebellion of 1403, as Henry IV insisted that the prisoners taken at the battle should be handed over to royal authority. Indeed, the Earl of Douglas actually fought with Hotspur at the battle of Shrewsbury.

Hook Norton, battle of, 913 (after Easter)

Raid at Hook Norton by a Viking army moving south from Leicester and west from Northampton, killing many.

Hopton Castle, siege of, February–13 March 1644

On the surface a typical minor Civil War siege, but one which was characterised by the killing in cold blood of thirty-one captured Parliamentarians after its storming by Royalists led by Sir Michael Woodhouse.

Hopton Heath, battle of, 19 March 1643

Hard-fought encounter in Staffordshire which resulted in the death of the Royalist commander the Earl of Northampton.

KEY REFERENCE: Young, P. 'The Battle of Hopton Heath, 19 March 1643' in *Journal of the Society for Army Historical Research*, XXXIII.

Staffordshire was in a state of flux in 1643, with the Royalists and Parliamentarians vying for control. Lichfield had fallen to Parliament earlier in March, although that city was to be retaken shortly. One of the successful Parliamentarian commanders from Lichfield, Sir John Gell, arranged to meet up with the other main commander from the siege, Sir William Brereton, on Hopton Heath. Each commanded some 750 men. The Royalist Earl of Northampton was in Stafford with about 1,200 men, whom he moved to meet the Parliamentarian threat. The Royalist force was almost entirely composed of cavalry and dragoons, while the Parliamentarians had a more balanced command.

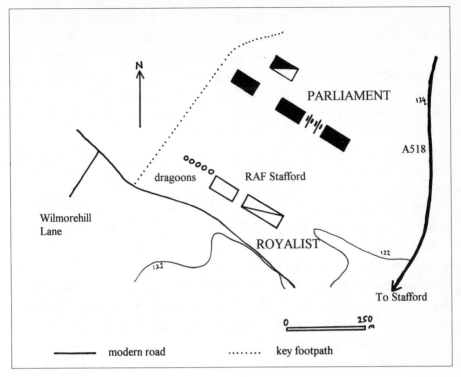

Battle of Hopton Heath, 19 March 1643.

The Parliamentarians were first onto the Heath, then largely open land, rather than the enclosed fields and woodland of today. Even in 1643 there were some hedges and solid walls which gave useful cover to the Parliamentarian musketeers, along with a rabbit warren which made the use of cavalry in that area almost impossible. As they were there first they elected to place their troops along the high ground running perpendicular to the A518 and parallel to Within Lane, about 600 metres to the north of it. Good views of the battlefield can be had from the footpath running north from Within Lane, running along the west side of the RAF depot. The Royalists in Stafford heard of the Parliamentarian arrival at about 11.00 a.m., but took until late afternoon to muster and march the four miles from Stafford. The Royalists formed up in battle order to the south, on the open heath, facing the Parliamentarians. After a lull of thirty minutes, during which time some dragoons were sent forward to clear the enclosures on the right of the Parliamentarian line, the artillery from both sides fired, with the Parliamentarian cannons firing from the highest part of the hill to the left of their position. The Royalist cavalry launched a charge against the Parliamentarian guns, capturing them. A guard of dragoons and horse was placed on them, but a reserve of Parliamentarian horse recaptured them. In the main charge the Earl of Northampton went on too far and ended up in the midst of the Parliamentarian army where he was killed. The Royalists mounted a second charge, which again captured the guns, although on driving the Parliamentarian horse back onto their foot Sir Thomas Byron received two wounds from pikes. Understandably, despite their success on the field the Royalists started to lose heart, due to the breakdown in command with the loss of two commanders. By that time it was also getting dark and no more attacks were launched. The Royalists had certainly had the better of the engagement, ending up with eight captured guns. They remained on the field through the night, expecting to renew the fighting at dawn. However, the Parliamentarians had retreated under cover of darkness, further reinforcing Royalist claims of victory.

The battle ensured that Stafford remained with the king and enabled Prince Rupert to mount a successful siege of Lichfield in April. It is of interest that a largely mounted force, apparently fighting by charging with swords drawn, were able to have the better of a balanced command in a defensive position. There is a plaque commemorating the battle at the edge of Hopton village on Willmorehill Lane. A further interpretation panel is expected on the main footpath across the battlefield.

Hornby Castle, siege of, June 1643

Minor siege during the First Civil War securing a local victory for Parliament in Lancashire.

Held for King Charles I by the Earl of Derby, Hornby Castle in Lancashire was stormed by Parliamentarians led by Colonel Assheton. A diversionary attack moved against the castle's gatehouse, while the main attack went in against the eastern defences. The Parliamentarians broke in there and set fire to the castle, securing it for Parliament. It was ordered to be slighted in October 1643. The castle ruins are not open to the public.

Ho(u)ghton Tower, siege of, February 1643

Brief siege of the First Civil War with an explosive finale.

This fortified manor house in Lancashire was held by the Royalists for two months in the First Civil War, ending in February 1643 when Colonel Starkie brought up a much stronger Parliamentarian force. Despite the surrender being agreed, somehow the gunpowder magazine exploded, killing Starkie and sixty of his men. Hoghton Tower opens to the public at various times (including Sundays) between Easter and the end of October.

Hoxne, battle of, 20 November? 870

Battle which led to the death of King – later Saint – Edmund of East Anglia and the widening of the Danish threat into Wessex.

Likely site in Suffolk where a Danish raiding-army met with an East Anglian army led by their king, Edmund. Edmund died either in the battle or afterwards while a captive, leading to his rapid sainthood and establishment of a cult around his grave at Bury St Edmunds. His commemorative day soon became established as 20 November, suggesting that as the correct date for the battle. The Danish army went on from this battle to subdue the remainder of the kingdom of East Anglia, from where they went on to encounter the army of Wessex at Ashdown on 8 January 871.

Hull, siege of, 10–30 July 1642

First siege of the First Civil War, securing this important arsenal for Parliament.

In April 1642 a Royalist party nominally led by James, Duke of York went to Hull to secure it and its arsenal for King Charles I. However, the Governor Sir

View of Hull in the seventeenth century showing the width of the River Humber and the strength of the defences, with frequent towers and bastions along the curtain wall, partly explaining why the Royalists were unable to capture this important port and arsenal in 1642.

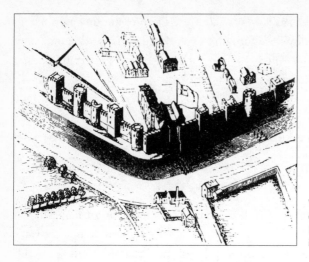

View of the Beverley Gate and defences at Hull. It was here that King Charles I was denied entry into the town in 1642.

John Hotham closed the gates on them, thus keeping the town for Parliament, as well as earning for himself the label of 'traitor' and providing the country with the first clear indication that open warfare could break out. Even when King Charles I approached the Beverley Gate (part of the gateway's excavated remains are still visible) of Hull on 23 April it remained closed.

On 10 July 1642 a siege of the town began, although negotiations carried on away from Hull, using the port as a bargaining chip between the two sides as the siege continued. The local Royalist commander, the Earl of Lindsey, had three forts built to help blockade the port, possibly in the nick of time, for Parliament reinforcements arrived by sea under the command of Sir John Meldrum, which prevented any attempt to hand over the town. He was further reinforced towards the end of July, which, together with the aid of a naval bombardment against the Royalist forts, put the defenders in a strong position. On 30 July Meldrum launched an assault from the town against the Royalist positions, driving the men away and forcing the abandonment of the siege.

Hull, siege of, 2 September–11 October 1643

Failed attempt by the Royalist Earl of Newcastle to capture this important Parliamentarian port and arsenal.

Having won the battle of Adwalton Moor in June 1643, the Earl of Newcastle marched towards East Anglia, taking the town of Gainsborough just after Colonel Cromwell had left. However, instead of pressing on into the

Parliamentarian heartland, he decided first to tackle Hull. The Parliamentarians were relatively safe behind strong defences and were further strengthened by receiving constant supplies by sea. Newcastle gave up the siege in October, after receiving news of the Royalist defeat at Winceby.

Humbleton Hill, battle of, *see* Homildon Hill

Ipswich, raid of, 991

Large raid by the Danish King Swein 'Forkbeard', (or possibly, according to one version of the Anglo-Saxon Chronicle, the Norwegian Olaf Tryggvason) against Ipswich with a fleet of ninety-three ships, going on to raid other coastal towns, and culminating in the Battle of Maldon in August.

Isle of Wight, battle of, 530

Battle, possibly at the site of Carisbrooke Castle on the Isle of Wight, where West Saxons Cerdic and Cynric broke into Wihtgar's stronghold and took it.

Isle of Wight, battle of, 12 March 1672

Captain Sir Richard Holmes with a small squadron attacked and disrupted a Dutch convoy off the Isle of Wight at the beginning of the third Anglo-Dutch War.

Isle Moors, skirmish of, 9 July, 1645

A preliminary to the Battle of Langport fought on 10 July.

George Goring for the Royalists and Thomas Fairfax for Parliament had detached forces under Porter and Massey respectively. These two bodies met at Isle Moors to the south-west of Langport. Massey split his cavalry force into two parts which then surprised Porter's men and routed them, causing fifty casualties and capturing a further 100. Goring took more men from his main force to check the Parliamentarian advance, but at the cost of a wound to his ear. This action persuaded Goring to retreat after a holding battle, which would be fought at Langport the next day. He sent the bulk of his artillery and stores away after the fight at Isle Moors and his cavalry must have been considerably demoralised.

Kenilworth, battle (2 August 1265) and siege of, 1266

Central to the campaign which saw the downfall and death of Simon de Montfort at the Battle of Evesham.

Kenilworth was one of the main fortresses of Simon de Montfort, who strengthened its defences. Prince Edward, son of Henry III who was the prisoner of de Montfort, moved against de Montfort's son (also called Simon) who was camped at Kenilworth and expecting to join his father rather than to face a battle. At dawn on 2 August Edward's men surprised the part of the younger Simon's army who were lodged in the town rather than the castle. Simon only escaped from the Priory by finding a boat to take him across to the castle. This raid ensured that Simon would not be able to join his father before Edward would be able to bring the latter to battle. In addition, Edward's men had captured armour and standards from Simon's men, which would be used to deceive and demoralise Earl Simon's army at Evesham on 4 August.

After Evesham, Kenilworth Castle (now under the care of English Heritage) became a focal point for any surviving rebels. The surviving Simon left the castle in November 1265, agreeing to hand it over to Henry III. However, the garrison decided to fight on and the king and Prince Edward were at the siege between 23 June and 16 December 1266. Various attempts at storming the defences were made, including a plan to use boats to cross the wide water defences. This width made the use of siege engines less effective, although a siege tower was nearly successful before being destroyed by the defenders' stone-throwers. Eventually, the large garrison was starved into submission, with them accepting terms of surrender on 13 December 1266.

Kempsford, battle of, 802

Battle between two Saxon Earls, Aethelmund and Weohstan, in which the latter with his Wiltshire men won the victory, despite both leaders being killed.

Kentish Knock, battle of, 28 September 1652

Naval battle of the first Anglo-Dutch War in which Admiral Blake in the Resolution and with a fleet of some sixty ships defeated Admiral de Witt, who had a similar sized force.

Keynsham, skirmish of, 25 June 1685

Fought in the late afternoon of 25 June 1685 during Monmouth's rebellion. His forces crossed the River Avon at Keynsham, having repaired the bridge, only to be driven back into the town by bad weather. They were then surprised by 350 Royalist cavalry, who attacked from two sides, affecting the rebels' morale and persuading Monmouth to abandon any attempt to capture Bristol.

King's Lynn, siege of, late August–16 September 1643

Only major action in Norfolk during the Civil Wars.

KEY REFERENCE: Yaxley, S. *The Siege of King's Lynn 1643* (The Larks Press, Dereham, 1993).

The important port of King's Lynn was declared Royalist by local gentry on 13 August 1643, with Sir Hamon Lestrange as its governor. The town was well fortified, although the Royalists depended on support reaching them from the North if they were to be successful. Instead, a besieging force of the Parliamentarian Army of the Eastern Association led by the Earl of Manchester arrived to commence a siege. They set up cannon and mortars in Old Lynn, on the other side of the River Ouse from the main town. With Parliamentarian control of the river, this meant that shot and 'grenadoes' (mortar shells) could be fired into the town at will. Manchester also stationed troops around King's Lynn who dug trenches and sealed off the town, despite occasional sallies from the town. On Friday 15 September boats were made ready for a river-borne assault and carts of scaling ladders were prepared. On seeing this, the defenders sent a letter asking for a truce so that surrender terms could be agreed. This was accepted, with the Earl's forces entering the town the next day. It remained in Parliament's hands for the remainder of the war. A contemporary pamphlet estimates that eighty were killed in total.

L

Langport, battle of, 10 July 1645

Second major victory for Parliament's New Model Army in which they defeated one of the last Royalist armies of the First Civil War.

KEY REFERENCE: Edwards, G. *The Battle of Langport, A Short Historical Account* (Stable Design & Print, Langport, 1995).

Somerset, along with most of the West Country, had supported or at least been controlled by the Royalists for most of the First Civil War, certainly since the victory at Roundway Down in 1643. In Somerset, Parliament had only two garrisons by the summer of 1645. After his success at Naseby on 14 June 1645, Sir Thomas Fairfax, commanding the New Model Army, decided to move to the south-west to break the Royalist hold on the region, rather than pursuing King Charles I to Wales. Fairfax moved into the West Country through Dorset to enable supply via the southern coastal ports before swinging north into Somerset. His way was blocked at the River Yeo by the Royalist commander George Goring, but, thanks in part to superior numbers as well as superior manoeuvring, Fairfax marched and counter-marched before crossing the river at Ilchester on 8 July. Fairfax moved forward cautiously, dispatching a sizeable force of 4,500 under Colonel Massey to counteract a Royalist detachment under Porter which was moving towards Taunton. These forces met and fought at Isle Moors on 9 July, which resulted in Porter's defeat and Goring's cavalry being demoralised, convincing the latter to send his heavy wagons and most of his artillery away before fighting a holding battle.

This battle was fought just to the east of Langport on the road to Somerton. Some writers have placed the battle on the more direct route from Ilchester through Long Sutton, but it is widely accepted now that the battle was fought at the crossing of the Wagg Rhyne, between Pitney Hill where the New Model formed up, and Ham Down, which was occupied by the Royalists. There are many contemporary accounts of the battle which agree on the progress of the fighting. They also provide sufficient evidence to place the battlefield as outlined above, although further archaeological and landscape work are necessary to enable the location to be fixed with absolute certainty. The key landscape features are that both armies formed up on opposite hills, that there was boggy ground in a valley between them with a stream running along it and that there was only one crossing or 'pass' across it. One source gives the place name of 'Issebury [Pibsbury] Bottom', which drew some to place the pass on the Long Sutton road, but that location does not have the necessary hills. Pibsbury Bottom could easily be extended to cover what would have been boggy ground across the Somerton road. Certainly the terrain on the Somerton road fits the fighting perfectly, with the Wagg Rhyne crossed at the 'pass' by what would have been a deep ford in 1645. The battlefield is still largely unspoilt, although views across the field are difficult due to the busy main road which has high hedges and no safe stopping places. The best safe viewpoint is from Tengore Lane, running onto the main road from behind the Parliamentarian left flank.

Goring had perhaps 7,000 men with him, but only two artillery pieces. He placed two regiments of foot at the ford, with his cavalry on the hill in the centre and further infantry towards Langport. By 10.00 a.m. Fairfax had begun deployment of his 10,000 men, although the main fighting did not occur until between noon and 1.00 p.m. A 'forlorn hope' of musketeers along with a full infantry regiment (presumably mainly armed with muskets) were sent forward to clear away their Royalist counterparts from the ford and the protective hedges on either side. At the same time the New Model's artillery opened fire, sending 'about fifty or sixty great shot' into the Royalist horse and foot on the opposite hill. This may explain the delay at the start of the battle, with the Parliamentarian artillery playing a more significant part than was normal for most battles of the First Civil War. By this point the Royalists must have been wavering. Major Bethel was given the honour of leading a cavalry charge across the ford. This he did, making some headway up the opposite hill before being forced back. In support of him were more cavalry, and a fresh charge broke the Royalists, forcing them to flee towards Bridgwater. A brief stand was attempted near Aller, but that was quickly swept aside.

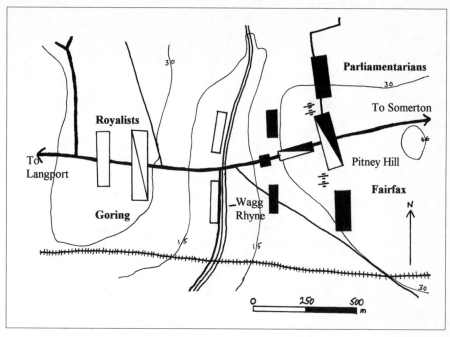

Battle of Langport, 10 July 1645.

The casualties were relatively light, although the Royalists lost nearly 300. However, some 2,000 prisoners were taken by the Parliamentarians, which effectively shattered Goring's command. Within days several Royalist garrisons in the area surrendered, bringing control of Somerset over to Parliament.

Lansdown (Hill), battle of, 5 July 1643

Bloody stand-off in which the Royalists of Hopton and the Parliamentarians of Waller fought themselves to a standstill.

KEY REFERENCE: Young, P. and Holmes, R. *The English Civil War* (Wordsworth Editions Ltd, 2000).

In the summer of 1643, the Royalists were vying for control of the West Country with Waller's Parliamentarian army. Hopton, overall commander of the Royalists, advanced towards Bath from the north on 4 July. This route led him to the foot of Lansdown Hill, from where it seemed that any attack up the steep slope would be tantamount to suicide. The modern road still winds its way up the wooded slope (it may not have been quite so thickly wooded in 1643), with traces of earlier, steeper routes being visible just above the modern road, behind the monument to the Royalist Cornish infantry commander Sir Beville

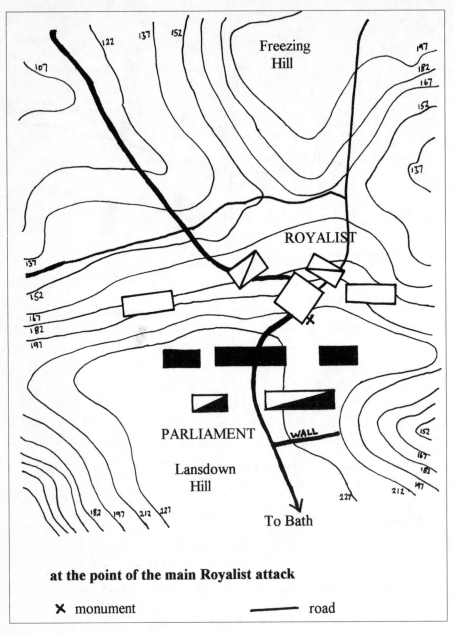

Battle of Lansdown, 5 July 1643.

Grenville. The Royalists withdrew to think again, but could not come up with a better plan, so on 5 July they attempted to reach the summit. Several small-scale assaults by dragoons failed during the morning, their task made more difficult by the erection overnight of some earthwork defences along the crest.

Hopton had a force of some 4,000 foot, 2,000 horse and 300 dragoons, with a large part of the horse being commanded by Prince Maurice (brother of Prince Rupert and a nephew of King Charles I), who had held an independent command until a month before Lansdown. This had led to friction between the two main components, with command of the army still in some doubt, although Hopton appears to have taken command in the field. Waller had an approximately equal force, except with more cavalry in the total, although the terrain of the battlefield was little suited to their use.

After the early Royalist failures, an attempt was made by Waller to clear the Royalists with cavalry, with fighting taking place at the foot of the slope and onto Freezing Hill to the north, but this was soon broken up by a good combination of foot, dragoons and horse, forcing the Parliamentarian cavalry to return to the top of Lansdown Hill. At about 3.00 p.m. the Cornish foot who had played the largest part in this fight demanded to attack up the slope. A flanking attack by musketeers worked its way up through the woods at either end of the Parliamentarian position. Then, an assault of pikes with cavalry in support moved up the road. Fired at by muskets and artillery, the Royalist infantry struggled, until an inspired advance of Cornish pikemen was led by Sir Beville Grenville. They reached the summit and there they stood, 'as unmovable as a rock' according to the Royalist Richard Atkyns, despite three cavalry charges against them, in the last of which Grenville fell, presumably close to the point where his monument now stands. Their resolution forced Waller to

Sir Beville Grenville, who died leading a Royalist assault of his Cornish foot up the hill at Lansdown in 1643.

withdraw from his breastworks to a stone wall 400 yards south of the crest, possibly on the line of a current wall. Gaps were made in the wall to allow sorties, with these being covered by the pikes and horse, while the muskets remained behind the wall. Firing continued on and off until after midnight. In the morning, the Royalists discovered that they had possession of the field, as Waller had withdrawn to Bath in the small hours, leaving lighted matches and pikes along the wall as a deception. The Royalists were unable to press forward as they were desperately short of ammunition and powder, so they retired down the hill so dearly won the day before, eventually reaching Devizes on 9 July, four days before the Battle of Roundway Down was fought just outside the town.

The battle had few direct consequences other than to lead to the more decisive battle at Roundway Down, although on the morning of 6 July Hopton suffered a near-fatal injury as a result of an accident vividly described by Richard Atkyns. Hopton was passing near an ammunition wagon on which were some Parliamentarian prisoners. While lighting their pipes one of them managed to let sparks ignite the gunpowder, with an obvious result. Hopton was 'miserably burnt' (indeed, he was temporarily blinded and paralysed) while another officer, Major Sheldon, complained 'that the fire was got within his breeches, which I tore off as soon as I could, and from as long a flaxen head of hair as ever I saw, in the twinkling of an eye, his head was like a blackamoor'. As well as the large Grenville monument, there is a signed trail with interpretation panels erected in 2003 on the initiative of the local authorities.

Lathom House, siege of, 28 February–27 May 1644 and July 1644–2 December 1645

One of the few Royalist garrisons in Lancashire during the First Civil War, which withstood two sieges before falling at the end of 1645.

KEY REFERENCE: Young, P. & Emberton, W. *Sieges of the Great Civil War* (Bell & Hyman, 1978).

Lathom House was defended stoutly for King Charles I throughout nearly two years of continual sieges. In 1644 a garrison of 350 led resolutely by Lady Derby held off a much stronger force of some 2,500 men for three months, in the face of a prolonged bombardment by six pieces of artillery including a massive mortar, before being relieved by Prince Rupert. This respite was short-lived however, as 4,000 Parliamentarians led by Egerton renewed the siege later in 1644. This proceeded for over a year, until the castle's final surrender then under Colonel Rosthern. The moated and fortified manor house or castle was then destroyed on the orders of Parliament.

Launceston, battle of, 23 April 1643

The Royalists temporarily thwarted Parliament's attempts to enter Cornwall at this encounter battle.

KEY REFERENCE: Peachey, S. *The Battles of Launceston and Sourton Down 1643* (Stuart Press, 1993).

Over the winter of 1642–1643 the Royalists secured Cornwall for King Charles I. In spring 1643 the Parliamentarians decided to challenge this by crossing the River Tamar at Poulson (or Polston) Bridge and advancing into Launceston. James Chudleigh led this force of about 1,500 men (mainly musketeers) across the bridge to the east of Launceston, as soon as a forty-day truce had ended, which had prevented the Parliamentarians from crossing the Tamar. Their few troops of horse pushed aside the Royalist guard on the bridge at about 10.00 a.m. on 23 April, enabling the rest of the column to press forward. News of this reached the Royalist commander Sir Ralph Hopton while he was at morning prayers in Launceston. Once finished, he ordered half of Sir Beville Grenville's regiment of foot out of Launceston and onto Beacon Hill just to the south of the town, where they were met by other Royalist units, bringing their strength up to about 1,000. Some of these were stationed at the foot of the hill facing the Parliamentarian advance, with musketeers lining hedges. The Parliamentarians managed to drive these back up the hill after some prolonged skirmishing, although they were unable to make headway against the main Royalist position. With the arrival of more reinforcements Hopton took the offensive in the early evening, forming his men into three columns and ordering them to advance. One of these, probably the column on the Royalist left, broke through and threatened to cut off the Parliamentarian line of retreat to the bridge. At that point Chudleigh received a fresh regiment in the form of Merrick's greycoats, who secured the bridge, enabling their comrades to retreat back into Devon and safety. As the Royalists started to advance in the dark, a gunpowder store in a barn exploded, causing casualties. Two nights later Hopton's own offensive was thrown back in disarray at Sourton Down.

Leicester, siege of, 943

Following the Viking Olaf's victory at Tamworth, King Edmund besieged Olaf in Leicester, capturing the town but failing to capture Olaf, who had slipped away during the night.

Leicester, siege of, 29–31 May 1645

Storming of Leicester by the Royalist Prince Rupert after the refusal of the Governor Sir Robert Pye to surrender, leading to a day's artillery bombardment and a night assault, which at first failed in the main breach on the south side until a further attack was mounted on the opposite side of the town, leading to its sack.

Leominster, raid to, 1052

Raid by King Gruffydd ap Llywelyn of Wales into Herefordshire and as far as Leominster.

A force of English and Normans, the latter of whom had been invited over by King Edward 'the Confessor', tried to defeat the Welsh force in battle by coming out from a local un-named castle. However, the Welsh routed them and then turned back across the border.

Lewes, battle of, 14 May 1264

Battle which established Simon de Montfort as the *de facto* ruler of England, although he made moves to have this rule sanctioned by a Parliament.

KEY REFERENCE: Carpenter, D.A. *The Battles of Lewes and Evesham* (Mercia Publications Ltd 1987).

King Henry III had been forced to move towards a more consensual form of government after accepting the Provisions of Oxford in 1258. By 1264 Henry had decided to break from this agreement, which clearly would not be tolerated by the baronial opposition, led by Simon de Montfort. War broke out in April 1264, with Henry moving against various rebel castles in the Midlands, while Simon led an army to besiege Rochester. This siege had to be raised as the king moved towards London and then to Lewes. Simon wanted to bring the king to battle and so marched out of the capital, reaching the vicinity of Lewes by 12 May, when a half-hearted attempt at reconciliation was attempted. Once this had failed the Barons decided to fight, moving out of Fletching at dawn on 14 May. They reached Offham and then ascended the Downs above Lewes, which they cannot have climbed until about 8.00 a.m. Simon's army was deployed in four divisions or 'battles', although it is difficult to be precise about their deployment from the sources. It seems that on his right was Henry de Montfort, in the centre Gilbert de Clare and on the left a large group of

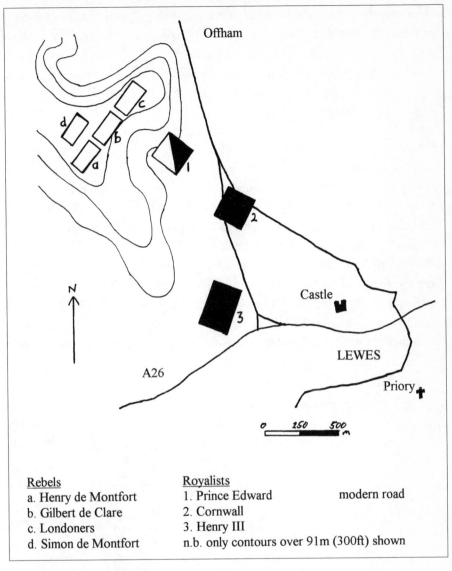

Offham

N

Castle

LEWES

A26

Priory

0   250   500
m

Rebels
a. Henry de Montfort
b. Gilbert de Clare
c. Londoners
d. Simon de Montfort

Royalists
1. Prince Edward
2. Cornwall
3. Henry III
n.b. only contours over 91m (300ft) shown

modern road

Battle of Lewes, 14 May 1264.

poorly trained and armed Londoners under Nicholas Segrave. Behind the centre was Simon de Montfort with a command chariot or wagon as well as troops. It is likely that these totalled something in the region of 5,000 men. The Royalists had perhaps twice this number, but they were caught rather unawares.

The location of the battlefield is open to interpretation, although it seems reasonable to side with writers such as Colonel A.H. Burne, who has Simon's army deployed on the top of the Down, to the north-west of Lewes and to the east of the old racecourse on what is a flat 'parade ground'. As Simon's men came over the brow of the hill they would have been observed by men in Lewes Castle, from where one can still gain views of the battlefield and see interpretation panels explaining some of the action. The king's army had Prince Edward (later Edward I) commanding cavalry in the van, Richard Earl of Cornwall (also styled King of the Romans), who was Henry's brother, with the second 'battle' and King Henry with the third. Edward, displaying his headstrong nature and determination, if not his later tactical awareness, pressed ahead and launched an attack against the Londoners on de Montfort's left. Not surprisingly they quickly broke and fled, with Edward's cavalry pursuing them off the battlefield. It is likely that his cavalry also fell in with de Montfort's baggage train in the vicinity of Offham. Meanwhile, Henry and Richard had little option but to press on up the hill. This movement would have been difficult with large bodies of men, as the slope is steep and access difficult. By the time they were close to the top, de Montfort's army had been able to recover from any shock they must have felt from their early losses. It is also likely that they charged forward, especially as they would have wanted to conclude the fighting before Edward could act against their exposed and open

Thirteenth-century English knight. At the Battle of Lewes in 1264, Prince Edward's mounted knights carried out a successful charge using the impact of their lances (here shown with a pennon together with the knights' heraldic device displayed) against the Londoners, who were mainly on foot. However, carried away with their success, they pursued the men off the battlefield only to return too late to win the battle for the King.

left flank. With Simon throwing his reserve into the action, the balance tilted against the king. His men were forced back down the slope, with them breaking as they reached the town. Much killing then took place, especially around the site of the later prison, where mass graves containing some 1,500 skeletons were unearthed in the nineteenth century during construction of a turnpike. The killing continued through the town, with another 500 skeletons being found next to the priory, where the king ended up seeking safety. Indeed, it is the location of the former graves that has convinced some historians that the battle was fought lower down the hill or to the west of the town, which is a possibility.

Prince Edward returned and apparently was able to gain access to the castle and then to the priory, where he contemplated launching another attack. Instead negotiations were begun which resulted in Simon ruling the country until his downfall at the Battle of Evesham in 1265. King Henry and Prince Edward were little more than prisoners, although it was the latter's escape from Hereford in May 1265 which was to lead to Simon de Montfort's premature end.

Lichfield, siege of, 2–5 March 1643

Parliamentarian capture of this important Midlands city.

Lichfield, situated in the heart of England, was of strategic importance during the Civil Wars, sitting between King Charles I's capital of Oxford and the more northern garrison at Newark. Moreover, it was relatively easy to defend, as the central Cathedral Close had been fortified by Bishop William de Langton in the fourteenth century.

In 1643 Lichfield's Cathedral Close was garrisoned by the Royalists under the Earl of Chesterfield with 300 men. Early on 2 March, a strong Parliamentarian regiment of perhaps 1,200 led by Lord Brooke entered the town and proceeded to set up a demi-culverin nicknamed 'Black Bess' to fire at the south gate of the close from Dam Street. As this was being done, Lord Brooke was shot through the left eye by a Royalist marksman called Mr Dyott from the cathedral's battlements around the bottom of the central spire. A plaque marks the spot where Brooke fell and one can appreciate the superb accuracy or perhaps the good luck of Dyott, firing as he did with a matchlock musket. With 800 Parliamentarian reinforcements under Sir John Gell, an assault on the gate failed, despite using a number of townspeople as 'human shields' in advance of the troops. On 3 March a further 3,000 Parliamentarians arrived with Sir William Brereton, but the heavily outnumbered Royalists managed to sally out and disrupt their enemies. On 4 March a large mortar arrived and began to lob shells into the close. This, combined with a shortage of supplies, forced the Royalists to surrender on 5 March. Parliament garrisoned the close under Colonel Russell, but they were attacked the following month.

The cathedral and close are well worth visiting, as is the excellent Heritage Centre in St Mary's Church, which includes a detailed video about the Civil War in Lichfield and four cases of documents presented by the Staffordshire Archive Service relating to the three Civil War sieges.

Lichfield, siege of, 8–21 April 1643

Royalist recapture of Lichfield led by Prince Rupert.

Following the capture of the Cathedral Close by the Parliamentarians in March 1643, Prince Rupert (nephew of King Charles I) was ordered to recapture the city. By 8 April the close had been invested and it is likely that earthworks were built to protect the attackers. The one visible Civil War earthwork in the city is 'Prince Rupert's Mount' situated at the end of Prince Rupert's Way on the hill overlooking the north of the close, with one corner of the fortification surviving. Whether this belongs to Rupert's siege or to the more substantial Parliamentarian works of the third siege is not clear. An assault on the south gate on 15 April failed, but miners from nearby Cannock Chase had been tunnelling under the north wall. On 20 April their mine was blown under the north-west tower of the close, leaving a breach 'wide enough for six men to enter abreast'. Forty musketeers defended the breach, with others on the walls who were able to repel the storming party, according to the Parliamentarian Captain Randolph. However, on 21 April they came to terms and surrendered, leaving the city in the hands of the Royalists for the next three years. The Parliamentarians were allowed to leave with eleven wagons and audaciously managed to remove the treasures from the cathedral, which were never recovered.

Lichfield, siege of, 9 March–10 July 1646

Third Civil War siege of this important Midlands city.

By 1646 the Royalist cause was nearly lost, with garrisoned castles and towns providing the main resistance to Parliament. On 9 March Sir William Brereton surrounded the Close of Lichfield Cathedral with a force of about 3,000 men, who began to construct a series of earthworks, possibly including the surviving 'Prince Rupert's Mount', which is usually ascribed to the second Siege. As well as a semi-circle of earthworks around the northern part of the close, the Parliamentarians set up cannon to fire from the south from Dam Street. These opened fire on 7 May, with some shots being directed at the cathedral spire, which was brought crashing down onto the roof of the nave and choir on 12 May. Eventually news reached the garrison that Charles I had given permission to his remaining garrisons to surrender, which they did at Lichfield on 10 July, marching out on 16 July.

As previously mentioned, the cathedral and close are well worth visiting. Inside the cathedral, in the south-eastern corner, is a memorial tablet to Colonel Richard Bagot, who died as a result of wounds gained at Naseby.

Lilleshall Abbey, storming of, 23 August 1645

This former Augustinian abbey in Shropshire (currently cared for by English Heritage with free admission) was garrisoned by the Royalists under Sir Richard Leveson for much of the First Civil War, until it fell to artillery fire and a storming party led by Colonel Braine.

Lincoln, battle of, 2 February 1141

Most important battle of the Civil War between King Stephen and Matilda, resulting in the capture of Stephen.

KEY REFERENCE: Bradbury, J. *Stephen and Matilda, the Civil War of 1139–53* (Alan Sutton, 1996).

Lincoln was a key city with an important castle in the twelfth century, making possession of it important during a period of unrest. Although the exact circumstances are unclear, Lincoln had come into the hands of Ranulf, Earl of Chester, whose governing of the city managed to upset the citizens. They sent a request to King Stephen to come to their aid, which he duly did, despite the fact that it was in the Christmas season of 1140. Stephen then besieged the castle until a rebel army led by Robert, Earl of Gloucester, accompanied by Ranulf, appeared before the city in an attempt to raise the siege.

The rebels managed to cross the marshy land beside the Fosse Dyke and formed up for battle. Stephen accepted, despite it being a Sunday, drawing up his men to the west of the city. The sources are not clear about the exact

Mounted knight of King Stephen's reign at the Battle of Lincoln, 1141, where such troops led by Earl Ranulf broke through Stephen's cavalry.

location of the battle, although this interpretation is widely accepted. There is also disagreement in the chronicles about the dispositions of the armies, although the most thorough account given by Henry of Huntingdon is followed here. He places the rebels in three lines, presumably because they marched in the usual three 'battles' and had not at the beginning of the fight wheeled out into a right hand, centre and left division on the battlefield. Earl Ranulf led the first line, William of Roumare the second and Earl Robert the third. Large numbers of Welsh infantry who were 'greater in courage than in knowledge of arms' were placed on each flank. As the armies drew closer it seems likely that the rebels did deploy into the more usual formation of three 'battles' (divisions) across the battlefield, with Ranulf taking his men to the right, as was usual for the foremost division. Stephen had his mailed knights dismounted and in close formation at the centre of his 'battle'. Probably in front of them were placed two rather thin lines of cavalry.

Earl Ranulf attacked and broke through the lines of cavalry, although, on Stephen's side, William of Ypres and William of Aumale routed the Welsh troops opposite them. This success was short-lived, as Ranulf's charge carried away Stephen's cavalry, including William of Ypres, who fled the field. This left the central formation of dismounted knights with Stephen in their midst. The rebels encircled and attacked them on all sides 'as if they were assaulting a castle'. If the chronicle account is to be believed, and it may well be exaggerating the role of named individuals, Ranulf charged directly towards the king. Stephen fought bravely, at first with a 'great two-handed battleaxe' and then, once that broke, with a sword. When that also broke, William de Chesney grabbed Stephen, taking him prisoner. The remaining Royalists were either killed or captured, with Stephen being taken to Bristol. If Stephen's rival Matilda had been more diplomatic at this point the war could well have been ended. Instead, Stephen's supporters managed to raise more troops and carried on the war.

Lincoln, battle of, 20 May 1217

Battle fought by William the Marshal against a largely French army, after the latter had besieged several English castles.

KEY REFERENCE: 'The History of William the Marshal' (part) in *English Historical Documents* vol. III ed. Rothwell, H. (Eyre and Spottiswood, London, 1975).

Prince Louis's army was already besieging Dover Castle when he ordered a force to move against Lincoln. After the death of King John in 1216 William

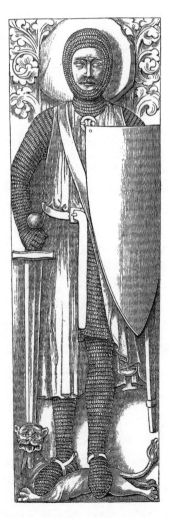

William Marshal, who led the royal army at the Battle of Lincoln, 1217. He would have carried the straight broad sword as a secondary weapon as a mounted knight; his primary weapon would have been a spear or lance.

the Marshal was regent for Henry III. We are told in the understandably biased 'History of William the Marshal' that the relief force consisted of 406 knights and 317 crossbowmen, presumably in addition to other foot soldiers. They were commanded by William, along with the Earl of Chester in the van, the Earl of Salisbury with the third formation or battle, and the Bishop of Winchester with the reserve. Opposing them were 611 French knights and at least 1,000 French foot, along with various English supporters, although these figures are likely to be inflated. By the time William's army arrived, the French were behind the city walls, although the battered castle still held out. It appears that the relief force entered the castle and then moved into the city, beating away the French besiegers. A large body of the French force then attacked up the hill to William's men, to be met before they reached the top by William's troops moving from the flat ground between castle and cathedral. The defeat of this force was completed when the Earl of Chester moved against their right flank, forcing them to flee towards Wigford. This victory effectively ended Louis's invasion and attempt to take the English throne.

Lindal-in-Furness, skirmish of, 1 October 1643

Impressive victory against a larger force in this small skirmish of the First Civil War.

A small force of Royalists under Colonel Huddleston moved against Colonel Rigby's Parliamentarians, who were besieging Thurland Castle in Lancashire. However, Rigby realised what was afoot and moved part of his force to meet Huddleston. This meant a march through Ulveston and Lindal, before encountering Huddleston's 1,600 men on the road to Dalton in the early afternoon. Although Rigby only had 500 foot, about 150 horse and two small cannon, they were better armed and trained than the Royalists. One determined charge was all it took to break Huddleston's force, with Huddleston himself being captured along with many men and supplies as they fled beyond Dalton.

Lindisfarne, raid of, 793

First Viking raid on a named place in Britain, sacking the monastery on Lindisfarne off the Northumbrian coast. It occurred in the same year as terrible portents such as 'fiery dragons' were seen in the air, according to the Anglo-Saxon Chronicle.

Lindsey, battle of, 1014

Fought as part of the struggle for the crown between the English and the
Danes.

Following the death of Swein 'Forkbeard' on 2 February 1014, the crown was
disputed between Cnut and Aethelred, with the latter gaining the most
support, not least as he had been king from 978 until Swein's assumption of the
kingship in 1013. However, Cnut was determined to continue to press his
claim, staying at Gainsborough with his army until Easter and making an
agreement with the people of Lindsey in Lincolnshire to supply him with
horses and men. Aethelred moved against Lindsey before Cnut was ready. The
people there were caught, the settlement raided and many were killed, while
Cnut made for his ships and slipped away down the coast to Sandwich with a
group of hostages. Cnut then put them ashore, but only after removing their
hands and noses. Aethelred's success was short-lived, as he died in 1016, with
the English line losing the Battle of Ashingdon against Cnut.

Lindsey, raid of, 1066

Attack by Tostig, brother and enemy of King Harold Godwinson, before linking up
with Harald Hardrada.

Tostig had left England in 1065, having been outlawed and driven from his
earldom. In 1066 Tostig was at Sandwich, but moved north once he heard that
Harold was marching towards him. Landing with a force most probably of
sixty ships on the shores of the Humber estuary, he raided Lindsey in
Lincolnshire. Again he was driven away, this time by the Earls Edwin and
Morcar, forcing him north again, to find refuge with King Malcolm III of
Scotland. From there he joined with Harald Hardrada to launch an invasion
of the North, leading to the battles of Fulford Gate and Stamford Bridge later
in the year.

Liverpool, siege of, 7–11 June 1644

Storming of the town by Prince Rupert during his march to York and Marston
Moor, following brief resistance by the Parliamentarian garrison under Colonel
Moore, many of whom escaped by boat during the night of 10 June before the
port was taken.

London, battle of, 851

Having over-wintered in England for the first time, a Viking force of 350 ships stormed London and Canterbury, routing Beorhtwulf of Mercia.

London, battle of, 994

An attempt by the forces of the Norwegian Olaf Tryggvason and the Danish King Swein 'Forkbeard' to capture London with ninety-four ships. They failed, but turned their attention to the coasts of Essex, Kent, Sussex and Hampshire.

London, siege of, beginning 7–9 May 1016

Part of a long-running Viking attempt to capture and loot London.

An army of Danes moved up the Thames to Greenwich and then dug a ditch around London to besiege it, even digging a ditch around the southern end of the bridge over the Thames to allow their ships to get upstream, presumably because the bridge itself was heavily defended. Despite these measures, London was not captured. Later in the year the Danes returned after battles at Penselwood and Sherston but were then driven off by King Edmund 'Ironside'.

Losecoat Field, battle of, 12 March 1470

Crushing of a rebellion organised by Warwick 'the Kingmaker' and George, Duke of Clarence against Edward IV.

KEY REFERENCE: Haigh, P. A. *Where both the hosts fought* (Battlefield Press, 1997).

After the Battle of Edgcote in 1469, King Edward IV surrendered himself to the Nevilles, led by the Earl of Warwick. However, it soon became clear that Warwick would not be able to rule the country with Edward in captivity, so he was released. Warwick and Edward's brother George, Duke of Clarence decided to attempt a further rebellion in 1470, as they saw Edward gathering more and more support. Unlike the previous year, Edward reacted quickly and decisively, attacking a large force of rebels near Empingham on the Great North Road (A1) in Leicestershire (Rutland).

Edward marched from Stamford on 12 March and was able to catch Sir Robert Welles, who had decided to confront Edward, rather than waiting for an opportunity to unite with Warwick and Clarence. This was because Welles hoped to liberate his father, Lord Welles, who was being held by Edward. However, as the king approached Sir Robert's force, which was probably deployed beside what is now the A1 on slightly higher ground just to the south of the line of the lane to Pickworth, this plan badly backfired. For as Edward readied his troops to the south on the slight rise in the ground to the south of Tickencote Warren, the king ordered the execution of Lord Welles and Sir Thomas Dymmock, presumably in full sight of the rebels opposite. The sources are at odds as to what happened next. Edward Hall and Polydore Vergil tell us that the rebels advanced to attack and that the battle was hard-fought and lasted for several hours. Others, however, paint a different picture, with the battle being over much more quickly, largely thanks to the use of the royal artillery train. If this is the correct interpretation, which is indeed the account followed by most modern authors, it sees one of the earliest successful and decisive uses of artillery on an English battlefield. It is reasonable to assume that the royal cannon demoralised an already shaken force, which fled once the more disciplined king's army came to blows. Numbers are also difficult to estimate, with 30,000 being a grossly inflated figure for the rebels. It is likely that the defeat and rout came quickly, and that it was then that many of the rebels fled, casting away their liveried jackets to help avoid detection, thus giving the battle its name of Losecoat Field. It is also possible that many were cut down on the other side of the Great North Road, in the wood which is still known as Bloody Oaks, as they tried to escape. This could indicate that the main Royalist attack came on the rebels' left, where the ground is more open, forcing their line to cave in on that side first and allowing them to flee to their rear and rear-right. Sir Robert Welles was taken and later executed, while letters were captured which clearly implicated Warwick and Clarence, if further proof were needed after hearing the rebels' battle cries of 'Clarence, a Clarence, a Warwick, a Warwick'. Edward duly pursued the two lords around the country, forcing them into exile, before the climactic battles of Barnet and Tewkesbury in 1471.

Lostwithiel, battle of, 19 January 1643, *see* Braddock Down

Lostwithiel, battle of, 21 August–2 September 1644

A decisive victory for King Charles I, going some way to offsetting the Royalist reverses at Marston Moor and Cheriton in the same year.

KEY REFERENCE: Holmes, R. *Civil War Battles in Cornwall, 1642 to 1646* (Mercia Publications Ltd, Keele, 1989).

The 1644 Battle of Lostwithiel was quite unlike any other major battle of the Civil Wars, sharing much more in common with numerous sieges, not least in the length of time over which the battle was fought. Indeed, action began in outlying areas on 11 August 1644, providing a case for extending this time still further. The decisions which led to a major engagement being fought in Cornwall are many and varied, with the Royalists seemingly unsure as to how to proceed after their victory at Cropredy Bridge near Oxford on 29 June 1644. King Charles I heard on 12 July of the major Royalist defeat at Marston Moor outside York, just after he had set out to the West Country from Oxford. Instead of returning, he carried on, in part to prevent the fall of largely Royalist Devon and Cornwall to a Parliamentarian army commanded by the Earl of Essex, which had started to move west during June 1644. The revenue from tin as well as the raw material itself and doughty Cornish foot were important resources for Charles and can be used to justify his decision to move against the Earl of Essex.

Essex forced the Cornish Royalist commander Richard Grenville to abandon the Siege of Plymouth, and then forced his way across the River Tamar into Cornwall on 26 July. However, once inside Cornwall there were only two easy land routes out, and these could easily be blocked by the king's large forces moving west, although a sea route was a possibility so long as Parliament controlled a port. Essex was aware of this priority as he secured Fowey on the South Coast, while his main force occupied nearby Lostwithiel on 2 August. He then garrisoned various outlying strongpoints overlooking Lostwithiel, including Restormel Castle, which is now under the guardianship of English Heritage.

The town itself sits in a natural bowl and as such could not be held for long if an enemy possessed the high ground nearly surrounding it. However, it had the lowest bridge on the River Fowey and so was of local strategic importance. The Royalists started to tighten the noose around Lostwithiel on 11 August, by taking the town of Bodmin to the north and then moving towards Lostwithiel on the west side of the River Fowey. Shortly after this Polruan was taken on the east side of the Fowey estuary, making relief by sea all but impossible for Essex, while a relief force by land was turned back in Somerset. This left Essex with around 10,000 men, while King Charles I had perhaps 14,000, having linked up with his nephew Prince Maurice on his way west, in addition to Grenville's 2,400.

Shortly after dawn on 21 August Grenville stormed Restormel Castle, while to the east of the Fowey other Royalist forces took the commanding Beacon Hill. The Royalists established redoubts into which artillery was positioned and the 'siege' proper began. At this point a determined breakout may have

O horrable Murder

Royalist propaganda depicting King Charles I as a martyr. After a hesitant start to the war he emerged as a competent commander in the field, especially at Lostwithiel in 1644.

succeeded as the Royalist forces were widely dispersed, with movement and communications between the various components slow. However, morale started to ebb away in Essex's army at the same rate as their dwindling supplies. Essex organised a breakout on the night of 30 August, which was betrayed to the Royalists by deserters. This enabled precautions to be taken, although surprisingly some 2,000 horse led by Balfour managed to slip through the Royalist lines and made their way to Plymouth. The bulk of the army still led by Essex planned to march to Fowey, which they started to do, destroying various properties in Lostwithiel as they left, including blowing off the roof of the church in a heavy-handed attempt to persuade Royalist prisoners to leave the building. The Royalists pursued, taking Lostwithiel at about 7.00 a.m. on 31 August, with the king fording the Fowey just to the south of the town shortly afterwards. The Parliamentarian retreat plodded on for about three miles down the western side of the Fowey until it reached the prehistoric fort of Castle Dore, which still guards the narrow neck of land between the towns of Lostwithiel and Fowey. A major attack was undertaken on this position at 2.00 p.m. on 31 August, once a large number of Royalist troops were available. This was beaten off, as were successive attacks later on that day. The scene is easy to imagine, with the high and thick banked and walled hedges providing ideal cover for the defenders while making the use of horse difficult. The earthwork defences no doubt were utilised by Essex, with traces of a possible gun platform still being visible between the two ringed ramparts of the fort. Whatever the skill of the defenders, their escape was now impossible with their pursuers in close contact. This persuaded Essex to slip away during the night, leaving in a fishing boat at dawn on 1 September, with his command handed on to Skippon. He was aided in this by the very wet weather, which had plagued much of the campaign. Just before the Royalists renewed their assault on 1 September Skippon requested a parley. This was granted and terms were discussed during the day, being finally agreed on 2 September. The 6,000 remaining Parliamentarian soldiers were escorted back to Portsmouth, but on their long journey many hundreds died from a combination of disease, hunger and attacks. One account claimed that only 1,000 made it back, which if true makes this episode one of the most disreputable of the war. On the other hand the reputation of the king increased dramatically, for he had been largely personally responsible for the Royalist strategy and leadership during the campaign. He marched back to fight again at Newbury in October before wintering in Oxford, handing back the initiative to Parliament in 1645.

Lowestoft, battle of, 3 June 1665

First major engagement of the second Anglo-Dutch War.

KEY REFERENCE: Haswell, J. *James II* (Hamish Hamilton Ltd, 1972).

The English fleet of about 100 ships under James, Duke of York (later King James II), moved to counter a Dutch fleet of 113 ships led by Admiral van Opdam to the south-east of Lowestoft. The two fleets met at about 1.00 p.m. on 1 June, with the east wind aiding the Dutch. James followed the Dutch down the coast on 2 June and just before dawn at 3.00 a.m. on 3 June the battle began. At the start the two fleets were on opposite tacks, with the English attempting to go about to sail parallel and in the same direction as the Dutch. This caused a good degree of confusion, taking up to six hours for the English to realign. Some firing took place during this stage, but it was at 10.00 a.m. that the fleets fell to a general mêlée. By 2.00 p.m. it was clear that Dutch losses were heavier than those of the English, despite the loss of three high-ranking officers to the same cannon shot as they stood next to James. The victory was secured when van Opdam's flagship exploded and a chase ensued across the North Sea into 4 June.

Luddite attacks, *see* Rawfolds Mill

Ludford Bridge, battle of, 12 October 1459

More rout than battle, this encounter early in the Wars of the Roses was a defeat and nearly a disaster for the Yorkist cause.

KEY REFERENCE: Hodges, G. *Ludford Bridge and Mortimer's Cross* (Logaston Press, 1989).

Following the bloody battle at Blore Heath in Staffordshire on 23 September the armies of York and Lancaster had manoeuvred and gathered strength in the West Midlands and Marches. The Lancastrian King Henry VI was following the Yorkists with a large army, which, according to one chronicle, had 30,000 harnessed men as well as others listed as 'naked', meaning men not from lordly retinues but probably recruited by a commission of array. As is usually the case, this figure is bound to be inflated, but it is clear that the king had a sizeable force with him, seeing as it included the retinues of many important lords. Modern accounts tend to estimate an army of 12,000 for the Lancastrians, while the Yorkists under the Duke of York and the Earl of Warwick had perhaps 6,000 between them.

The Yorkists took a somewhat circuitous route from Worcester to Kidderminster, to Tewkesbury and then into Herefordshire via Ledbury and Leominster, arriving at Ludford, just across the River Teme from Ludlow, in the wet on the evening of 12 October. The road in 1459 curved to the west of the current road where the latter moves down to Ludford Bridge. Therefore, the Yorkists positioned their forces across the old road, with their artillery behind a fortified ditch, no trace of which remains today. They must have felt trapped, with the river to their backs and a larger army facing them. What made the situation even worse was the presence of Henry VI opposite them, as this was the first time for most of the Yorkists that they had to bear arms against the anointed king in person. The final straw came with the defection of part of the Yorkist vanguard. Warwick had brought most of the Calais garrison over to England, which was commanded by Andrew Trollope. He took these men over to the Lancastrians, probably at this point, after receipt of a letter from the Lancastrian Duke of Somerset, with whom he had fought in France. The remaining Yorkists realised that the game was up, and after a hasty council of war they decided that the sensible option was to flee. This the leaders duly did at midnight, going through Ludlow and off into Wales, leaving the Lancastrians in charge of the field and their army with little option but to surrender.

This could well have been the end for Richard Duke of York, as his credibility was badly damaged by the fiasco at Ludford Bridge. He escaped to Dublin, while his son Edward, Earl of March (later Edward IV), went to Calais with Warwick. In November an Act of Attainder was passed against the Yorkists, but they managed to rally support to return to fight again, firstly at Wakefield and then at Mortimer's Cross just over a year later.

Ludlow, siege of, 24 April–29 May 1646

Capture of this important Royalist town and castle at the end of the First Civil War.

Ludlow remained in Royalist hands for nearly the entire First Civil War, despite Parliamentarian raids from time to time. It fell to the Parliamentarian Colonel Birch with 600 foot and 450 horse, who stormed it on 24 April 1646, burning part of the town as a consequence. Sir Michael Woodhouse (who could be blamed for the killing of Parliamentarians in cold blood at Hopton Castle in 1644) with a garrison of 250 foot and 100 horse attempted a raid on Birch at Eyton, but they were caught and suffered casualties as a result. The castle (now open to the public) held out for a month until it surrendered on terms without Birch having to deploy any siege guns, although positions for these had probably been prepared on Whitcliffe Common, on the other side of the River Teme from the castle.

Ludlow castle at the end of the seventeenth century, showing some exaggeration in the scale of the cliffs. The castle was more easily approached from the townward side of the castle. It surrendered on terms in 1646, helping it to avoid damage from siege guns as this engraving supports.

Luton, battle of, 913

Viking raid against Luton which was met by a local force who put the raiders to flight.

Lydford, raid of, 997

Raid by a Viking force moving east from the Tamar to attack Lydford in Devon, burning and killing before sacking the monastery at Tavistock.

Lyme (Regis), siege of, 20 April–15 June 1644

Siege of this Parliamentarian port, which demonstrated the importance of having sea-borne supplies.

KEY REFERENCE: Young, P. & Emberton, W. *Sieges of the Great Civil War* (Bell & Hyman, 1978).

Lyme was one of the few Parliamentarian garrisons in the West Country during the First Civil War, making it all the more important for that reason.

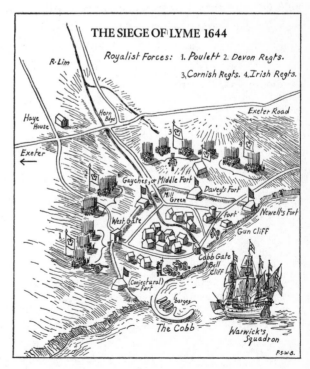

Siege of Lyme, 1644.

Parliament's navy controlled the Channel, making supply of the port relatively easy to maintain. On the other hand, Lyme was surrounded on its landward side by hills, suggesting that it should have been an easy target for enemy artillery. A Royalist army of 6,000 led by Prince Maurice (younger brother of Prince Rupert and a nephew of King Charles I) arrived outside the town's earthen defences on 20 April 1644. The garrison was led by Colonel Were, who was vigorous in organising sallies out of the town, which ensured that, even though only some 1,200 in number, they made life for the attackers as difficult as possible. Various attacks were attempted but all failed, with Maurice's frustration becoming greater as ships continued to arrive, bringing supplies and even reinforcements to the garrison. The closest Maurice got to capturing Lyme was on 21 May when a small force got over the defensive rampart on the western side of the town and made its way to the Cobb, Lyme's stone mole forming the harbour. This force destroyed the majority of the craft alongside and in the harbour, which could have led to the town's surrender had it not been for the timely arrival of the Admiral the Earl of Warwick with a squadron of seven ships. After landing much-needed gunpowder and match for the muskets, Warwick sailed to Charmouth to draw the Royalists' attention away from Lyme. Once this was discovered as a feint, the Royalists sent in another attack on the western side of Lyme, but the three separate assaults were just held off. The crisis had passed, although further trouble soon followed in the form of fire arrows, which destroyed many houses in the town. Relief was sought by the garrison, but they had to survive for another six weeks until help arrived in the form of the Earl of Essex. He marched his army to Blandford, persuading Maurice to abandon the siege of Lyme by 15 June.

Maiden Castle, siege of, *c.* AD 43

Storming of one of the most impressive hill forts in England by the invading Romans.

It is accepted that Vespasian's legion moved through the south-west, in particular moving against the Durotriges tribe, located mainly in modern Dorset and South Somerset. Maiden Castle just outside the Roman foundation of Dorchester is one of the largest and most impressive of the hill forts or oppida within this tribe's territory. Confirmation that it was indeed the scene of one of Vespasian's attacks came from a famous excavation by Sir Mortimer Wheeler in the 1930s. Most startling were the skeletons found just outside one of the main entrances into the fort, in what became known as the war cemetery. Suspicions that these were bodies from the assault on the fort were confirmed when one skeleton was found with a Roman ballista bolt embedded in its spine. Others had clear sword cuts, especially to the head. Some of these, including the unfortunate ballista victim, can be seen in Dorchester Museum. The defences also appear to have been deliberately slighted by the Romans after their success, with large stones being toppled from the entrances and ramparts. Tactics are not known for sure, but concentrated artillery fire followed by an infantry assault, presumably in *testudo* or tortoise formation against the entrance, would seem logical.

Maidenhead, battle of, January 1400

After a failed attempt to assassinate King Henry IV at Windsor, the Earl of Salisbury fled to Reading, while his forces held the bridge over the Thames at Maidenhead, fighting against the king's forces for three days until Salisbury was captured and executed.

Maidstone, battle of, 1 June 1648

Only major field action of the Civil Wars in Kent.

Parts of Kent rose in support of King Charles I shortly before the rising in Essex in the Second Civil War. Upnor Castle was seized, while the main Royalist force of about 7,000 under the Earl of Norwich (Lord Goring) took Maidstone. Parliament responded quickly, sending Sir Thomas Fairfax with part of the New Model Army to deal with them. Fairfax bypassed the main blocking force at Aylesford crossing the Medway at East Farleigh instead, which was only lightly defended. Reaching Maidstone in the evening of 1 June, Fairfax ordered an immediate assault on the barricades, breaking into the town from the south until the Royalists were hemmed into St Faith's Church. This was taken after a bloody fight, which only ended at about 11.00 p.m. Upnor Castle was retaken shortly afterwards.

Maldon, battle of, 917

Attempt by a Danish army to seize this fortified English *burh*.

Maldon had been fortified by King Edward of Wessex in 916. In 917 the English had already defeated the East Anglian Danes at Derby, Tempsford and Colchester, suggesting that this attack on Maldon could have been as a reprisal. Whatever the reason, the attack failed, despite reinforcements from the sea. A relief force arrived and the Danes were driven off, suffering very heavy casualties.

Maldon, battle of, 10 August (probable) 991

This defeat of the East Saxons and the slaying of Earl Byrhtnoth gave rise to the fine epic poem known as *The Battle of Maldon*, and to the first payment of *danegeld*.

KEY REFERENCE: Cooper, J. (ed.) *The Battle of Maldon: Fiction and Fact* (Hambledon Press, 1993), Scragg, D. (ed.) *The Battle of Maldon* (Blackwell, 1991).

A Danish Viking army led probably by Swein 'Forkbeard' (or possibly by Olaf Tryggvason) embarked upon a series of raids along the English coast. Arriving in the Blackwater estuary, the *burh* and mint at Maldon were an obvious target. Using Northey Island as a secure base for their ships, the Vikings were prevented from marching to the town, probably early in the morning, by an army of East Saxons led by their Earl Byrhtnoth, who blocked the landward end of a causeway linking the island to the mainland. With the tide coming in, the armies were forced apart and reduced to shooting arrows at one another. As the tide turned in the afternoon the Vikings pressed along the causeway, but this was held by three Saxon warriors, Wulfstan, Aelfhere and Maccus. Due in part to pride, but also to the need to bring the Vikings to battle before they could cause more damage along the coast, Byrhtnoth then allowed the Vikings to cross so that a battle could be fought.

This took place just to the north-west of the landward end of the present causeway, with the Saxons probably forming up on the slightly rising ground, with Byrhtnoth's household companions around their earl in the centre of the line. With a probable 2,500 to 3,000 men on each side, the armies would have formed in lines some 300m long, with the Saxon shield wall being six men deep with a reserve to the rear. According to the epic poem *The Battle of Maldon*, most of the weapons used were spears and swords, with bows also being used, while defensively shields and chainmail are mentioned (but perhaps

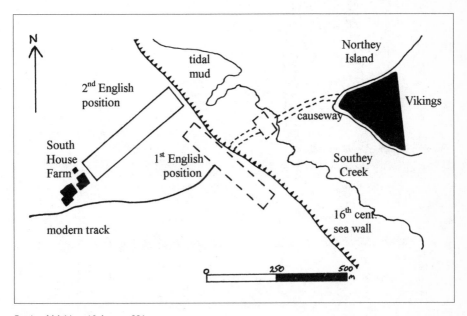

Battle of Maldon, 10 August 991.

Above: Part of a twelfth-century manuscript detailing the payment of danegeld by Aethelred II following the Battle of Maldon in 991.

Left: Archer typical of the Anglo-Saxon period, for example those described in the epic poem *The Battle of Maldon* (991) where 'bows were busy'. Unarmoured and equipped with a short bow around 120cm long, archers rarely formed a decisive element in battles throughout this period.

Reconstruction of a typical Viking long sword showing heavy straight blade, simple guard and decorated pommel. Such swords were relatively high-status weapons compared to the more commonly used spears and javelins. In the epic poem *The Battle of Maldon* (991), the most detailed description of a Viking battle mentions the use of both swords and spears ('darts').

oddly, not helmets). The fighting was fierce, with Byrhtnoth becoming a target, no doubt in part due to his position in the centre of the line, but also due to his great height and grey or white hair. He fell, having been wounded several times, with possibly his head being cut off (his headless corpse was later buried at Ely, with a ball of wax where the head should have been). His household companions fought on to avenge their fallen lord, while the remainder of the Saxon army lost heart and left the field. After the battle, the Vikings did not attempt to attack Maldon, but left, later being paid off with the sum of 10,000 pounds. This was an unfortunate precedent with many future Viking raiders being bought off in a similar fashion.

The location of the battlefield is very widely accepted as described here, although there are other much less convincing local candidates. The key to the location is the length of causeway and the fact that the incoming tide meets on either side of the causeway at Northey Island: something which is clear from the poem. Although coastal changes and the building of later sea walls have changed the nature of the battlefield, it is still a rewarding site to visit. Access is from the B1018 to the south-east of Maldon, along a private road leading to South House Farm. Alternatively, visitors can walk from the town along the coastal path which leads to the causeway at Northey Island. This is now a nature reserve managed by the National Trust, with access to the island only possible after contacting the warden. Maldon has the Maeldune Centre, which has some information about the battle, including a modern tapestry depicting Maldon's history.

Malmesbury, siege of, 1153

Early siege in Henry of Anjou's campaign of 1153 against King Stephen.

KEY REFERENCE: Bradbury, J. *Stephen and Matilda, the Civil War of 1139–53* (Alan Sutton, 1996).

Henry of Anjou, who had recently become Duke of Normandy (later Henry II), crossed to England, arriving on 6 January 1153. Henry brought a relatively small force with him, consisting of 140 knights and 3,000 infantry, although he knew he would gain a reasonable amount of support from various barons in England. He moved to attack the town of Malmesbury, which he took by storm. However, he was unable to capture its castle, which was stoutly defended by King Stephen's supporter, Jordan. Having repelled the first attack, Jordan slipped away to summon help from King Stephen. He responded by marching to Malmesbury with an army. However, a river not far from the walls of the town (probably the Avon) separated the two armies, although Stephen formed

Armoured foot soldier with a bundle of throwing spears rather than a single longer, stouter, thrusting spear. This soldier is typical of those who fought on both sides of the Civil War of Stephen's reign, for example at the battle of Malmesbury, 1153.

up ready for battle. Stephen had the larger army, but could not cross due to very heavy rain which had made the river impossible to ford. The rain drove into the faces of Stephen's men and they did not try to force the issue. Instead they retired back to London, leaving the keep at Malmesbury to surrender to Henry.

Manchester, siege of, 24 September–2 October 1642

Early Royalist siege of the First Civil War.

Manchester was for Parliament at the onset of the First Civil War in 1642, leading to local Royalists under the Earl of Derby besieging it with 2,000 foot, 800 horse and eight or nine cannon. The town's governor was Richard Holland, who held Manchester for Parliament throughout the war. The siege was abandoned once Derby received orders to join King Charles I at Shrewsbury in preparation for confronting the main Parliamentarian field army commanded by the Earl of Essex.

Marshall's Elm, skirmish of, 4 August 1642

The first action of the First Civil War, predating the skirmish at Powick Bridge by nearly three weeks.

This skirmish would merit no more than a footnote were it not for the fact that this action was the first of the Civil Wars following Sir John Hotham's refusal to allow King Charles I entry into Hull. The skirmish was fought in the West Country, between Wells and Somerton, just to the south of Street. A small force of about eighty Royalist cavalry and dragoons was stationed at the top of the scarp, between Walton and Collard Hills. A much larger force of some 600 Parliamentarians moved forward, not knowing the advantage they held due to their assumption that there were more Royalists behind those that could be seen on the crest. A small volley from the dragoons on either flank made the Parliamentarians waver, which was followed by a downhill charge by the horse, scattering the larger unit and killing twenty-five men.

Marston Moor, battle of, 2 July 1644

Largest battle of the First Civil War, which secured the north of England for Parliament.

KEY REFERENCE: Newman, P.R. and Roberts, P.R. *Marston Moor 1644, the Battle of the Five Armies* (Blackthorn Press, Pickering, 2003), Barratt, J. *The Battle for York: Marston Moor 1644* (Tempus, 2002).

One of the best known battles of the English Civil Wars, Marston Moor outside York is still open countryside and easy to interpret on the ground. In addition to the historical sources there has been research based on the distribution of shot, started by Peter Newman in the 1970s and continued in depth by Paul Roberts, which has helped interpret the battle. There is just one interpretation panel next to the monument to the battle, which was put up by the Cromwell Association in the 1930s. On the other side of the road running from Long Marston to Tockwith is a small lay-by large enough for one coach or three cars.

The city of York, held for King Charles I, had been under siege since 21 April 1644, when a Scottish army led by the Earl of Leven and allied to Parliament had joined forces with Parliament's northern army under Lord Ferdinando Fairfax outside York. On 3 June the Parliamentarian Army of the Eastern Association led by the Earl of Manchester arrived and made the encirclement of the city complete. The Marquis of Newcastle had retreated before the Scottish army and had become the besieged force inside York. To relieve the city and to take the war to Fairfax and the Scots, Prince Rupert (nephew of King Charles I) determined to swing to the west from the Midlands collecting troops as he went, before crossing the Pennines to reach York. He did this on 1 July, after the Allied army had raised their siege and withdrawn to land between Long Marston and Tockwith, hoping to intercept Rupert before he reached York. However, Rupert cleverly slipped past their armies by swinging round them to the north, brushing aside minor opposition as he went.

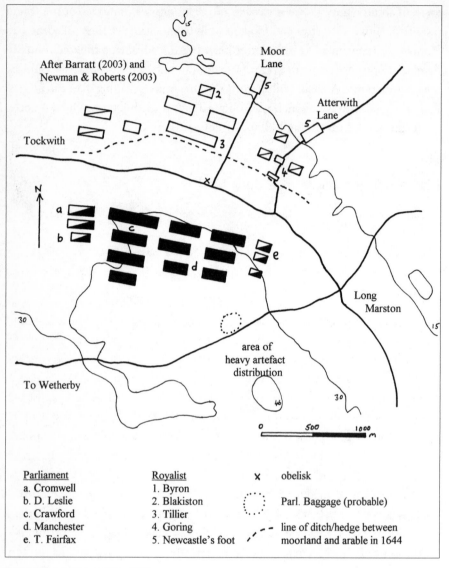

Battle of Marston Moor, 2 July 1644.

On discovering this the Allies agreed to pull back to link up with further reinforcements, which they started to do on 2 July. With just a rear-guard of 3,000 horse left on the ridge above Long Marston and Tockwith, the Parliamentarians observed Rupert's cavalry arriving on the moor below, leading to skirmishes at the western end of these slopes where the moorland gave way to agricultural land and a rabbit warren. Realising that Rupert's arrival could put their own withdrawal and that of the entire army under threat, the Allies ordered their retreating armies to 'about turn' and return to take up positions on the high ground. This consisted of the long ridge of Braham Hill between Long Marston and Tockwith, marked by 'Cromwell's Plump' at the Long Marston end, just to the south of the modern monument. The land consisted of large open fields, although near both of the villages were smaller enclosures and, at the Tockwith end, the already noted warren at Bilton Bream. This cultivated land continued just to the north of the road between the villages where the landscape gave way to moorland, with the boundary between the two marked by a hedged bank and ditch. Rupert had the king's authority to fight against the allies having relieved York, and he sensed an opportunity to destroy part of the Allied forces above Marston Moor before they could deploy their entire force. However, Newcastle did not stir himself or his men quickly enough to make the most of this chance, and by the time the Royalists were ready for battle on the Moor, his enemies had been in position for some time, as Parliamentarian artillery had opened fire at about 2.00 p.m.. By 4.00 p.m., when the last of the Royalist infantry started to arrive, Rupert appears to have given up any prospect of battle and retired to the rear for supper. However, on seeing preparations for cooking and eating being made along the enemy's lines and taking confidence in their own numerical superiority and position, the Allies decided upon an attack. This took the

Sir Thomas Fairfax, commander-in-chief of the New Model Army from 1645 and formerly a thorn in the Royalists' side in Yorkshire, playing a prominent role in the 1643 campaign before commanding the parliamentary horse at Marston Moor in 1644 on the right wing. Of Fairfax, John Milton wrote: 'Fairfax, whose name in armies through Europe sings, filling each mouth with envy or with praise.'

Illustration suggesting that war was not far away in 1642 as the Royalist or Cavalier dog squares up to the Parliamentarian or Roundhead dog. Note that the Royalist dog is portrayed as a poodle belonging to Prince Rupert. This dog, named Boy, was a target for Parliamentarian satire throughout the war, until the poodle's untimely death at Marston Moor in 1644.

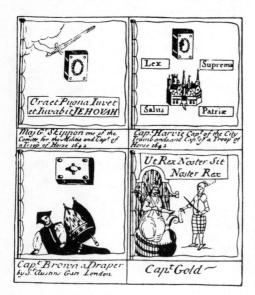

Parliamentary standards. Each troop of horse during the Civil Wars would usually carry its own standard. These often reflected the personality and personal tastes of their commander to a greater extent than the more stylised colours of foot companies and regiments. There would have been numerous standards at large-scale actions such as that at Marston Moor in 1644.

Royalists very much by surprise, as they had assumed that the day was too far gone for a full-scale battle to be fought, but even with the action starting at about 7.00 p.m. this gave three hours with enough light for action. It is also possible that Rupert had miscalculated the strength of the allies, as it would have been difficult to keep track of all their movements during the afternoon. The Allies' ridge was in fact two ridges, one lower and parallel to the first, with a long 'channel' of dead ground between them, which would have hidden a whole line of the Allies' troops, although they would have been observed taking up such a position.

The Allies formed up as follows: on their right was Sir Thomas Fairfax with 3,000 horse in three lines. In the centre were some 20,000 foot in four lines, while Cromwell commanded the left flank of 4,000 horse and 1,000 dragoons, giving an overall total of about 28,000 men. On the Royalist side against Thomas Fairfax were 2,100 horse and 500 musketeers under Lord Goring. In the centre were 11,000 foot, probably in three lines along with some reserve horse under Blakiston, although most of the third line consisting of Newcastle's men was still entering the Moor when the battle began in earnest. On the Royalist right against Cromwell were 2,600 horse and 500 musketeers under Lord Byron, giving a total of nearly 17,000 men. It would appear that the greater number of horse at the Tockwith end of the battlefield indicates that the terrain there was more open, with the boundary hedge and ditch between the moor and fields being less substantial, as well as there being fewer enclosures.

At about 7.00 p.m. the Allied army moved down the slope to attack, supported by artillery fire and by a shower of rain, which must have led to a number of misfires among the Royalist musketeers lining the boundary hedge and ditch to their front. As the infantry advanced, Manchester's men on the left-centre cleared the hedge, which probably did not have a ditch or bank at that point, while Lord Fairfax in the right-centre had initial success, but was then forced back in retreat when his infantry came up against the experienced men of Newcastle's foot. Some Royalist cavalry from the centre under Blakiston, seeing the gap in the Allied line, pushed through and reached the top of the ridge before being charged in their flank by some allied reserve horse. Meanwhile on the allied left, Cromwell and David Leslie led their cavalry against Byron with great success, driving him from the field with ease, if the lack of archaeological finds in that area is anything to go by, which supports the historical references. Even the arrival of Prince Rupert to rally his own regiment failed to stem the retreat. However, on the Parliamentarian right Sir Thomas Fairfax was pushed back, no doubt in part because of the difficult nature of the hedged lanes and enclosures on that part of the battlefield. In particular, it seems from Captain Stewart's (a Scottish officer on the Allied side) account that the main problem came when Fairfax attempted to charge up what was almost certainly Atterwith Lane, behind Long Marston, where he could only deploy three or four abreast. As Fairfax's men fell back, some of the Parliamentarian and Scottish infantry were caught up in the retreat as well, leading to a large gap appearing on the Allied right wing, with many troops and Lord Leven fleeing from the battlefield and the Royalist horse under Goring pursuing up the ridge to the south and south-east. The battle was saved by the Allied left, who continued to push opposing units away until they had swung right round to fight over the same ground as their own right wing had fought on earlier in the evening, being joined in this move by the successful foot from the left-centre. The cavalry regiments of Cromwell and David Leslie broke the previously successful regiments in front of them from the Royalist left, presumably having sighted them on the crest of the ridge. This involved crossing much of the battlefield, with one having to admire the discipline and tactical acumen of Cromwell and Leslie in carrying out this manoeuvre. The work of Roberts has proved that there was heavy fighting to the south of Long Marston, presumably from this phase of the battle, as Goring's men tried to fight their way back to the main Royalist lines. The distribution of artefacts, including much musket shot, demonstrating that reserve or rallied Parliamentarian foot were also involved, is particularly dense just to the south of the road from Long Marston to Wetherby. This area has until now not been thought of as part of the battlefield, but now clearly should be included in future interpretations of the battle, as well as being understood to have important implications for the area of the currently registered battlefield. Amidst the confusion towards the end of the battle, two groups of units of Royalist foot put up a brave defence from within enclosures, which were probably to either side of Moor Lane from the heavy distribution of shot found there, and possibly by Atterwith Lane, although many still favour the more central White Syke Close to be the site of this resistance. First Newcastle's Whitecoats were cut off, followed by a regiment of (possibly Tillier's) greencoats. Both suffered heavy casualties as the battle reached its bloody conclusion and fire was poured into their massed but thinning ranks, the Royalists in the words of a Scot, James Somerville: 'having refused quarters, every man fell in the same order and rank wherein he had fought.' It certainly seems unlikely that there was an enclosure at White Syke Close at the time of the battle, making it likely that both of these regiments were cut off beside Moor Lane, or perhaps more likely that the Whitecoats were stationed there while the greencoats were in one of the enclosures by Atterwith Lane, explaining why the latter are mentioned later in Stewart's account.

The battle was a decisive victory for the three Allied armies. York was soon taken, while Prince Rupert's reputation had disappeared with his fleeing regiments. On the other hand Marston Moor was very much the making of Oliver Cromwell, helping him to rise to the position of second in command of the New Model Army.

Maserfield, battle of, 5 August 641

King Oswald of Northumbria was killed at this battle, probably at Oswestry, by the army of Penda of Mercia.

Mearcred's Burn, battle of, 485

Unidentified battle in which Aelle fought against the Britons.

Medway, battle of the, AD 43

Arguably the most important battle and victory for the Romans during AD 43, which enabled the establishment of Britannia as a province of the Empire.

KEY REFERENCE: Manley, J. *AD 43 The Roman Invasion of Britain: A Reassessment* (Tempus, 2002).

For long accepted as historical fact, the Battle of the Medway has recently become the focus of much debate, especially since an article in 1989 by J.G.F. Hind in *Britannia* and two conferences in 1999 and 2001 on the subject of the invasion. Much of the debate is summarised and parts expanded upon in Manley's book listed above. The extent of this debate is due to there being no direct historical or archaeological evidence which pinpoints fighting to a crossing of the River Medway in Kent during the Claudian invasion of AD 43, although there is circumstantial evidence. We learn from the Roman writer Cassius Dio that the leader of the invasion, Aulus Plautius, encountered a British force at a river crossing, which was presumably some distance from the site of the landing as Plautius had already fought two actions against Caractacus and Togodumnus of the Catuvellauni before coming up against this defended crossing. Richborough has some archaeological evidence to suggest that it was used as a landing place in AD 43, although whether this was during the first phase or later in the campaign is impossible to say. One of the problems with Richborough being the place used for the entire invasion force of about 40,000 soldiers is that the landing area simply would not have been large enough to cater for the 1,000 necessary ships: even if the landings were staggered during a day the logistical and organisational problems would have been too great. One solution to this problem is that Richborough was used as the main landing, while Chichester Harbour was used for a secondary force, centred on the future Emperor Vespasian's II legion. A more radical option is to see the Chichester landings as the main thrust, with Richborough as secondary or later. Certainly the archaeological evidence for landings in the Chichester area in AD 43 is as strong as for Richborough.

What happened at the battle itself is clearer thanks to Dio's account, which tells us in some detail about this two-day encounter. The river was wide and unbridged, which had led to over-confidence on the Britons' part, as they were careless with their deployment. This allowed Plautius to send over his German (probably Batavian) auxiliary cohort(s) who were trained to swim while wearing armour. Vespasian's II legion then got across, possibly by using a ford. This does add weight to the argument that the army was together at this point, although it is equally possible that Dio had mixed up his facts or his sources on this point. If Vespasian was with the main force, then the question arises whether this was at the Medway, or at a river crossing between Chichester and the Thames. At this point the battle died down for the day, to be renewed on the morrow, as the Britons had re-grouped. It would seem that there was an opportunity for a counter-attack while the Roman force was divided by the river, but Dio gives no indication that this was attempted. Instead we learn that Hosidius Geta, presumably with a fresh legion, won the battle for Plautius, despite being nearly captured. The Britons then retreated to beyond the River Thames.

Unless clear archaeological evidence is discovered to pinpoint the battle, it is difficult to locate it at the Medway, despite this being the accepted orthodox view. It is certainly ironic that there is a memorial stone to the battle erected in 1998 at the Medway near the village of Burham, when many other well-documented and located battlefields have no such marker.

Medway, raid in the, 10–14 June 1667

Impressive raid by the Dutch against the English fleet at anchor during the second Anglo-Dutch War.

Following losses in battle, the devastation caused by the Great Plague and the Fire of London and escalating costs of the war started in 1665, the English fleet was laid up in the River Medway at and downstream from Chatham. The Dutch Admiral de Ruyter led the audacious raid in 1667, which first of all captured the fort at Sheerness on 10 June, as well as landing a small force on the Isle of Grain. This enabled the Dutch fleet to sail up the Medway on 12 June, breaking through a defensive chain at Gillingham soon after 10.00 a.m. by using two fireships, while two English ships were captured (including the flagship the *Royal Charles*) and two destroyed. On 13 June the Dutch proceeded further upstream and sank three more large ships close to Chatham before calmly sailing back to the Thames on 14 June. A Dutch fleet kept up a blockade of the Thames for a month before the Treaty of Breda was signed, bringing an end to the war.

Meretun, battle of, March 871

King Aethelred of Wessex and his brother Alfred were defeated after having the upper hand for much of the day.

Merrington, skirmish of, 17 October 1346

Preliminary skirmish to the Battle of Neville's Cross when a Scottish raiding party stumbled into the main English army.

The Scottish army led by King David II had invaded England largely due to the absence of King Edward III, who was fighting in France. The northern English lords assembled an army to meet this invasion and moved to intercept the Scots. On 17 October a force of about 500 Scots raided the town of Merrington near Durham, but then fog set in and the force became confused when they heard a large force of men somewhere near. Sir William Douglas, leading the raid, stumbled into two of the main columns of the advancing English, led by the Archbishop of York and Sir Thomas de Rokeby. The *Lanercost Chronicle* claims that less than half the Scottish force escaped to fight later the same day at Neville's Cross.

Middlewich, skirmish of, 13 March 1643

In 1643 Parliamentarians and Royalists vied for control of Cheshire, which resulted in this success for the Parliamentarians against a force of Royalists under Sir Thomas Aston. The Royalists were defeated by Sir William Brereton, with the action concluding when some of the Royalist foot were holed up in Middlewich Church and forced to surrender after the doors were blown in.

Modbury, battle of, 21-22 February 1643

Skirmish winning some measure of local control for Parliament, after the Royalist success at Braddock Down.

KEY REFERENCE: Peachey, S. *The Battle of Modbury 1643* (Stuart Press, 1993).

Plymouth in Devon was an important garrison for Parliament throughout the First Civil War, holding firm despite Royalist control of Cornwall and much of Devon for most of the war. Modbury to the south of Dartmoor was being held by a Royalist garrison of about 1,500 men in February 1643, under the

command of Sir Nicholas Slanning and Colonel Trevanion as part of their plans
to capture Plymouth, standing as it did on the eastern route from that port. To
counter this the Parliamentarians launched a coordinated attack on the town
by sending around 1,500 men from Plymouth to attack from the west, while a
large column of up to 8,000 had come from north Devon via Totnes and
Kingsbridge to attack Modbury from the east.

Although heavily outnumbered, the Royalists held up the Parliamentarians
throughout the afternoon of 21 February helped in part by the thick
hedgerows, banks and stone walls around the town. Once darkness fell, sporadic
firing continued until the majority of the Royalists slipped away during the
night to Plympton, leaving a small force of dragoons to carry on the action. At
dawn on 22 February the surviving dragoons tried to make good their own
escape, but some were captured and some Parliamentarian horse started a
pursuit. The Royalists left behind five pieces of artillery and 1,100 muskets,
with perhaps eighty men captured, 100 killed and 200 wounded, while
Parliamentarian losses were very much lighter. With the arrival of the
Parliamentarian force from north Devon the Royalist commander in the area,
Sir Ralph Hopton, called off the Siege of Plymouth.

Mons Badonicus, battle of, *see* Badon

Morpeth Castle, siege of, 10–30 May 1644

This castle in Northumberland changed hands five times in 1644, with the
most lengthy siege being when the Royalist Scot Montrose captured it from a
garrison of 500 Scottish Covenanters, before Montrose retreated to Scotland
and the Battle of Marston Moor was lost by the Royalists, leading to the
recapture of Morpeth later in the year.

Mortimer's Cross, battle of, 2 (or 3) February (Candlemas) 1461

Wars of the Roses battle which helped to establish the reputation of Edward of
York (later Edward IV), as a great commander.

KEY REFERENCE: Hodges, G. *Ludford Bridge and Mortimer's Cross* (Logaston Press, 1989).

Edward became the Yorkist claimant to the throne occupied by King Henry
VI after the death of Edward's father at the Battle of Wakefield on 30

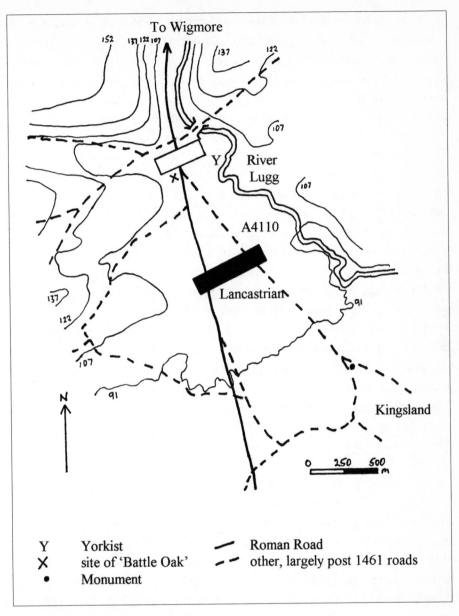

Battle of Mortimer's Cross, 2 February 1461.

December 1460. Edward was at Shrewsbury, where he recruited an army from the Marches. News arrived of a Lancastrian landing in South Wales led by the Earls of Pembroke and Wiltshire. Their forces advanced towards Edward, so the latter decided to block them at the defile of Mortimer's Cross in the Lugg valley.

When reading about the Battle of Mortimer's Cross in the majority of twentieth-century accounts, the battle is described as having been fought from west to east, with the Lancastrians from the west attacking the Yorkists deployed with their backs against the River Lugg. However, it is clear that in fact the Yorkists formed up from west to east, facing the Lancastrian attack coming from the south. This interpretation is reinforced by the displays in the small battle museum in Mortimer's Cross Mill on the battlefield. The route the Lancastrians took in 1461 emerged just to the south of Mortimer's Cross, or else they came up directly from Hereford along the old Roman road: they could not have approached from the west, because there was no road there, apart from the fact that it would have been impossible to deploy an army of the period on the steep slopes in that direction. The position chosen by Edward at the entrance to a narrow defile was well suited to a smaller army taking on a larger one. It seems likely that there was no bridge at Mortimer's Cross over the River Lugg in 1461, further supporting the interpretation that the battle was not fought by Edward with his back to the river.

The Yorkists formed up on the morning of 2 February (or possibly 3 February), 1461 (Candlemas) to witness a strange meteorological phenomenon called a parhelion. This event gives the appearance of a triple sun, and was seized upon by Edward of York (later Edward IV) to be a good omen representing the Trinity shining upon the Yorkists. He deployed his army in three 'battles' as was the custom of the period. One source tells us that the Yorkists numbered 15,000, while the Lancastrians had 8,000. However, from the lists of named followers it would appear that the Lancastrians held the advantage, with perhaps 3,500 against 2,500 Yorkists. On the Yorkist side there were no great lords other than Edward himself, whereas on the Lancastrian side there were the two Tudors, Jasper and Owen (Jasper was the later Henry VII's uncle, Owen was Jasper's father, Henry VII's grandfather) and the Earl of Wiltshire with contingents from Ireland, France and Wales. The Lancastrians would also have deployed in three 'battles', with the Irish under Wiltshire on the left, the centre under Jasper Tudor, Earl of Pembroke, and Owen Tudor on the right.

The battle commenced with an arrow storm, which provoked the Lancastrians into an advance into the bottle-neck caused by the terrain against the Yorkist lines, where heavy hand-to-hand fighting took place. After a savage, but probably relatively short mêlée, the Lancastrian line broke, at first on their right, with men fleeing back towards the village of Kingsland. There, and for several miles along the banks of the Lugg, men were cut down and prisoners taken, including Owen Tudor, who was later executed in Hereford. We are told that 4,000 Lancastrians were killed, but this Yorkist figure must be greatly exaggerated, especially if their starting numbers were the 3,500 suggested earlier!

Mortimer's Cross was a decisive battle and helped Edward on the path to becoming one of the most successful and inspirational commanders of the Wars of the Roses, as well as helping him to become King Edward IV. Coming so soon after the death of Edward's father at the Battle of Wakefield, Mortimer's Cross was vital in keeping Yorkist hopes alive.

Mount Badon, battle of, *see* Badon

Myton (-on-Swale), battle of, 20 September 1319

Fought five years after the Battle of Bannockburn, Myton represents another low water mark for Edward II of England.

KEY REFERENCE: English Heritage: *Battlefield Report: Myton 1319* (English Heritage, London, 1995).

Although Bannockburn was a crushing defeat for the English, Edward II was still able to continue the war albeit from England rather than in Scotland. By 1319 King Edward was based in York from where he moved to besiege Berwick in August. The Scots launched a diversionary invasion of England with perhaps 15,000 men under the Earl of Moray and Lord James Douglas, to relieve pressure from the defenders of Berwick. A captured spy was brought in to York with news of where the Scottish invading force was located. It was decided to attempt a surprise attack based on this information, although the force which was hastily assembled lacked any real quality, discipline or cohesion, as it largely consisted of townspeople from York, because many of the trained fighting men must have been with Edward to the north. This force, also consisting of about 15,000, marched towards Myton-on-Swale under the command of the Archbishop of York and the Bishop of Ely.

The English arrived at Myton village to the south-east of the River Swale on the afternoon of 20 September. They could see the Scots drawn up beyond the river, probably on the low ridge running broadly parallel to the river to the west. The narrow timber bridge of 1319 was sited around 200 metres to the south-west of the current footbridge. The English crossed the bridge, finding themselves in the pasture of Myton village, which may well have made their advance difficult and no doubt accounts for the fact that the Scots had camped some way back from the river where the ground was drier and higher. The modern landscape is

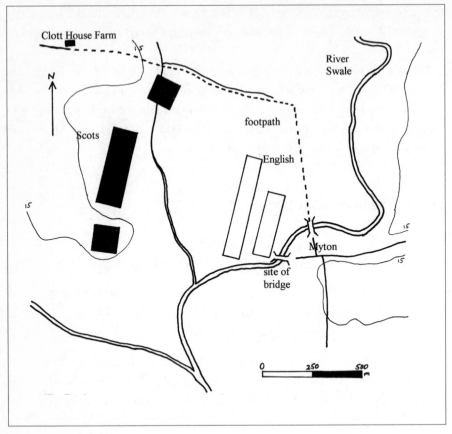

Battle of Myton, 20 September 1319.

probably better drained than it was in 1319, with the water-course running into the Swale on the line of the Scots' advance perhaps not having been present at the time of the battle. Further confusion was caused by the Scots firing three haystacks, with the resulting smoke obscuring their movement. The Scots formed up in one large schiltron (see the Battle of Boroughbridge entry) and advanced. This demonstrates that the Scots could see how poorly organised and equipped the English were, as the schiltron was usually employed as a defensive formation. This formation smashed into the English mass and predictably broke it, killing many and forcing the rest to flee back towards the river, where more were cut down or captured. As the *Life of Edward the Second* tells us, 'many of our [the English] men …were untrained in the art of war, and were readier to flee than to fight'. The defeat was made all the worse because a group of Scots had worked round behind the English and cut their line of retreat to the bridge, leading to many drowning in the Swale as they attempted to escape.

By the time of the Battle of Myton in 1319, plate armour was becoming a more common sight on the battlefield. This figure has a particularly well-articulated suit of armour, especially in the gauntlets and foot pieces.

The defeat at Myton persuaded Edward II to raise the Siege of Berwick, so that the troops employed there could be used to protect the northern counties. It also led to more problems between the king and some of his powerful subjects, especially the Earl of Lancaster who was to end up in open rebellion, fighting royal forces at the Battle of Boroughbridge in 1322, just a few miles from Myton. The battlefield is arable farmland, with good access onto the site from Ellenthorpe Lane on the west side of the river, as well as from the village of Myton-on-Swale, so long as there is access across the bridge. The original pastureland can be traced from the more recent drainage ditch and flood bank, suggesting that the main fighting took place at the foot of the gentle slope up to the Scots' position.

Nantwich, battle of, 25 January 1644

Royalist defeat which ended hopes of securing the North-West for Charles I.

KEY REFERENCE: Barratt, J. 'A Happy Victory': The Siege and Battle of Nantwich, 1644 (Caracole Press, 1995).

Parliament held the town of Nantwich at the beginning of 1644, but found themselves under threat from a Royalist army of 3,500 led by Lord Byron. Sir Thomas Fairfax marched all the way from Lincolnshire with a force of some 5,000 to relieve the town, to prevent the king's forces from gaining control of Cheshire and the North-West.

The two armies met to the north-west of Nantwich in fields beside the later Shropshire Union Canal, from whose bridges good views of the battlefield can be gained. In particular one should park in Acton (there is a small public car park opposite the church) and then walk down to the canal and follow the tow-path to the north. The Royalists occupied the low ground by the canal, while Fairfax appeared on the low ridge to the north-east, having marched his men down the Chester road to an earlier position to the north of Burford. The low ground in January must have been very wet, especially as the River Weaver had burst its banks on 24 January, causing problems for the Royalists, who had a temporary bridge swept away, and making communications between the various besiegers of Nantwich difficult. It even appears that some of the Royalist defenders were unable to reach the battlefield, at least at the beginning of the battle, due to this problem.

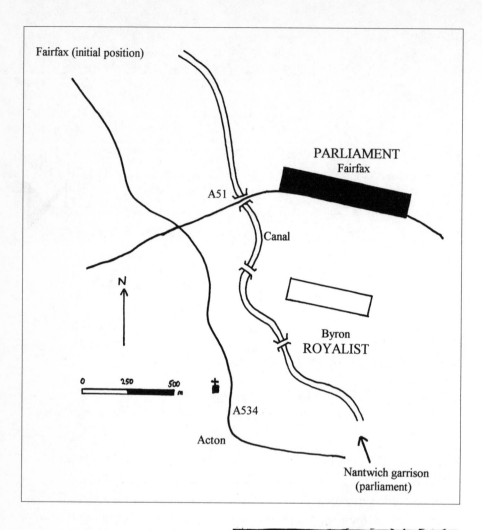

Fairfax (initial position)

PARLIAMENT
Fairfax

A51

Canal

N

Byron
ROYALIST

0   250   500
              m

A534

Acton

Nantwich garrison
(parliament)

Above: Battle of Nantwich,
25 January 1644.

Right: The Battle of Nantwich,
1644, was fought in very
damp conditions which would
have made misfires from the
matchlock muskets very likely;
this near contemporary
illustration shows the
musketeer ensuring that his
match is still burning.

Blow your Cole

28

With Fairfax pushing through a Royalist advance force of 200, the Royalists had to fight on poor ground and with inferior numbers. They were soon defeated, despite an attempt to drive the Parliamentarians from their low hill. A sally from the Parliamentarian garrison of Nantwich against Byron's rear sealed the fate of his army. Although Byron himself escaped with the bulk of his cavalry, the majority of the Royalist foot were taken prisoner, with many of them going into the Parliamentarian army. The Siege of Nantwich was ended and the townspeople celebrated by putting sprigs of holly in their headgear. This is commemorated every year with Holly Holy Day in the town, along with a re-enactment of the battle by the Sealed Knot on the Saturday closest to the 25 January. The museum in Nantwich has a display relating to the battle. As a result of the battle, the Parliamentarian cause remained very much alive in the North-West and Sir Thomas Fairfax's stock continued to rise.

Naseby, battle of, 14 June 1645

The decisive battle of the First Civil War, which saw the blooding of the New Model Army and the destruction of King Charles I's main field army.

KEY REFERENCE: Foard, G. *Naseby, The Decisive Campaign* (Pryor Publications, 1995).

Although it is difficult to rank English battles and battlefields in order of importance, it is tempting to place Naseby at the top of both such lists. It was at Naseby in Northamptonshire that the result of the First Civil War became inevitable, thus securing a form of parliamentary government for England. It also saw the successful if not entirely smooth debut of what can be called England's first nominally red-coated army: Parliament's New Model, under the command of Sir Thomas Fairfax. The battlefield is a most rewarding one to visit, as it is largely undeveloped, with the key areas and views unspoilt. On the other hand, the A14 dual carriageway allows traffic to thunder across the southern edge of the field, separating the village of Naseby and site of the Parliamentarian baggage train from the remainder of the battlefield. It was due to the building of this road in the early 1990s that led to battlefields in England being taken seriously as an important part of the historic environment. The publication of the *Register of Historic Battlefields* in 1995 by English Heritage was partly a consequence of the building of the A14, as was the formation of the Battlefields Trust, a registered charity dedicated to the preservation and better interpretation and presentation of battlefield sites. Naseby is also important as it is a battlefield where responsible metal-detecting has led to a better understanding of the events, the positioning of units and the extent of the battlefield. This work was carried out by two local farmers, Mike Westaway and Peter Burton, and is interpreted in detail in the key reference by Glenn Foard. Ever since the battle, other artefacts have been recovered from the battlefield, but only a handful survive in a known location and with good provenance. Most notable of these are a small collection in Northampton's museum, including a coin hoard found in Sibbertoft, along with a sword and spur in Naseby Church. The small Naseby Battle museum in the village only opens on rare occasions such as Bank Holidays.

In an attempt to gather support and gain the initiative, the Royalist army had left its headquarters at Oxford and moved north on 7 May 1645. Despite defeating Parliamentarian garrisons and storming Leicester, King Charles I decided to return to Oxford. Sir Thomas Fairfax, in command of the New Model Army, had at first been ordered to raise the Siege of Oxford by Parliament and had subsequently been given the freedom to act as he thought best. This meant locating the king's army and bringing it to battle. The Royalists hoped to increase the strength of their army before fighting Fairfax, but were caught sooner than they had anticipated. By the night of 13 June the Royalists were in and around Market Harborough, while the Parliamentarians were centred on Guilsborough to the south, with their forward parties already exchanging blows in the village of Naseby. On the morning of 14 June, before first light, the Royalists marched out to a hillside just to the south of East Farndon, while the New Model pushed through Naseby along the Clipston Road, where they halted and started to form up on a commanding hill. However, the battle was fought just to the west of these positions, between Sibbertoft and Naseby villages, as the Royalists had no intention of attacking the Parliamentarians in such a strong position. It is not clear whether it was the New Model which moved first, realising that they needed to bring the Royalists to battle, or whether it was the Royalists led by the king's nephew, Prince Rupert, who sought to move round the left flank of the Parliamentarians. Certainly it was the Royalists who had further to march to reach what was to become the battlefield. It is more than likely that it was Fairfax who moved to the slightly less commanding position of Mill Hill to the left of the Naseby to Sibbertoft road first, as it appears that it was Parliament who in effect chose the ground. This is because the ground consisted largely of open fields, with the right flank of the New Model guarded by a walled rabbit warren and the left flank by the thick Sulby hedges. If Rupert had been able to choose the ground then, even taking into account his headstrong nature, he would have tried to fight over enclosed ground which was available close by rather than in the open, given that he knew his army was outnumbered overall and in particular in cavalry.

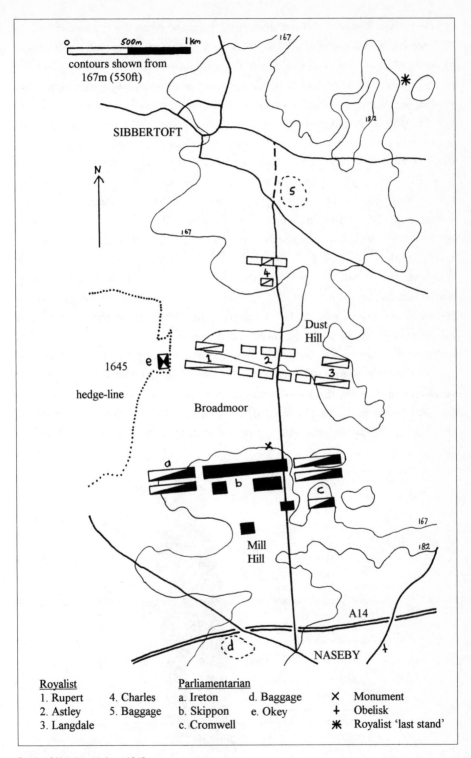

500m · 1 Km

contours shown from
167m (550ft)

N

SIBBERTOFT

1645

hedge-line

Dust
Hill

Broadmoor

Mill
Hill

A14

NASEBY

Royalist
1. Rupert   4. Charles
2. Astley   5. Baggage
3. Langdale

Parliamentarian
a. Ireton   d. Baggage
b. Skippon   e. Okey
c. Cromwell

✕ Monument
✛ Obelisk
✳ Royalist 'last stand'

Battle of Naseby, 14 June 1645.

Glenn Foard, working from the contemporary maps (or picture-maps) of Streeter and de Gomme, as well as from the dimensions of the terrain, frontages from drill books and from the archaeological record, has been able to place the units on the landscape and to calculate their numbers with a high degree of confidence. Standing by the Cromwell Monument just to the west of the Naseby to Sibbertoft road, one can view most of the main battlefield stretched out to the north across what was known as Broadmoor but was then one of the large open fields of Naseby, known as Turmore Field. The hill on whose southern slope the monument has been erected is where Fairfax drew up his infantry, although they were placed higher up behind (to the south of) the post-battle hedge and monument. This position is found in the sources as 'the ledge of a hill' or a 'plain on an eminence' rather than the perhaps more obvious position of Mill Hill just to the south. Cromwell, with over half of the cavalry, was to the right (east) of the road, with Ireton (Cromwell's son-in-law) with the remainder of the cavalry to the left. In the centre were the infantry under Skippon with Fairfax and the reserve. Running perpendicular to the main line of battle on the western edge are the Sulby hedges. A regiment of dragoons under Colonel Okey was dispatched along them to a hedged close to pour flanking fire into any Royalist attack. From the scatter of carbine shot it would appear that Okey ventured a considerable way north, some distance away from the relative safety of the main Parliamentarian lines. Facing the Parliamentarians, the Royalists formed up on the southern slopes of Dust Hill, across Broadmoor. Fewer in numbers, they still

Musketeer of the New Model Army, showing the soldier wearing characteristic shoes, stockings and breeches along with a soft, probably knitted, hat. Individual charges for each shot hang in wooden cases, the lead tops of which have proved to be useful archaeological finds in helping to pinpoint formations of musketeers on the battlefield, for example at Naseby (1645).

A contemporary woodcut showing Sir Thomas Fairfax in council with officers of the New Model Army. In part propaganda, this is suggestive of a democratic spirit within the Parliamentarian forces. This spirit arguably reached its zenith in 1647 with the Putney Debates. Fairfax continued as Lord-General of the New Model Army until 1650. Much of the responsibility for the New Model's success at the Battle of Naseby in 1645, the most decisive battle of the Civil War, lies with its commander-in-chief Sir Thomas Fairfax.

adopted a deeper formation, with Rupert on the right (facing Ireton), Astley in the centre and Langdale on the left (opposite Cromwell). The overall commander King Charles I was to the rear in the centre with a reserve. Throughout their formations the Royalists combined infantry with cavalry, possibly in an attempt to offset their lack of numbers with superior training and unusual tactics. In total the Royalists put some 9,000 men into the field, comprising 4,500 each of foot and horse. Against these Thomas Fairfax was able to deploy about 13,500 of the New Model Army, consisting of 6,000 foot, 6,500 horse and 1,000 dragoons. This disparity in numbers would greatly affect the outcome of the battle. Artillery was present, although with the rapid movement just before the battle and a lack of cannon balls found on the southern side of the battlefield, it seems that few Royalist guns were in position. The dispositions of these forces appear to have been completed by 9.00 or 10.00 a.m., when the battle proper began.

Colonel Okey's Dragoons were quickly in action, as an attempt was made to force them out of their well-protected flanking position. However, they stood firm and Rupert's cavalry then charged past the dragoons to come into contact with Ireton's cavalry, who counter-charged down the hill. Ireton had initial success, and possibly turned some of his regiments against the advancing Royalist foot. However, Rupert, leading a second charge, broke some of Ireton's forces,

Marmaduke, Lord Langdale, who commanded the Royalist left-wing horse at the battle of Naseby in 1645, where he was outnumbered by Cromwell's wing of horse opposite him. He was a key Royalist commander in the North during the Second Civil War, but had difficulties coordinating with the Duke of Hamilton.

leading to their withdrawal. At this point, Rupert's men pursued the broken Parliamentarians towards the baggage train, which was drawn up just to the north-west of Naseby village. However, they would have been better employed against the rear of Fairfax's infantry, or against the remainder of Ireton's cavalry, as many of the latter still remained on the battlefield in good order.

In the centre the Royalist infantry also advanced, first against the Parliamentarian 'forlorn hope' at the foot of the slope, and then against the main body of foot which had come forward to a position just above the current monument. Fire from the muskets had little effect, with both sides closing with their pikes. With the Royalists outnumbered they were unable to make headway at first. However, a second charge helped by regiments from their second line, as well as cavalry from Rupert's wing or from those ordered forward with the infantry, made more progress. The Parliamentarian front line, especially Skippon's Regiment on the left, started to buckle under the pressure and to give ground. However, Skippon was able to bring up the second line to plug any gaps and to bolster the hard-pressed front line. The Royalists had already committed their second line and were unable to press home their advantage due to lack of numbers. A fire-fight seems to have taken place, as indicated by the heavy scatter of musket shot. One suspects that at some point the greater numbers of the Parliamentarians would have forced the Royalists back down the slope, from a combination of fire and then pikes. This moment came sooner rather than later, due to the arrival of some of Cromwell's cavalry from the right. At the start of the battle Cromwell's cavalry had met with Langdale's. With the advantages of slope, numbers and probably discipline, Cromwell was able to drive Langdale from the field. Keeping his reserves in check, Cromwell turned to the left and brought these men to bear against the Royalist infantry. This turned a probable defeat for the king into an inevitable one. Already outnumbered, the Royalist infantry were unable to fight off this new threat, and they started to retreat. The battle did not break down into a disorderly rout as many accounts suggest, but instead there was a fighting retreat for several miles, at least by some Royalist regiments. This started with a stand by Prince Rupert's Bluecoats, probably on the southern slope of Dust Hill. The evidence for this retreat is compelling and clear, consisting of concentrations of shot back to Sibbertoft and then to the north-east. At Wadborough this concentration is particularly dense, suggesting a final last stand by the Royalist infantry, perhaps covering the departure from the field of the king. The pursuit was thorough and savage, with the Irish women with the Royalist baggage train being treated particularly badly. In this decisive battle Parliament lost perhaps 150 dead with just under 500 seriously wounded. The Royalists, on the other hand, lost about 1,000 killed, a further 1,000 seriously wounded and some 5,000 captured as prisoners. A memorial to one of those Royalists who died as a result of his wounds can be found in the south-eastern corner of Lichfield Cathedral, where there is a commemorative tablet to Colonel Richard Bagot. As well as the aforementioned monument near the centre of the battlefield is another, taller obelisk, on the Naseby to Clipston road, just to the south of the A14. Charles I's main field army no longer existed, and as a result he was to surrender himself and his crown.

Naseby not only marked the end of any realistic chance of victory for the Royalists in the First Civil War, but saw the experiment that was the New Model Army grow and evolve into the modern British Army. It was also a significant step on the road towards becoming Lord Protector for Oliver Cromwell, although his role in the battle should not be over-exaggerated, as much of the responsibility for the New Model's success lies with its commander-in-chief Sir Thomas Fairfax.

Nesbit Moor, battle of, 22 June 1402

Attempt by the lowland Scots to raid northern England, although overshadowed by a second invasion which ended at the Battle of Homildon Hill.

Henry IV had fought off a number of rebellions, but in 1402 the situation became very serious as he had to face Owain Glyndwr as well as Scottish invasions. A force of lowland Scots invaded Northumberland on 7 May, led by Sir Patrick Hepburn. A large-scale raid took place until they were caught unexpectedly by an English force led by the Earl of Northumberland and his son Sir Henry 'Hotspur' Percy at Nesbit Moor north of Wooler, where they were decisively beaten. Presumably, the English had taken up a position to block the return of the Scots to Scotland after the latter had crossed the River Till. The Scots launched a larger invasion later in the year, which resulted in the Battle of Homildon Hill (just three miles south of Nesbit Moor) and indirectly to the Percys' rebellion of 1403.

Neville's Cross, battle of, 17 October 1346

Crushing defeat for the Scottish army of King David II outside Durham.

KEY REFERENCE: Brown, C. *The Second Scottish Wars of Independence, 1332–1363* (Tempus, 2002).

With the main English army in France under Edward III gaining the famous victory of Crécy earlier in the year, the French King Philip appealed to David II of Scotland for help, in the form of a diversionary invasion of the north of England. David was happy to oblige and his forces raided through Northumberland. The English had anticipated such trouble and Edward had given command of the northern forces to Henry de Percy, the Archbishop of York and Ralph de Neville, under a commission of array dated six days before the Battle of Crécy on 20 August. Given this preparation it is perhaps surprising that it was nearly two months before the English brought the main Scottish force to battle, which they did by positioning themselves across the main route of the Scots to the west of Durham, where a series of small cross ridges go across the main north-south plateau. Earlier in the day a Scottish raiding party had stumbled into the main English army in the fog outside Merrington, giving the Scots their first clear indication that a battle would be fought on 17 October.

It is likely that the English positioned themselves on the cross ridge a few metres to the north of the railway line running just to the north of Neville's Cross itself, which now stands slightly to the east of its original position, and with only its original socket in place.

The Scots had camped in nearby Bearpark and marched out to meet the English, forming their forces into three 'battles' or divisions: the Earl of Moray on the right, King David II in the centre and Robert the Steward on the left. However, it seems from the *Lanercost Chronicle* that the left wing was slow and may have arrived late, unless this was part of a deliberate plan to attack in echelon. Certainly there was not enough room to deploy a large army of

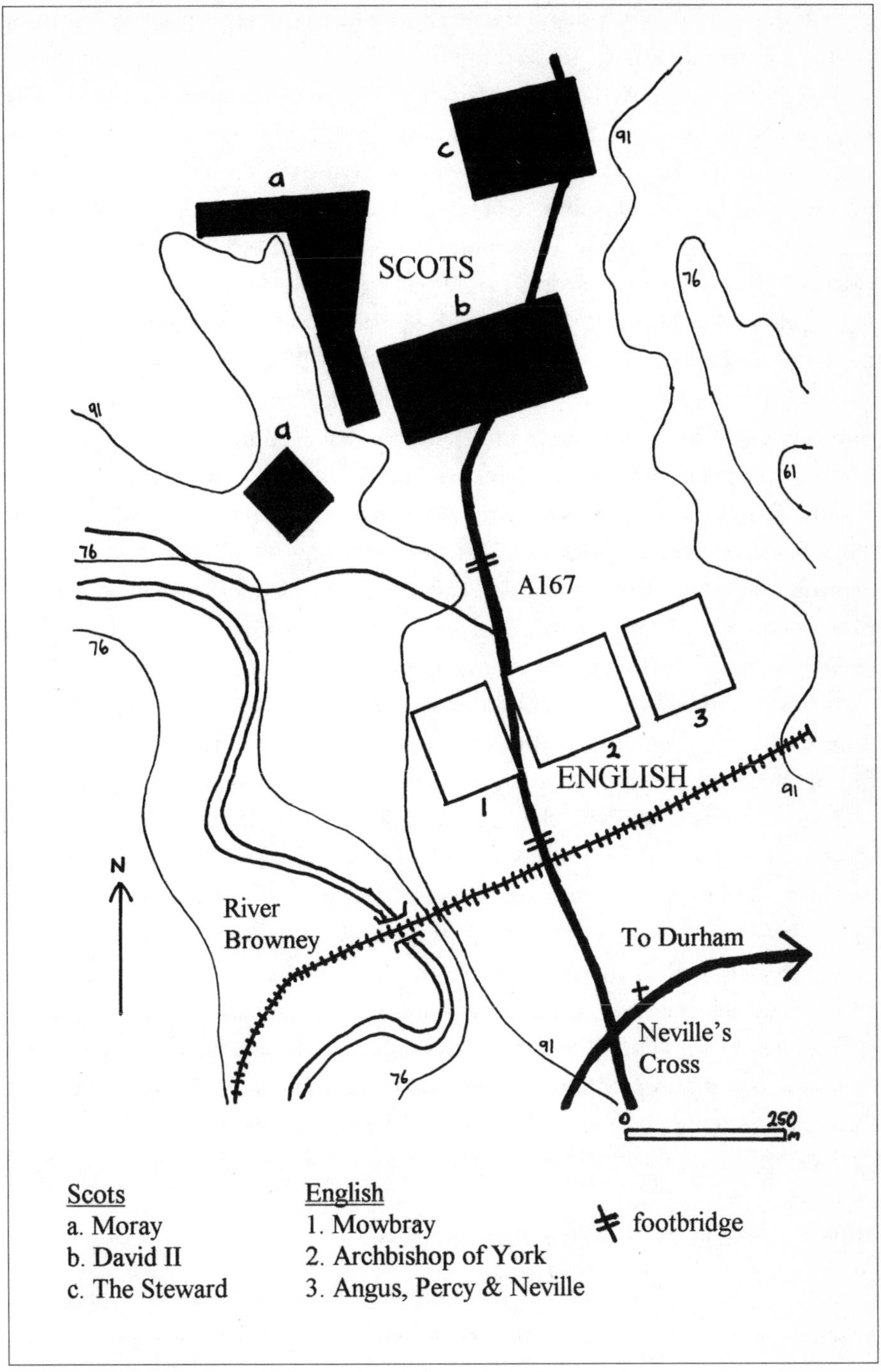
c
a
SCOTS
b
a
91
91
76
76
61
76
A167
1
2
3
ENGLISH
91
N
River
Browney
To Durham
Neville's
Cross
91
76
0
250
m
Scots
a. Moray
b. David II
c. The Steward
English
1. Mowbray
2. Archbishop of York
3. Angus, Percy & Neville
footbridge

Battle of Neville's Cross, 17 October 1346.

probably around 10,000 men on the next cross-ridge to the north (approximately running perpendicular to the A167 just to the north of the point where the second footbridge travelling north from Neville's Cross spans the road). The English had about 8,000, but had the advantage of having chosen their position. On their left was Sir John de Mowbray, in the centre the Archbishop of York and on the right the Earl of Angus, Sir Henry de Percy and Sir Ralph de Neville.

Although each army faced each other from their respective cross-ridges, it was very difficult for the Scottish right to engage the English left, as there is a steep-sided valley between their respective positions. The battle started at around 9.00 a.m. and lasted until 6.00 p.m. if we are to believe the *Lanercost Chronicle*, although this seems too early a start when the skirmish at Merrington is taken into account. The Scottish right under Moray managed to put in an attack, but had great difficulty with the terrain, presumably because of the English archers and the fact that they were forced to attack down and then up the steep slopes. This attack was forced back and the survivors appear to have moved to the Scottish left, where the ground was easier and where perhaps there was more room due to the slow approach of all of the third division. The battle was decided in the centre where the main commanders clashed. This must have been hard-fought, with several attacks and counter-attacks, with pauses in between, until finally the English gained the upper hand. Twice the English archers and foot had been forced back, but had rallied each time with the support of men-at-arms. The end came with the capture of King David by Sir John Coupland, who lost two teeth in the process according to Wyntoun's *Orygynale Chronicle of Scotland*. The retreat became a rout, largely because the Steward had taken his men away early and did not cover the retreat. As many Scots fell in the retreat as had died in battle: perhaps 500 in each.

The battlefield is now almost entirely built over, with the exception of the difficult terrain on the English left flank and Scottish right. Good views can be obtained from the footbridge already mentioned, which also has a helpful interpretation panel fixed to its railings facing north towards the nearby Scottish position.

Newark, siege of, 27–28 February 1643

Attempt by the Parliamentarians to seize this key town from Royalist control.

KEY REFERENCE: Warner, T. *Newark, Civil War and Siegeworks* (Nottinghamshire County Council, 2000).

The Royalists garrisoned and fortified Newark towards the end of 1642, as it was a key town situated at the junction of the Great North Road and the Fosse Way, as well as being on the River Trent. A Parliamentarian force of about 6,000 with ten cannon commanded by Thomas Ballard moved to assault the town, whose garrison was under Sir John Henderson. The Parliamentarians approached over Beacon Hill to the east of Newark, forcing the Royalists behind their defensive works. Ballard ordered a three-pronged attack which made some progress until Byron ordered a counter-attack in the evening. This was successful, driving off the Parliamentarians, who abandoned the siege the next day. The assault which had come close to success persuaded the Royalists to strengthen the defences of Newark, which was carried out in time for the second siege in 1644.

Newark, siege and battle of, 29 February–21 March 1644 (battle, 21 March 1644)

Second of three Civil War sieges of this important Royalist-held town, ending with a set-piece battle.

KEY REFERENCE: Warner, T. *Newark, Civil War and Siegeworks* (Nottinghamshire County Council, 2000).

Newark was the 'key to the North', positioned as it was at the junction of the Great North Road and the Fosse Way, as well as being on the River Trent. As a result it had been garrisoned and fortified by the Royalists since 1642. The Royalist commander at Newark in 1644 was Sir Richard Byron, who was besieged on 29 February by 7,000 Parliamentarians under Sir John Meldrum. The siege was pressed home by eleven cannon and two mortars, one of the latter setting fire to the mayor's house. Meldrum managed to capture one of the Royalist redoubts, at Muskham Bridge, allowing him to push troops and artillery across the 'island' between the two arms of the River Trent and closer to the town. With the net closing, it was clear that Newark might fall, and so an appeal for help was made from the local Royalist commander outside the town to Prince Rupert, King Charles I's nephew.

Rupert advanced from Balderton with a force of around 6,000, sweeping down from Beacon Hill at dawn on 21 March into Meldrum's more dispersed forces. At the same time Byron attacked onto the island and forced the Parliamentarians back over Muskham Bridge. Meldrum had little option but to surrender to this well-planned and surprise onslaught. His men were allowed to leave, but large quantities of supplies and guns were left to the Royalists, including the thirty-two-pounder cannon nicknamed 'Sweet Lips' apparently after a well-known prostitute from Hull from where the gun had come.

Newark, siege of, 26 November 1645–8 May 1646

This third siege of the 'key to the North' was one of the most important of the
First Civil War, its end coinciding with the surrender of King Charles I to the Scots.

KEY REFERENCE: Warner, T. *Newark, Civil War and Siegeworks* (Nottinghamshire County
Council, 2000).

Newark had been garrisoned by the Royalists since the beginning of the First
Civil War in 1642 and by 1645 had already witnessed two sieges. As a
consequence of its position at the junction of the Great North Road and the
Fosse Way, as well as being on the River Trent, it was well fortified and
considered to be the 'key to the North'. The Royalists had constructed a full
circuit of earthen ramparts with artillery positions some distance from the town,
as well as outlying forts and two very large forts or 'sconces' called the King's
Sconce to the north-east and the Queen's Sconce to the south-west of the main
ring of defences. The castle, which now houses a useful exhibition including
information on the Civil War, stands in the town next to the river. The Queen's
Sconce is the most impressive surviving Civil War earthwork in the country and
can be found off Boundary Road, where the Sconce Hills car park services a
children's play area and recreation field. Many of the other earthworks survive,

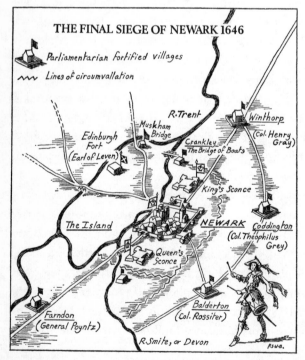

The final siege of Newark, 1646.

Alexander Leslie led the Scottish forces, which linked up with General Poyntz, to besiege the key town of Newark late in 1645.

but many can only be clearly seen from the air, as well as being on private property. We are fortunate in having two contemporary siege maps, including the very detailed map of Richard Clampe, which shows the works of both sides.

Following the Royalist's heavy defeat at Naseby in June 1645, the Parliamentarians began to mop up remaining garrisons, moving towards Newark by November. Before the town could be properly besieged the Parliamentarians had to force their way past the Royalist outposts. This began on 3 November when Shelford Manor was stormed by an overwhelming force against less than 200 defenders. Part of the site has been excavated in 2001 for the television series *Two Men in a Trench* but little directly relating to the siege was found other than the flattened remains of part of the defensive rampart. It seems likely that most of the defenders were put to the sword, possibly as a grim warning to the citizens of Newark. Wiverton Hall was besieged on 4–10 November, with its garrison surrendering on terms. Its fall allowed the Parliamentarians to tighten the noose around the town, greatly assisted by the arrival of a Scottish army under Alexander Leslie from the North. King Charles himself had been in the town, but slipped away just before he would have been trapped.

The Parliamentarians commanded by General Poyntz linked up with the Scots and started to dig their own earthwork line of circumvallation around the town, with the Scots on the 'island' between the two arms of the river Trent, where they constructed a large camp they named 'Edinburgh'. *Two Men in a Trench* found that all traces of the ramparts of the camp had been obliterated by subsequent generations, but a metal-detector survey turned up some evidence of occupation and certainly use during the Civil War period, including the likely manufacture of musket balls. As the winter progressed, the Parliamentarians edged closer by digging a second, inner line of circumvallation, and from Clampe's map it is clear that Poyntz set up his headquarters almost against the Queen's Sconce. Earlier excavations have demonstrated that this inner line was a relatively simple yet effective affair, with a bank and inner ditch which together were about 8m across with the ditch 1m deep. By March 1646 the Royalist commander Lord John Belasyse must have realised that time was running out, as his force became thin and weak through hunger and disease, while the Parliamentarians received reinforcements. An artillery bombardment commenced from twenty-three pieces of artillery, and led to further misery. Poyntz called upon Belasyse to surrender on 28 March 1646 but Belasyse refused. However, matters were taken out of his hands with King Charles' realisation that the game was up. The king decided to surrender himself to the Scots around Newark rather than to Parliament, so he travelled from Oxford to Southwell where he gave himself up on 5 May. He was 'persuaded' to order the surrender of Newark, which he did by sending a message to Belasyse, who was permitted to march out of the town on 8 May. This ended the siege and with this came the virtual end of the First Civil War. The Parliamentarians captured what remained of the Royalists' military supplies and cannon, including the thirty-two-pounder gun nicknamed 'Sweet Lips', captured from the Parliamentarians at the end of the second siege in 1644.

Newburn Ford, battle of, 28 August 1640

Only set-piece battle of the Second Bishops' War fought by the forces of Charles I to prevent a Scottish army crossing the River Tyne.

KEY REFERENCE: English Heritage: *Battlefield Report: Newburn Ford 1640* (English Heritage, London, 1995).

With the refusal of the Scots to adopt the new prayer book favoured by King Charles I and Archbishop Laud, the first Bishops' War had broken out in 1639, leading to a rapid climb-down by Charles, as he had inadequate forces to defend England from invasion. In 1640, encouraged by the Earl of Strafford, Charles went to war again, in an attempt to impose his will on his Scottish kingdom. However, it was a Scottish army of around 20,000 men under Alexander Leslie, the Earl of Leven which invaded England. Charles's main force was preparing in Yorkshire, while he had about 12,000 men in Newcastle led by Lord Conway. The latter sent a small force of 2,000 foot and 1,500 horse to block a Scottish crossing of the Tyne at Newburn Ford, just to the west of Newcastle, on 27

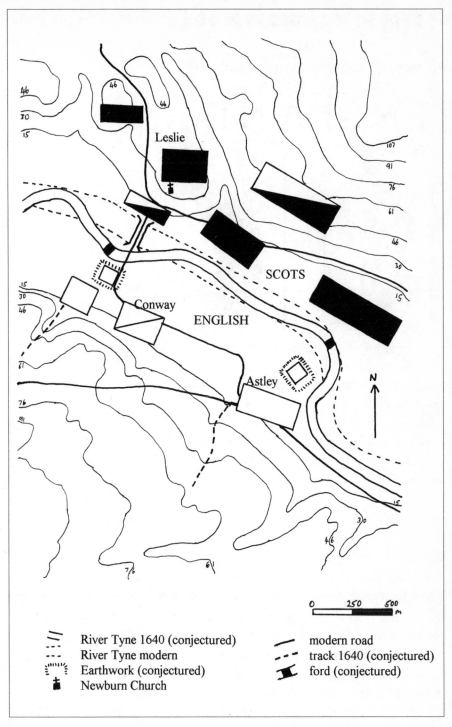

Battle of Newburn Ford, 28 August 1640.

These militiamen were typical of the poorly trained English army which fought in the Bishops Wars against the Scots, for example at Newburn Ford in 1640.

August, with further reinforcements of 2,000 foot under Sir Jacob Astley joining them on 28 August. By then the large Scottish army had assembled on the north bank, with artillery on the slopes and the tower of Newburn Church overlooking the ford at Newburn and a further ford half a mile downstream (east) at Kelshaw. These crossings were guarded by two earthwork emplacements or sconces, occupied by 400 musketeers and four cannon each, on the flood plain by the south bank. The Scottish artillery forced the Royalists to withdraw from their first earthwork (presumably the one at Newburn), in the afternoon as low tide on the river was approaching, enabling Scottish horse to cross the ford at Newburn, which was sited just to the west of the current bridge. The English horse counter-attacked, but were driven off by more Scottish artillery fire, with the Scots taking the second work, helped again by well-directed cannon fire. It seems that the English retreated from the flood plain to the hills to the south, where modern rights-of-way probably mark the old trackways as they climb these slopes. Having being rallied in a wood by Sir Jacob Astley, some of the English foot marched forward to the top of this slope, where they met six troops of their own horse. However, as the foot advanced down the slope to engage the enemy, the Scottish horse caught them in a narrow lane and broke them. The rest of the English army retreated, allowing the Scots to march into Newcastle on 30 August, while Charles made a humiliating treaty which included the payment of £850 per day to the Scottish army. This was largely the reason for Charles having to call what became known as the Long Parliament and was thus an important short-term cause of the First Civil War.

This registered battlefield is partly built over, with the river and flood plain greatly altered since 1640. However, the land to the south of the ford is still surprisingly open, and the slopes to the south and, to a lesser extent, to the north can be explored.

Newbury I, battle of, 20 September 1643

Battle in which a Parliamentarian army led by the Earl of Essex managed to win a victory against King Charles I and force a safe passage to London.

KEY REFERENCE: McNair-Wilson, M. *Battle for a Kingdom* (Deidre McNair-Wilson, 1993).

The year 1643 had gone badly for Parliament in the west, with them leaving the field at Lansdown, effectively losing Waller's army at Roundway Down and then losing the important city of Bristol. However, the city of Gloucester managed to stay with Parliament despite a siege, which was raised as the Earl of Essex approached with a relieving army. Once it was clear that Gloucester was safe, Essex started to return to London, knowing that he would be harried all the way. He was keen to avoid battle, but the Royalists were able to outwit him by delaying him at the Skirmish of Aldbourne Chase on 18 September and by arriving in Newbury in strength on the morning of 19 September led by Prince Rupert (a nephew of King Charles I), just as the Parliamentarian quartermasters were beginning to sort out billets in the town. Newbury blocked the passage of Essex's army and so battle became inevitable once the Royalists arrived in the town in force.

The armies deployed through the afternoon and early evening of 19 September, with the Royalists taking up positions facing west from the River Kennet in the north to the steep slopes at the southern end of Wash Common. Opposite them to the west on largely lower ground were the Parliamentarians around one mile distant. Each army totalled about 14,000, although the composition varied, with the king's army having 6,000 horse to Essex's 4,000. Both sides had twenty pieces of artillery. Rupert appears to have taken most responsibility for the Royalists' deployment, although King Charles was present and in allowing this he made a serious oversight. In front of the centre of the Royalist lines was a feature referred to as 'Round Hill'. This almost certainly must have been part of Wash Common, which appears from some parts of the Royalist lines to be cut off from the main plateau and to be round. It can be found by following the road off the Andover Road between the Gun Public House and the Falkland Memorial. As this road swings left there is a right turn towards Skinners Green. This road moves across the western part of Round Hill as it starts to descend. A better and safer view of this feature and most of the battlefield can be gained from a footpath leading off the road from the Falkland Memorial to the remaining open space of Wash Common.

Essex saw the importance of Round Hill, as well as realising that much of the battlefield, with its many hedged 'closes', was better suited to infantry than cavalry, which played to his army's strength. A wet evening on 19 September would have made the ground more difficult for the cavalry, but could also have caused problems for the musketeers and their powder and matches. Essex moved some infantry up the slopes of Round Hill while it was still dark, so that at dawn on 20 September the Royalists found themselves faced by determined enemy infantry behind the hedges. Byron was ordered to move against them at 5.00 a.m. with Falkland in support. They located a hedge with a very narrow gap in it, which held the key to their advance on the hill. Falkland charged out on his own and was hit by musket fire, which killed him (hence the memorial to the rear of where he must have been hit). Byron's men continued to push forward, driving the Parliamentarians from Round Hill. Essex then ordered forward some of his cavalry under Stapleton in an attempt to break through the Royalist lines and open up the route to London. After some initial success, the Parliamentarian cavalry were driven back, largely through a large-scale counter-charge led by Prince Rupert. This swept the Parliamentarians from Wash Common, returning them pretty much to their earlier positions. Throughout this major phase of the battle the sources are not always clear, as indeed the fighting must have been chaotic, given that much of the action was carried out in hedged closes or small fields. One of the noticeable features of the battle is the impact of artillery fire, with most sources commenting upon it, especially with regard to casualties caused by it on both sides. Having driven the Parliamentarian infantry from Wash Common, Rupert took his cavalry down the slopes in an attempt to break Essex's right wing and to break into his baggage train. Essex plugged the gap with infantry reserves who were able to stem Rupert's advance. At this point some of Rupert's men attempted to trick their way through the Parliamentarian lines by placing sprigs of fern and broom in their hats, copying the recognition symbol used by Parliament. However, they were discovered and quickly repelled.

The battle was by this time extending into the evening, and Essex still had no way through to the road to London. Although Rupert had not managed to break the Parliamentarians, he had prevented their escape, which would lead to

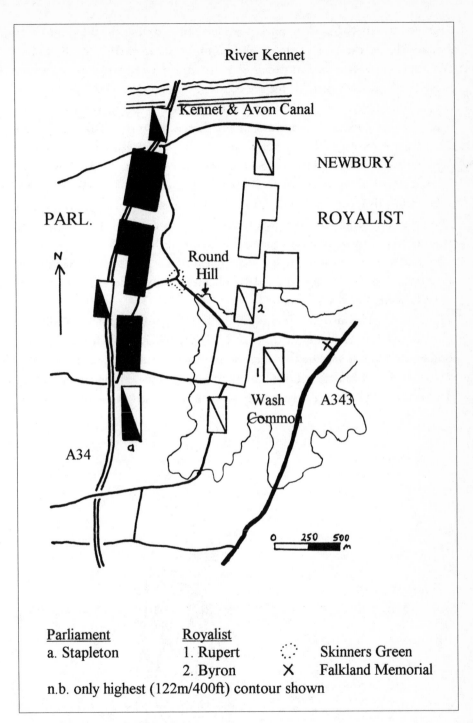

River Kennet

Kennet & Avon Canal

NEWBURY

PARL.

ROYALIST

N

Round
Hill

2

Wash
Common

A343

A34

1

a

0 250 500
m

Parliament   Royalist
a. Stapleton   1. Rupert   Skinners Green
                 2. Byron   ✕ Falkland Memorial
n.b. only highest (122m/400ft) contour shown

Battle of Newbury, 20 September 1643.

their defeat, especially as supplies were low. In addition, the Royalists held Round Hill at the end of the day's fighting, making their position secure. Overnight, both sides had to decide whether to carry on. From the summary above it would seem obvious for the Royalists to continue. However, supplies were also a problem for the Royalists, with Lord Percy reporting that they were reduced to ten out of their original ninety barrels of powder. This, along with King Charles probably losing heart after a bloody day, led to the Royalists deciding to withdraw, which they did around midnight. As 21 September dawned, Essex must have been relieved as the situation became clear. He ordered his army forward onto Wash Common and then onto Greenham Common, bypassing the Royalists in Newbury and Speen. One can easily imagine how Prince Rupert must have felt, as he had understandably been keen to continue the battle. He harried the rear of Essex's army, achieving some success against the London Trained Bands in a narrow lane called Padworth Gully, now known as Red Lane.

The battle had ended in a draw, although the Royalists were definitely in the stronger position. Estimates of the casualties vary wildly in the contemporary sources, although it appears that there were more Royalist losses. Strategically, victory went to Parliament. Even though their army escaped there was still talk of a negotiated peace in Parliament. Had the king pressed home his advantage

Drawing from the statue of Lord Falkland in St Stephen's Hall, Westminster. He was killed by musket fire during the first battle of Newbury in 1643. The Falkland Memorial in Newbury is close to the point where he met his death.

at Newbury and then advanced on London this could well have been the result. Instead, Parliament was able to recover and strengthen its resolve and its armies.

Newbury II, battle of, 27 October 1644

Confused and disjointed battle fought a year after the larger first Battle of Newbury.

KEY REFERENCE: Young, P. and Holmes, R. *The English Civil War* (Wordsworth Editions Ltd, 2000).

King Charles I had spent a successful summer out-manoeuvring and defeating the Earl of Essex in the South-West. However, the heavy defeat of the large Royalist army at Marston Moor and the king's failure to relieve Basing House meant that the war was still in the balance. Several forces converged in the Newbury area by mid-October, with the prospect of a decisive battle being fought as the king moved towards Donnington Castle with its Royalist garrison, which had been under siege by the Earl of Manchester. The Parliamentarian forces consisted of nearly 20,000 men, made up of the armies of the Earl of Manchester, Sir William Waller and a few remnants of Essex's command. They faced the king's 10,000, including a large artillery train. With the Parliamentarian command structure confused and with the Earl of Essex ill, their superior numbers gave them less of an advantage than they should have done. Despite these problems, they came up with an ambitious plan to echo Waller's impressive night flanking march undertaken at Alton the previous winter.

Charles' horse reached Newbury on 21 October, while the rest of the army concentrated in the area the next day. After a reconnaissance on 21 October, the Parliamentarians withdrew to Reading, but came up in strength from the east on 25 October, to find the king's army massed between Newbury and Donnington Castle to the north. The Parliamentarians decided to attempt an ambitious outflanking manoeuvre by sending Waller on a thirteen-mile march with well over half their forces round the Royalist's northern flank during the night of 26 October. They were to appear at the rear in the morning, just as Manchester attacked with the remainder of the army against the Royalist front around Shaw House, from their positions on Clay Hill to the north-east of Newbury. Waller set off, defeating a Royalist outpost at Boxford, which helped to alert the garrison at Donnington. Meanwhile, Manchester launched a diversionary attack against Shaw House, which was repelled while helping to exhaust Manchester's relatively small command. Waller's force seems to have made very slow progress from Boxford, as they were only in position to attack by about 3.00 p.m. on 27 October. At first this force was held at Speen, but after some fierce fighting the Parliamentarians forced the Royalists back, while at 4.00 p.m. Manchester's troops renewed their attack from Clay Hill against Shaw House and the surrounding area. Royalist cavalry pushed back the horse in Waller's command, led by Balfour on the right and a strangely inactive Cromwell on the left. Manchester was also forced back, with the Royalists maintaining both fronts as darkness fell. Charles knew he was outnumbered and in danger of being surrounded, so after half an hour at Donnington Castle he rode with his horse towards Bath, while the foot made its way to Oxford via Wallingford, leaving Manchester to resume his siege of Donnington Castle. By the end of 1 November the king also reached Oxford, where he rested for a few days before leading his forces south to Donnington Castle to relieve the garrison on 9 November.

The second Battle of Newbury was indecisive but could have been otherwise, especially if Waller had been in position to make his attack earlier than he did. The battlefield is now largely built-over, with housing estates covering most of Clay Hill from where Manchester attacked. However, Shaw House is still much as it was, although currently empty, while the remains of Donnington Castle are open to the public. The route of Waller's march via Hermitage, Chieveley, Winterbourne, Wickham Heath and Boxford can still be followed, while the museum in Newbury has displays relating to the Civil Wars.

Newcastle (upon Tyne), siege of, 3 February–late October 1644

Fought as a result of the Scottish Covenanting army joining the First Civil War against King Charles I.

The Scottish army of some 18,000 men led by Alexander Leslie, Earl of Leven, crossed the border into England on 18 January 1644, coming up against the forces of the Royalist Marquis of Newcastle. Their first major obstacle was Newcastle-upon-Tyne and the river itself. Initially, in difficult weather conditions, the Scots settled down to besiege the town. At first they captured the outlying fort of Shieldfield, but the defenders moved back, burning the surrounding houses to give them a good field of fire. Over the following weeks the Scots attempted to cross the River Tyne, but Royalist reinforcements prevented them from doing so. Eventually, on 28 February, the Tyne was crossed and Leven went south with the bulk of his army, leaving only a small masking force outside Newcastle.

Newcastle-upon-Tyne, 1644. This frontispiece records the early consequences of the Scottish Covenanters' intervention in the First Civil War. They agreed to send a force of 18,000 foot and 2000 horse into England, crossing the border on 19 January 1644. This pamphlet carried on the story up to 12 March 1644.

Newcastle-upon-Tyne in the seventeenth century showing part of the circuit of walls on the left, with housing spreading beyond the defences. The castle where the Royalist die-hards remained until the bitter end in 1644 can be seen on the right.

In June 1644 another Scottish force commanded by the Earl of Callander crossed the border to conduct the siege in earnest. He took the southern end of the Tyne Bridge at Newcastle, although his numbers were insufficient to press the siege too closely. This was rectified on 12 August, when some of Leven's men returned to help after their victory at Marston Moor outside York. Attempts at mining commenced, as well as employing artillery. Eventually, on 19 October, a large breach was made in the walls after one of the mines was exploded (excavations have discovered evidence for one of these mines near White Friars Tower), leading to a successful storming of the town. The governor, John Marley, and some of his men held out in the castle for a few more days, but in the end they too had to surrender.

Newnham (-on-Severn), storming of, 8 May 1644

Minor siege and storming fought as part of the ongoing struggles in and around Gloucester during the First Civil War.

The Royalists fortified the Church of St Peter at the south end of the village on the banks of the River Severn by constructing earthwork defences, some of which can still be traced. The small garrison was attacked by the Parliamentarian Massey on 8 May 1644, when he took the outer defences before storming the church itself, capturing over 100 men.

Nibley Green, battle of, 20 March 1470

The last private battle fought on English soil, bringing to a violent end a long-running legal dispute.

KEY REFERENCE: Fleming, P. and Wood, M. *Gloucestershire's Forgotten Battle: Nibley Green 1470* (Tempus, 2003), Haigh, P.A. *Where both the hosts fought* (Battlefield Press, 1997).

Fought during the Wars of the Roses, Nibley Green was really a private battle resulting from the disputed inheritance of the Berkeley estates dating back to the death of the 4th Earl of Berkeley in 1417. He had died without a male heir and his estate was contested between his daughter and her descendents on the one hand and his nephew and his descendents on the other. After many twists and turns, the nineteen-year-old Thomas Talbot Lord Lisle, descendent of the Earl's daughter, issued a challenge to William Lord Berkeley received on 18 March 1470 in an attempt to settle the issue once and for all, by fighting for the land with their retainers. Berkeley replied on

19 March, accepting the challenge, no doubt in part because he knew he had more retainers and more experience than this man he must have considered as a young upstart. In his reply, Berkeley told Lisle to be 'at Nibley Green at eight or nine of the clock'.

Both men had a very short time to gather their forces, a factor which would have gone against Berkeley, who had more to gain by a delay as he had more retainers. Instead he had to rely on those in the immediate vicinity, which he claimed were but a tenth of his force, but this may have been a ploy to lull Lisle into over-confidence.

Nibley Green is on the scarp to the east of the modern M5 between Gloucester and Bristol, between Berkeley Castle and Lisle's manor at Wotton. Berkeley arrived in the area first, deploying his men at the edge of Michaelwood Forest, now marked by the motorway service station of the same name. Lisle took his 300 or so men down the steep hill from North Nibley towards Berkeley's force. It is likely that Berkeley had brought enough of his men out of the forest to tempt Lisle down the hill, while keeping a substantial number of archers at the edge of the wood. Certainly Berkeley outnumbered Lisle, perhaps by three to one. The steepness of the slope would have made it difficult for Lisle to keep his men in check, and their disorder would have increased as they neared Berkeley's men to be met by a storm of arrows, shot both from the men who had been sent out in advance and by those on the wood's fringes. Lisle himself was killed by being hit in the face by an arrow from the bow of one Black Will. The forces met briefly, probably at the stream just to the east of the modern Bush Street Farm, but Berkeley's retainers quickly gained the upper hand, forcing Lisle's demoralised troops to run back up the hill, where many were slaughtered in the narrow lane leading up to the church.

Berkeley conducted a vigorous and ruthless pursuit to Wotton, which was sacked. Legally the issue was still not settled, with Edward IV intervening and then the matter continuing in the courts until 1609, making the lawyers the real victors.

Norham Castle, siege of, late August 1513

This extremely strong castle by the River Tweed was taken by the army of King James IV of Scotland after an artillery bombardment, which was begun from across the river on the Scottish bank, followed by an assault, enabling the army to advance south where it fought the Battle of Flodden.

Sculpture showing the massive mid-fifteenth-century gun known as Mons Meg on the left, still to be seen at Edinburgh Castle along with two other, later, artillery pieces (sixteenth-century culverins). Pieces such as the latter pair formed James IV's impressive modern artillery train of seventeen guns for the campaign of 1513 which included the siege of Norham Castle.

Depiction of a sixteenth-century siege from Raphael Holinshed's *Chronicles of England, Scotlande and Irelande*, published in 1577, showing the use of heavy siege artillery behind gabions. James IV's army had an impressive modern artillery train. Note the use of light pieces and hand-guns by the defenders. The extremely strong castle of Norham by the River Tweed was taken in a similar fashion by the army of James IV of Scotland at the Siege of Norham Castle in 1513.

Naval battle at North Foreland in 1666 between Monk and de Ruyter, from a contemporary Dutch print.

North Foreland, battle of, 25 July 1666

Temporary breaking of the blockade of the Thames during the second Anglo-Dutch War, which enabled a break-out by the English fleet to conduct a successful raid on Dutch merchant shipping.

An English fleet of about ninety ships under Prince Rupert and the Duke of Albemarle clashed with de Ruyter's slightly smaller Dutch fleet, to the south-east of Orfordness at 10.00 a.m. on St James' Day. The battle developed into two separate actions, with the two rear squadrons moving west, while the main fleets drifted eastwards. The main engagement ended at 3.00 p.m. with twenty Dutch ships having being lost to one English ship.

North Luffenham, siege of, spring 1643

This fortified manor house in Leicestershire was garrisoned by the Royalists, but fell to Parliamentarians led by Grey and Wray who then sacked and destroyed it, leaving only traces of the moat visible today.

North Walsham, battle of, June 1381

Crushing of the last major peasant rebellion of 1381.

KEY REFERENCE: Hart, R. 'A translation of Thomas of Walsingham's account of Littester's [sic] Rebellion in 1381, with an explanatory reference to preceding and subsequent events' in *Norfolk Archaeology* (vol. 5, 1859).

With the earlier defeat and death of Wat Tyler, there were further disturbances of commoners to be dealt with by the supporters of Richard II. The most serious of these, and one which led to a small battle, was the rebellion in Norfolk led by the 'King of the Commons', John Littester, a dyer from Norwich (or quite possibly Geoffrey Lister from Felmingham, which is close to the final battlefield) according to the account left by Thomas of Walsingham. Probably protesting against poor wages, Littester gathered a 'multitude' together and then tried to force the Earl of Suffolk to join him to give the rising more credibility and even respectability. The Earl escaped in disguise to the king at St Albans, leaving Littester having to be content with the capture of five or more local knights instead, although one of these, Robert de Salle, objected and was promptly 'knocked on the head by a countryman'. Two of these knights and three commoners were sent to parley with the king, but were intercepted by the fearsome Henry Despenser, Bishop of Norwich, in full military rig, who had two of the commoners' heads struck off while he went to deal with the third. Gathering his small force of eight knights and 'a very few archers', the bishop marched towards the rebels, who had retired to North Walsham from Norwich, gaining more troops as he went from his starting point near Newmarket.

Littester had protected his camp with a ditch and bank, reinforced with miscellaneous items of furniture and fences, about a mile to the south of North Walsham on the Norwich road, which in 1381 was just to the west of the current main road. On sighting this position, the bishop charged on horseback, reaching the top of the bank apparently 'before the arrows of his followers' could reach the same spot. His men were soon over the obstacle and then a hard-fought but quick encounter ensued, as the bishop carried on fighting, 'grinding his teeth like a wild boar'. The rebels soon fled, but were hampered in this by their own wagons to the rear. Littester was captured in a cornfield, along with three other named rebels: Sceth, Trunch and Cubitt, according to John Capgrave, a monk of (King's) Lynn. Littester met the fate of most rebels and was hanged. Two crosses on the current main road from North Walsham to Norwich traditionally mark the site of the battle, as does a third ruinous cross just to the south-west on private land. One of the crosses stands over 3m tall and is about 1km south of North Walsham at a minor road junction, while the other, consisting of just a stump, is on the edge of North Walsham by the water tower, along with a commemorative plaque. The roads in the area and the wood to the south have been greatly modified since the battle, largely as a result of the creation of the park, ponds and woodland for Westwick House and the construction of the eighteenth-century turnpike from Norwich to North Walsham (now the current road). The route of the fourteenth-century road, however, is probably traced by the footpath running north from Perch Lake Plantation into North Walsham, emerging where the cross stump mentioned above was reset next to the road by the local council in 1932. Therefore, the battle was likely to have been fought on the land between the modern water tower and the woods to the south of North Walsham across the line of the footpath.

Northallerton, battle of, 22 August 1138

Also known as the Battle of the Standard, this battle marked a bloody end to the Scottish King David I's invasion of England.

KEY REFERENCE: English Heritage *Battlefield Report: Northallerton 1138* (English Heritage, London, 1995).

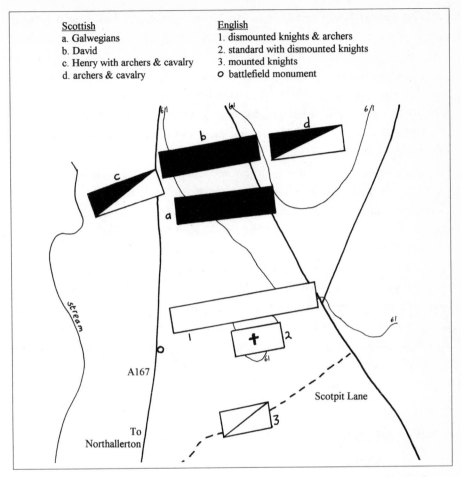

Battle of Northallerton, 22 August 1138.

Stephen had taken the crown of England in 1135, but was faced by civil war and a rival claimant in Henry I's daughter, Matilda. King David I of Scotland, as Matilda's uncle, had a good excuse to interfere nominally on her behalf. Accordingly, raids and then a full-scale invasion were carried out, with the Scots reaching Durham by 21 August. An attempted parley failed, leading to the Scots moving further down the great North Road before coming up against an English force two miles to the north of Northallerton.

The English had been energised by the Archbishop of York, who had turned his attempt to repel the Scots into a religious crusade. As part of this a large standard was erected on a wagon consisting of a ship's mast with a silver pyx hanging from it and the banners of St Peter, John of Beverley and Wilfrid of Ripon. The English were at the battlefield first, very early in the morning and probably before dawn, having bypassed Northallerton on their way, deploying on the low hill next to the current Standard Hill Farm, just to the east of the A167 and the battlefield monument. There was a slight delay before the Scots came into view and deployed on the hill just to the north, on which is placed the modern Standard Farm. The English adopted a flexible defensive formation, with dismounted knights 'interspersed with archers', according to Richard of Hexham's *Chronicle*. Behind these in the centre and probably at the brow of the hill was the standard with a protection force of further dismounted knights, together with assorted clerics and other non-combatants. In addition there was a small mounted reserve, which along with the horses of the dismounted knights was positioned to the rear, away from the 'shouting and uproar of the Scots', probably on the line of Scotpit Lane. The Scots appear to have argued about their dispositions according to Ailred of Rievaulx, culminating with the fiery Galwegians (sometimes referred to as Picts, but more properly as Galloway men) taking the front line. The two main sources fail to agree on the remaining alignment of Scottish troops, but it seems reasonable to suggest that King David took the centre of the second line, with a force mainly of dismounted knights, but also including some French and English knights in his service. On either flank of the second line were mixed forces of archers and cavalry, with David's son Prince Henry taking the right.

The standard eponymous to the battle known more commonly as the Battle of Northallerton, 1138, from a near contemporary manuscript of the Abbot of Rievaulx, along with a description of the battle. Prior Richard of Hexham described the standard as being made from a ship's mast.

Numbers are even more difficult to assess, with Richard of Hexham giving us the figure of 26,000 Scots, which is no doubt an exaggeration. Numbers of about 15,000 in King David's army and 11,000 English are probably as good an estimate as any.

The battle began shortly after sunrise and lasted for two hours. The Galwegians launched a ferocious charge against the English front line, but many did not make it to close quarters due to the efficiency of the English bows and the lack of armour of the Galwegians, leading to them appearing 'like a hedgehog with its quills, so you would see a Galwegian bristling all round with arrows' (Ailred of Rievaulx). Those who reached the English line found themselves met by the dismounted knights, who with superior armour and order were able to drive the Galwegians back in disorder. Prince Henry attempted to rectify the situation by charging the English left and breaking through and round them, the horse holders and reserve at the rear. This can only have been a temporary success as we read that the main Scottish line broke, with the English able to press forward, seemingly without needing to fear Prince Henry's men to their rear, who had perhaps been dealt with by the English reserve. Some Scottish troops from Lothian fled without fighting, but King David was prepared to fight on in person, although his knights urged him to retire, which he did. Once the royal standard was seen to withdraw, the army fell back, with even Prince Henry realising that he had to pull back, given that he was then hopelessly cut off. The Scots moved to Carlisle and the invasion was over, leaving Northumbria in English hands and allowing Stephen to pursue his war in the South.

The battlefield is well preserved although now enclosed, rather than being the open moor which it probably was in 1138. Views can be had across the battlefield from either side, although the only safe parking place on the A167 is the small lay-by next to the battle monument. No public footpaths cross the battlefield, which is a frustration, and even Scotpit Lane is a private track. Scotpit Lane is so named after the discovery of burial pits, which have traditionally been ascribed to Scottish dead. The position of these pits to the south of the English position poses something of a problem, as it seems unlikely that the Scottish dead would have been carried up over the hill and down the other side. It could be more likely that these are in fact pits for the English dead, but when they were first discovered it was assumed that they were for Scottish casualties, or that the pits originally spread up and over the hill rather than just beside the lane and so would have been used for the dead of both sides.

Northampton, battle of, 5 April 1264

Successful capture of Northampton by Prince Edward (later King Edward I) for King Henry III against forces supporting Simon de Montfort, thanks in part to help from the Prior of St Andrew's, leading to the sack of the town.

Northampton, battle of, 10 July 1460

This Yorkist victory of the Wars of the Roses saw a well-defended Lancastrian force defeated in part by treachery.

KEY REFERENCE: English Heritage: *Battlefield Report: Northampton 1460* (English Heritage, London, 1995).

After their defeat at Blore Heath in 1459, most of the losing Yorkist leaders fled to Calais. They returned in June 1460, quickly winning Kent and London to their cause. King Henry VI with the main Lancastrian force waited in Northampton for reinforcements. The Yorkist leader Edward, Duke of York determined to force the issue before Henry's army became too strong. The royal army waited, according to *An English Chronicle* (ed. J.S. Davies), in a 'strong and a mighty field, in the meadows beside the Nunnery'. *A Short English Chronicle* adds that the battle was fought beside Northampton in the Newfield between Hardingstone and Sandyford. Although there are problems in identifying the latter, it is accepted that the battle was fought on what is now a municipal golf course, to the south of the River Nene. Unfortunately, there are new plans to build further mounds and banks on and around the golf course, which if permitted will hinder interpretation of the battle and damage and obscure the remaining ridge and furrow along the western part of the registered battlefield. The nunnery was Delapré Abbey, which is now owned by the local authority and may soon in part become a visitor centre. This field is overlooked by a wooded ridge on which is sited an Eleanor Cross, from where the Archbishop of Canterbury viewed the fighting, although this viewpoint is now screened from the battlefield by a belt of trees. The king's army was entrenched, with an extinct field boundary called 'Battle Dyke' giving a possibly vital clue as to the location of these defences, being between the nunnery and the foot of the ridge. Henry then had his position 'arrayed with guns'.

We are told that the Yorkist earls approached with 60,000 men (certainly an exaggeration) and through bishops acting as intermediaries they attempted a parley. This failed, and battle commenced at 2.00 p.m. on 10 July. It seems likely that Lord Grey of Ruthin was on the right of the Lancastrian position, with

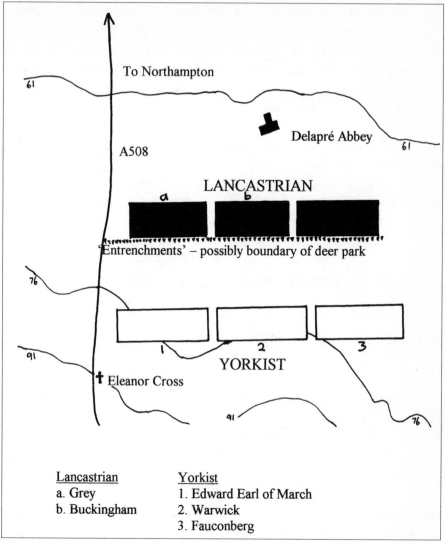

To Northampton

61

Delapré Abbey

61

A508

LANCASTRIAN

a b

'Entrenchments' – possibly boundary of deer park

76

91

YORKIST

1 2 3

✝ Eleanor Cross

91 76

Lancastrian
a. Grey
b. Buckingham

Yorkist
1. Edward Earl of March
2. Warwick
3. Fauconberg

Battle of Northampton, 10 July 1460.

the Duke of Buckingham commanding the centre. On the Yorkist side we are told that Lord Fauconberg commanded the advance guard, then Edward, Earl of March (later Edward IV) and the Earl of Warwick 'the Kingmaker' with the main 'battle' (see below). The Lancastrians, despite being in an apparently strong position, had serious problems. Firstly, there was heavy rain, which meant that their artillery and hand-guns were 'quenched and might not be shot'. Secondly, Grey performed an act of treachery after a short period of fighting, which had probably been pre-arranged. We are told that he allowed the Earl of March into the camp, which effectively decided the outcome. This implies that Edward must have been commanding the Yorkist left, or the left part of the centre, with perhaps Fauconberg on the right. We are also told in Waurin's chronicle that Grey gave the Yorkists entry into 'the park'. This suggests that the defensive bank and ditch may have been the boundary around a possible deer park, rather than a fortification constructed specifically for the battle. Once the Yorkists were inside, mayhem ensued, with many Lancastrians being killed in the camp or as they tried to cross the river, including the Duke of Buckingham. King Henry VI was captured by an archer.

The battle gave Edward, Duke of York the opportunity to press home his claim to the throne and it led to a bloody series of battles, ending at Towton in 1461.

Northwich, skirmish of, *see* Winnington Bridge

Norton St Philip, battle of, 27 June 1685

Small action in the Duke of Monmouth's campaign, leading to the Battle of Sedgemoor.

KEY REFERENCE: Chandler, D.G. *Sedgemoor 1685* (Spellmount, 1999).

Having landed at Lyme Regis on 11 June 1685 in an attempt to seize the throne from James II, the Duke of Monmouth (who was the bastard son of Charles II) marched through the West Country gathering an army. By late June he may have had some 6,000 men armed with an assortment of weapons, while the Royalist army commanded by Lord Feversham had about 2,500 of better trained and equipped soldiers. Monmouth decided against an attempt at Bristol and was refused entry into Bath. He led his army to Norton St Philip, where they camped for the night of 26 June before setting off towards Frome.

In the early hours of 27 June Feversham ordered forward a forlorn hope of forty-five grenadiers commanded by Captain Hawley. Monmouth's rearguard put up stout resistance, leading Monmouth to return and deploy more troops against the advancing Royalists. His Red Regiment on the right and Green Regiment on the left moved against the Royalists, who had reinforced the forlorn hope with the remainder of the guards under the Duke of Grafton. These units pushed the guards away from the village to the north, following up by manning the hedges with musketeers. The guards were nearly cut off but were rescued by the arrival of the Royalist Horse Grenadiers. Monmouth placed two cannon at the mouth of the lane exiting from the village, with two more on a slight rise to the right.

The Duke of Marlborough
from a Dutch engraving of
the early eighteenth
century. In 1685 he was
still Major General John,
Lord Churchill and second
in command of King
James II's army during
Monmouth's rebellion
which included the action
at Norton St Philip in 1685.

Feversham pulled back, but stayed within artillery range as he also brought up cannon in the late morning. Fire carried on throughout the day but with little effect, although overall this engagement was a victory for the rebels. Neither side was willing to risk an attack across difficult terrain, and during the night both withdrew: Feversham to Bradford-upon-Avon and Monmouth to Frome.

Norwich, raid of, 1004

Attack by the Danish King Swein 'Forkbeard' which captured, looted and burned the town.

Nottingham Castle, siege of, early March–28 March 1194

Siege conducted by King Richard 'the Lionheart' on his return from the Holy Land.

KEY REFERENCE: Foulds, T. 'The Siege of Nottingham Castle in 1194' in *Transactions of the Thoroton Society of Nottinghamshire* (vol. XCV, 1991).

Prince John, younger brother of King Richard I, took Nottingham Castle in 1191 while Richard was on crusade. John had been given the county of Nottinghamshire by Richard to add to his considerable titles and estates, although he had not been given Nottingham castle. Richard, having been taken prisoner during his return journey from the Holy Land, had eventually been released on payment of a large ransom to his captor Emperor Henry. He returned to England on 13 March 1194, while John was in France. Richard immediately went to join the Siege of Nottingham Castle, which had been begun on his orders by the Earls of Huntingdon and Chester and Earl Ferrers. The besieged refused to surrender at first, mainly because they thought they were being attacked by John's enemies and definitely not by their king. Richard reached Nottingham on 25 March with considerable reinforcements, and took over the conduct of operations himself. It seems that Richard placed himself in the thick of the fighting, clad only in a light coat of mail and an iron hat on his head, leading an assault against the gates of the castle. The outer gates were burnt down and the outer bailey taken before the king's forces moved against the next gate with its barbican. Night came before they could make any more real headway and so they withdrew to the outer gateway. On the next day, 26 March, Richard planned his next moves against the middle and upper baileys (little remains of the twelfth-century castle, although the site is still an impressive one). Siege engines were built and prisoners hanged in sight of the walls to demoralise the defenders. Although our two contemporary accounts differ in their details, it appears that on 27 March further reinforcements arrived with the Bishop of Durham, which persuaded some of the defenders to come out to discuss terms and then throw themselves on the king's mercy once they realised that Richard himself was present. The siege then ended, or possibly continued until the next day if only some of the garrison had surrendered on 27 March. Richard remained in Nottingham following the siege to hold a council at which several important judgements were given.

Nunney Castle, siege of, summer–20 August 1645

Siege through the summer months of 1645 leading to the fall of this Somerset stronghold to Parliament.

Nunney Castle had a very small garrison of perhaps nine soldiers, but certainly no more than twenty-four. However, they apparently also had a secret weapon: a pig! The defenders took this wretched animal to one of the towers every day and made it squeal as if it was being slaughtered, to convince the attackers that they had plenty of food in the castle. This ruse failed to defeat the heavy artillery brought up by the Parliamentarian general Sir Thomas Fairfax, leading to the surrender of the garrison once breaches were made in the walls.

Ockley, battle of, 851

Possible location of the Battle of Oak Field, fought between King Aethelwulf of Wessex and a large Danish army, which had come fresh from the routing of a Mercian army, with the English being victorious.

Orfordness, battle of, *see* North Foreland

Oswestry, siege of, 21–22 June 1644

Dramatic capture of this Shropshire town and castle by Parliamentarian forces.

Oswestry in Shropshire was garrisoned for King Charles I by Colonel Lloyd, who was attacked by a local Parliamentarian force led by the Earl of Denbigh. They stormed the town by battering the gates with artillery fire. The Parliamentarian guns were then brought forward and some were positioned in or by St Oswald's Church. The following day a petard was exploded by the castle gates, forcing a way in and leading to the Royalists' surrender.

Otford, battle of, 776

Battle between the Mercians and men of Kent at Otford in Kent, with no further known details.

Otterburn, battle of, 19-20 August 1388

Heavy defeat for the Percy family against a Scottish army, although the battle had few long-term consequences.

KEY REFERENCE: English Heritage: *Battlefield Report: Otterburn 1388* (English Heritage, London, 1995).

A large Scottish army invaded northern England in 1388, with the bulk of the force moving against Carlisle, leaving Sir James Douglas to take the eastern route towards Durham. The Scots reached the gates of Durham, but were not strong enough to think about a storming or a siege in the face of a larger English force led by Sir Henry ('Harry Hotspur') Percy. There was some confused skirmishing as the Scots retreated to Newcastle, which continued outside the walls for three days. In one of these encounters Douglas took the pennon from Percy's lance, which Hotspur took as a personal slight on his honour. He vowed to win it back by pursuing and fighting Douglas' army, while Douglas hoped that Hotspur, given his impetuous nature, would come after him and in his rashness make a mistake.

The events are vividly described by Froissart in his *Chronicles* as well as in several other contemporary sources from both sides. Although none of these gives a clear location for the battlefield, it is reasonable to follow the majority view of later historians to put the fighting close to the Percy Cross, just to the west of Otterburn. The cross was moved a short distance and the monument reconstructed in 1777, but it still stands at the centre of what was almost certainly the battlefield, although in 1388 it would not have been in its current atmospheric copse. Instead the field would have been open rough pasture, becoming quite boggy as the bottom of the slope leading down to the River Rede was reached, suggesting that the bulk of the fighting would have taken place on the higher, drier ground around the current site of the Percy Cross.

Douglas started his retreat along Redesdale, making his camp before attacking Otterburn Tower on 19 August. He failed to take it, but decided to stay for another attempt the next day and to fight Percy if he arrived. It appears that Percy reached the Scots much more quickly than expected, but the Scots' dispositions made up for this. According to Froissart the camp nearest to Percy's advance was that of the servants and baggage, which meant that when the English arrived at nightfall on 19 August they assumed this was the main camp of the Scots. As the English cleared the camp the Scottish troops had time to form up beyond the camp to the west and await battle. It seems that Douglas had about 6,000 men (although Froissart puts their numbers at only 600 knights and 2,000 infantry), while Percy had some 8,000. According to some contemporary sources, Percy ordered a flanking march by Sir Matthew Redman or Sir Thomas Umfraville to move round the Scottish (left) flank to attack their rear. However, even though there was a bright moon and there would have been men with local knowledge present with Percy, it seems an extremely ambitious plan to propose at that juncture. Given the fact that Froissart does not mention this and the difficulties in explaining how this English flanking force failed to bump into a Scottish movement on the same flank, together with the other problems already mentioned and Percy's impetuous nature, it would seem likely that this English manoeuvre never took place. This interpretation is strengthened further when one hears little of the force later in the battle, even in those sources which include its setting off.

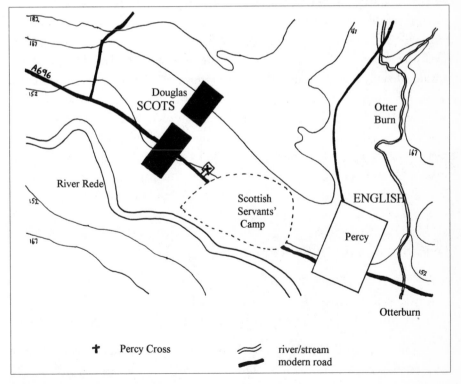

Battle of Otterburn, 19–20 August 1388.

This standard was said to have been carried by Archibald Douglas of Cavers at the battle of Otterburn in 1388. However, it has been identified to date from the sixteenth century, and is therefore more contemporary with Flodden.

Even though it appears that the Scots were initially caught by surprise, they had planned for the possibility of an English attack. Therefore, Douglas was able to put his own pre-planned flank attack into operation. While the two main forces engaged and the Scots were pushed back by weight of numbers, Douglas took his men up the slope to his left and down and round Percy's right. This crucial part of the battle could well have occurred around the site of the original 'Battle Stone', just to the north-east of the present cross position. Douglas fell under a torrent of blows wounded in the shoulder, stomach and thigh. At the time the Scots did not realise that their commander had fallen, and the fighting went on. It was still possible that the superior numbers of the English would win the battle, but in a last Scottish attack Hotspur was captured after fighting with Lord Montgomery. With this the English fell back, leaving well over 1,000 dead on the field. Later on 20 August the Bishop of Durham advanced with a large body of reinforcements, but as stragglers passed them most of his force melted away, leaving him with no option but to retreat. The Scots, with their leader dead, recommenced their own retreat, reaching Melrose Abbey where Douglas was laid to rest. The battle had achieved little, but it merits attention not least because of the rich sources for the battle and the strong echoes of chivalric warfare they contain. The battlefield has clear on-site interpreation, with car parking and a picnic site just below the Percy Cross.

Oxford, siege of, 29 September 1142–end 1142

Siege of the Civil Wars of King Stephen's reign, where the king came into direct contact with his adversary the Empress Matilda.

KEY REFERENCE: Bradbury, J. *Stephen and Matilda, the Civil War of 1139–53* (Alan Sutton, 1996).

After the capture of Wareham, King Stephen moved to besiege Matilda's main base at Oxford. The castle was behind the river, but this did not afford the defenders the protection they assumed. Stephen personally led his troops across a deep ford, pushing the defenders back behind the castle walls. They set fire to the city and laid siege to the castle for the next three months. Just before surrender became inevitable, Matilda decided to attempt an escape. This was just before Christmas 1142, with snow on the ground and the river frozen. She slipped out during the night with an escort of four knights, crossing the river in a white cloak for camouflage. She managed to get away but the garrison at Oxford then surrendered.

Oxford, siege of, May–24 June 1646

Capture of King Charles I's 'capital' of the First Civil War.

KEY REFERENCE: Gaunt, P. *The Cromwellian Gazetteer, an Illustrated Guide to Britain in the Civil War and Commonwealth* (Alan Sutton, 1994).

Oxford had been held continuously for King Charles I since October 1642, after the city was seized initially by the Parliamentarian Lord Saye and Sele. Charles entered Oxford on 29 October 1642 and from then on it effectively became his capital for the duration of the war. The University was predominantly Royalist, although much of the city sympathised with Parliament. The college buildings made very useful and suitably grand and secure buildings for the court and various departments, not least the Royal Arsenal. Oxford was threatened at various points during 1644 and early 1645, with elements of the New Model Army closing in from late April 1645. Oliver Cromwell took various outposts, including Bletchington House at midnight on 24 April. The Royalist Colonel Windebank surrendered his force, along with up to 300 muskets and seventy-one horses to Cromwell's force consisting of just a few dragoons. For this perceived act of cowardice the unfortunate Colonel was shot in Oxford Castle's garden on 3 May. On 7 May the king left the city for the Naseby Campaign, with the Parliamentarians following his forces, thus removing the threat from Oxford. King Charles returned on 5 November and wintered there, before leaving for the last time on 27 April 1646. A regular siege ensued, with the city's fall inevitable once it had been stripped of most of its garrison. The surrender duly arrived on 24 June 1646. Many of the buildings used by the king and his court during the war still stand. In particular, Christ Church was the home of the court and Charles, as well as being the formal centre and meeting place. The cathedral has a number of Royalist memorials, largely in the Lucy Chapel. Henrietta Maria, Charles' Queen who arrived in July 1643, was housed at Merton College. Both the Oxford Museum and the Ashmolean Museum contain a number of artefacts from the Civil Wars.

P

Padstow, raid of, 981

Attack from the sea by a Viking force against Padstow and other settlements along the Devon and Cornwall coasts.

Pen, battle of, *see* Penselwood, 1016

Pendennis Castle, siege of, March–16 August 1646

This siege holds claim to being the last stronghold to surrender to Parliamentarian forces in England in the First Civil War.

Even after the defeats of King Charles I's field armies at Naseby, Langport and Rowton Heath in 1645, a number of garrisons held out. One of these was Pendennis Castle, commanded by Sir John Arundell, known as 'Old Tilbury' as he had reputedly been present at Tilbury Docks when Elizabeth I gave her rousing speech in 1588. Just before the start of the siege led by Sir Thomas Fairfax, Prince Charles (later Charles II) stayed at Pendennis before leaving for the Scilly Isles. The garrison had little chance, especially as the castle had been built to dominate the sea approaches rather than face an attack from the land. With a large number of non-combatants inside, food became a problem, so terms were agreed after five months as starvation started to set in. These terms were favourable and reflect creditably on Arundell and the defenders, although Fairfax was no doubt just glad to be finished as news filtered through of Charles I's surrender to the Scots at the beginning of August 1646.

Penselwood, battle of, 658

Battle, probably near Gillingham in Dorset, in which Cenwalh defeated the British and then drove them west of the River Parret.

Penselwood, battle of, 1016

King Edmund 'Ironside' fought against a Viking army at Penselwood near Gillingham in Dorset, which he defeated and put to flight.

Peterloo, *see* St Peter's Fields

Pevensey Castle, siege of, 1088

Result of an attempt to wrest the throne from William II for Robert of Normandy.

With the death of William I in 1087 the crown of England passed to William II, but there was wide support for his older brother Robert's claim to the throne. After taking the castle at Tonbridge, the king's supporters moved against Rochester, but found that Odo had moved to Pevensey. The castle withstood a siege of six weeks, but then the garrison ran short of food, forcing them to surrender. Odo came to an agreement, giving up the castle to the king, and then travelled to Rochester, seemingly to surrender the castle. However, his men continued to revolt, forcing William to besiege Odo inside Rochester Castle. The castle was duly taken and Odo went into exile, leaving William to capture the last main stronghold of the revolt, Durham Castle.

1 Contemporary woodcut showing the devastation caused by a mine or mortar during the Siege of Colchester, 1648.

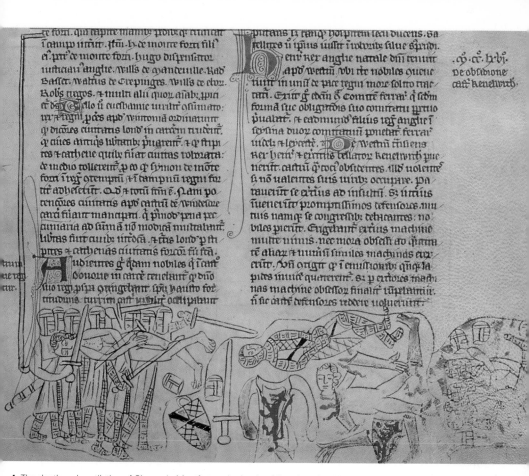

re fom. qui capue manib; probe q; cruuca
i campo nuttur. iftu li; de monte fom fili'
ei. prt' de monte fom. hugo difpinfator
iufticiar' anglie. wills de cgandeuille. Rad
Baffer. waltus de Crepinges. wills de clor.
Robs negos. + multi alii quoz asiab; ipia
et oa. G Ello u euefhanue nurltr ofiumato:
ur. + regni pces apd' wintomia ordinanur
q diones cuutatis lond'in carcem truduit.
q ciues eiuttgs libranb; puarent. + q; ftipi
tes + carhene quib; fuat cuutas tolurata.
de medio tollerent. p q q; fymon de morte
fom i regt orenupti. + i tampnu regni for
ut adheferut. O.d + totu ffm e. Nam po
tencores cuutatis apd castru de wundefore
card fuiaut manapan. q pinod' prua pce
cunaria ad fuma uo modica muttaluut.
libras fuit cuib; iurdca. + tbs lond' p th
pites + carhenias cuutatis forcor fui fca.

A udientes g q̃dam nobiles q̃ i carce
douone in carce tenelaur q duo
fuo regi pfpa oringelaur. fpu hauffo for
ttudunis. turrim gatt uiftul ocupraur

putans li tanq; dolprtem tecu ducens. Ba
lellires u ipfius iuffu i robonb; filue s̃prnd.
env'ker anglie natale dni tenuit
apd' weftm̃. ubi ne nobiles queue
nient in unu de pace regni more folito trac
tatu. Erutr g̃ edm̃ o comitte ferrar' q fcdm
forma fue obligatibis fuo comitatu prtio
puatur. + eadminus' filius reg anglie i
fcrina duoz comitatuu ponetur. ferrar'
uidel; + leyceftr. G e weftm̃ tueiens
ker hen' + einus bellatoz kenetwrth pue
nienit. castru q̃ toci obfidentes. illd' uolente
fi no ualentes fuis unib; occupare. pa
tauerut fe ertius ad infultu. S; utrius
fueneriit promptiffimos defenfores. mu
tuis namq; fe congreffib; debicantes: no
biles pierut. Engelanit ertius machino
multe unus. nec moza obfefti ad q̃am
te aliaz + uuruu ffmiles machinds exti
erut. Non ongit q̃ i eniiffionibz q̃q̃ la
pides uuue quererent. S; p ertiores mach
nas machine obfeffoz finanr iupetamur.
ñ fic carhe defenfores reddere uolueruut.

.ců .cc. l̃vi.
de obfidione
caftr kenetwrth.

4 The death and mutilation of Simon de Montfort at the battle of Evesham in 1265.

2 *Opposite above:* Cropredy Bridge, 1644. This view from Cropredy Bridge towards Hays Bridge (off the picture to the far left) shows the flat-topped hill on which sits the village of Wardington, and demonstrates that any troops in and around that village would be invisible to troops just across Cropredy Bridge.

3 *Opposite below:* Edgehill, 1642, looking north from the top of Edgehill by the Castle Inn over the village of Radway onto the battlefield.

5 The firing of an English 'serpentine' from the Piper's Hill position outside Branxton village at Flodden, 1513. The English had five such pieces with them, along with eighteen lighter guns, while the Scots deployed generally heavier siege pieces.

6 Flodden, 1513. The view from the right-centre of the Scottish position towards the Piper's Hill monument, which is visible in the middle distance. The ridge running to the right of the monument is where the English formed up.

7 Flodden, 1513, looking from the right-centre of the Scottish position towards the village of Branxton, nestling behind the low ridge occupied by the English.

8 Fornham St Genevieve, 1173, showing the tower of the ruined church of Fornham St Genevieve – the only spot from which the church can be seen from public rights of way.

9 Hastings, 1066, Bayeux Tapestry. The Norman cavalry ride up against the English shield wall.

10 *Battle of Hastings, 1066* by Frank W. Wilkin (1800?-1842). This painting was originally commissioned for the Great Hall at Battle Abbey and the canvas measures 27ft by 17ft. It was recently discovered under floorboards in a gallery in Hastings.

11 Lansdown, 1643, looking up the hill with the modern road following the line of trees on the left. The Royalists had to attack up this slope towards the waiting Parliamentarians at the top.

12 Lichfield, April 1643, showing the faint remains of a Civil War earthwork in the modern Prince Rupert's Way with the cathedral spire to the left.

13 Lostwithiel, 1644. Shown is Restormel Castle, which was stormed by Royalist troops led by Richard Grenville on 21 August 1644.

14 Lostwithiel, 1644. The prehistoric remains of Castle Dore where Parliamentarian forces made their last stand.

15 Lostwithiel, 1644. The view from the prehistoric fort of Castle Dore towards the advancing Royalists.

16 *Cromwell after Marston Moor* by Ernest Croft. As Cromwell and his weary troopers drew rein after routing Goring's horse on the evening of 2 July 1644, they had played a decisive role in winning Parliament's greatest victory of the war so far.

17 Mortimer's Cross, 1461, from beside the River Lugg looking towards the Yorkist lines. Note the steep hills in the left background, which would have made an advance from that direction all but impossible.

18 George Cruikshank's depiction of the Peterloo 'massacre' in 1819. Maximum sympathy for the crowd is gained through showing them harmless and helpless under the sabres of the cavalry.

19 Rochester Castle, 1215, showing the rebuilt circular south-east tower, which was necessary after King John's mining operation during the siege of 1215.

20 Roundway Down, 1643, looking from the rear left of Waller's position, close to the Battlefield Trust's interpretation panel, towards Morgan's Hill.

21 Roundway Down, 1643, looking from the foot of the Down towards Oliver's Castle showing the steep gullies down which some of the Parliamentarian horses tumbled.

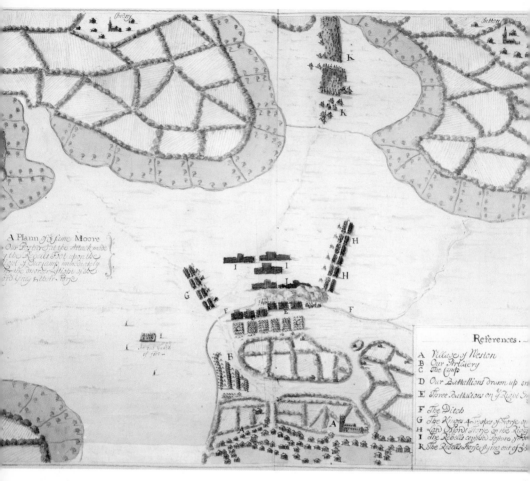

Text visible within the map image:

(Chedzy)

Sutton

K

K

A Plann of ye same Moore
Our Posture at the Attack made
by the Rebells Foot upon the
right of Our Camp immediately
before the Break of day of the
first ... their Horse

H

I I

I

H

G

F

E

F

i

i

In full Quarte
of fire

i

B

i

E

A

A

References.

A   Village of Weston
B   Our Artillery
C   The Camp
D   Our Battallions drawn up on ...
E   Three Battallions on ye Right ...
F   The Ditch
G   The Kings 4 Troopes of Horse ...
H   Lord Oxford Horse on his Right ...
I   The Rebells repulsed Posture of ...
K   The Rebells Horse flying out of ye ...

22 The second of the Dummer maps of the Battle of Sedgemoor, 1685, showing the nature of the historic environment (e.g. Chedzoy 'island' at the top left-centre) and the detailed dispositions of the troops after the Royalist cavalry were sent across the Upper and Lower Plungeons.

23 *Opposite above:* Stoke Field, 1487, showing the hill up which Henry VII's army advanced to attack the rebels at the top of the slope.

24 *Opposite below:* Stratton, 1643, showing one of the deep lanes up which the Royalists advanced to attack.

27 Queen Margaret of Anjou taken prisoner after the Battle of Tewkesbury, 1471.

25 *Opposite above:* Tewkesbury, 1471. This view shows the surviving part of the Gastons Field, spared from housing after a Public Inquiry.

26 *Opposite below:* Tewkesbury, 1471. The narrow 'Bloody Meadow' which proved to be a death trap for many retreating Lancastrians.

28 Worcester, 1651, showing Powick Bridge, the scene of one of the earliest skirmishes of the First Civil War. Powick Bridge was also fought over in the battle of Worcester at the end of the third Civil War.

29 Winwick Pass, 1648, showing the steep rock-cut bank to the south of the stream, which would have formed a difficult obstacle for the advancing Parliamentarians coming from the right of the picture.

30 Blake's three-day engagement with van Tromp in 1652.

Pinhoe, battle of, 1001

Following their unsuccessful attack on Exeter earlier in the year the Viking army marched on to Pinhoe where they met an army made up of men from Devon and Cornwall, led by Kola. The Vikings won quickly, burning nearby manors before taking their loot back to the fleet.

Piper Dene, battle of, 10 September 1435

Battle just to the south of Wark by the River Tweed in which the Earl of Angus defeated the Earl of Northumberland.

Plymouth, siege of, 30 September–22 December 1643

Failed Royalist siege of this important West-Country port during the First Civil War.
KEY REFERENCE: Young, P. & Emberton, W. *Sieges of the Great Civil War* (Bell & Hyman, 1978).

Just across the county border from Cornwall, Plymouth in Devon was always within striking distance of Royalist forces in the former county. However, Parliamentarian control of the Channel meant that supplies could be fed into Plymouth despite Royalist batteries on either side of Plymouth Sound. Throughout 1643 until the formal siege began in September, the Royalists under Hopton had done their best to clear Devon of Parliamentarian forces, which despite the occasional setback (as at Modbury), had led to success with the exception of the garrison of Plymouth, which continued to hold out. With the fall of Exeter and Dartmouth to the Royalist forces of Prince Maurice (younger brother of Prince Rupert and nephew of King Charles I) the situation looked grim for Plymouth's garrison. At that point the garrison received a new and vigorous commander in Colonel Wardlaw along with some reinforcements. This was just as well, as Maurice soon arrived with a large enough force to cut off the town by land, building a string of forts and batteries, including one near Plymstock, which was positioned to fire into the town from across the Catwater. A major attack was launched on 16 November against Plymouth's northern defences, but this failed to break through or to cower the garrison into accepting terms of surrender. A further attempt was made on 18 December, but that too was beaten off, leading the Royalists to abandon the siege four days later.

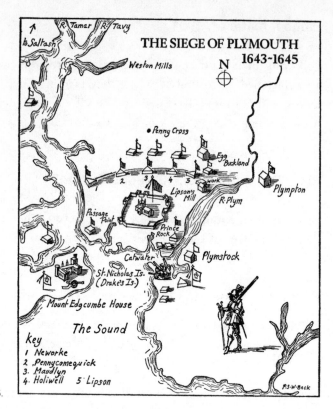

Siege of Plymouth, 1643–1645.

Pontefract Castle, siege of, 1648–March 1649

One of the few sieges of the Second Civil War and the longest and most serious of those endured by Pontefract Castle during the Civil Wars.

This great medieval castle had already fallen somewhat into disrepair by the time of the Civil Wars, but nonetheless withstood three sieges during the 1640s. Of these, the most serious was during the Second Civil War, when the castle was seized by northern Royalists from Sir Marmaduke Langdale's army, the bulk of which linked up to join the Scots under the Duke of Hamilton. While the latter headed for defeat at Preston in August 1648, Pontefract Castle remained in Royalist hands. After ensuring a change in government north of the border by going to Scotland himself, Cromwell travelled back south and paused for a few weeks at the Siege of Pontefract Castle before returning to London. The siege continued under Lambert, who had been the commander in the area at the start of the war. Pontefract held out until March 1649, two months after the execution of Charles I on 30 January. Once taken, the castle was slighted on the orders of Parliament, with the townspeople gladly carting off vast quantities of stone for building projects. Although little remains of the castle today, it has been the subject of archaeological excavations. One of these found deposits from the Civil War period at the base of the Constable Tower, including large amounts of body armour and military equipment, which could well have been thrown there by the defeated Royalists at the end of the siege. Excellent dating evidence for this third siege has been found at the castle in the form of lozenge-shaped siege money cut from silver plate.

Poole Harbour, battle of, 896

Possible location of a naval battle between King Alfred and the Danes.

The Danes had long been unchallenged at sea, but Alfred had ordered the construction of a number of ships which were longer and faster than their Danish counterparts, having at least sixty oars. A flotilla of six Danish ships had been raiding along the South Coast in 896. Alfred dispatched a squadron of nine of his new ships, which trapped the Danes by blocking their exit to the sea, making Poole Harbour a likely location, although other sites such as the mouth of the Exe are possible. The Danes tried to reach the open sea with three ships, while the other three beached. The English captured two of the escaping ships, killing the crews. However, the falling tide beached all the ships, with six of the English ships some way away from the other three and the stranded Danes.

The surviving Danes grouped together and crossed the flats to the three beached English ships. A battle ensued, with sixty-two English with their Frisian allies being killed and 120 Danes. The tide started to rise, enabling the Danes to float first, probably because their ships had a shallower draught, with the three ships which had been beached from the start escaping. Two of these ships then ran aground as they sailed along the Sussex coast. Their crews were led to Winchester where Alfred ordered them to be hanged. The remaining vessel limped around the coast to East Anglia.

Porlock, battle of, 1052

Raid by Saxon earls against Somerset and Devon.

Earl Harold Godwinson (later the King Harold who was killed at Hastings), along with the majority of his family, had been exiled from England in 1051.

Harold and his brother Leofwine had fled to Ireland but they returned the next year to raid the coasts of England. They landed at Porlock, where a battle was fought. Harold's force won, apparently killing thirty thegns during the battle. Harold and Leofwine then re-embarked and sailed round Land's End to attack the South Coast.

Porlock, raid of, 914

Raid by a Viking fleet from Brittany, which had been driven away from the River Severn earlier in the year. The raid was unsuccessful, with the survivors having to swim back to their ships.

Portland, battle of, 840

Earl Aethelhelm attacked a Danish army at Portland in Dorset, but was killed in the attempt along with many of his men, thus losing the battle.

Portland, raid of, 982

Viking raid by three ships against Portland in Dorset.

Portsmouth, battle of, 501

Early Anglo-Saxon victory against the Romano-Britons.

Port, with his two sons, came with two ships to Portsmouth, or possibly Portchester, where they defeated a Romano-British force, killing a young nobleman. This gives a good indication of the small scale of the majority of these early 'dark age' battles.

Powderham Castle, siege of, January 1646

Impressive castle in Devon, heavily restored after the Civil Wars and open to the public, which fell to Parliamentarian forces as they moved through the West Country, culminating with the fall of Pendennis Castle.

Powick Bridge, battle of, 23 September 1642

First battle or more accurately an early cavalry skirmish of the Great Civil War, which established the reputation of Prince Rupert's cavalry.

KEY REFERENCE: Peachey, S. *The Battle of Powick Bridge* (Caliver Press).

A month after the raising of the Royal Standard at Nottingham, both the Royalists and Parliamentarians were attempting to collect resources while trying to bring their main army into a favourable position. King Charles I was at Shrewsbury, expecting a convoy of treasure from Oxford to reach him via Worcester. To help secure the convoy, he dispatched Prince Rupert with a force of horse before they could be intercepted by Parliamentarian forces detached from the Earl of Essex's main army. On 22 September the Parliamentarian Captain Fiennes made a weak attempt to enter the city of Worcester but was repelled. At this he moved to the south bank of the Teme, to the village of Powick. The 1,000 horse, dragoons and commanded musketeers were under the overall command of Colonel Brown, while on the north bank of the Teme was part of Rupert's newly arrived force, who had been sent to guard the crossing, probably also 1,000 strong. It appears that the Parliamentarians secured the bridge, which still exists despite later damage (largely before the Battle of Worcester, 1651) and rebuilding.

Inaction then set in, until a message came from Essex the following afternoon. This spurred Fiennes, Brown and a Colonel Sands into action. The latter pressed forward before waiting for Brown with the dragoons to come up from the village of Powick, and even before the horse at the bridge had finished singing their psalm! Due to the narrowness of the bridge and the confines of the hedged lane the other side, there was no room for manoeuvre. Accordingly, the Royalists were able to cause some confusion and casualties by opening fire with their own dragoons with short muskets, who were lining the hedges. Despite this the Parliamentarians reached the open spaces of Wick field, where they were able to deploy their first troops of horse before being charged. The Parliamentarians appear to have remained stationary, probably waiting for all their troops to debouch from the lane. However, before this was able to happen the Royalists came forward, exchanged pistol fire and then charged home with the sword. Although Fiennes' troop made a spirited resistance, the other Parliamentarians were quickly scattered. The narrow lane must have become a scene of chaos, with men from all formations being mixed together as one. Colonel Brown was able to restore some order at the bridge, as he had kept a few dragoons under his command, who were able to prevent the Royalists from crossing. However, the routed troops continued to flee for several miles until they met the main army, having panicked Essex's lifeguard on the way. The Parliamentarians suffered around 150 casualties, with a further eighty captured, while the Royalists lost very few, although Rupert himself and several other commanders received sword cuts. The Royalists were able to escort the treasure convoy safely to Shrewsbury, having gained a psychological advantage over the Parliamentarian cavalry which was to last for much of the war. Had it not been for the fact that this was the first major engagement of the war, Powick Bridge would scarcely merit a line in most histories of the conflict.

The 'old bridge' at Powick is worth a visit, although the site of the main action at Wick field is under housing and other development. See also Worcester, battle of, 1651.

Preston, battle of, 17 August 1648

Decisive battle of the Second Civil War, where an invasion by a Scottish army supporting King Charles I was defeated.

KEY REFERENCE: Bull, S. and Seed, M. *Bloody Preston* (Carnegie Publishing Ltd, 1998).

By the end of 1647 King Charles I had made an agreement with the Scots promising to introduce Presbyterianism into England for an initial three-year period, in return for a Scottish army helping to restore him to the throne. Charles had been held by Parliament since May 1646 after he had surrendered to the Scots Covenanters who at that point were fighting on the same side as Parliament. By spring 1648 a number of Royalist revolts had broken out in South Wales, Kent and Essex in particular. In May 1648 Sir Marmaduke Langdale crossed into England and proceeded to recruit in Cumbria, raising some 3,000 foot and 1,200 horse for the king's cause. Major-General Lambert was sent to track him with the Parliamentarian forces of the Northern Association, who were joined by the end of June by the Lancashire militia, bringing Lambert's numbers to some 5,000. However, on 8 July the Duke of Hamilton crossed the border with an army of 6,000 foot and 3,000 horse, which forced Lambert to fall back. Hamilton decided to invade using the western route rather than moving to the east of the Pennines, gathering more men to him as he went, with around 6,000 reinforcements from Scotland reaching him by 26 July. Fortunately for Parliament, Hamilton hardly made rapid progress, which enabled Cromwell to conduct an impressive march from South Wales where he had been dealing with the revolt there, while the Lord General Sir Thomas Fairfax moved against the rebels in Kent and Essex. Some units were sent to Lambert in advance, although Cromwell brought the bulk of his army with him when he moved north after the fall of Pembroke Castle on 11 July. By 1 August Cromwell had reached Leicester with a force of around 4,000. He then moved north into Yorkshire, meeting Lambert at Wetherby on 12 August. Lambert had expected Hamilton to follow him from Lancashire, but instead the Royalist army had continued to follow the western route south through Lancashire. At that point Hamilton still outnumbered the Parliamentarian forces by about two to one, with some 20,000 men against a combined total of around 10,000 Parliamentarians.

Having lost contact with Lambert, one would expect Hamilton to have kept his forces close together, but instead they were spread out over many miles of road and still made little progress. At that point Cromwell and Lambert had the choice either to fall back and hopefully block Hamilton's advance to London, or to take the more daring step of crossing into Lancashire and attacking the Scots' flank. They chose the latter course, marching to Skipton and then down the Ribble valley, making contact with Langdale's scouts on the night of 14 August. Both sides gathered more information on 15 August, but the messages sent on to Hamilton by Langdale were largely dismissed. Certainly, Hamilton discounted the idea that Cromwell could have appeared so far north so quickly, and by the time this truth was realised in the early hours of 17 August it was too late to concentrate his forces.

Langdale was with the rear-guard just to the north-east of Preston when serious contact was made later on 17 August by Longridge Chapel. The battle

General John Lambert, the prime Parliamentarian General in the north of England during the Second Civil War, see Preston, 1648.

started there, as Parliamentarian dragoons and mounted skirmishers pressed the Royalists, who made a fighting retreat across the open ground towards Preston with its enclosures, which would have given some cover to Langdale's men. No doubt Langdale hoped that he would be joined by other units of Hamilton's army, but the River Ribble to the south of Preston was an obstacle even with a bridge at Walton (the current bridge is slightly upstream or east from that of 1648). By noon Langdale was in position on the south side of Eaves Brook on Ribbleton Moor to stand and attempt to fight off the Parliamentarians. Cromwell deployed his troops into battle lines either side of Longridge Lane (now Road) and advanced to attack Langdale's force. With the ground being enclosed and quite wet, Cromwell kept his horse on the road in the centre, with the foot to their right and left. The battle began with slow progress being made by the Parliamentarians. If Hamilton had responded quickly, the situation could have been turned to his advantage, but instead of recalling most of his Scottish horse from the south, all he did was to order some of his Scottish foot to the north side of the River Ribble by Walton Bridge, meaning that they were still separated from the action, which was taking place over a mile to the north beyond the floodplain and scarp to the north of the Ribble. By 4.00 p.m. Langdale's left was beaten, with it heading back towards the bridge, although his right had proved most stubborn, only being beaten when Parliamentarian cavalry turned from the defeat of the centre to attack them from the rear. At that point Langdale's force dissolved and headed for Preston or the Ribble behind them.

The battlefield on Ribbleton Moor is now entirely developed apart from a narrow strip along Eaves Brook, although the floodplain of the Ribble beneath the scarp leading to Walton Bridge is still open. Good views can be gained across this part of the battlefield from the various side streets leading to the top of the scarp in Fishwick. On seeing Langdale's men streaming towards them, most of the Scottish foot crossed to the south side of the Ribble, although some remained on the north side to be caught, defeated and mainly captured by the pursuing Parliamentarians. Others fled into Preston from where they were driven, with Hamilton himself only just escaping by fording or swimming the river to the west. During the evening, fighting continued south of the Ribble, where various units of Scots and northern Royalists continued to stand. However, the game was up, with the bulk of the remaining Scots' foot being defeated at Winwick Pass on 19 August and Hamilton surrendering with the remaining horse at Uttoxeter on 25 August. What should have been a serious threat to Parliament fizzled out in the face of indecisive leadership from Hamilton and a determined seizing of the initiative by Cromwell. Although the battlefield is not particularly rewarding to visit, the Harris Museum and Art Gallery in Preston have interesting displays relating to the Civil Wars and later Jacobite invasions.

Preston, battle of, 12–14 November 1715

Major action of 'the '15' to be fought in England as the Jacobites proclaimed 'the Old Pretender' as King James III.

KEY REFERENCE: www.lancashire.gov.uk/environment/oldmap/others/pres1715.gif

The Earl of Mar raised the Jacobite standard at Braemar on 6 September 1715 against King George I, but then did very little in the following month, allowing Hanoverian forces to secure important cities in Scotland. A detachment of around 2,000 Jacobites was sent south to gather further support, reaching Preston with perhaps 3,000 men on 10 November. On 12 November the Government's Major-General Wills attacked the Jacobites in Preston, but found his way blocked by barricades. Unknown to them, on the next day the main Jacobite army was defeated at Sheriffmuir to the north of Stirling, leaving the Jacobite cause hopeless. Further Hanoverian reinforcements under Lieutenant-General Carpenter arrived on 13 November, enabling a complete encirclement of the town, as shown in an excellent contemporary plan of the battle (see key reference above). Despite losing few men compared to the 200 or so Hanoverian casualties, the Jacobites surrendered on 14 November, bringing 'the fifteen' in England to an end. The Harris Museum and Art Gallery in Preston have displays relating to both 'the '15' and 'the '45'.

Radcot Bridge, battle of, 20 December 1387

Defeat of the Earl of Ireland who was trying to reach London to free Richard II
from the clutches of the Lords Appellant.

A group of nobles, including the Earl of Derby (future King Henry IV),
rebelled against King Richard II, as they did not want to relinquish control of
the kingdom once Richard had become old enough to rule. Known as the
Lords Appellant because they had appealed that various supporters of the king
should be declared traitors, they took control of London and the young king.
The Earl of Ireland gathered a force of around 4,500 men at Chester and
marched to rescue Richard. However, the Lords Appellant blocked his route in
most directions, forcing him to turn to the west to cross the River Thames.

He moved to cross the river at Radcot Bridge (probably without a
preliminary skirmish at Witney) to the west of Oxford, but his way was blocked
both by the bridge which had been broken in three places and also by a larger
force under the Earl of Derby, including archers stationed on the bridge. The
bridge of 1387 still stands, although the central arch has been altered, with
another bridge just to the north, which spans a later canalised stretch of the
river. Ireland had the Royal Banner unfurled, but many of his army were
unwilling to advance. Probably at this point another force of the Lords
Appellant arrived under the Duke of Gloucester. They threatened to trap
Ireland's men, which persuaded the Earl and some of his closest followers to

attempt to cross the river on horseback, which must have been extremely difficult given that the ground was marshy and the water probably high due to the time of year. However, Ireland managed to escape, abandoning his men. One of his followers, Sir Thomas Molyneux, was pulled back from trying to cross the river and was killed by Sir Thomas Mortimer. There is confusion in the contemporary sources about the exact sequence of events, but it would appear that the main action was fought at Radcot Bridge. The result was that Richard II remained in the hands of the Lords Appellant and his supporters were rounded up and punished by the subsequent 'Merciless Parliament'.

Rawfolds Mill, attack on, 11–12 April 1812

Largest disturbance involving the Luddites in West Yorkshire.

KEY REFERENCE: Bailey, B. *The Luddite Rebellion* (Sutton Publishing, 1998).

Although the greatest concentration of Luddite (named after their mythical leader Ned Ludd) attacks and riots were in the Midland counties of Nottinghamshire, Derbyshire and Leicestershire, where workers were largely protesting against the arrival of stocking-frames, the most famous incident of these troubles was in West Yorkshire, where the protests were focused on shearing frames, which were being introduced and seemingly taking away employment from the shearmen or 'croppers'.

The climax came with an organised attack on Rawfolds Mill at Liversedge on the River Spen, owned by a Mr Cartwright who was also a captain in the Halifax Militia. He had anticipated an attack and had taken various precautions including sleeping on the premises, having armed workers and militiamen on patrol and even keeping acid ready to pour on any attackers. On the night of 11 April there were six workers and five soldiers as well as Cartwright in the four-storey mill, when a force of between 150 and 300 Luddites (probably nearer 150) approached from their meeting point at the 'Dumb Steeple' monument about two and a half miles away to the south-west. They were formed up in two bodies led by George Mellor and William Thorpe as they moved against the mill. They appear to have been surprised by the organised defence of the mill, which is strange given that most must have been local men. As they tried to force a way in, the defenders opened fire, wounding two of the Luddites, while others threw stones from the roof and rang a warning bell to alert a local unit of cavalry. This was enough to persuade the attackers to retreat and disperse, leaving their wounded comrades to be taken captive. Both died from their wounds. Following this attack and other disturbances close by, the

Government sent many regular troops into the area, but problems continued for several months, until the problems died down in the aftermath of executions and other harsh punishments for convicted Luddites. The attack on Rawfolds Mill is immortalised as Hollow's Mill in Charlotte Brontë's *Shirley*.

Reading, battle of, 4 January 871

King Aethelred of Wessex and his brother Alfred attacked the Viking army encamped at Reading. They were beaten off by Viking reinforcements sallying out of the encampment, but turned at bay to fight at Ashdown four days later.

Reading, siege of, 15 – 28 April 1643

First major siege of the First Civil War.

King Charles I spent most of November 1642 at Reading, as his army at first attempted to march on London and then retreated to Reading after the stand-off at Turnham Green. On the king's retreat to Oxford at the end of the month, Reading was left with a garrison of 2,000 foot and a regiment of horse under Sir Arthur Aston, who spent the winter months strengthening the town's defences. The Parliamentarian Earl of Essex moved to besiege the town on 13 April 1643, using Southcote House as his headquarters. He had a force of at least 4,500 (mainly horse) including siege artillery, which opened fire on 16 April. On 18 April a small relief force approached Reading, but they were unable to cross by Caversham Bridge just to the north of the town, as part of it had been taken up by the Parliamentarians. A few hundred Royalist musketeers got into the town by boat, but the bulk of the force was driven away. However, a larger relieving force under the king had left Oxford and was almost in sight of Reading when the garrison under Feilding (Aston being wounded) made a truce on 25 April, partly because the messenger sent by the king to bring news of the relief had failed to get through the Parliamentarian lines. The king's force, not knowing of the truce, still attempted to charge across Caversham Bridge, but they were stopped and pushed back. Feilding surrendered on 27 April, and his forces marched out the next day, thus ending the siege, although Essex's troops then proceeded to sack the town.

Excavations have found evidence of a large defensive ditch from the Civil War in the grounds of Reading Abbey, while an earthwork in Forbury Park may be one of Aston's forts.

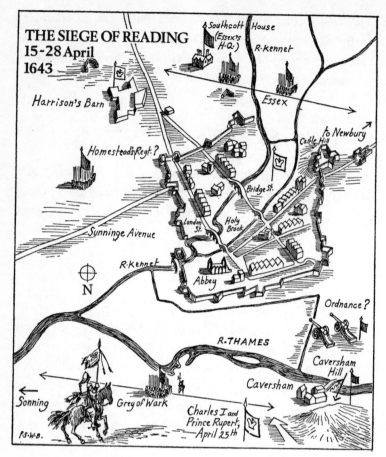

Siege of
Reading,
15–28 April
1643.

Reading, skirmish (or fight) of, 9 December 1688

Largest fight of 'the Glorious Revolution'.

With the landing of William of Orange at Torbay, King James II at first looked to defeat him. However, the hand-over of power was carried out largely through negotiation, although there was serious fighting after William's accession culminating in the Battle of the Boyne in 1690. In December 1688 a body of Irish troops loyal to James garrisoned Reading, blocking William's approach to London. William sent 300 Dutch troops into the town from an unexpected direction, as the townspeople had provided intelligence as to where the Irish troops were stationed. Fighting ensued in the town, especially in Broad Street after which the 'battle' is sometimes known, but the Irish were forced out after losing around fifty casualties, some of whom were buried in St Giles' churchyard.

Reidswire, raid of the, 7 June (?) 1575

Dispute which spilled over into a skirmish between the English and the Scots at the modern border point called Carter Bar, then named Reidswire, which the Scots won. The English began the fight by shooting a volley of arrows, but then fell into disarray when Scottish reinforcements arrived, as described in the ballad 'the Raid of the Reidswire'.

Ribbleton Moor, battle of, see Preston, battle of, 17 August 1648

Ringmere (Pit), battle of, 5 or 18 May 1010

A large Viking army attacked East Anglia, first taking Ipswich before moving on to defeat the English at Ringmere, probably near Thetford. This victory allowed the Vikings to pillage further, looting and burning Thetford and Cambridge before moving on to Northampton, the Thames and into Wiltshire.

Ripon, raid to, 948

King Eadred of England raided Northumbrian territory, burning Ripon Minster, because the Northumbrians had accepted the Viking Eric 'Blodaxe' as their king.

Ripple Field, battle of, 13 April 1643

Largely cavalry action of the First Civil War, which saw a victory for Prince Rupert's younger brother Prince Maurice.

The Parliamentarian General Sir William Waller moved into the West Country in March 1643 taking Winchester, Malmesbury and Gloucester. This provoked a reaction from King Charles I stationed at Oxford, who ordered his nephew Prince Maurice to harass Waller. Maurice crossed the River Severn at Tewkesbury via a bridge of boats to catch Waller to the east of the river. However, Waller doubled back, crossed the river and destroyed Maurice's bridge. Maurice moved north to cross at Upton Bridge, while Waller moved to intercept him. The Royalist Maurice moved more quickly and was over the bridge before Waller could meet him. The two forces met between Tewkesbury and Upton at Ripple Field.

Waller deployed just to the north of Ripple village (to the west of the modern A38), with a force of around 1,300 and a few ill-served guns. Maurice had around 2,000 men, mainly cavalry, who moved forward once they detected that Waller was trying to withdraw, having realised he was outnumbered. Their charge was successful, forcing away Waller's 'forlorn hope' of dragoons from the hedges by a lane and driving into the main body. The situation was only rectified by the arrival of a reserve regiment of armoured cavalry: Hesilrige's 'lobsters'. They held up Maurice's advance long enough to allow the bulk of Waller's men to retire to the safety of Tewkesbury, although some died attempting to ford the Severn.

River Idle, battle of, 617

Bede gives us the location of this battle 'fought in Mercian territory on the east bank of the River Idle', in which King Raedwald of East Anglia's army (the man probably buried in the richest of the Sutton Hoo burials) defeated and killed Aethelfrith of Northumbria, leading to the reinstatement of Edwin as King of Northumbria and Raedwald becoming 'High King'.

River Lea, battle of the, 895

The Danes had rowed their ships up the River Lea in 894 from Mersea Island and the River Thames. They fortified a site near Hertford on the River Lea, which was attacked by the English in the summer of 895, but they were driven away with heavy losses.

River Parret, battle of the, 848

A combined force of men from Somerset under Earl Eanwulf and from Dorset under Earl Osric and Bishop Ealhstan defeated an army of Danes at the mouth of the River Parret.

Rochester, battle and siege of, 999

The Viking raiding force which had operated throughout the 990s turned its attention to the River Medway and Rochester, besieging it 'for a few days' before being met by a Kentish army which was defeated, resulting in the capture of Rochester.

Rochester, siege of, 884

An army of Danes besieged Rochester in 884, protecting themselves from a relieving force by building an outer work. The city held out, and in 885 Alfred arrived, driving the Danes away to their ships.

Rochester, siege of, 1088

Result of an attempt to wrest the throne from William II for Robert of Normandy.

With the death of William I in 1087 the crown of England passed to William II. However, a group of bishops and barons preferred to put Robert, his older brother on the throne. The revolt was widespread, starting at Easter 1088, with the rebels taking station at their castles around the country, with Bishop Odo the leader of the rising moving to his castle at Rochester. After taking the castle at Tonbridge the King's supporters moved against Rochester, but found that Odo had moved to Pevensey.

After a siege of six weeks and the failure of an attempted invasion by Robert's supporters from Normandy, Odo came to an agreement. Odo travelled to Rochester, seemingly to surrender the castle. However, his men continued to revolt, forcing William to besiege Odo inside Rochester Castle. The castle was duly taken and Odo went into exile, leaving William to capture the last main stronghold of the revolt, Durham Castle.

Rochester Castle, siege of, 11 October–30 November 1215

Dramatic siege involving the technique of mining, which led to the fall of this impressive castle.

KEY REFERENCE: Allen Brown, R. *Rochester Castle* (1986, English Heritage).

King John had an ongoing feud with Stephen Langton, Archbishop of Canterbury and a wide range of barons. This in part led to the signing of Magna Carta on 15 June 1215, but also to John's unwillingness to allow Langton to take over Rochester Castle, which had traditionally been held by the Archbishop. At the end of September 1215 a number of barons led by

Rochester Castle, 1215. The seal
of Rochester shown in around
1300, showing the massive square
keep with its forebuilding just to
the right. The keep had to be
repaired following the successful
mining operation under the south-
east corner during the siege of
1215.

William d'Albini seized Rochester and held it against John, leading to this siege. The defenders had between ninety-five and 140 knights, with supporting troops including crossbowmen. John's forces moved up from Dover and cut Rochester off from London, from where relief for the rebels would have come, by taking the Medway bridge and besieging the castle on 11 October. John himself arrived on 13 October to supervise the attack, ordering the construction of five large siege engines. These battered the walls while a mining operation was begun, helped by the provision of many picks from nearby Canterbury on the order of King John. The curtain wall was broken down, forcing the defenders to seek refuge in the massive square keep (now cared for by English Heritage and open to the public). The mine continued under the south-east corner of the keep, with the gallery being fired with the fat from forty pigs. This brought down the angle of the keep (it was rebuilt later, evidence of which can be seen in the masonry), allowing John's men to storm inside. The defenders held out for a while in one half of the keep behind the dividing cross-wall, but once inside, the castle had to fall. John then threatened to execute the rebels, but he was restrained by advice from one of his supporters, seemingly only executing one of the crossbowmen. The castle was taken by Prince Louis of France the following year, although he left in 1217, with the castle returning to the English king. The keep was repaired during the reign of Henry III, ready for the next siege in 1264.

Rochester Castle, siege of, 17–26 April 1264

Fought during the prelude to the Battle of Lewes, as Simon de Montfort and the forces of King Henry III went to war.

KEY REFERENCE: Allen Brown, R. *Rochester Castle* (1986, English Heritage).

While King Henry III started to capture various rebel castles in the Midlands, Simon de Montfort moved out of London to besiege the important fortress at Rochester, along with Gilbert de Clare on 17 April 1264. He had some success, fighting his way across the River Medway the next day with the use of a fire ship (possibly to create a smokescreen), and taking the city. However, despite taking the castle bailey on 19 April, de Montfort failed to capture the massive square keep, which held out under the command of the Earl de Warenne. Henry made as if to attack London, which forced de Montfort to raise the Siege of Rochester to protect the capital. At the same time, Prince Edward (later Edward I) made a forced march with cavalry to enter Rochester, before rejoining his father for the Battle of Lewes.

Romney Marsh, battle of, 798

Although details are lacking, it appears that King Cenwulf of Mercia raided through Kent, which included the fighting of an action in or near Romney Marsh. According to one version of the Anglo-Saxon Chronicle, the Kentish leader was captured and taken off to Mercia, where his eyes were put out and his hands cut off.

Rottingdean, raid of, June 1377

Following the burning of Folkestone and Rye, a landing by French and Castillian raiders was made at Rottingdean, leading to a skirmish and the burning of the church of St Margaret and other parts of the town.

Roundway Down, battle of, 13 July 1643

Arguably the most decisive Royalist victory in the field during the Civil Wars.

KEY REFERENCE: Haycock, L. *Devizes in the Civil War* (Wiltshire Archaeological and Natural History Society, 2000).

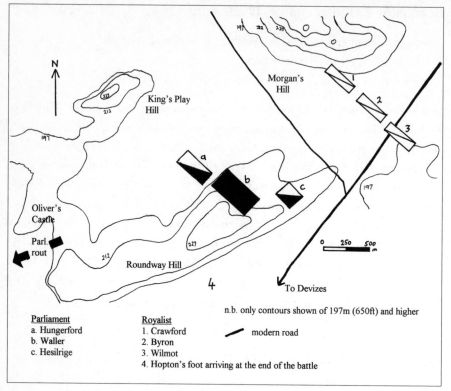

Battle of Roundway Down, 13 July 1643.

Having fought themselves to a standstill at the Battle of Lansdown north of Bath on 5 July, the Royalist army of Sir Ralph Hopton retired to Devizes. The morale of the army and not least of Hopton himself had lowered, after he was temporarily struck blind and paralysed after being caught by an exploding gunpowder wagon. The Parliamentarian army of Sir William Waller followed and moved to besiege Devizes, while trying to ensure that they could block any attempt at relief of the Royalist force from Oxford. However, Waller's numbers were insufficient to maintain a tight blockade and in the darkness in the early hours of 11 July the Royalist cavalry under Prince Maurice (Prince Rupert's younger brother and a nephew of King Charles I) broke out towards Oxford.

A small independent mounted force under Crawford attempted to enter Devizes on 11 July, but they were beaten away by Waller. By the morning of 13 July, news reached the Parliamentarians that a stronger body of cavalry was approaching from Oxford. This meant that Waller had to postpone a second assault on the town, after the first had failed on 12 July, so that he could meet this new threat. To do so he took his army onto Roundway Down above Devizes, across which the road from Oxford ran at that time.

Roundway Down is a large, open, saucer-shaped plateau, bounded by 'four hills, like the four corners of a die', as we are told by Captain Richard Atkyns, who was with the relief force. There is some dispute about the exact positions taken by both sides, although the area of the battlefield is clear. However, the contemporary sources do provide vital clues as to the initial dispositions. Firstly, one of the Royalist cavalry commanders, Byron, tells us that signal cannon were fired to alert Hopton in Devizes 'from an high hill that overlooks the town'. This suggests Roughridge Hill to the east of Roundway Hill, with the Royalist force of three brigades of cavalry of about 600 men in each brigade forming up next to these two guns, filling the gap leading to the slopes of Morgan's Hill. Secondly, several sources are clear that Waller drew up his army on a hill, in a tightly packed formation. This ideally fits Roundway Hill, with his men facing north-east towards Morgan's Hill. This also explains why it was the Parliamentarian right which came into action first, as it was the closest to the advancing Royalists. Waller had 2,500 infantry in his centre, with about 1,000 armoured cavalry (cuirassiers, known as 'lobsters') on his right under Hesilrige and another 1,500 cavalry and dragoons on his left. Given his superiority in numbers, it is at first difficult to see how Waller could lose, although the reasons soon become apparent as Wilmot's (Wilmot commanded the Royalists on the field at the start of the battle) manoeuvrable cavalry brigades were able to defeat the two wings of cavalry in detail without being troubled by the Parliamentarian infantry.

Hesilrige moved his densely packed cavalry forward in the early afternoon, probably to save Parliament's 'forlorn hope', which had been bettered in the initial exchanges. His six-deep line was met by a three-deep line, which overlapped him at both ends. Wilmot's cavalry broke Hesilrige's lobsters with Richard Atkyns capturing Hesilrige as they fled, although his attempt to shoot him with his pistols failed due to the thickness of his armour, even though one shot went off as he touched his pistol to Hesilrige's helmet. On seeing their commander captured, some of the lobsters rallied and rescued Hesilrige, which suggests that their flight was not out of control. Waller then advanced down the hill, presumably wheeling to the right, so that his left wing cavalry led the advance. Byron, commanding a second brigade of Royalist cavalry supported by Wilmot and Crawford with the third brigade, met the left wing cavalry of Waller. The Royalists pushed the first line back onto the second line, despite having being fired at by artillery as they advanced. This led to both lines of Parliament's horse becoming mixed together and both broke. This quickly became a rout, with Byron chasing them from the field and down the precipitous slopes to the west by Oliver's Castle (a local misnomer, as Cromwell was not at the battle and the feature dates from the Iron Age). Many men and horses were killed as they tumbled down the hill into what became known as 'bloody ditch'. It seems most likely that this was the steep re-entrant just to the south of Oliver's Castle rather than just to the north, or else surely the fleeing cavalry would have reached the safer descent provided by the nearby Bath Road. This just left Waller's infantry on the field and stalemate set in, as Wilmot charged them with cavalry but was fought off. However, their fate was sealed as Royalist Cornish infantry from Devizes arrived on the Down to their rear. Some, including Waller, escaped, but the bulk were killed or captured, shattering his command. Two grave pits have been found on the battlefield, and there is one named burial of William Bartlett, a Parliamentarian, at Rowde Church.

The battlefield is an extremely rewarding one to visit, being open and unspoilt. It has a marked trail, round which one can be aided by an illustrated leaflet available in Devizes. Moreover, there is an interpretation panel erected by the Battlefields Trust to the rear left of Waller's position. In Devizes one should visit the museum and information centre, which both have displays relating to the Civil War, as well as gazing up at the tower of St James's Church, which has clear cannon ball holes from the siege.

The battle effectively secured the West for King Charles I, although he did not make the most of this opportunity. The Royalists had a commemorative medal struck in Oxford and the battle became known as Runaway Down, making this an important propaganda victory as well. It also did much to discredit William Waller, although this seems rather harsh today for the general formerly known as 'William the Conqueror'.

Rowton Heath, battle of, 24 September 1645

Royalist attempt to break the Siege of Chester and turn the tide after serious defeats at Naseby and Langport.

KEY REFERENCE: English Heritage: *Battlefield Report: Rowton Heath 1645* (English Heritage, London, 1995).

King Charles I had an ever-decreasing number of troops available to him by September 1645, with his main field army having been defeated at Naseby and then Goring's force in the South-West losing at Langport. Accordingly, the Royalists decided to attempt to muster at the besieged city of Chester, with Charles entering the city on 23 September. His main force in the field of 2,500 horse was to the south of the city under Sir Marmaduke Langdale, with orders to trap the Parliamentarian besiegers. To counter the threat of these newly arriving enemies, the Parliamentarians sent out messengers to look for their own reinforcements. These were found in the guise of General Poyntz, who began to march towards Chester from Whitchurch in the early hours of 24

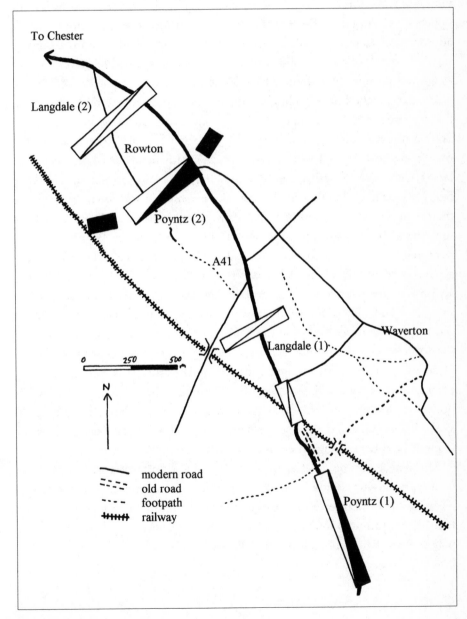

Battle of Rowton Heath, 24 September 1645.

September. Langdale intercepted a message from Poyntz which convinced him to fight the latter before turning his attentions to the besieging force.

Poyntz approached from the south along the line of the present A41. Before reaching Rowton from the south, and just before the road crosses over the railway, there is a public footpath across the road, which roughly marks the point where the first clash occurred. If travelling by car, it is best to park in the village of Waverton to the east and then walk along the (muddy) footpath from opposite the church to the A41. There is a footbridge over the railway which affords good views to north and south. Between this bridge and the current A41 is a stretch of old road, lined with very thick hedges, which gives a useful indication of how the road may have looked in 1645.

Having marched since midnight with around 2,500 cavalry and 500 infantry, the Parliamentarians advanced straight along the road at about 6.00 a.m., hoping to catch the Royalists unawares, but found it very difficult to deploy owing to the hedged lane. Despite this, the Parliamentarian horse came to blows with their Royalist counterparts after discharging their pistols. After fighting for fifteen minutes the Royalists were pushed back down the road, but their main force then pushed the Parliamentarians back. There was then something of a stand-off until about 4.00 p.m., when Poyntz received reinforcements from the besiegers outside Chester. Langdale had by then fallen back towards the city onto what was then called Rowton Heath, where the action is harder to follow on the ground. Langdale advanced to attack, but was met first by a volley of fire and then with a cavalry charge. The Parliamentarian musketeers were formed up on the flanks of their force and managed to bring fire to bear on the Royalist reserve, forcing it to flee. A final encounter took place just outside Chester, fought against Langdale's survivors who had by then been reinforced by a regiment from the Chester garrison, but this site now lies under later development. Among the Royalist dead was Lord Bernard Stuart, aged twenty-three and a cousin of King Charles I, who was buried in Christ Church Oxford, although there is no visible memorial to him there.

This defeat outside Chester made it clear that Charles I would not be able to mount another serious military challenge from within England, although the war was to drag on into 1646 as garrisons continued to hold out against Parliament. Although much of the battlefield is built over, the southern section where the initial clash occurred is well worth a visit.

St Albans, First Battle of, 22 May 1455

The first major encounter of the Wars of the Roses.

KEY REFERENCE: Watson, H. B. 'The First Battle of St Albans, 1455' in *Battlefield* (vol. 7 issue 2).

King Henry VI planned to hold a council at Leicester, possibly in an attempt to avert war breaking out with the Duke of York and his faction. However, the latter fearing a trap, he marched towards London with 3,000 men to confront Henry. Henry marched out from London, his small army of around 2,000 men commanded by the Duke of Somerset. On 21 May the Yorkists were at Ware, from where they swung west to march towards St Albans and the king, who was at Watford. After some delay and debate, Henry, urged on by the Duke of Buckingham, marched to St Albans to parley with York. The king reached St Albans first, at about 9.00 a.m., taking up positions at the top of the town in and around the Market Place, while the Yorkists made camp in Key Field to the east of the town.

Negotiations began between Buckingham and York, but they soon fell out as York demanded that Somerset should be put on trial for treason. Henry raised his standard in the Market Place, making it clear that any attack on him would constitute treason, while his men blocked the streets on the eastern side of the town, which were further guarded by small barricades and the vestiges of a town ditch. Many of the streets can still be traced today, but what was then open land to the east of the town is now entirely built-up.

York decided to move into the town to take Somerset by force, thus starting the battle and the war. At 10.00 a.m. the action began, with arrows falling on both sides. The Yorkists sent forward at least two columns: one up Shropshire Lane (now Victoria Street) and one further to the south up Sopwell Lane. Both of these faltered at the barricades on the line of the town ditch, but at that point the Yorkist reserve led by the Earl of Warwick came into action. He manoeuvred his men across the ditch between the two main columns, then slipped through the houses and plots leading towards the Market Place (probably along the line of the modern main London Road), emerging there unexpectedly. Finding themselves outflanked, the Lancastrians at the barricades fell back, while many others were caught unprepared and unarmoured in and around the Market Place. The fight was short but decisive, with Warwick's men wounding and capturing the king and Buckingham. Somerset was even less fortunate, being cut down and killed outside the Castle Inn on the corner of St Peter's Street and Victoria Street (now a building society branch office with a commemorative plaque on the outside wall to the Duke of Somerset). Fewer than 200 men were killed, most of them being Henry's Lancastrians.

After the battle, both parties went to London, where York promised allegiance again to the king, but also became 'Protector and Defender of the Land'. This uneasy truce staggered on for four years until open warfare broke out again in 1459 at Blore Heath.

St Albans, Second Battle of, 17 February 1461

A complex action fought in and around St Albans, in what many thought should have proved to be a decisive victory for the Lancastrians.

KEY REFERENCE: Watson, H. B. 'The Second Battle of St Albans' in *Battlefield* (vol. 7 issue 3).

St Albans had the misfortune to be the site of two battles during the Wars of the Roses, with the second battle being wide-ranging across the town. Although St Albans has inevitably spread since 1461 with most of the locations being built-up, it is still possible to follow the course of the battle on the ground. The key Yorkist supporter the Earl of Warwick took up position in and to the north of St Albans on 12 February, anticipating the advance of the main Lancastrian army. Lord Montagu was stationed across the road from Harpenden, defended by a large (still visible) Iron Age earthwork known as Beech Bottom. The Duke of Norfolk was beyond Sandridge to the north of St Albans, with Warwick in Sandridge. In addition, a body of archers was in the centre of St Albans. Further precautions were taken in the form of scattering caltrops (four-spiked pieces of iron to break up charges) and even placing nets at likely points where the hedges had gaps. In total the Yorkists probably had around 10,000 men including a unit of Burgundian mercenaries armed with handguns – the first time a formation of these new weapons made their appearance on an English battlefield. Against them the Lancastrians had perhaps 15,000 and were under the nominal command of Queen Margaret and the Duke of Somerset, although in practice led on the day by Andrew Trollope (who was knighted after the battle).

The Lancastrians must have gained information regarding Warwick's deployment, for they swung round to the north-west of St Albans, taking Dunstable, which had been held by a small detachment, on their way on 16 February. They continued their advance through the following night, appearing to the west of St Albans as dawn arrived on 17 February. Having outflanked the carefully prepared Yorkist defence lines, the Lancastrians were able to enter the town unopposed, until reaching the Market Place at the centre of the town, where they were met by the Yorkist archers. Although the initial attack stalled, a second column of Lancastrians forced its way into the town and moved against the rear of the archers from the north. Isolated and nearly surrounded, the archers were defeated. What is surprising is that at this point the main Yorkist force did not make an appearance, as they must have realised what was happening in the town, especially as the fighting there carried on until noon. However, the situation must have been very confused and it would have taken some time to confirm reports of the attack and then to re-deploy, let alone advance the Yorkist forces. Montagu had to turn his troops around and away from their strong defences at Beech Bottom, crossing Bernard's Heath and then deploying in a line across the main road leading north from St Albans. This is now partly open recreational ground, although with built-up development around it.

The main clash took place in that area, with everything conspiring against Montagu. Firstly, his 'secret weapon' the handguns caused more casualties to his own forces than to the enemy, as the guns misfired and some then exploded. The misfires had occurred in part because of the adverse weather of sleet, snow and high winds. Then, part of his force led by Sir Henry Lovelace changed sides, contributing to the collapse of the remainder of Montagu's command, which fled back across Bernard's Heath and also north towards Warwick's force. Perhaps realising that Trollope's attack from the town was the main Lancastrian force, Warwick finally moved his men towards the fighting. However, as they advanced they came across the fleeing remnants of Montagu's force, which together with the usual fears of treachery and the surprise and discomfort they felt with abandoning their well-prepared positions, meant that they were at best half-hearted when it came to facing the Lancastrians. The latter, with their blood up from their initial successes, had no difficulty in sending Warwick's men back up the road, through Sandridge and beyond. It was in this area known as Dead Woman's Hill that Victorian navvies uncovered many skeletons, probably casualties from the battle. As the Lancastrians finally gave in to exhaustion, Warwick extricated those he could – presumably largely Norfolk's command – and retreated to join forces with the new Duke of York. Although they did not realise it at the time, this was to prove costly to the Lancastrians, as it enabled both Warwick and Norfolk to fight at Towton at the end of March. Queen Margaret was also not strong enough to hold London for any length of time, so Edward Duke of York was able to enter the capital and be proclaimed king.

St Peter's Fields, encounter of, 16 August 1819

Bloody quashing of an initially peaceful demonstration in an attempt to prevent radicalism and parliamentary reform.

A meeting was organised by the Manchester Patriotic Union Society under the banner of 'Universal Suffrage', to be held on open ground in Manchester known as St Peter's Fields. The organisers were concerned that the meeting should be peaceful and so the crowd of about 50,000 men, women and children turned up in their Sunday best to hear the speakers, which included the radical Henry 'Orator' Hunt. The local magistrates were determined not to let the meeting proceed as planned and had deployed a number of regular and yeomanry units in the surrounding streets. Yeomanry cavalry moved in to arrest Hunt, but trampled a young girl to death in the throng, as they struggled to control their horses and themselves. Some of the crowd responded by throwing brickbats and jostling the horsemen. In response, a regular unit of hussars was ordered to help the yeomanry withdraw. The line between battle and crowd control in the early nineteenth century was not a clear one, and the hussars cut their path through the crowd with sabres drawn and busy. The crowd panicked, with many being injured in the crush. Eleven demonstrators were killed, while 162 suffered sabre wounds out of a total of over 400 wounded, many of them women and children. The event was ironically named 'Peterloo', comparing this episode to the great victory of four years before.

Salcombe Castle, siege of, February–May 1646

Successful Parliamentarian siege of this castle known as 'the Bulwark', defended by Sir Edmund Fortescue, with the garrison surrendering on terms, leaving only the garrison at Pendennis holding out for King Charles I in the West Country.

Salisbury, battle of, 552

Battle at the hill fort of Old Sarum to the north of Salisbury, in which the West Saxon Cynric defeated an army of Britons.

Salisbury, skirmishes of, December 1644

Two running fights through the city of Salisbury as Royalists and Parliamentarians vied for control.

Salisbury, without any walls or other substantial defences, was a city which could be taken more or less at will during the First Civil War. There were two skirmishes in the city itself in the winter of 1644–1645. In the first of these the Parliamentarian Colonel Ludlow charged into and routed a body of Royalist horse in the Cathedral Close. Later in the month the same thing happened to Ludlow and his men in the streets of the city, when they were surprised by more Royalist horse under Langdale.

Sampford Courtenay, battle of, 16 August 1549

Final act of the Western Rebellion against the reformed prayer book of Edward VI.

KEY REFERENCE: Gould, M. 'Conflicts of the 1549 Western Rebellion' in *The Battlefields Trust Newsletter* (April, 1997).

The rebel cause was as good as lost after their defeats at Fenny Bridges and Clyst St Mary, along with the failed siege of Exeter. Sampford Courtenay was effectively their last stand against the royal, largely mercenary, forces led by Lord Russell. It is likely that the rebels were outnumbered by this stage of the campaign, so they tried to make up for this inequality by entrenching their positions. The royal forces drove the rebels under Arundell from these positions and through the village. A final charge dispersed the rebels, resulting in possibly

700 being killed and the same number captured. The rebellion was over, save for the trial and inevitable execution of Arundell and the other leaders.

Sandwich, battle of, 850

King Athelstan attacked a large Danish force at Sandwich, capturing nine ships and putting the remainder to flight, although the Danes over-wintered in England for the first time despite this defeat.

Sandwich, battle of, 1009

Naval battle between two Saxon forces in a rare lull during the Viking Wars.

The English had formed a large fleet off Sandwich to guard against a Viking attack. However, the South-Saxon Prince Wulfnoth turned against them and formed his own fleet of twenty ships with which he raided the South Coast. The Saxon commander Beorhtric took eighty ships to trap Wulfnoth, but was caught in a storm, losing many ships. Wulfnoth then came upon the stricken fleet and burned the ships, forcing the remainder to retreat to London.

Sandwich, battle of, 1048

A Viking raiding fleet attacked the South-East but were met by an English fleet under King Edward 'the Confessor', which drove the Vikings away.

Sandwich, battle of, 24 August 1217

Naval battle off the then port of Sandwich, in which a French force bringing troops to England to aid Prince Louis of France in his campaign against King Henry III was defeated.

The French fleet was commanded by Eustace the Monk, 'a most infamous man' according to Matthew Paris' account. His aim was to sail to London, but his ships were intercepted by the English led by Hubert de Burgh off the Kentish coast. Hubert with sixteen ships was able to attack the rear of the French formation, boarding at least one ship. His men cut the sails down and the French on board were caught 'as a net falls over trapped birds'. Eustace himself was dragged out and summarily beheaded.

Sandwich, raid of, 991

Large raid by the Danish King Swein 'Forkbeard', or possibly according to one version of the Anglo-Saxon Chronicle, the Norwegian Olaf Tryggvason, against Sandwich with a fleet of ninety-three ships, going on to raid other coastal towns, culminating in the Battle of Maldon in August.

Sandwich, raid of, 15 January 1460

Attack on Lancastrian shipping at Sandwich by the Earl of Warwick, before he returned to Sandwich again with Edward, Earl of March from Calais in June 1460, leading to the Battle of Northampton.

Scarborough Castle, siege of, 18 February–25 July 1645

Impressive defence by a resolute and resourceful Royalist commander.

By 1645 Scarborough was the only useful East-Coast port left to the Royalists, and as such became a target for the Parliamentarians of Sir John

Eighteenth-century depiction of Scarborough Castle, showing its formidable situation but surprisingly little evident damage from the siege of 1645.

Meldrum. They captured the town on 18 February and moved to besiege the medieval castle, which is now under the guardianship of English Heritage. The Royalists under Sir Hugh Cholmley had built a battery known as Bushell's Battery just in front of the main entrance to the castle. The Parliamentarians took over the church of St Mary's (whose tower collapsed after the Civil War due to damage during the siege) a little further down the road and turned this into a fortified battery of their own. After various delays and sorties by the garrison, the Parliamentarian cannon began to batter the castle walls, breaching them. Cholmley patched up the defences enough to withstand an assault, although Bushell's Battery fell. This allowed Meldrum to move guns closer to the walls and at a range of no more than 100m they soon made an even wider breach. Despite this, the Royalists mounted more sorties, including one which destroyed Bushell's Battery, and then on 11 May Meldrum was mortally wounded. After this the Parliamentarians kept their distance with artillery fire only. Eventually Cholmley negotiated good terms and left by ship to the Netherlands, handing over a much ruined castle to Parliament.

Seacroft Moor, battle of, 30 March 1643

Fought as part of the ongoing struggle for the control of West Yorkshire between the Parliamentarian Fairfaxes and, in this case, the Royalist Lord Goring.

KEY REFERENCE: Cooke, D. *The Forgotten Battle: The Battle of Adwalton Moor 30 June 1643* (Battlefield Press, 1996).

A Parliamentarian force under Sir Thomas Fairfax raided Tadcaster, but then realised they were in danger of being intercepted by a force of Royalist horse under Lord Goring, who had been sent by the Earl of Newcastle. It seems that Goring had about 1,000 horse, including some dragoons, while Fairfax had about 200 horse and maybe 200 musketeers and a further 800 or so poorly armed and trained locals. The Parliamentarians managed to get across Bramham Moor, but were then caught in the open as they tried to cross Seacroft Moor. The Royalist horse charged their flank and rear, having got onto the moor by a different route to Fairfax, causing the untried Parliamentarian foot to throw down their weapons and run. Many prisoners were taken – possibly as many as 800 if the Duchess of Newcastle's account is to be believed – while the remainder made their escape to Leeds.

31 Prince Rupert in the regalia of a knight of the garter. Some of this flamboyance was taken into battle (for example at Aldbourne Chase in 1643), as Rupert's horse swept all before them at the start of the Civil War.

32 Somewhat fanciful version of Richard III's charge at Bosworth in 1485 with anachronistic weapons, armour and equipment. From Abraham Cooper's *The Battle of Bosworth Field,* 1825.

33 Bosworth, 1485. The view from the top of Ambion Hill showing the position of Richard III's 'battle' as marked by the standard in the foreground, following the Bosworth Battlefield Centre's current interpretation of the battle.

34 Barnet, 1471, showing modern Hadley Common where the centre divisions probably clashed and which in 1471 would have been treeless.

35 Blore Heath, 1459. The Hempmill Brook flows through the gully across the centre of the photograph, which is taken from the Lancastrian right-centre as it advanced down the slope.

36 Blore Heath, 1459, showing the Hempmill Brook looking west. Note the steep slope to the north up which the Lancastrians attempted to attack.

37 Bosworth, 1485. Michael K. Jones' favoured site for the battle taken from the top of a windmill mound with Fenny Drayton in the left middle distance, looking west.

38 Braddock Down, 1643. This is part of the site favoured for the battle until publication of Wilton's article – the Parliamentarians would have deployed on the far slope, which would have been open ground if it was then part of the moor.

39 Cheriton, 1644. The view from the Parliamentarian left towards Cheriton Wood on the skyline, showing the valley between the southern ridge (out of shot to the right) and the 'intermediate' ridge, where much of the fighting took place.

40 Cheriton, 1644, from the 'intermediate ridge' towards the Parliamentarian-held ridge in the distance, with Cheriton Wood on the left.

41 Cheriton, 1644, from Hinton Ampner and the likely site of some Parliamentarian artillery towards the southern of the three ridges, with Cheriton Wood to the right. The valley to the front is the site favoured by John Adair for the main fighting.

42 Clifton Moor, 1745, looking south out of the village. Government troops attacked down the slope towards the spot from where the photograph was taken.

43 The tower of St Mary's-at-the-Walls in Colchester showing the brick rebuilding of the top of the structure, necessary after the 1648 siege. The tower became a target as it served as a gun platform for a Royalist saker.

44 Evidence of shot holes in timber of the 'Old Siege House' in East Street, Colchester. The Royalists attempted a break-out past this house on 5 July 1648, but were driven back.

45 Evesham, 1265, looking north from a position just to the west of the houses along Greenhill.

46 Halidon Hill, 1333. The view from the right of the English position looking across to Witches Knowe from where the Scots advanced. The land around the farm on the right of the photograph would no doubt have been boggy ground at the time of the battle, as would the valley off the photograph to the right.

47 Hastings, 1066. The view from the modern terrace walk about half the way up Senlac Hill, looking down to the centre of William's lines.

48 *Above:* Homildon Hill, 1402. The photograph is taken from where most of the English were formed up, with Homildon (Humbleton) Hill on the left and Harehope Hill to the right. The English archers formed up on the latter, with the protection of the wooded gulley between them and the Scots.

49 *Right:* Admiral Robert Blake, who was the key English admiral during the first Anglo-Dutch War and achieved a mixed record against the able Admirals van Tromp and de Witt, winning at Kentish Knock in 1652.

50 *Above:* Langport, 1645, looking towards the Parliamentarian positions on Pitney Hill, taken from the Royalist left flank. Note the thick hedges flanking the modern road.

51 *Left:* Ralph, Lord Hopton, long time friend and, during the First Civil War, sparring partner, of Sir William Waller. Hopton was badly wounded two days after the Battle of Lansdown in 1643 when an ammunition wagon exploded nearby.

52 Lewes, 1264, at the top of the Downs above Lewes, showing Burne's 'parade ground' where de Montfort probably formed up his army.

53 Maldon, 991. The view from Northey Island held by the Vikings across the causeway towards the East Saxon position.

54 Marston Moor, 1644, looking from the rear left of the Royalist position towards the slope of Braham Hill on which the Parliamentarians and Scots deployed. The trees on the skyline mark 'Cromwell's Plump'.

55 *Right:* David Leslie, first Lord Newark, Scottish commander who led the Scottish contingent of horse on the triumphant allied left-wing at the Battle of Marston Moor in 1644.

56 *Below:* Myton, 1319, showing the flat field across which the Scots advanced to meet the English, once the latter had crossed the River Swale.

57 *Above:* Naseby, 1645. The view from the Cromwell Monument towards Dust Hill, looking across Broadmoor. Much of the infantry fight would have taken place in the area in the foreground.

58 *Right:* Henry Ireton, Cromwell's son-in-law who commanded the left-wing of Parliamentarian horse at the battle of Naseby, 1645.

59 Newark, 1645–46. The view of the Queen's Sconce, constructed by the Royalists as protection for the town.

60 Nibley Green, 1470, showing the steep slope down which Lisle advanced.

61 Imaginative depiction of the Battle of Northallerton in 1138 with the standard at the midst of the English army. Accounts do not mention a large crucifix.

62 Otterburn, 1388. The view from the edge of the copse with the Percy Cross looking towards the Scottish lines.

63 Solway Moss, 1542, looking from the furthest forward position of the Scots towards the main English line to the right centre.

64 Towton, 1461, looking towards the Yorkist-held ridge in the distance from close by Dacre's Cross.

65 Towton, 1461, looking towards the River Cock showing the steep slopes down which many retreating Lancastrians must have slid and tumbled, before being caught by their pursuers.

66 Towton, 1461. Evocative portrayal of the rout of the Lancastrians at the Battle of Towton in 1461. Many died trying to cross the swollen and close-to-freezing waters of the River Cock.

67 Wakefield, 1460. The view from the foot of Sandal Castle's mound over the area where the fighting took place.

68 Wakefield, 1460. The chantry chapel outside which the Earl of Rutland was probably killed by Lord Clifford.

69 Winceby, 1643. The view from the line of the 1643 road down which the Royalists advanced towards the ridge in the distance occupied by the Parliamentarian horse.

70 Worcester, 1651. This standard was carried at the Battle of Worcester. It is the Royal Banner of Scotland, which would have been a target for Parliamentarian attacks if it was brought close to the front line.

THE
SOULDIERS
Pocket Bible :

Containing the moft (if not all) thofe places contained in holy Scripture, which doe fhew the qualifications of his inner man, that is a fit Souldier to fight the Lords Battels, both before he fight, in the fight, and after the fight ;

Which Scriptures are reduced to feverall heads, and fitly applyed to the Souldiers feverall occafion, and fo may fupply the want of the whole Bible, which a Souldier cannot conveniently carry about him :

And may bee alfo ufefull for any Chriftian to meditate upon, now in this miferable time of Warre.

Imprimatur, *Edm. Calamy.*

*Jof.*18. This Book of the Law fhall not depart out of thy mouth, but thou fhalt meditate therein day and night, that thou maift obferve to doe according to all that is written therein, for then thou fhalt make thy way profperous, and have good fucceffe.

Printed at *London* by *G.B.* and *R.W.* for *Aug : 3* *G.C.* 1 6 4 3.

---

71 Parliamentarian army soldiers were sporadically issued with Bibles. This is the title page of the *Soldiers' Pocket Bible* (1643).

Sedgemoor, battle of, 6 July 1685

Decisive battle which brought the rebellion of the Duke of Monmouth against James II to a bloody end.

KEY REFERENCE: Chandler, D. G. *Sedgemoor 1685* (Spellmount, 1999).

King Charles II died in February 1685, leaving his younger brother James, Duke of York to be crowned as King James II. However, Charles' bastard son the Duke of Monmouth had hoped to succeed himself, although his chances had been decreased when he had taken himself into exile in 1684. His claim rested on the fact that he was a Protestant unlike the Catholic James, and that his mother had secretly married Charles II. Monmouth decided to press his claim and sailed from the Netherlands to Lyme Regis in Dorset, where he landed on 11 June 1685, with only a very small force. In 1680 Monmouth had carried out a very successful tour of the West Country and so must have hoped for a warm welcome. Volunteers did arrive, but not in the numbers hoped for. It seems that this contributed to Monmouth's indecisiveness as he marched towards Bristol via Taunton. He decided not to attempt to storm Bristol and despite winning a skirmish at Norton St Philip he retreated to Bridgwater, where more hoped-for recruits failed to materialise in the numbers expected. By this time (3 July) a Royalist army was closing in, reaching Westonzoyland on 5 July, under the Earl of Feversham. Monmouth observed their arrival from the church tower of St Mary's in Bridgwater and sent out a scout for more information. On his return, Monmouth decided to gamble on a night-march and attack, rather than face a siege in Bridgwater. The Royalist army was not entrenched, although it was behind a watercourse called the Bussex Rhyne, a feature of which Monmouth must have been aware. Although post-battle drainage has altered the line of the drainage ditches in the area, we know the lie of the Bussex Rhyne, largely from aerial photography. The current ditches run straight, with the best viewing point being from the 1927 memorial beside the Langmoor Drove, which is waymarked from Westonzoyland as part of the 1985 'Pitchfork Rebellion' trail. If one stands facing away from the memorial field, the line of the Bussex Rhyne runs almost directly away into the field opposite. With this field laid down to pasture the Bussex Rhyne can be picked out, as the grass grows higher and more lushly along its course, particularly when it meets the fence at the far end of the field. Indeed, the silted-up channel can still be picked out, while excavations for the *Two Men in a Trench* television series have shown that the Rhyne was some 15m wide and in places just 1m deep. It is certainly useful to have a map which marks both the modern features and the contemporary ones. With Sedgemoor we are fortunate in having contemporary plans drawn shortly after the battle,

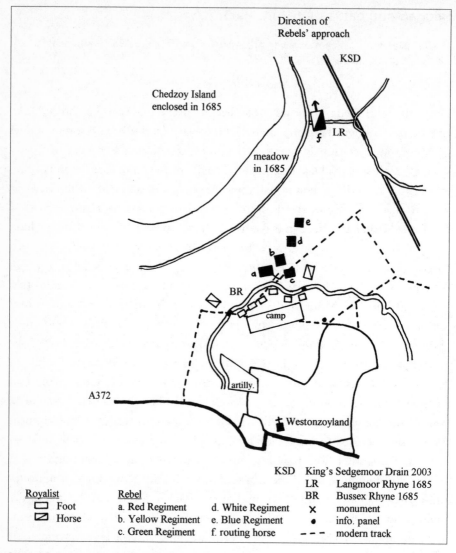

Battle of Sedgemoor, 6 July 1685 at around 3.30 a.m.

especially those by Andrew Paschall, the rector of nearby Chedzoy, and the astonishingly detailed series of three maps by Dummer.

Monmouth organised his army of 800 cavalry and approximately 2,500 foot with three serviceable cannon into a column to march out at about 11.00 p.m. on 5 July. They were to take a circuitous route, hopefully to avoid detection and the Royalist guns which were drawn up across the most obvious line of approach on the road from Bridgwater to Westonzoyland. In this they were aided not only by the dark of night, but by a thick mist on the moor. However, the Royalists had taken precautions with scouts and patrols. Moreover, Monmouth's men had to cross not only the Bussex Rhyne but also the Langmoor Rhyne, a mile further back in their march. It was while trying to find the stepping stones across the latter at around 1.00 a.m. on 6 July that Monmouth's cavalry, under the command of Grey, were detected. A cavalry trooper quickly warned the Royalist camp, with the result that their five regiments of foot (around 1,900 men) were able to take their pre-arranged positions along the Bussex Rhyne. The Royalist cavalry amounted to some 700 men including the outlying patrols and dragoons, not all of whom were present. On either flank were easy crossings of the Rhyne, called on the right the Upper Plungeon and on the left the Lower Plungeon. It was the former of these that Grey's cavalry had been ordered to make for. However, after being discovered at the Langmoor Rhyne it must have been difficult to remain clear-headed, while their passage was blocked by the timely arrival of one of the mounted scouting detachments. At this point Monmouth's chances of victory had virtually evaporated, as surprise had been lost and they had a defended obstacle to cross. Added to this was the imbalance between the morale and equipment of the two forces, with Feversham's Royalists being superior. All but one of Dumbarton's regiments had their musketeers equipped with flintlock muskets, while many of Monmouth's rebels had farm implements as weapons.

Grey took the bulk of his cavalry to his right across the front of the Royalist army, while the remainder fought with opposing cavalry at the Upper Plungeon. Grey's men passed across the front of Dumbarton's regiment unharmed, but the next unit fired upon them, causing them to flee. At this early stage of the battle Feversham was not on the field, and it appears that it was Lord

Battle of Sedgemoor, 1685.

Sedgemoor, 1685. An interesting engraving showing the Duke of York's horse guards from part of the coronation procession of Charles II in 1661. As one would expect, the uniforms are a cross between those worn during the Civil War and at Sedgemoor during the 'Pitchfork' or Monmouth's rebellion of 1686. By then the Duke of York had become King James II and the Duke of York's Troop of Horse Guards had become the third Troop of the Horse Guards.

John Churchill (later Duke of Marlborough), his second-in-command, who ordered their two left-flank regiments of foot to march behind their line to take up position on the right near the threatened Upper Plungeon. The rebels did well to bring their three cannon into play against Dumbarton's regiment, who presented a target due to the glow of their slow matches for their matchlock muskets. The rebel infantry started to arrive, first the Red Regiment, followed by the Yellow and the Green, adding their fire against Dumbarton's regiment. The re-deployment of the Royalist regiments, along with the arrival of six cannons, tipped the balance their way. With the light increasing, the gunners and musketeers could be more sure of their aim and it must have been obvious that the rebels would be unable to mount a serious attempt to cross the Rhyne, even with the arrival of their White and Blue regiments. By 3.00 a.m. Feversham could see enough to launch his cavalry across the Lower and Upper Plungeons to perform a double outflanking manoeuvre on the rebels. Despite some resistance, the rebels were beaten, especially as Monmouth had escaped with Grey and one or two others once it was clear that they could not win. Finally, the Royalist foot were ordered across the Bussex Rhyne when 'the pikes of one of their [the rebels] battalions began to shake'.

The pursuit was thorough, with many rebels being killed or taken in the ground immediately beyond the Rhyne. Many were buried in a large pit beyond the memorial and covered with sand. Some 500 prisoners were brought to Westonzoyland Church, which is well worth a visit, as is Chedzoy Church, from whose tower a good view of the battlefield can be gained so long as the key to the tower is requested in advance of a visit. Monmouth himself was captured on 8 July at Woodlands near Blandford Forum in Dorset, which still has 'Monmouth's Ash' under which he was taken. He was executed on Tower Hill in a botched execution, when his head was not severed from his body after five axe blows, the executioner Jack Ketch having to complete his grisly task with a knife. Monmouth's army suffered perhaps 1,500 killed in the battle and immediate aftermath, while the Royalists probably lost about eighty, mainly coming from Dumbarton's regiment. Judge Jeffreys was then sent into the West Country with the result that many more were executed or transported, although it is difficult to know how many of the final figure of 333 death sentences were carried out. The battle was the last large-scale action to be fought on English soil and was decisive in bringing this early threat to James II to an end.

Selby, battle of, 10 April 1644

Battle largely fought in the streets of Selby, with the Parliamentarians forcing out the Royalist defenders.

KEY REFERENCE: Baker, C.M.A. 'Selby 1644: The Key to Marston Moor, part 2' in *The Battlefields Trust Newsletter* (April, 1995).

Despite losing the battle of Adwalton Moor in 1643, Lord Ferdinando Fairfax and his son Sir Thomas continued to fight for control of Yorkshire. Selby commanded the River Ouse and important routes to and from York and Hull. The Royalist defenders under Belasyse garrisoned the town and barricaded the main access roads, with the added protection of the flooded Dam Fields outside the town. Lord Fairfax formulated a risky plan, by splitting his attacking force into three parts, making co-ordination difficult. Colonel Needham led an attack against the barricaded west end of Gowthorpe, Sir John Meldrum attacked the barricade at the east end of Brayton Lane, while the Fairfaxes moved round the town to attack Ousegate. After initial resistance, Thomas Fairfax broke into the town at Ousegate, leading to the rapid collapse of its defence. Escape was difficult, with the result that 1,600 Royalists were captured, including the wounded John Belasyse, along with large quantities of munitions. The way was then more open for the Siege of York and the much larger clash at Marston Moor later in the year. The battlefield is now largely developed within modern Selby, although the streets still mainly survive, enabling the action to be traced on the ground.

Senlac (Hill), battle of, *see* Hastings

Severn, raid of the River, 910

Raid by a fleet from Brittany up the River Severn, resulting in the deaths of most of the raiders.

Severn, raid of the River, 914

Following a similar raid in 910 another Viking fleet from Brittany pillaged northwards up the River Severn.

The Viking force was met by an army from Hereford and Gloucester and forced to retreat. Despite this, part of the fleet attacked at Porlock and near Watchet later in the year.

Sheffield Castle, siege of, 1–11 August 1644

Capture of Sheffield and its castle following the Royalist defeat at Marston Moor.

Although only fragments of the castle remain today in and below Sheffield's Castle Market it was still an imposing structure in 1644. The attacking Parliamentarians, led by Major-General Crawford, attempted to drain the castle moat, but had to wait for success until their heavy artillery arrived on 9 August. The castle then quickly fell, with the surrender being agreed on 11 August.

Shelford House, siege of, 1–3 November 1645

Storming of this large house in Nottinghamshire, protected by earthworks and a ditch, by the Parliamentarian Colonel Poyntz with 2,000 men who heavily outnumbered Sir Philip Stanhope's 200 defenders.

Sherborne, siege of, 6–12 September 1642

Early siege of the first English Civil War, which was aborted by Parliament after a spirited Royalist defence.

KEY REFERENCE: Morris, R. *The Battle of Babylon Hill, Yeovil 1642* (Stuart Press, 2000).

One of the earliest actions of the Civil War was fought out at Sherborne in Dorset. The Royalists had garrisoned the Old Castle at the beginning of

August, under the command of the Marquis of Hertford and Sir Ralph Hopton. However, the surrounding area tended to sympathise with Parliament and a force was quickly assembled for a siege, led by the Earl of Bedford. The Royalists skirmished with the advancing Parliamentarians on 6 September, despite being heavily outnumbered. Hertford contented himself with setting up camp just to the north of the town, presumably on the hill overlooking the Old Castle, with the New Castle beyond, where there are still traces of an earthwork, while the Royalists manned the streets as well as the castles. An assault was attempted on 7 September, but musketeers in the houses and gardens of the town, supported by cavalry in the streets, forced them back. At night the Royalist cavalry attacked the pickets at the Parliamentarian camp, causing confusion and a small number of casualties. An effort was made to construct a battery closer to the castle, but this was disrupted by a small counter-battery. By 12 September Bedford decided he had had enough, especially as he was facing a large number of desertions, so he withdrew to Yeovil, leading to the skirmish at Babylon Hill on 15 September.

Sherburn-in-Elmet, skirmish of, 16 December 1642

Skirmish as a result of a raid which helped to establish the reputation of Sir Thomas Fairfax.

The Parliamentarian commander Sir Thomas Fairfax carried out a raid on the local Royalist force, which was temporarily based at Sherburn-in-Elmet, near Tadcaster. Fairfax attacked across the common from the east, with about 300 horse and dragoons, brushing aside a small detachment, probably at Cross Moor Bridge. The Parliamentarians continued along the road towards the church, situated on higher ground, but came up against a manned barricade. Leading from the front, Fairfax forced a way through and the Royalists then broke. Once reserves arrived in the shape of Lord Goring with Royalist cavalry, Fairfax made an orderly withdrawal to Selby.

Sherburn-in-Elmet, skirmish of, 15 October 1645

Defeat of a demoralised Royalist force of cavalry towards the end of the First Civil War.

KEY REFERENCE: Barratt, J. 'Lord Digby's Last Ride' in *Miniature Wargames* (no. 148, September 1995).

The Royalist Lord Digby took command of some 1,500 northern horse in an attempt to reach Scotland and the Marquis of Montrose, before news came of the latter's defeat at Philliphaugh. The march continued, slipping over the River Aire at Ferrybridge, when a report arrived telling Digby that a large force of Parliamentarians was moving to intercept him from York. Digby, together with Sir Marmaduke Langdale, determined to smash their way through the small garrison of around 1,200 men at Sherburn-in-Elmet before they could be caught. This they did, capturing many of the Parliamentarian foot, although many more fled east towards Cawood. A small body of Parliamentarian horse (two troops) was also broken up to the north of Sherburn. However, the Royalists lingered in and around the town, with their forces scattered. This enabled a Parliamentarian pursuing force under Colonel Copley to catch the Royalists, bringing them to battle just to the south of Sherburn. The fight was confused, but led to Digby being routed through the town, despite Langdale fighting bravely. The remnants of the Royalist force regrouped and continued to march north, reaching Scotland five days later.

Sherston, battle of, 1016

Bloody battle, apparently lasting two days, between King Edmund 'Ironside' and the Danes, possibly led by Cnut (Canute) with the latter breaking off the fight and retreating to besiege London.

Shirburn Castle (or House), siege of, May 1646

Fall of this fortified manor house, which had stood for the Royalists throughout the First Civil War after a brief siege, to forces led by Sir Thomas Fairfax.

Shrawardine Castle, siege of, October 1644–29 June 1645

Capture of this Shropshire castle by Sir Thomas Mytton for Parliament.

Sir William Vaughan known as 'the Devil of Shrawardine' for his successful raids against Parliamentarians in Shropshire held this castle for King Charles I, until he was captured in October 1644, when he and some of his men were surprised at the local church. The Parliamentarians then besieged the castle with it surrendering in June 1645. Very little survives of the castle today.

Shrewsbury, battle of, 21 July 1403

Battle seen as the classic victory of the longbow, in addition to having
Shakespearean connections with King Henry IV and Prince Hal defeating 'Hotspur'.
KEY REFERENCE: English Heritage *Battlefield Report: Shrewsbury 1403* (English Heritage,
London, 1995).

The battlefield at Shrewsbury is easy to locate, with the Battlefield Church
having been built on the site, and the later settlement which is now the suburb
of 'Battlefield' to the north of the town spreading onto the fringes of the area
its name commemorates. In addition, a battlefield viewing platform looks
towards the church from the south, beside the recently built bypass link-road,

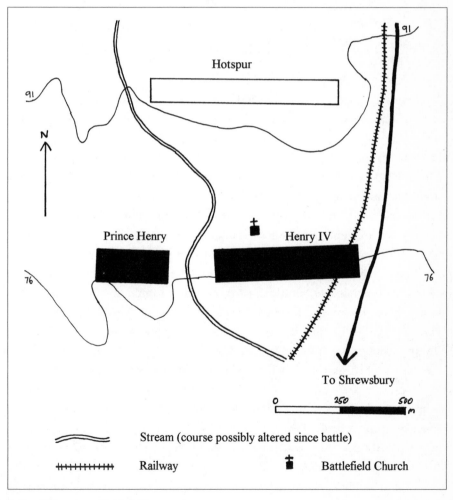

Battle of Shrewsbury, 21 July 1403.

Battle of Shrewsbury, 1403, taken from the 'pictorial life' of Richard Beauchamp, Earl of Warwick, who died in 1439. Although attention is drawn to the mounted knights and men-at-arms, the importance of the longbow-armed archers is also clear. The brutality of early fifteenth-century warfare is demonstrated in the centre foreground, where dismounted men-at-arms 'finish off' a helpless opponent.

along with a signed trail, constructed in time for the 600th anniversary of the battle in 2003. Despite this, there has been some dispute over the exact position of the battlefield and the two opposing armies, although research suggests that the picture is now clear.

The Percy family, as the most important in the North, had been key supporters of Henry Bolingbroke when he had taken the throne in 1399, becoming King Henry IV. Moreover, they had long fought against the Scots, recently commanding the English army which was defeated at Otterburn in 1388 and turning the tables on the Scots at Homildon Hill in 1402. However, the Percys embarked on rebellion, stung by Henry's insistence on taking over custody of the valuable Scottish prisoners from Homildon Hill, along with a royal refusal to arrange for the release of Edmund Mortimer (Sir Henry 'Hotspur' Percy's brother-in-law), who was the prisoner of the Welsh leader Owain Glyndwr.

Henry IV had started to march north to help the Percys against the Scots, but on his way he received news of Hotspur marching to Cheshire in rebellion, to link up with his new ally Glyndwr. Accordingly, Henry IV turned west to bring Hotspur to battle. This aim became all the more urgent once it became clear that Hotspur was advancing on Shrewsbury, which was garrisoned by Prince Henry (later Henry V). Henry IV moved with great speed, reaching his son in Shrewsbury before Hotspur. Moreover, the latter was now at a disadvantage, as he was separated from potential reinforcements led by

Glyndwr by the River Severn, leaving the two Henrys with the opportunity to defeat Hotspur on his own. This was a chance they did not turn down, advancing out of Shrewsbury on the morning of 21 July to bring Hotspur to battle.

Henry's combined force probably numbered around 14,000, while Hotspur was certainly outnumbered, with perhaps 10,000. Both armies possessed large numbers of archers equipped with the longbow, leading to Shrewsbury becoming the first English battle to witness longbow versus longbow. Hotspur had drawn his army up on the low ridge just to the north of the current Battlefield Church, while Henry IV advanced from the south. The ground in 1403 would have been open, rather than enclosed as it is today, with the battlefield probably extending just to the east of the current railway. After a failed attempt at negotiations to prevent fighting, Hotspur opened the battle, ordering his archers to fire down the slope, while Henry's bowmen did likewise. The king's men fell 'as fast as leaves fall in autumn after the hoar-frost' (the *Annals of Henry IV*), with Prince Henry receiving a wound to the face, while Hotspur's army also suffered. Moving forward in the confusion, Hotspur and the Earl of Douglas (who had fought against Hotspur the previous year)

The death of Sir Henry 'Hotspur' Percy at the Battle of Shrewsbury in 1403. Notice elements of an 'arrow storm', an important feature of the battle.

charged downhill towards the king's standard, no doubt realising that they had to win by such a bold stroke before numbers told against themselves. It is possible that Henry himself was not easy to detect, as Adam of Usk's chronicle tells us that decoys had been dressed as the king. Whatever the truth of this, in the mêlée the king's standard-bearer was killed, while Hotspur also fell and Douglas was captured. Rebel resistance then ended, with many being cut down or taken prisoner. Their defeat was hastened by the actions of Prince Henry's division, which appears to have been to King Henry's left. Finding few opponents to their front once Hotspur and Douglas advanced down the slope (possibly due to a stream forcing the rebels to incline to their left), Prince Henry, despite his wound, swung his men round to their right, thus outflanking Hotspur's right. This must have made escape difficult for the men involved in the mêlée, leading to the large number of casualties and prisoners, including Thomas Percy, Hotspur's uncle, who was beheaded in Shrewsbury after the battle and his head then displayed on London Bridge. The king also lost many men, both from the arrow storm and during the mêlée, with probably some 2,000–3,000 casualties on each side. The density of the fighting at the foot of 'Hotspur's Ridge' can be seen from the mass of metal artefacts found in that area by metal-detector surveys for the television series *Two Men in a Trench*. These included buckles, spurs and bodkin-headed arrows, which helps to confirm that the battle was fought to the north of Battlefield Church. Certainly the longbow had made its bloody mark on the battlefield, with Prince Henry in particular learning much from these events, which he was to put to good use twelve years later at Agincourt.

Shrewsbury, siege of, 22 February 1645

Capture from a surprise attack of this depleted Royalist garrison.

Earlier in February 1645 the Royalists had weakened the garrison of Shrewsbury to strengthen their field army. This did not pass unnoticed by the local Parliamentarians who planned an attack. This was carried out in the early hours of 22 February when a party of carpenters in a boat started to saw their way through a palisade by the castle. It is possible that they were detected but not stopped due to treachery, or perhaps it was simply that darkness hid their activities. A small party led by Captain Benbow went through the breach and probably opened the nearby north gate to allow in a larger force under Reinking, who proceeded to secure the town for Parliament.

Skipton Castle, siege of, July 1644–21 December 1645

Held since the beginning of the First Civil War for King Charles I, Skipton Castle (now privately owned but open to the public all year) survived a long siege, until finally surrendering on terms after suffering some damage due to artillery fire and running very low on supplies.

Skipton Moor, battle of, 29 May 1405

'Battle' near York, in which King Henry IV's forces led by the Earl of Westmorland defeated the Archbishop of York, Richard Scrope and Thomas Mowbray, who had a force largely made up of men from York, by agreeing to a parley and then having the rebel leaders arrested.

Slapton Sands, encounter of, 28 April 1944

The most costly exercise in Britain during the Second World War.

KEY REFERENCE: Small, K. *The Forgotten Dead: Why 946 American Servicemen Died Off the Coast of Devon in 1944* (Bloomsbury, 1988).

As part of the training for D-Day, American ground forces and British and American naval forces were involved in Exercise Tiger as a simulation of the landing which would take place at Utah Beach in Normandy. The main 'attacking' force landed on Slapton Sands in South Devon on 27 April, with a second wave due to arrive early on 28 April. This force consisted of eight large LSTs (landing ship tanks), five from Plymouth and three from Brixham, plus HMS *Azalea* as an escort (which suffered damage from a collision and had to return to port before a replacement could arrive), along with a widely spread protective net of warships which would hopefully stop any German raiders. However, a force of nine German E-boats from Cherbourg evaded the naval defences and got among the convoy, sinking two of the LSTs with torpedoes and damaging the others, at a cost of 749 allied deaths. A memorial to the local population who had been displaced was unveiled at Slapton Sands on 6 June 1954 by the US Army, although no mention was made of the casualties. To help redress this, a salvaged Sherman tank from an earlier training accident was erected as a memorial to the dead in 1984.

Sole Bay, battle of, 28 May 1672

Naval battle off Southwold in Suffolk, marking the beginning of the Third Anglo-Dutch War.

KEY REFERENCE: Haswell, J. *James II* (Hamish Hamilton, 1972).

Following the victory off Lowestoft in the previous Anglo–Dutch War, James, Duke of York (later King James II) took up command of England's fleet at the outset of the Third Anglo–Dutch War in March 1672. In this England was aided by France, with whom a treaty had been signed, promising naval aid. However, before the allied fleets could combine, news arrived of de Ruyter's Dutch fleet, forcing James to sail to attempt to intercept him. This failed, but the Dutch withdrew, enabling James to link up with d'Estrées' French squadron. After much manoeuvring throughout May, the Dutch moved to attack James in Sole (Southwold) Bay off the Suffolk coast. James was re-supplying when de Ruyter moved in with the advantage of the wind. James was caught on a lee shore, with little chance to escape as the Dutch moved in shortly after dawn on 28 May. The action commenced at 7.00 a.m. with the Dutch using fireships as well as the tactics of broadsides and boarding. During the morning, while the allies were still out of formation, James commanding the Red Squadron and the Earl of Sandwich commanding the Blue Squadron had a severe fight on their hands. Sandwich, in his 100-gun ship *Royal James* fought against the ninety-gun *Great Holland* while at the same time sinking three approaching fireships. Just after this fight was won, *Royal James* was caught by a further fireship, which burnt and sank the English ship, with Sandwich being drowned. Meanwhile, another Dutch squadron had engaged the French slightly to the south-east, with the French being criticised for not coming to aid the English. This seems unwarranted, as they were also in action, although rumours circulated that d'Estrées had been given orders to let the Dutch and English batter each other without endangering his own ships. However, this may well be a case of traditional Anglo–French suspicion and should therefore be discounted as a genuine factor. By 7.00 p.m., when the firing died away, the English had lost five ships and the Dutch four. Despite the Dutch having the tactical advantage, this was not really pressed home, with the result being a minor victory for de Ruyter, although James' fleet had certainly taken more damage. The artist William van de Velde the elder was present with the Dutch fleet and made a number of sketches during the battle. The battle is commemorated not least by the Southwold-based Adnams' Sole Bay Brewery and their 'Broadside' ale, which was first brewed for the tercentenary of the battle.

All-action Dutch print of the battle of Sole Bay in 1672 at the start of the Third Anglo-Dutch War. Although a confused action, the fleets would have been more dispersed than shown here.

Solway Moss, battle of, 24 November 1542

Fought just south of the Anglo-Scottish border as a result of a major raid by King James V of Scotland.

KEY REFERENCE: English Heritage: *Battlefield Report: Solway Moss 1542* (English Heritage, London, 1995).

Despite the crushing defeat at Flodden in 1513, fought largely as a result of James IV's alliance with France, the links between Scotland and France continued into the reign of James V. By 1542 Henry VIII, who had been king of England when Flodden was fought felt obliged to move against the Scots, partly due to this policy. In retaliation for a raid led by the Duke of Norfolk James V raised a force to invade the north-west of England, despite significant problems in persuading the Scottish nobility to participate. On 24 November 1542 they crossed the border and moved south, to be met later the same day by an English force led by Sir Thomas Wharton.

We are fortunate to have a thorough account of the battle written by the English commander, from which it is relatively easy to follow the course of the battle. It seems that the Scots, without James in person, had intended to burn and raid rather than to fight a set-piece battle. As they crossed the River Esk and fired buildings, the English approaching from Carlisle saw the smoke. As a result, 'prickers' (mounted skirmishers with spears) moved forward from the

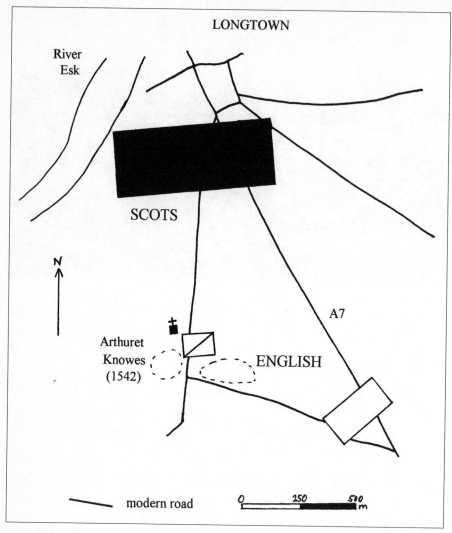

Battle of Solway Moss, 24 November 1542.

English force of 3,000 to harry the Scots, probably at around 9.00 a.m. They had some success, but weight of enemy numbers (the Scots' army had perhaps 14,000 men) drove them back towards the Arthuret Knowes. These were two outlying hillocks to the south of Longtown, either side of the modern minor road, which turns back to join the A7 as it enters the wood on Hopesike Hill. Only the eastern of these two mounds remains, as the other was removed for sand in the 1950s. It is almost certain that the road in 1542 followed the course of this minor road, as the A7's route across this part of the country was first laid out in the nineteenth century.

The main English force had deployed on Hopesike Hill, and it appears that once the advancing Scots caught sight of them, the latter panicked and started to retreat, possibly thinking that they were in fact part of the much larger army of the Duke of Norfolk. Lack of a clear commander must have caused further confusion as the English sent forward their cavalry once again. They turned the retreat into a rout, with many of the Scots being trapped against the River Esk, with the battle being over by noon. The English foot played little part in the fighting, but advanced as far as the Arthuret Knowes, where they witnessed the chaos before them. Many prisoners were taken, as well as a reported 5,000 horses and much ordnance, including 'twenty carted pieces'.

The battlefield is now largely arable farmland, with woodland covering the surviving Arthuret Knowe and Hopesike Hill. The visitor has to be careful not to be distracted by the line and noise of the A7, with the battle best being followed from the minor road leading beside the Arthuret Knowe. Solway Moss is on the north side of the Esk. Presumably those who managed to cross the river attempted to seek shelter in the boggy ground and to escape the pursuit.

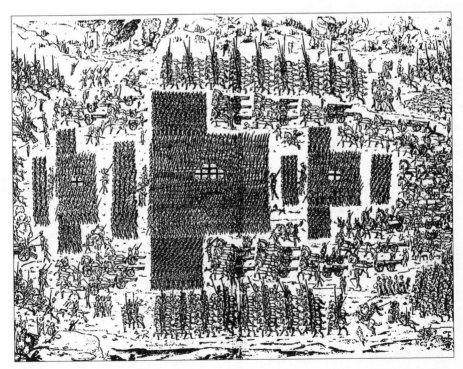

An English army on the march. The 3,000-strong force sent forward to encounter the Scots at the Battle of Solway Moss fought in 1542 would not have contained as much artillery as shown here. Note the solid central block of pikemen with smaller blocks of musketeers to either flank. This basic organisation remained for over a hundred years more, with just the proportions of pikes to muskets changing in the musketeer's favour.

The battle was an embarrassing defeat for the large Scottish army and possibly contributed to King James V's death in December.

Somerton, battle of, 733

Aethelbald, King of Mercia, took Somerton in Somerset as a result of this battle.

Sourton Down, skirmish of, 25–26 April 1643

Bold night-time skirmish in which 108 Parliamentarian horse caused havoc among the Royalist Cornish army of around 3,500.

KEY REFERENCE: Peachey, S. *The Battles of Launceston and Sourton Down 1643* (Stuart Press, 1993).

Following their success at the Battle of Launceston on 23 April, the Royalists under Sir Ralph Hopton advanced into Devon. News of this reached the Parliamentarian James Chudleigh in Okehampton shortly after 9.00 p.m. on a very stormy night. He quickly ordered out 108 horse in six troops to lie in ambush on the slope above the road being taken by the 3,500 Royalists. Once the Royalists had drawn level, the Parliamentarians fired a volley of carbines and then charged down the hill crying 'fall on, fall on, they run, they run'. Led by Captain Drake wielding a battleaxe, they swept through the column, causing the front of it to break. However, Hopton managed to rally the remainder, making use of an ancient ditch, and brought his four pieces of artillery together. Chudleigh had sent for his musketeers from Okehampton, but as they advanced Hopton's guns fired two shots on seeing their lighted matches in the dark. This was enough to cause them to panic and flee. Chudleigh acted quickly, gathering up the lighted matches and draping them on gorse bushes. This seems to have convinced the Royalists to retire back to Launceston, fearing a large enemy force in the dark. Despite there being few casualties, the Royalists were forced back into Cornwall, which in turn encouraged the Parliamentarians to advance in May, leading to the Battle of Stratton.

Southampton, battle of, 840

Rare English success against a raiding force of thirty-three Viking ships, with Earl Wulfheard gaining the victory.

Southampton, raid of, 980 or 981

Attack by a sea-borne Viking force of seven ships, which killed or captured most of the inhabitants of Southampton.

Southwark, battle of, November 1066

Aborted attempt by Duke William of Normandy to cross the River Thames at London Bridge, after resistance from English forces supporting Edgar the Aetheling forced the Norman army to swing to the west before crossing at Wallingford and after firing the suburb of Southwark.

Southwark, battle of, 3 July 1450

Jack Cade, leader of a force of Kentish rebels, fought his way through Southwark and into London, although he then lost a further fight on London Bridge, forcing him to flee back into Kent, where he was captured and then executed.

Victorian political cartoon calling upon the memory of Cade's rebellion from 1450 (see Southwark, 1450). Historical accuracy is not the aim, but it is interesting to note that there must have been awareness of this now largely forgotten episode of English history.

Stainmore, battle of, 954

Poorly documented battle in the kingdom of Northumbria, above Edendale, at
which the Viking King Eric 'Bloodaxe' was defeated and killed by Earl Maccus,
with his kingdom being taken over by the English King Eadred of Wessex.

Stamford Bridge, battle of, 25 September 1066

The second of the 'three battles of 1066', Stamford Bridge saw rapid revenge for
the English defeat at Fulford Gate, but sapped too much of King Harold's army's
strength before the conclusive Battle of Hastings.

KEY REFERENCE: Cooke, D. *'Seven Feet of Ground': The Battles of Gate Fulford and Stamford
Bridge, September 1066* (Battlefield Press, 1998).

While primarily concerned with meeting the expected invasion from
Normandy through the summer of 1066, King Harold was also concerned with
a possible threat from across the North Sea. This threat duly materialised with the
appearance of a fleet of 300 ships led by Harald Hardrada of Norway in the
North, which forced Harold to march north to face the threat, knowing that the
armies of the northern earls, Morcar and Edwin, may not have been strong
enough to repel an army of up to 12,000, although this number is probably
exaggerated. Further complications arose when Harold's brother Tostig, whose
position as Earl of Northumberland had been taken from him in 1065, allied with
Harald Hardrada in Scotland. The combined fleet sailed south to the Humber
estuary and then on to York. They landed at Riccal on the east bank of the Ouse
before beginning the nine-mile march to York. The brothers Morcar and Edwin
met them with a smaller army and were heavily defeated at the battle of Fulford
Gate on 20 September. At that stage Hardrada did not garrison York, instead
taking hostages and withdrawing to Stamford Bridge to the east, sending a
detachment of perhaps 1,000 back to Riccal to guard the fleet.

Despite this caution and perhaps over-confidence, Hardrada was caught by
surprise due to the rapid advance of Harold from the south and through York
without pause. Harold's army had marched from Tadcaster on 25 September,
suggesting that it must have been the afternoon by the time they reached
Stamford Bridge. Hardrada and Tostig must have been dismayed to see the large
dust cloud stirred up by the approaching army, seeing it as a sign that they were
to be attacked shortly. Messengers were dispatched to Riccal to summon
reinforcements, while foragers were called in and armour put on. It seems that
they deployed the bulk of their available forces (possibly around 5,000 men in

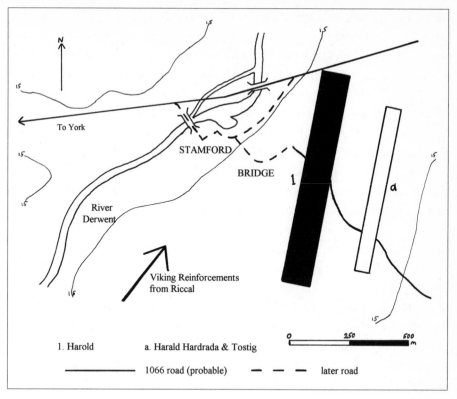

total) along the top of the low scarp to the east of Stamford Bridge, with a smaller detachment guarding the river crossing, although it is possible that the majority were at the river from the start.

The modern crossing is slightly downstream from the bridge of 1066, with the course of the river having being altered due to time and the construction of a large mill. It is likely that the bridge stood where the Roman road would have met the river bank, which could well have been where the current weir is now. The English of Harold's army forced their way across, possibly fording the river as well as fighting their way over the bridge, which according to one, probably romanticised, source was defended by a lone Norwegian until he was speared from below. Whatever the details of the crossing, it is clear that the main fighting took place once the English were across the river. Hardrada had for this second phase of the battle all his available troops formed up on what became known as Battle Flat, up the slope from the river. The main source for the battle is the thirteenth-century Icelandic *Heimskringla* of Snorri Sturlasson, which appears to give more details about warfare of that period than of 1066. However, certain details emerge which are probably correct. Namely, that the English (possibly around 8,000 strong) launched a charge against Hardrada's outnumbered forces, which was held until Hardrada fell from a wound in the throat which killed him. Tostig rallied the army around Hardrada's 'Landwaster' standard, rejecting an offer of a truce. The battle continued with fierce fighting until Tostig too was killed. At that point, too little too late, the Norwegian reinforcements arrived from Riccal, although they fought bravely, some of them without armour, as they had discarded their mail coats due to the heat and the efforts of the forced march. This furious counter-attack was held and turned back, with a rout occurring right back to the ships. The next day a truce was arranged and the Norwegians were allowed to sail home, but they needed only 20–24 ships of their original 300 to carry all their men. No doubt these figures overplay the scale of the victory, but it was certainly decisive and allowed Harold to turn south to fight a new invader. The brutality of warfare of the period is clear from a number of skeletons (possibly from a total of 600, although only around sixty have been recovered) from Riccal. Many of these have evidence of multiple wounds on the bones, including one with a sword point on the inside of the sacrum, indicating a thrust from the front, rupturing internal organs before stopping up against the bottom of the spine. Analysis of the oxygen isotopes in the teeth of these skeletons has enabled scientists to make a geographical plot of the areas inhabited by these people when they were infants, due to the unique signatures from the rainwater they were exposed to (as explained by Julian Richards in the book and television series *Blood of the Vikings*). This evidence clearly suggests that the Riccal skeletons were men from Scandinavia, and probably Norway, showing that they were casualties from the Battle of Stamford Bridge or its immediate aftermath.

The battlefield is now entirely built over, with encroachment and finally total coverage of Battle Flat taking place up to the late 1990s. There is a memorial in the centre of the village, along with a mural on the outside wall of the public conveniences.

Stamford Bridge, battle of, 31 October or 1 November 1454

Part of the long-running dispute between the Neville and Percy families, which spilled into the War of the Roses.

Following their altercation at Heworth Moor in 1453, the Nevilles and Percys continued to feud. At Stamford Bridge to the east of York, it appears that Lord Egremont (a Percy) clashed with Sir Thomas Neville and Sir John Neville. Part of Egremont's force fled, leading to the capture of Egremont and his brother,

Richard Percy. It is possible, although unlikely, that this action and that at Heworth Moor are one and the same.

Stamford Castle, siege of, 1153

Last of the three main sieges of Henry of Anjou's (later Henry II) campaign of 1153 against King Stephen.

After his limited success at Malmesbury and Crowmarsh, Henry of Anjou moved north to besiege Stamford. He took the town, but the castle continued to resist. A message was sent to Stephen asking for help, but he was too busy besieging Hugh Bigod in Ipswich Castle. When no help came the castle surrendered to Henry.

Standard, battle of the, *see* Northallerton

Stockbridge, battle of, September 1141

Fought during the rout of Winchester, as the Empress Matilda's force escaped from their Royalist besiegers.

KEY REFERENCE: Bradbury, J. *Stephen and Matilda, the Civil War of 1139–53* (Alan Sutton, 1996).

Earl Robert of Gloucester had helped Matilda in her escape from the besieged town of Winchester. He then led the rear-guard of her army as they continued to flee to safety. This force was caught at Stockbridge, some 12km to the west of Winchester, on the road to Salisbury, by troops led by William of Ypres. Most ran, but some were cut off and killed or captured, the latter fate befalling Earl Robert. This defeat for Matilda led to the Treaty of Winchester, signed in October 1141, which agreed to an exchange of prisoners, including the release of King Stephen on the Royalist side and Earl Robert on the Empress Matilda's side.

Stoke (Field), battle of, 16 June 1487

Final act of the Wars of the Roses, where the Tudor army defeated the forces fighting for the Yorkist Pretender Lambert Simnel.

KEY REFERENCE: English Heritage: *Battlefield Report: Stoke 1487* (English Heritage, London, 1995).

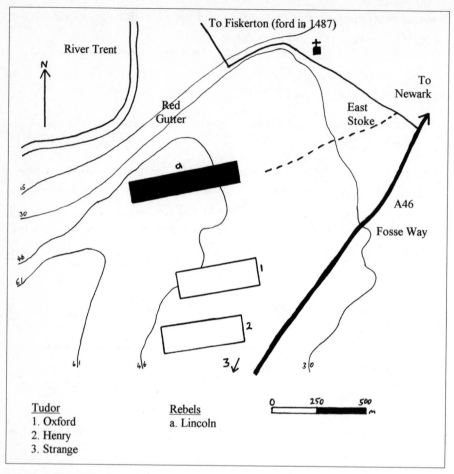

To Fiskerton (ford in 1487)

River Trent

N

Red
Gutter

East
Stoke

To
Newark

A46

Fosse Way

Tudor
1. Oxford
2. Henry
3. Strange

Rebels
a. Lincoln

0   250   500
                m

Battle of Stoke Field, 16 June 1487.

This battle was fought as a result of a determined Yorkist rising against the recently crowned King Henry VII. Yorkist support was rallied around Lambert Simnel, an impostor of Edward, Earl of Warwick, who the Yorkists proclaimed as King Edward VI, despite the fact that the real fifteen-year-old earl had been imprisoned in the Tower of London by Henry VII. The rebels' leaders were the Earl of Lincoln and Lord Lovell, who had brought troops from Ireland along with a force of German mercenaries. Altogether it seems the rebels had about 8,000 men by the time they formed up for battle on the then unenclosed land along the crest of the hill to the south-west of the current village of East Stoke, three miles to the south-west of Newark along the Fosse Way. It is likely that they had forded the River Trent at Fiskerton, choosing the best defensive position available from which to face the larger army of Henry, consisting of perhaps 12,000 men.

As at Bosworth, the Earl of Oxford commanded Henry's vanguard, with Henry and the main 'battle' (or division) and Lord Strange with the rear 'battle' lagging behind as they advanced from their overnight camp at Radcliffe. Although Polydore Vergil's account has Tudor moving south-west down the Fosse Way from Newark on the day of the battle, this has to be taken as an error, as the main and probably only eye-witness account of the battle has them advancing from the south-west to the north-east. On observing the rebels to the left of the road just before 9.00 a.m., Oxford swung his troops into line to face them, with cavalry on each wing of his 'battle' with Lord Scales on the right and Sir John Savage on the left, while he remained in the centre with his infantry. The Earl of Lincoln's rebel force also seems to have been in the usual three 'battles', one of English troops, one of the German mercenaries under Martin Schwarz and one of Irish troops with no armour. Probably because the rebels could see a gap between Oxford's vanguard and the rest of the army, Lincoln decided to give up the advantage of his uphill position and launched an attack against Tudor's vanguard. This had mixed success, with the mercenaries inflicting heavy casualties on Oxford's men, but with the Irish suffering badly from archery as they came down the hill. It seems likely that Oxford's foot bore the brunt of this early fighting, as we are told that a charge by his men then turned the tide. This could well have been by the cavalry of Scales and Savage, who would have been able to manoeuvre to an advantageous position once the foot were engaged. Whatever the true details of this mêlée, the result was that the rebels were forced back, seemingly without the need for Henry's other two 'battles' entering the fray. The fighting quickly turned to slaughter as the rebels broke off the hill towards the River Trent and the crossing at Fiskerton. It is likely that the feature still known as 'Red Gutter', leading off the hill now in private woodland, gained its name during the bloody pursuit.

Simnel was captured, and according to Vergil benefited from the king's mercy by being set to work as a turnspit in the royal kitchen, before being promoted to 'trainer of the king's hawks'. This engagement made the throne secure for Henry, who did not have to fight another battle.

The battlefield is largely unspoilt, although is now all fields and woodland. Public footpaths allow access to the main areas of fighting, including one which leads from East Stoke up to the lower slopes of the rebels' hill. Indeed, one can stand at the point where the main clash probably occurred. Unfortunately, there is no access to the Burrand Bush memorial, which is usually hidden by crops, or to 'Red Gutter'. There is a recent memorial to the dead of both sides just outside the church at East Stoke, which lists the notable casualties as well as commemorating the 7,000 English, Irish and German dead.

Stow (-on-the-Wold), battle of, 21 March 1646

Defeat of King Charles I's last field army in the last battle of the First Civil War.

KEY REFERENCE: English Heritage: *Battlefield Report: Stow 1646* (English Heritage, London, 1995).

King Charles I was becoming increasingly desperate by the early spring of 1646, especially once news of the defeat of Hopton's army at Torrington reached him. He clung to the hope that help would materialise from Ireland, Scotland, France or even from the Pope, but in reality there was little left for him, except to call upon Lord Astley to attempt to join him at Oxford from Worcestershire where he commanded some 1,000 horse and 2,000 foot. Astley reached the vicinity of Stow in the evening of 20 March after dark, pausing on a hill at some point in the night probably just to the west of the village of Donnington (although some favour one of the hills to the south of the village, between Donnington and Stow), a mile to the north of Stow. By that time the local force of around 2,300 under Colonel Morgan had been joined by the Parliamentarian commander from Cheshire Sir William Brereton with up to 1,000 horse, and they manoeuvred into position just to the north of Astley by first light at 5.00 a.m. on 21 March. The immediate surroundings would have been largely open fields or sheep pasture, providing good ground for cavalry, although the slopes leading to Astley's position were steep. The fight was a fairly straightforward affair, with the Parliamentarians attacking uphill. On the Parliamentarian left the Royalists pushed some of the Parliamentarian foot back down the slope, but on the right Brereton led a successful charge with his horse, accompanied by 'at least 200 firelocks', according to one of Brereton's troopers. The hill was a steep one to assault, with a false crest part the way up before the final climb. The slopes are now partially obscured by areas of woodland, which would almost certainly not have existed in 1646. Brereton's men chased the Royalist horse from the field, back towards Stow, leaving the foot in a difficult situation. They too were forced back into Stow, possibly after making a second stand at some point. An hour after the fight had begun, the battle had ended with most of the foot having been captured, although some must have carried on fighting in Stow if stories about Digbeth Street running with Royalist blood are to be believed. St Edward's Church was certainly used as a temporary prison after the battle. The battle's end was marked by a poignant moment as the defeated Royalist commander Lord Astley sat on an upturned drum and uttered these prophetic words: 'You have done your work, boys, and may go play, unless you will fall out among yourselves.'

Stratton, battle of, 16 May 1643

Impressive Royalist victory against the odds during the First Civil War.

KEY REFERENCE: English Heritage: *Battlefield Report: Stratton 1643* (English Heritage, London, 1995).

The see-saw campaign in Devon and Cornwall had started to tilt in the Royalist Sir Ralph Hopton's favour as he moved to lead his army across Devon to link up with other Royalist forces in the West Country. The Parliamentarian commander the Earl of Stamford learned of this move and went to block Hopton at Stratton in north-east Cornwall, arriving in the town on 15 May. Stamford occupied a prominent hill just to the north of Stratton, which since the battle has borne his name, thus giving no doubt as to where the battle was fought. Hopton, despite being heavily outnumbered, decided to attack Stamford, as he knew his enemy would only get stronger as Stamford had detached nearly all his horse to Bodmin, while Hopton's own men were short of supplies. Therefore, on the evening of 15 May, Hopton brushed aside Stamford's outposts at Efford Mill just to the south-west of Bude and moved into Stratton itself, using the Tree Inn as his headquarters. The following night must have been extremely tense as the two forces were only a short distance apart. Hopton had ordered the majority of his men into enclosures ringing Stamford's hill from the south and around the west side to the north, leaving only the east side clear due to the steepness of its slope.

Hopton decided to gamble further by dividing his already outnumbered attacking force into four columns of foot, while leaving his 500 horse and dragoons under Digby as a reserve, placed on a 'Sandy-Common' according to Hopton's own account. This would be towards Bude, where the golf course now lies, although the common may well have extended closer to Stamford Hill in 1643 than it does today. Hopton had only 600 men in each column, with two cannon per group, while Stamford had well over 5,000 men and fourteen pieces of artillery on a steep hill, defended by Cornish banked hedges and with the added protection of a prehistoric circular earthwork at the summit. Hopton was aided by the fact that there were four or five separate lanes leading up the hill, with each lane providing cover from the high hedges on either side. The enclosure walls would have given further protection to defender and attacker alike, and may have helped to deceive Stamford as to the true strength of his opponents.

Presumably, each column put its pikemen on the lane itself, with musketeers to either side in the enclosures. From dawn at 5.00 a.m., fighting broke out as the early light revealed opposing musketeers only about 40m apart. Hopton

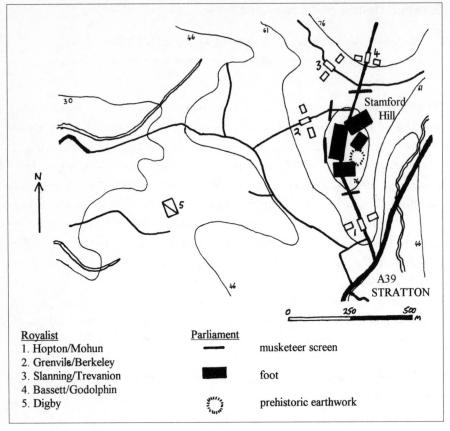

Battle of Stratton, 16 May 1643.

and Lord Mohun led the column from Stratton in the south. There was then a gap before the next column in a clockwise direction, under Grenville and Berkeley, then the third led by Slanning and Trevanion and the fourth under Bassett and Godolphin. The attacks began soon after dawn and fighting continued until around 3.00 p.m., with no breakthrough being achieved. The nature of the ground with its high-walled, banked and hedged enclosures and lanes must have made it difficult to close to hand-to-hand fighting, while casualties from musketry would have been light. The turning point came when James Chudleigh led a force of Parliamentarian pikemen against Grenville's pikemen in the second column. The Parliamentarians made some headway, even knocking Grenville to the ground, but Berkeley, with his musketeers to either side, threw the Parliamentarians back up the hill and captured Chudleigh. Shortly after this all four columns converged near the summit, probably just to the north, where they were able to re-form and launch a final combined assault. It is quite possible that most of the Parliamentarian guns were unable to fire due to the dense formations of their own foot screening the Royalists. The exact course of the final attack is not clear, and one Parliamentarian account puts this down to the arrival of the Royalist horse who had already routed Stamford's few horse, although it is difficult to imagine horse operating effectively in the overcrowded environment on the hill. It is clear that the end came quickly, with the capture of thirteen cannon, one mortar and 1,700 men, with the Parliamentarians losing possibly 300 dead. The detached horse retreated into Devon, while Hopton was able to re-supply his men with captured provisions and munitions to march on and fight later in the year at Lansdown and Roundway Down. Most importantly the revenue and material from the Cornish tin industry remained with King Charles I, as the Parliamentarian threat to the county had been removed.

The battlefield today has suffered from some development on Stamford Hill's southern slopes, but the summit and nature of the enclosures and lanes are easy to appreciate. Interpretation panels can be found on the hill, while a leaflet with a marked trail is available locally. At the summit the earthwork still stands, with a monument to the battle inserted into its bank on the western side.

Sudeley Castle, siege of, 27–28 January 1643

Good example of a well-planned and executed capture of a Civil War stronghold, albeit with a strongly superior attacking force.

KEY REFERENCE: Morris, R. *The Storming of Sudeley Castle 1643* (Stuart Press, 1999).

Sudeley Castle in Gloucestershire was held by the Royalists at the beginning of the First Civil War, with Captain Bridges and just under sixty men as its garrison. In late January 1643 a Parliamentarian force of around 400 horse and dragoons from Cirencester (later reinforced by 200 musketeers and one gun), along with 300 musketeers, two guns and eighty horse from Gloucester, were sent to capture the stronghold. This attempt began on the evening of 27 January, when the Parliamentarian artillery opened fire. A first summons to surrender was rejected, so during the night the Parliamentarians surrounded the castle and formed up for an assault. They advanced, rolling bundles of wool in front of them to protect themselves from enemy fire, while their horse rode up and set fire to hay to provide further cover. During this phase the Parliamentarian guns were brought forward, leading to a Royalist surrender on terms. The castle was then garrisoned for Parliament by Lieutenant Colonel Forbes. Following the fall of Cirencester to the Royalists led by Prince Rupert on 2 February, Sudeley was abandoned by Forbes, to be re-garrisoned by the Royalists until its surrender to Waller's overwhelming forces on 9 June 1644 during the Oxford or Cropredy Bridge campaign.

T

Tadcaster, battle of, 7 December 1642

Bungled Royalist attack on a weaker Parliamentarian force during the First Civil War.

The Royalist Earl of Newcastle advanced through York and onto the Parliamentarian force under Lord Ferdinando Fairfax, who was awaiting him at Tadcaster. Fairfax positioned his force on the east side of the River Wharfe, covered by artillery, while Newcastle moved to attack with a greatly superior force of foot – probably around 4,000 to 1,000. Newcastle sent his horse to Wetherby to cross the Wharfe there, before moving to cut off Fairfax from the rear. However, this outflanking force failed to arrive, and the fighting went on from 11.00 a.m. until dark at Tadcaster, with the Parliamentarians just holding their ground. During the night, Fairfax withdrew to Selby, realising that he was doomed if he stayed at Tadcaster.

Tamworth, siege of, 943

The Viking Olaf from Ireland raided Tamworth, winning the battle and capturing the Mercian noblewoman Wulfrun.

Tavistock, raid of, 997

Conclusion of the Viking raid of that year which had earlier focused on Watchet and Lydford, culminating with the destruction of Tavistock Abbey.

Temple Bar, skirmish of, 7 February 1554

Skirmish in London which saw the end of Wyatt's rebellion against Mary I.

Sir Thomas Wyatt staged a rebellion largely against the proposed marriage of Queen Mary I to Philip of Spain. Despite a set-back for some of his supporters at Wrotham Hill, Wyatt took Cooling Castle in Kent before moving on London. Wyatt found the gates of London closed to his force of some 3,000 men. His force quickly dissolved, leaving only around 300 men with him when fighting broke out at Temple Bar. A force of Royalist cavalry broke up Wyatt's remaining force, killing around forty and capturing many more, including Wyatt, who was executed on 11 April.

Tempsford, battle of, 917

The English, fresh from their success at Derby, attacked and killed many Danes at Tempsford in Bedfordshire in the late summer, including their king of East Anglia.

Tetbury, siege of, 1144

Siege of the Civil War of King Stephen's reign, in which Stephen's besieging force was forced to give up upon the arrival of a relief force led by Robert of Gloucester.

Tettenhall, battle of, 5 or 6 August 909 or 910

Battle at the end of a major raid by Northumbrian Danes.

Edward of Wessex had fought a campaign against the Danes in 909, but in 910 the Danes from Northumbria took the initiative. Raiding deep into Mercia, they followed the Severn back north to Bridgnorth. It seems that a combined army of Wessex and Mercian English caught up with this army near Tettenhall in Staffordshire. An account in *Aethelweard's Chronicle* claims that the precise location was at Wednesfield just to the east of Tettenhall. The raiding army lost, with three of its Northumbrian kings being killed.

Tewkesbury, battle of, 4 May 1471

Decisive battle of the second main phase of the Wars of the Roses, which secured the throne for Edward IV and heralded a period of peace for the next twelve years.

KEY REFERENCE: Hammond, P.W. *The Battles of Barnet and Tewkesbury* (Alan Sutton, 1990).

Following the Yorkist victory at Barnet the previous month, including as it did the death of the Earl of Warwick 'the Kingmaker', the Lancastrian cause in the Wars of the Roses was suddenly struggling. Henry VI's queen, Margaret, landed at Weymouth with more supporters, but had to gather an army before attempting another advance on Yorkist-held London. This took her to Wales, where she could link up with Jasper Tudor, uncle of the future Henry VII, and possibly with the Stanleys (later to play a key role at Bosworth) in Cheshire. Edward IV moved west supplied with information from spies, which enabled him to shadow Margaret's movements. By the beginning of May the two armies were close, with Edward keen to force battle before Margaret could meet up with her reinforcements. However, on 2 May, Margaret managed to give the Yorkists the slip by encouraging them to think that battle would be given at Sodbury but instead marched north towards Gloucester, where the Severn could be crossed. Not to be outdone, Edward sent messengers to Gloucester, where the governor Sir Richard Beauchamp closed the gates of the city to the Lancastrians. This forced the latter towards the next river crossing at Tewkesbury, which was reached by late afternoon on 3 May.

Margaret had little option but to fight, but at least had the advantage of choosing the ground, based on the site occupied by her camp the night before the battle. This was in a field called 'Gastum', part of which still survives intact and is now known as 'The Gastons'. This field was bounded by thick hedgerows and ditches, with approach from the south difficult. The Lancastrian line extended east of this field to cover the approach of Edward's army, reaching the then marshy ground beside the River Swilgate. From west to east (their right to left) the Lancastrian 'battles' (or 'divisions') were commanded by Somerset, Wenlock (with the Prince Edward) and Devonshire, while facing them respectively were Gloucester, Edward IV and Hastings. In addition, Edward IV had sent 200 (mounted?) spearmen into Tewkesbury Park to the

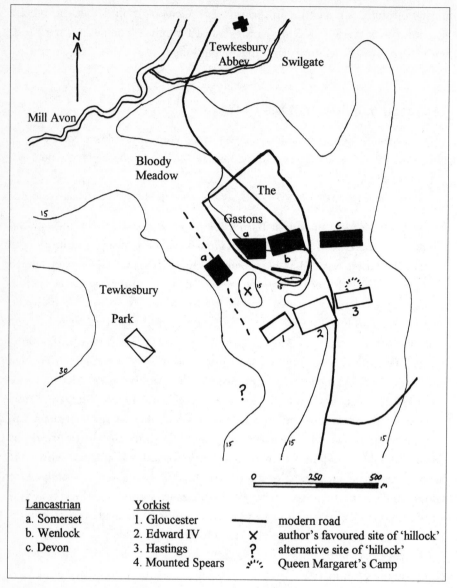

Battle of Tewkesbury, 4 May 1471.

west of the battle lines, in case of a Lancastrian attempt at ambush. As no such attempt was made, these spearmen were then ordered to 'employ themselves in the best ways as they could' (from *The Arrivall of Edward IV*). From casualty lists and records of payments made to components of the Yorkists, it would seem that the Lancastrians had a slight advantage in numbers, although the Yorkists probably outnumbered their foes in archers and mounted men, as well as in guns. The latter includes both artillery pieces of various calibres and various hand-guns. Overall figures of 6,000 Lancastrians against 5,500 Yorkists cannot be far from the mark.

The battle began early in the morning with an exchange of missiles, both arrows and shot, with the Yorkists bettering their opponents. Most of the guns appear to have been with Gloucester's left, with deployment possible, as the course of the road in 1471 cut across the battlefield rather than bisecting it across the centre as it does today. Presumably their superior number of missiles must have more than outweighed any advantages of cover held by the Lancastrians. Somerset's 'battle' appears to have suffered the most, indicating that the Yorkist archers and gunners of Richard of Gloucester's 'battle' were certainly effective. Due to this and also a pre-arranged plan, Somerset's men came out of 'The Gastons' and followed the lane through Lincoln Green, with a park boundary on their right-hand side. This movement somehow went undetected by the Yorkists, suggesting that only some of Somerset's men were involved: possibly a detachment which had been out of sight and waiting on the lane since the beginning of the battle. They appeared on the top of the slight hill by Lincoln Green just to the left of the Yorkists, possibly as Gloucester was still extending and deploying his line to the left. Some modern accounts suggest that Somerset's men marched further along the lane until they appeared on a round hillock to the rear of the Yorkists. This certainly fits the topography described in *The Arrivall*, but if this is followed it makes a surprise attack and the direction of Somerset's subsequent flight difficult to accept. It seems more likely that the slope leading down to the Yorkists' left is the hillock referred to in the sources. Certainly, this still fits the next part of the battle well. As a consequence of this flank attack, Gloucester was initially taken by surprise, but his men (they are termed 'Edward's men' in *The Arrivall*, but this is probably because all of the Yorkist army were 'Edward's men' and calling them so gives more credit for the victory directly to the king) soon forced Somerset's detachment back across a ditch, through a hedge and up the slope. Then, aided by the sudden appearance of the hitherto hidden 200 spearmen at the backs of the Lancastrians, the Yorkists turned Somerset's men to rout. Turning back the way they came, the Lancastrians were funnelled into the long strip of land known as 'Bloody Meadow', from which there was no easy exit as it met high banks and then the Mill Avon. Many must have been cut down in their blind panic. This may have been averted had the Lancastrian centre under Wenlock advanced to attack at the same time as the right. However, they remained on the defensive, relatively secure behind the cover of the hedgerows, banks and ditches. This may even have been due to treachery on Wenlock's part, as is suggested by *Hall's Chronicle*, where it is reported that Somerset rode up to the dilatory earl and dashed his brains out with his axe. Certainly the Yorkists were able to regroup after Somerset's initial attack and, led by Edward IV, the centre and right met the remaining Lancastrian forces. Although keen to talk up Edward's prowess, *The Arrivall* is accurate in emphasising the difficulties faced by the Yorkists as they had to assail the main Lancastrian position. However, spurred on by the success of their left, the Yorkists breached the line and from that time it became a general rout, with the Lancastrian centre and left fleeing the field. They sought to escape but many failed, including Prince Edward and the Earl of Devonshire, who probably fell at this point. Some escaped through the town, while others, including Somerset, claimed sanctuary in Tewkesbury Abbey. This was refused, with Somerset and many of his supporters being tried by the Dukes of Norfolk and Gloucester and then executed two days after the battle. Yorkist casualties in the battle were very light, but the Lancastrians probably lost some 2,000, mainly in the rout. Edward of York as Edward IV was now secure on his throne after such a decisive victory. He further ensured this thanks to the capture of Queen Margaret after the battle and by the killing of Henry VI in the Tower of London shortly afterwards. Edward did not face another serious challenge while he lived.

The battlefield is still largely unspoilt on the crucial Lancastrian right, with Bloody Meadow and the lane to Lincoln Green still intact, along with the positions where Gloucester deployed. The opposite side has not fared so well, with nearly all lost to housing, although the earthwork known as 'Margaret's Camp', next to which Hastings' 'battle' would have deployed, is still open ground. Tewkesbury Museum in the High Street is also well worth a visit, with a room dedicated to the battle.

Thames, battle of the River, 54 BC, *see* Caesar's second expedition

Thames, battle of the River, AD 43

Crossing of this important river during the Roman invasion which helped to establish Britannia as part of the Roman Empire.

Having beaten the Britons in three battles before reaching the River Thames, the Roman army led by Aulus Plautius had established some form of superiority over their foes, at least for the initial campaign. The Roman writer Cassius Dio tells us that they arrived at the Thames 'where it empties into the Ocean and at flood-tide forms a lake'. With the environmental changes of the past 2,000 years it is difficult to be certain where this places the crossing from Tower Bridge eastwards. Just as at the previous battle, possibly at the River Medway, the Romans sent across German (probably Batavian) auxiliaries who were trained to swim in armour. At the same time another force was sent upstream to cross by a bridge (which they may have constructed themselves – possibly in pontoon form having been supplied by the navy), enabling them to outflank the defenders. Many Britons were killed at this point, although the Romans suffered in their pursuit, as they over-reached themselves in the difficult marshy terrain.

Thames Estuary, battle of, 992

An attempt by the English to trap a fleet of raiding Vikings, but only one ship was caught as the raiders were forewarned by the Saxon Earl Aelfric.

Thanet, battle of, 853

Ealhhere of Kent and Huda of Surrey fought against the Vikings at Thanet killing many, but were both killed themselves.

Thetford, battle of, 1004

Part of a large-scale Danish raid led by Swein 'Forkbeard'.

Having raided Norwich three weeks earlier, a Viking army moved south to Thetford, which they moved into at night, looting and burning it. An English force led by Ulfcytel came up to the town the following morning, bringing the Danes to battle. Many were killed on both sides, but it appears that the Danes still held the ground at the end of the action.

Thurland Castle, sieges of, June–October 1643

Series of minor sieges which saw this castle change hands three times in less than a year.

Thurland Castle in Lancashire was held by Royalists at the start of the First Civil War, but was taken by Parliament in June 1643, only to be retaken by Sir

John Girlington. By August, the Parliamentarian Colonel Rigby started a siege of the castle, which led to its fall in October, despite Rigby having to take most of his force away to defeat a small Royalist force at Lindal on 1 October.

Tickhill Castle, siege of, 1193–1194

Siege of Prince John's castle near Doncaster by Barons loyal to King Richard I.

With King Richard I in prison abroad, his younger brother Prince John attempted to gain control of England. A number of barons moved against him, led in the North by the Archbishop of York. At first other nobles were unwilling to commit themselves, but in early 1193 a force led by the Bishop of Durham besieged Tickhill. This siege was abandoned in April following a truce, but was resumed in February 1194. The garrison surrendered once it became clear to them that King Richard had returned to England in March 1194.

Tiverton, siege of, 17–20 October 1645

Short siege towards the end of the First Civil War providing Parliament with Tiverton to use as a winter base.

Following Naseby and Langport, the New Model Army of Parliament continued to march west, mopping up garrisons as it went. In October 1645 it reached Tiverton in Devon, where a force of only 250 or so Royalists defended the castle. After three days of siege, a cannon shot brought down the drawbridge, having smashed the holding chain, and this led to the castle's surrender. Tiverton Museum's Britton Gallery has a model of the castle as it would have appeared in 1645, as well as replica Civil War armour. Parts of the castle survive, which are open to the public on an occasional, largely seasonal basis, when more armour can also be viewed.

Torrington, battle of, 16 February 1646

This battle saw the end of the First Civil War in Devon.

KEY REFERENCE: Young, P. and Holmes, R. *The English Civil War* (Wordsworth Editions Ltd, 2000).

By 1646 Parliamentarian forces were largely engaged in mopping up the remaining Royalist garrisons. An exception to this was in the West Country, where Hopton led a field army of some 2,000 foot and 3,000 horse for King

Charles I. The Parliamentarian New Model Army commanded by Sir Thomas Fairfax outnumbered Hopton's force and moved in on the town which Hopton had fortified with a series of earthworks and barricades, after clearing a detachment of dragoons from nearby Stevenstone House. After nightfall the Parliamentarians forced their way into the town, but as the fight was still raging a stray spark exploded the Royalist gunpowder magazine stored in the church (since rebuilt as the Church of St Michael and all Angels), killing some Royalists and their 200 Parliamentarian prisoners. The bulk of Hopton's army was able to escape in the resulting confusion to be pursued by Fairfax, leading to Hopton's surrender agreed at Truro in March 1646 and leaving only the garrison at Pendennis Castle to fall in Cornwall.

The Battle of Torrington is re-enacted each year and a trail and centre named 'Torrington 1646' mark these climactic events.

Towcester, siege of, 917

A Viking army from Northampton and Leicester attacked the newly built stronghold at Towcester, but were driven off by a resolute defence.

Towton, battle of, 29 March (Palm Sunday) 1461

The biggest and bloodiest battle of the Wars of the Roses, ending the first major phase of fighting and leading to the coronation of Edward IV.

KEY REFERENCE: Boardman, A. *The Battle of Towton* (Alan Sutton, 1994).

Fortunes had been mixed over the months preceding March 1461, but Edward, by then Duke of York and earlier Earl of March (later Edward IV), held the stronger hand, especially as he had proved himself as a capable commander and controlled London. He was determined to secure the throne, which meant a battle had to be fought against the main Lancastrian army. Accordingly, Edward set off north and, following a clash at Ferrybridge, arrived close to the Lancastrian camp at Towton, near Tadcaster in the evening of 28 March 1461.

The battlefield is still open agricultural land, not dissimilar from its appearance in 1461, except that the open fields would then have been farmed as ridge and furrow, making any manoeuvre difficult, although this may have been eased by frozen ground. The battle took place on Palm Sunday between the villages of Saxton and Towton, with the Lancastrians forming up on a slight rise to the north of Towton Dale (to the east of the battle cross), leaving the Yorkists to advance onto the slightly higher rise to the south.

Estimates of the forces vary wildly, and depend on how much faith is put in the various chronicle sources. Edward Hall puts the total for both sides at just over 100,000, with several contemporary sources agreeing on 28,000 deaths. It would appear that these are highly inflated, given the recruiting power, availability of supplies and the likely size of the population. Modern estimates of 25,000 Lancastrians and 20,000 Yorkists still make this an exceptionally large battle for the period. There is a major problem when translating these figures to the battlefield, particularly where the Lancastrians are generally accepted to have formed up. With a less than generous 1m frontage per man, they would have to have formed up about thirty deep to fit into the 800m or so available, although a reserve and the possible ambush party should be subtracted from the equation. From this one should surmise that in all probability the numbers involved were smaller still. The Lancastrians formed up with Northumberland on the left and Somerset on the right, together with Sir Andrew Trollope, and in addition possibly had a small ambush party hidden behind what would be the Yorkist left flank in Castle Hill Wood. Opposing them were the outnumbered Yorkists with Edward, Duke of York on the left and the Earl of Warwick in the centre/right. Both sides had their archers with longbows to the fore, those of the Yorkists commanded by Lord Fauconberg. The Yorkists were not at full strength at the start of the battle as they were still waiting for the Duke of Norfolk to arrive with his men on their right.

The action started at 9.00 a.m. with a large-scale archery duel. The Yorkists had the better of this, due in part to a blizzard of snow, which drove into the faces of the Lancastrians, causing their arrows to fall short. The Yorkists then advanced and shot not only their own arrows but returned those of their enemy. This provoked a full-scale advance from the Lancastrians, who stumbled forward into the blizzard. The Yorkist left started to give way to Trollope's advance, which became perilous for the Yorkists after much fighting, possibly because of the arrival of the Lancastrian ambush party. Certainly, the Lancastrians must have forced the Yorkists back through sheer weight of numbers. Fortunately for the Yorkists, Norfolk arrived at noon, throwing his men into the struggle on the Yorkists' right. Slowly but surely the Lancastrian left was forced back, although the fighting apparently lasted for ten hours – a phenomenal effort given not only the normal effects of fighting a late medieval battle, but also because of the weather and lack of food and water. One of the notable casualties during this hard fighting was Lord Dacre

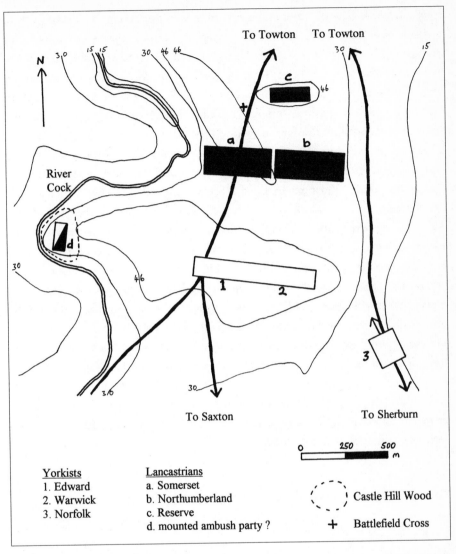

Battle of Towton, 29 March 1461.

on the Lancastrian side, who was shot in the neck by an arrow as he was pausing for refreshment. He was later buried in Saxton churchyard, where his grave can still be seen. He was apparently buried with his charger, which along with the lord was possibly interred upright. Finally the Lancastrian line started to crack, with their lines having wheeled round so that their rear now faced towards the steep-sided valley of the River Cock. As men started to flee more gaps appeared, until the whole line disintegrated. It then became a case of 'every man for himself' and there must have been carnage, as men tried to escape towards Towton or across the river. Many died trying to cross; indeed, bridges of bodies are said to have been caused by the high number of casualties. The sheer brutality of the fighting at Towton, as indeed any other battle of the period, is demonstrated by the horrific wounds discovered on the (probably) thirty-seven skeletons unearthed in the grounds of Towton Hall in the 1990s. Nearly all had suffered multiple head wounds from the battle, although it is possible these men were 'executed' rather than killed in combat. There are several other known battlefield graves marked on the county's sites and monuments record, with others in and around Saxton Church, the latter being commemorated next to Lord Dacre's tomb. Many other artefacts have been found on the battlefield, although few have found their way into museums. An exception to this is a small axe which is now in Alnwick Castle. Every year the Towton Battlefield Society organises a walk of the battlefield on Palm Sunday, viewing the site from either side's perspective. Dacre's cross on the B1217 stands on the right wing of the Lancastrian position, with good views across the battlefield towards the Yorkist ridge. A small, (currently) unsurfaced pull-in by the cross allows access to a short track which leads to an interpretation panel standing above the River Cock with 'Bloody Meadow' in view. It is a most rewarding battlefield to visit, with the landscape much as it must have been in 1461.

Towton was certainly decisive. Edward was able to return to London to be crowned as Edward IV, while the Lancastrian cause was unable to mount a serious challenge for nearly ten years.

Turnham Green, stand-off of, 13 November 1642

The battle for London that never was.

After the Battle of Edgehill the Royalist army of King Charles I advanced towards London via a circuitous route. Prince Rupert's successful attack on Brentford on 12 November encouraged the king to push his troops towards Turnham Green to the west of London. However, the Royalist success at Brentford roused many Londoners to take this threat seriously and, led by the Earl of Essex, some 24,000 men were in position on 13 November to stop this thrust for the capital. They were enough to dissuade the Royalists from attempting to advance, as their numbers were too few to force the issue, leading to a withdrawal to Hounslow and then to Reading. Only a small remnant of the 'Green' or common survives in this part of London's suburbia.

Tutbury Castle, siege of, 1153

Successful siege by Henry of Anjou in the same year as further sieges at Malmesbury and Crowmarsh, leading to a truce with Stephen.

Tynemoor(e), battle of, 920 or 921

Battle in Northumbria where a Scottish force defeated some Danish raiders.

Tynemouth, siege of, October 1648

Brief but violent siege and storming of the Second Civil War.

The garrison of Tynemouth went over to the Royalist cause during the Second Civil War. However, Sir Arthur Hesilrige was in the area and moved to take the castle by storm, killing most of the garrison and their commander Henry Lilburne in the process. The ruins of the castle are under the care of English Heritage.

Upnor Castle, siege of, May–early June 1648

This sixteenth-century castle (now open to the public) protecting the entrance to the River Medway was taken by a group of Kentish rebels during the Second Civil War, although they were dislodged by Parliamentarian forces after the battle of Maidstone.

Upton Bridge, battle of, 28 August 1651

Fought as a prelude to the Battle of Worcester, enabling a Parliamentarian force to cross to the west bank of the River Severn.

KEY REFERENCE: Spicer, T. *The Battle of Worcester, 1651* (Paddy Griffith Associates, 2002).

With the largely Scottish army of Charles, son of King Charles I, at Worcester, Oliver Cromwell gathered his forces at Evesham. These included men he had marched with from Scotland and more local forces, including those under Major-General Lambert. To invest the city of Worcester, Cromwell needed to get troops onto the west bank of the River Severn, which was difficult as the Royalists held the bridges. Rather than facing a delay by going as far south as Gloucester or possibly crossing at Tewkesbury, Cromwell ordered Lambert to move against the bridge at Upton. The bridge in 1651 was slightly to the south of the modern bridge and the Royalists had taken down an arch, leaving only a plank on which to cross. Lambert gathered his men at Ryall and sent forward eighteen dragoons at around 10.00 a.m. on 28 August. They managed to cross and reached Upton church, where they found themselves besieged by the Royalist Scots. A force of perhaps 500 horse and dragoons forded the Severn a little to the south and came to the eighteen men's rescue, with more Parliamentarians crossing over the bridge on hastily laid planks. The bridge was adequately repaired by 29 August, enabling General Fleetwood to cross to take command of the Parliamentarians on the west bank of the Severn and leading to the Battle of Worcester on 3 September.

Viking raid, first, 786?

Important turning point in English history, ushering in three centuries of
Scandinavian influence and partial control.

The *Anglo-Saxon Chronicle* tells us that the first raid by the Vikings, or
Northmen, took place between 784 and 800, probably in 786, in part because
the raid against Lindisfarne in 793 was certainly later, as well as due to the order
and sequence of entries. One account informs us that they landed at Portland,
while from the *Chronicle* we hear that the force consisted of three ships, with
the Vikings killing the local reeve.

Wakefield, battle of, 30 December 1460

Crushing Yorkist defeat in the Wars of the Roses, which saw the death of Richard, Duke of York.

KEY REFERENCE: Haigh, P. *From Wakefield to Towton, the Wars of the Roses* (Leo Cooper, 2002).

With the capture of the Lancastrian King Henry VI at the end of the Battle of Northampton earlier in the year, the Yorkists were in a very strong position, being able to have the Act of Accord passed which acknowledged that the crown would pass to the Duke of York and his heirs on the death of Henry VI. However, their position was not entirely secure. Richard, Duke of York had only returned from exile in Ireland in September, two months after Northampton and with high-handed behaviour which had not endeared himself to many. This no doubt made it easier for Queen Margaret, wife of the 'captive' Henry to raise further Lancastrian forces, largely in Wales and the North. The forces in Wales were to clash with the Yorkists under the future Edward IV at Mortimer's Cross in February 1461, while Richard, Duke of York marched north to deal with the main Lancastrian threat.

His intention was to confront the Lancastrians at Pontefract Castle, but for some reason (possibly because he intended to use Sandal Castle as his base) diverted slightly to the west where his forces encountered those of the Lancastrian Duke of Somerset, who had marched all the way from Corfe Castle in Dorset, at Worksop. York's army moved on to Sandal, just to the south of

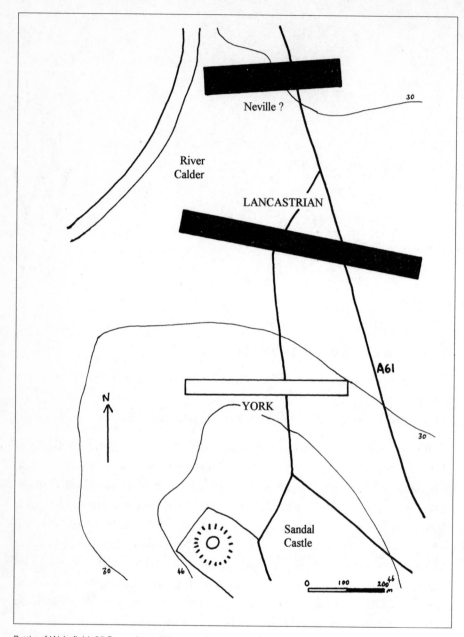

Battle of Wakefield, 30 December 1460.

Wakefield, which was a relatively small castle and did not have the necessary supplies to feed an army of 5,000 men for long, nor enough room to house them all. The fact that it was late December and there was a Lancastrian army close by at Pontefract meant that York had marched into a difficult situation.

The stronger Lancastrian army of perhaps 15,000 marched from Pontefract on 28 December, reaching Sandal on the same day. The Yorkists must have camped on the flat area immediately in front of the castle to the north, while the Lancastrians formed up to the south of the River Calder. By 30 December supplies must have been running low, with both sides sending out foraging parties. One of the Yorkist parties was caught by the Lancastrians and chased back to the castle, which may have provided the catalyst for the battle.

The exact sequence of events and directions taken by the forces are not clear from the contemporary sources, other to say that the main fighting took place on flat ground between Sandal Castle and Wakefield, i.e. on and around modern Wakefield Green. Two other factors may have contributed to the Yorkists coming down from the castle to give battle. The first is that they may have under-estimated the size of the Lancastrian army, possibly because some of them were hidden in dead ground or in woods. The other is that York perhaps hoped and even expected Lord Neville to arrive with reinforcements. Neville had requested permission from York to recruit forces under a Commission of Array, and this had been granted. Accordingly, it is possible that Neville was sighted close at hand with some 8,000 men, leading York to think that victory could be achieved. However, Neville had changed sides and his men would ensure York's defeat rather than victory. It is not clear if Neville joined the battle, but it is a possibility, being one which is put forward by Philip Haigh in particular. Whatever the reason for his decision, York certainly moved down the slope from the castle to meet the main Lancastrian force in battle.

Following the slope down along the line of the current Manygates Lane, the Yorkists crashed into the Lancastrian line. Being outnumbered, the Yorkists were soon outflanked and attacked on all sides. The arrival of Neville's men in the fight sealed the Yorkists' fate. It is possible, as many historians argue, that the Lancastrians planned an ambush, with the Duke of Somerset leading the main 'battle' or division and with the two flank 'battles' in ambush under Lord Clifford and the Earl of Wiltshire, if Edward Hall's later chronicle is to be believed. With their large advantage in numbers, such an ambush was unnecessary other than to lure York to attack, thinking that the Lancastrian force was smaller than it actually was. Whatever the exact sequence of events, Richard, Duke of York was killed in the fighting, along with the majority of his men who found escape difficult. Somehow, the Earl of Rutland, the seventeen-year-old son of the Duke of York, reached the bridge leading over the River Calder into Wakefield. There, probably just outside the still-standing chantry chapel, Rutland was killed by Lord Clifford's own hand.

Although the site is largely built over, there are excellent views from the top of Sandal Castle, with the course of the battle being traceable along Manygates Lane across Wakefield Green right to the old bridge over the Calder. On Manygates Lane, by the school at Wakefield Green, is a Victorian monument to the battle, which replaced an original cross put up by Edward IV to commemorate his father. A new visitor centre has been built at the castle in 2002, which hopefully includes information about the battle. With the death of the Duke of York the Yorkist claim passed to his older son, Edward Earl of March, who became the new Duke of York and later King Edward IV. Richard, Duke of York's body was dismembered after the battle, with his head, along with those of other fallen Yorkist lords, being displayed in York. Richard's head was adorned with a mocking paper crown and put on a spike at Micklegate Bar.

Wakefield, storming of, 21 May 1643

Taken by the Fairfaxes as they attempted to secure West Yorkshire for Parliament before the setback at Adwalton Moor on 30 June 1643.

KEY REFERENCE: Cooke, D. *The Forgotten Battle: The Battle of Adwalton Moor 30 June 1643* (Battlefield Press, 1996).

Lord Fairfax (who stayed at Howley Hall during the assault) and his son Sir Thomas decided to attack Bradford, thinking that its Royalist garrison was much smaller than the 4,000 or so it actually contained. Two simultaneous attacks were planned and delivered in the early morning with a total of 1,500 men: one along Warrengate from the east and the other down Northgate. It took the Parliamentarians up to two hours to break into the town, as the Royalists had not been caught by surprise and had placed defensive works at the ends of both streets. Gifford with Sir Thomas broke through and, capturing an enemy cannon and turning it round to fire on its former owners, made progress towards the centre of the town, although for a time Sir Thomas was cut off from his men. Firing the cannon into the packed market place decided the outcome, with the Royalists running or surrendering by 9.00 a.m. For a short time it looked as if West Yorkshire would remain with Parliament, but the next month the Earl of Newcastle went on the offensive for the Royalists, leading to the Battle of Adwalton Moor.

Wallingford, siege of, 1153, *see* Crowmarsh Castle

Wallingford, siege of, 11 May–July 1646

One of the last strongholds to fall at the end of the First Civil War.

After holding out for the Royalists throughout the First Civil War, Wallingford fell to Thomas Fairfax and the New Model Army after a seven-week siege. The large castle was demolished, with only traces of the masonry surviving today, although extensive earthworks remain, including a semi-circular Civil War outwork. Information about the siege is available in Wallingford Museum (open March–November).

Wareham, siege of, 1142

Successful siege by King Stephen during the 'castle war' phase of the Civil Wars of his reign.

After the Treaty of Winchester in 1141, both sides – King Stephen's Royalists and the Angevin supporters of the Empress Matilda – built up their strength. One of Matilda's main supporters was Earl Robert of Normandy. While Robert was in his earldom, Stephen attacked Wareham in the early summer. He captured the castle and town, setting fire to the latter.

Watchet, raid of, 914

Raid by a Viking fleet from Brittany, which had been driven away from the River Severn earlier in the year. The raid ended with many casualties for the attackers.

Watchet, raid of, 988

Large-scale Viking raid against Watchet, causing the death of Goda of Devon and many other English.

Watchet, raid of, 997

The Viking raiding army which had been successful since 991 turned its attention to Devon, Cornwall and the Severn estuary, raiding Watchet before turning back to Land's End, the Tamar estuary and Lydford in Devon.

Wetherby, skirmish of, 30 November 1642

An outnumbered Thomas Fairfax was surprised by a force of Royalist cavalry, but the latter fled after being scared away by the chance explosion of the Parliamentarian gunpowder store.

Whalley, battle of, 2 April 798

Viking attack against a Northumbrian force, leading to a big battle at Whalley on the River Ribble, in which Alric of Northumbria was killed and the English defeated.

Wheathampstead, battle of, *see* Caesar's second expedition

White Battle, the, 1319, *see* Myton

Whitehaven, skirmish of, 10–11 April 1778

Last action involving a foreign force fought on English soil.

John Paul Jones, born in Scotland under the name John Paul, was apprenticed as a seaman in Whitehaven in Cumbria. Before the American War of Independence broke out, Jones fled to America after killing an alleged mutineer in the West Indies. He joined the fledgling 'Continental Navy' of Congress, fighting against Britain. In 1778, during the American War of Independence and after a spell in France, Jones sailed from Brest in his ship, *Ranger*, to Whitehaven. He landed two shore parties close to midnight on 10 April 1778. His party captured and destroyed the guns at one of the forts overlooking the harbour, while the other party appears to have gone to the pub! Jones captured and disabled the other fort, before sinking three ships in the harbour and then sailing away. On the way back he was encountered by the sloop HMS *Drake* off Northern Ireland, which he captured.

Wigan, skirmish of, 25 August 1651

Small Royalist force caught as it attempted to join the main army during the Third Civil War.

The main Scottish army had marched south a few days previously *en route* to Worcester, when the Earl of Derby marched to join it with some Lancashire volunteers. However, he was intercepted just to the north of Wigan along Wigan Lane by Robert Lilburne, who badly cut up his force, capturing many. Derby was wounded and forced to hide, although he was captured after the Battle of Worcester and then taken to Bolton where he was executed for his part in the massacre which had taken place after the Storming of Bolton in 1644.

Wigingamere, siege of, 917

Raid by a Viking army into Mercia against this stronghold, possibly another name for Wigmore, in which they fought for most of a day but were driven off.

Wilton, battle of, 871

The first battle fought by Alfred 'the Great' as King of Wessex.

Having succeeded to the throne of Wessex after the death of his brother Aethelred, Alfred took a raiding party against two Viking forces at the town of Wilton in Wiltshire. Fighting on a hill on the south bank of the River Wylye (quite possibly the hill in the current Wilton Park upon which a tumulus is situated), the Saxons pushed the larger Danish army back. However, either by the guile of a feigned retreat as suggested by Bishop Asser, or by the use of reserves, the Vikings turned the tide and won the victory.

Wilton, battle of, 1143 (possibly 1142)

One of the few pitched battles of the Civil Wars of King Stephen's reign, although details of the action are scant.

KEY REFERENCE: Bradbury, J. *Stephen and Matilda, the Civil War of 1139–53* (Alan Sutton, 1996).

The battle at Wilton was fought as King Stephen attempted to fight his way clear of a besieging Angevin force. He faced an Angevin army under Earl Robert of Normandy, who had deployed his men in three groups. His cavalry were launched at Stephen's main body, pushing them back. Perhaps remembering what had happened at the end of the Battle of Lincoln, Stephen decided to attempt to flee rather than risk capture. This he did successfully, thanks to one of his men, William Martel, who held off the attackers while his king escaped. Stephen, once in safety, agreed to hand over the important castle of Sherborne in return for the release of Martel.

Winceby, battle of, 11 October 1643

Cavalry battle which helped build the reputations of Thomas Fairfax and Oliver Cromwell.

KEY REFERENCE: English Heritage *Battlefield Report: Winceby 1643* (English Heritage, London, 1995).

After their victory at Adwalton Moor in June 1643, the Royalists hoped to drive a wedge between the main Parliamentarian bases to the south and their garrison at Hull, leading to the capture of the latter. To prevent this, the Parliamentarian Earl of Manchester moved north from King's Lynn with his army of the Eastern Association, strengthened by Yorkshire cavalry under Thomas Fairfax, who joined him at Boston. The Royalists had a garrison at Old Bolingbroke which was under threat from Manchester's force. To relieve Bolingbroke and to catch Manchester, the Royalist commander in the North, the Earl of Newcastle, dispatched Sir William Widdrington from Lincoln with a force of up to 3,000 mounted men. They moved east to Horncastle, where they skirmished with Parliamentarian scouts. These retired back towards Bolingbroke where they met with Manchester, who decided to carry on to observe and probably fight the Royalist force.

Winceby is on the Lincolnshire Wolds, while Horncastle from where the Royalists advanced is on low-lying ground. It appears that Manchester's cavalry, who also numbered about 3,000 men, advanced and saw the Royalists approaching. They thus had the opportunity to choose the ground for the battle, although they would have had to fight before their infantry had time to come up. The Royalist advance took them along the current A158 towards Spilsby. However, the road in 1643 to Winceby did not turn off at the same spot as it does today. Instead, it followed a straighter line from Horncastle, turning off the Spilsby Road just to the east of High Toynton Grange. This route is still a footpath which emerges on the same alignment as Slash Lane just to the north-west of Winceby. This is important, as it helps the visitor to align the armies in their correct positions rather than being influenced by the current road as it turns off the A158. At this point it is best to dismiss the other possible location for the battle just to the south of Winceby, as that is on too broad a position for the Parliamentarians to have chosen it, as we know from the sources that the Royalists had a narrow front. Cromwell was in charge on the

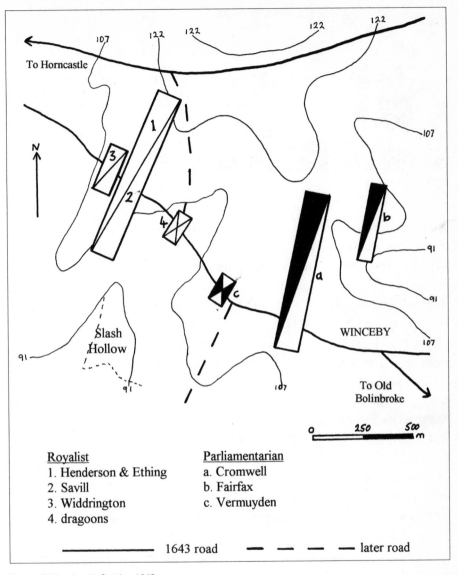

Battle of Winceby, 11 October 1643.

field with around the same number of horse and dragoons as the Royalists, as Manchester was with the infantry. He sent forward a forlorn hope of dragoons under Quartermaster General Vermuyden, who were met by a similar Royalist force. Cromwell took the first line consisting of his own and the Earl of Manchester's regiments, who would have formed up on the ridge just to the north-west of Winceby, across the road, with Fairfax behind with the second line. Facing them on the opposite, slightly less imposing hill were the Royalists,

Mounted dragoons of the First Civil War. Mounted dragoons were issued with shorter muskets than foot musketeers, and were mounted on smaller horses than cavalry troopers. Dragoons rarely fired from horseback, preferring to use cover when dismounted. Parliamentarian armies tended to have more dragoons than Royalist armies, and were often deployed as the advance guard, a highly dangerous formation, as at the battle of Winceby, 1643.

with Henderson and Ething on the left, Savill in the centre and right and probably Widdrington with a small reserve behind.

As Cromwell moved forward to charge, the Royalist dragoons opened fire, and as they were 'so nimble' they got off a second volley which killed Cromwell's horse. He was in trouble as Sir Ingram Hopton moved in, but fortunately for Cromwell Hopton was killed (his memorial is in Horncastle Church) and he was given a remount – probably a dragoon's horse as it is remarked upon as being 'poore'. This first charge appears to have broken most of the Royalists, although it is possible that the latter had made progress on their left. No doubt because of this, Fairfax led his second line towards the right, possibly in part hidden by the crest of the ridge, and routed Henderson's and Ething's men. Fairfax continued his attack from right to left across the battlefield, joining with Cromwell's first line before the rout was complete. Many Royalists were driven against the thick parish boundary in the feature still known as Slash Hollow, where most of their 500 casualties occurred, along with some 800 being taken prisoner. The remainder fled back towards Horncastle and beyond.

The battle saw the first action in which Cromwell and Thomas Fairfax fought together, with Winceby showing how effective the Parliamentarian horse were becoming. The Siege of Hull was abandoned by Newcastle on the same day, so the land route from Norfolk to this important port was secured.

Winchcomb, siege of, 1144

Siege immediately after the aborted Siege of Tetbury, in which King Stephen took the castle at Winchcomb by ordering archers to loose their arrows while other men crept up the castle motte, ensuring its surrender.

Winchelsea, battle of, 29 August 1350

Naval battle in which the English defeated a Spanish fleet, partly through their first use of cannon at sea.

The Spanish were conducting a raid in strength, which was intercepted by King Edward III, with the battle beginning late in the day. Edward III according to Froissart headed for the first Spanish ship 'for I want to joust with it'. However, the Spanish were moving faster as they had the advantage of the wind, leading to serious damage for Edward's ship as they collided, with the English forecastle crashing down into the sea. Edward's men were able to grapple a second ship despite taking in water. Eventually his men captured this ship, which was higher and larger than their own, throwing their captives overboard. The Prince of Wales was grappled by another ship and was close to sinking when the Duke of Lancaster grappled from the other side shouting 'Derby to the rescue!' The Prince and his men were just able to cross to the captured ship as their own sank. Late in the evening the Spanish captured a ship containing the Royal Household commanded by Robert of Namur. Showing more mercy than the English, the Spaniards kept their prisoners on board. One of Robert's servants managed to cut down the sail of the Spanish ship with a sword, leading to confusion. The ship was recaptured and the English showed no mercy, summarily depositing the survivors into the sea. In all the Spanish lost fourteen ships, with the English making landfall off Winchelsea and Rye a little after dark. This battle also saw the first use by the English of artillery at sea.

Winchester, battle of, 860

A large Danish fleet attacked, captured and sacked Winchester, before being caught by a combined army of men from Hampshire under Earl Osric and from Berkshire under Earl Aethelwulf, who defeated and drove off the raiders.

Winchester, siege and rout of, 31 July–September 1141

Important action which lost the advantage that Matilda had gained following the Battle of Lincoln against the forces of King Stephen.

KEY REFERENCE: Bradbury, J. *Stephen and Matilda, the Civil War of 1139–53* (Alan Sutton, 1996).

After being less than diplomatic following her forces' success at Lincoln, Matilda quickly lost the support of London. She moved to Oxford and then to Winchester where the Bishop, Henry, had started to besiege the castle which was being held for Matilda. She arrived on 31 July and promptly started her own siege of the other castle in Winchester, which was held for Bishop Henry. She relieved the siege of her own castle, forcing Henry to flee the town, while she continued to besiege the bishop's castle of Wolvesey. Things soon turned against her, as the supporters of King Stephen laid siege to the whole town, with Matilda's forces within it. On 2 August the situation for Matilda became even more serious, with the setting on fire of part of the town, probably by the men at Wolvesey. By 14 September it was clear that the only solution for Matilda was to try and break out. This was duly achieved, thanks mainly to a diversionary attack by Robert of Gloucester. However, the royalists pursued Matilda's force in what is now known as the rout of Winchester. During this retreat an action was fought at Stockbridge, to the west of Winchester.

Winnington Bridge, skirmish of, 19 August 1659

The last action of the Civil Wars, fought after the death of Oliver Cromwell but before the Restoration of King Charles II.

With the death of Oliver Cromwell on 3 September 1658, Royalist plotters were encouraged to plan for the possible return from exile of Charles Stuart (later King Charles II). By the following summer the main group of plotters known as the Sealed Knot had organised a rising to take place in Cheshire and Shropshire. Despite the plot being discovered, the rising still went ahead, with the Royalist Sir George Booth seizing Chester. Booth had few trained or well-equipped troops to face the forces of General Lambert who was sent from London to end the rising. After some manoeuvring, Lambert pinned Booth down just to the north of Northwich at Winnington Bridge on 19 August 1659. Booth fell back across the bridge which he manned. This proved to be less of an obstacle to Lambert than Booth hoped, for musketeers and dragoons soon cleared its defenders. Once across the River Weaver (there was no canal there in 1659), Lambert's seasoned men made short work of the poorly armed rebels. The remaining strongholds quickly fell and Booth was captured trying to escape disguised as a woman, to be imprisoned in the Tower of London, from where he was released at the Restoration.

Winwedfeld, Winwaed or Winwoed, battle of, 15 November (?) 654

Large and important battle in which the pagan Penda of Mercia died.

This battle may well have been fought at Winmoor in Barwick-in-Elmet near Leeds. As well as the most powerful king in the country, many others of note were killed, including thirty royal children (or possibly generals) and Aethelhere of East Anglia. They were defeated by the army of the Christian Oswy, King of Northumbria. Bede tells us that the River Winwaed had been swollen by rain, leading to the drowning of many at the end of the battle.

Winwick Pass, battle of, 19 August 1648

Neglected but decisive victory of Cromwell fought after the battle of Preston in the Second Civil War.

KEY REFERENCE: Barratt, J. 'The Battle of Winwick Pass, 19 August 1648' in *The Battlefields Trust Newsletter* January, 1997.

Most modern accounts give the Battle of Preston as the decisive victory which ended the northern threat to Parliament in the Second Civil War. However, it was only part of Hamilton's army which had been defeated at Preston, leaving sizeable components of the Scottish invasion force largely intact. One of these elements was a large body of Scottish foot perhaps 4,000 men strong which pressed on south, until they were caught up by Cromwell's forces two days after Preston at Winwick Pass just to the north of Warrington.

The Scots chose to make a stand along a marshy valley called Newton Brook across the Wigan to Warrington road. They were aided further by the existence of a high sandstone bank along the southern edge of the valley, probably with a hedge on top. Cromwell ordered forward a 'forlorn hope', which was repulsed, to be followed by an infantry attack. The Scots seem to have had pikemen in the centre where the road crossed the brook, for the two sides came to 'push of pike', with the Parliamentarians again being forced back after a long fight. No doubt skirmishing took place across the valley as well, which artillery fire and cannon balls found on the battlefield and now in Warrington Museum testify. Locals gave Cromwell information that a route existed to take men around the right flank of the Scots. He quickly sent cavalry on this flank march, while ordering forward the newly arrived Pride's Regiment of foot. This, together with the appearance and rapid disappearance of their own cavalry, forced the Scots to abandon their position and retreat south. A rearguard made a stand in the village of Winwick on the green and then in the church (whose tower still bears musket-ball marks on its north face) where the New Model Army 'made a great slaughter of them'. Indeed, Cromwell claimed 1,000 enemy dead and 2,000 prisoners. The survivors made it to Warrington, where the foot surrendered, effectively ending the invasion.

Wipped's Creek, battle of, 465

Early Anglo-Saxon victory against the Britons.

The *Anglo-Saxon Chronicle* records this battle as having been fought near Wipped's Creek, although attempts to locate this feature have been unsuccessful. The army of Hengest and Aesc defeated the Britons (called Welsh in the *Chronicle*), killing twelve chieftains but losing their own thegn, Wipped.

Woden's Barrow, battle of, 592

Battle probably fought at modern-day Adam's Grave at Alton Priors, Wiltshire, in which the West Saxon Ceawlin was defeated by a British force.

Woden's Barrow, battle of, 715

King Ine of Wessex fought against King Ceolred of Mercia at the same site as the battle of AD 592.

Woodbury Hill, battle of, August 1405

Decisive defeat of Owain Glyndwr, who was camped on this prehistoric hill fort now beside the B4197 to the north-west of Worcester, by the forces of King Henry IV, forcing the former to withdraw to Wales.

Woodstock, siege of, 8–26 April 1646

Siege at the end of the First Civil War resulting in the fall of the town to Parliament after an artillery bombardment of the old palace.

Woolsthorpe, siege of, January 1646

In the build-up to the capture of nearby Belvoir Castle by Parliament, the church at Woolsthorpe was taken along with most of its small Royalist garrison after artillery fire had severely damaged it.

Worcester, battle of, 24 October 1055

A major raid into Herefordshire by the King of Wales and a rebel Saxon force.

King Gruffydd ap Llywelyn of Wales had been causing problems for the Saxons in Herefordshire for some time (see Leominster, raid of, 1052). An outlawed Saxon lord, Aelfgar, had fled to Ireland where he had built up a small army. In 1055 he crossed to Wales with 'eighteen pirate ships' according to Henry of Huntingdon. Joining forces with Gruffydd, the two forces moved into Herefordshire, raiding and looting as they went. They were met in battle by Earl Ralph 'the Timid' (son of King Edward the Confessor's sister, Goda) two miles from Worcester. The English were ordered to fight on horseback, 'contrary to their custom', although this seems only to have served the purpose of allowing quicker and easier flight. Earl Ralph fled first with his Norman and French cavalry, followed by the rest of the army, leaving 400 to 500 killed on the battlefield. Gruffydd and Aelfgar then went to Hereford where they forced their way into the cathedral, slaying seven canons who were guarding the door. Taking much loot with them, they returned to Wales.

Seal of Owain Glyndwr, who campaigned against the forces of King Henry IV at the beginning of the fifteenth century (see Woodbury Hill, 1405). Here he is shown as a heraldic knight on a fully caparisoned warhorse.

Worcester, battle of, 3 September 1651

Conclusive battle of the English Civil Wars, which was wide-ranging in its extent
and results.

KEY REFERENCES: Atkin, M. *Cromwell's Crowning Mercy: The Battle of Worcester 1651* (Sutton,
1998); Spicer, T. *The Battle of Worcester, 1651* (Paddy Griffith Associates, 2002).

With the execution of King Charles I on 30 January 1649, the Royalist claim
passed to his eldest son, also called Charles. He found support for his claim in
Scotland, due in large part to the English Parliament's refusal to introduce the
Solemn League and Covenant after Scottish help earlier in the First Civil War.
Charles took the Covenant himself and started to raise an army. Parliament
reacted to this by sending their New Model Army north under the command
of Oliver Cromwell, defeating the Scots at Dunbar on 4 September 1650.
Charles, outflanked at Stirling by the Parliamentarians crossing the River Forth
to the east by a bridge of boats, decided to march south and invade England.
Pursued by Parliamentarian forces, the Royalists reached Worcester on 22
August 1651, having left Stirling on 31 July. By the time it reached Worcester,
Charles' army consisted of some 10,000 Scots and 2,000 English Royalists,
although they reached the city in an exhausted and demoralised state, realising
that they were outnumbered and cut off as well as most of them being a long
way from home. Cromwell, who had also marched south, was met by
reinforcements, which gave him a total of 28,000 men concentrated around
Evesham to the south-east of Worcester. Cromwell must have felt he had the
opportunity to defeat this inferior enemy force in open battle, or to draw the
net more tightly around Worcester, which would enable a formal siege to begin
with defeat and surrender inevitable for the Royalists if this happened. This
helps to explain why Charles decided to fight before a full siege could be
started. It also explains why the fighting was conducted on a broad front, with
the Parliamentarians manoeuvring their force to outflank and eventually
encircle the Royalists.

Worcester was walled with further fortifications, most notably Fort Royal,
just outside the walls on the south-east side of the town on a knoll which can
still be climbed next to the excellent Commandery Museum, which focuses on
the Civil Wars. In an attempt to prevent encirclement, the Royalists held the
line of the River Teme and even land to the south of it, having lost control of
the important Upton Bridge across the Severn to the south on 28 August.
However, this gave their forces a long perimeter to defend, which even with
the advantage of having interior lines would be difficult to hold against such a
numerically superior opponent. The River Severn, running from north to

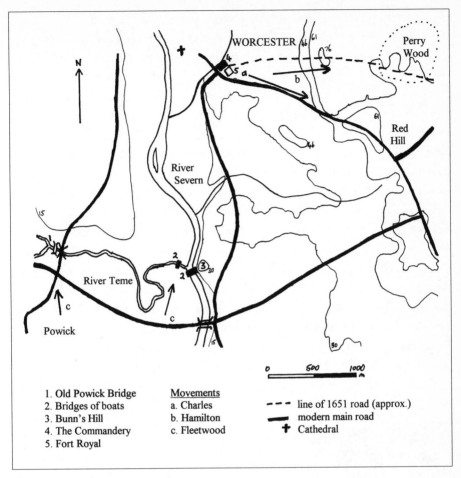

Battle of Worcester, 3 September 1651.

south, effectively bisected the battlefield, although Parliamentarian tactical ingenuity and planning helped to overcome this obstacle by building bridges of boats which made movements across the battlefield possible for their troops.

The Battle of Worcester began around the village of Powick to the south of Powick Bridge, where one of the earliest actions of the Civil Wars had taken place in 1642. The 12,000 Parliamentarians to the west of the Severn were commanded by General Fleetwood, who advanced from Upton to Powick, leaving the former location soon after 5.00 a.m. on 3 September, but only reaching the River Teme at around 2.30 p.m. This suggests that there was heavy skirmishing on the way, with Royalist musketeers lining the roadside hedges, while Fleetwood had to proceed with care and a lack of speed as he escorted a wagon train carrying boats for the bridge across the Teme. Held up at Powick by Scottish resistance around the church, Cromwell took decisive action. Artillery stationed on Bunn's Hill to the east of the Severn near the confluence of the Severn and Teme gave covering fire to allow the bridge of boats across the Severn to be swung into place by the current. Some contemporary sources favour a crossing just above (to the north of) the confluence, while most modern writers, including Tony Spicer, favour a crossing just below it. Arguments can be made for either, but the landscape and known course of the battle make the more southern crossing most likely. With the Royalists already under pressure from Fleetwood's advance and with close-range artillery support from Bunn's Hill (sadly now under threat from a proposed housing estate, despite this area being within the area of the registered battlefield), the Severn bridge of boats enabled Cromwell to reinforce Fleetwood. The small number of Highlanders under Pitscottie were unable to prevent this crossing and the Royalists were forced back to the north bank of the Teme via Powick Bridge by 3.00 p.m. The second bridge of boats was then constructed crossing the Teme, but this was difficult to cross, in part because of Scottish opposition but also due to the much steeper banks of the Teme. It is surprising that the Parliamentarians failed to force the Royalists back from the Teme at once, but instead Fleetwood sent men to the west of Powick Bridge, where they crossed the Teme at Bransford Bridge and also just to the east of the former bridge

Oliver Cromwell from a contemporary Dutch engraving, c.1651. Note the decapitated heads bottom left (Charles I) and right. The battle of Worcester in 1651 was one of Cromwell's greatest victories.

Charles II riding out of Worcester after a crushing defeat by the British Commonwealth on 3 September 1651.

where troops managed to ford the river. It would appear that the Royalists simply did not have the numbers to cope with these several crossings and they were forced back, in order at first, but as more Parliamentarians arrived the pressure increased, with retreat becoming an unruly rout as the troops rushed for the safety of the city via Town Bridge across the Severn. The meadows by the Teme, leading to the confluence of the two rivers, can now be viewed from a trail through land owned by Bennet's Dairy, or one can view this part of the battlefield from a viewing platform just to the east of the Severn at the meeting of the A422 and A38. The enthusiast can also gain access to the likely site of the Severn's bridge of boats by following a footpath along the east bank of the Severn.

The bulk of the fighting during the battle took place to the east of the Severn. Cromwell had taken possession of Red Hill on 29 August and had strengthened the site since then by spreading north into Perry Wood. Watching from the cathedral tower in Worcester, Charles and his commanders realised the importance of these positions. They also saw or were informed of the Parliamentarian troop movements to the west side of the Severn. This led them into launching an assault up Red Hill at around 4.00 p.m. Relatively few troops could be gathered together for this attack – probably 2,000 at the very most. The main attack went up the London Road from Sudbury Gate, past the Commandery (now traceable in the lanes just to the west of the modern road). The Duke of Hamilton peeled away to the left to attack Perry Wood, with both attacks meeting with initial success and capturing some cannon.

Cromwell managed to respond to this extremely quickly, leading to the suggestion that he was already on his way back to that part of the battlefield when news of the attack reached him. Perhaps the Royalist attack came too little too late, with Cromwell able to act decisively in the western sector of the battlefield before reaching the eastern action just in time. Certainly, Cromwell's arrival with cavalry began to turn back the Royalist advance, which had probably already run out of steam. The remaining Royalist reserves of cavalry sat out the battle to the north of the city wall on Pitchcroft Meadow, largely because they and their commander Leslie had decided that they could not win.

The battle quickly turned into a decisive victory for Cromwell. With no reserves forthcoming, the Royalists on Red Hill and in Perry Wood were soon exhausted and cut off. Retreat into the city followed, with the Parliamentarians pressing hard, gaining entry through Sudbury Gate and from the west over Town Bridge. Royalist resistance was maintained long enough for Charles to escape through St Martins Gate and thence after many an adventure, abroad. The battle finally brought the English, or more accurately British, Civil Wars to an end after nearly ten years of fighting. Worcester was a decisive victory which displayed tactical imagination and flexibility on Cromwell's part, although the failure to capture Charles was significant, not least in that this enabled him to return to be crowned King Charles II in 1660. Although the battlefield is largely within modern Worcester, there are many sites to visit as indicated above and in the key references.

Charles II and Jane Lane passing through a troop of Roundheads. Jane Lane acted as Charles' guide during a part of his flight in disguise after the Battle of Worcester in 1651. They are represented here making their way through a troop of Roundheads, who do not recognise the fugitive.

Worcester, siege of, (started 7 November) 1139

Failed siege by the Angevins during the Civil War of King Stephen's reign.

The attack began with an assault on the castle in Worcester, but this held out. The Angevins, who had come from Gloucester in an attempt to secure the important town of Worcester, then attacked the north walls. This was more successful, with some of the attackers getting into the town before escaping with loot and prisoners. However, the castle was not taken and the siege was raised.

Worcester, siege of, 1646

This important city fell to Parliament on 22 July 1646, three months after the surrender of King Charles I to the Scots.

Worksop, battle of, December 1460

Minor encounter fought between the Lancastrian Duke of Somerset and Richard, Duke of York on their way to the Battle of Wakefield. The Yorkist vanguard was defeated, but the encounter did not develop into a major action.

Wretham Heath, battle of, *see* Ringmere (Pit)

Wrotham (Hill), battle of, 28 January 1554

Fought as part of Wyatt's rebellion against the marriage of Philip of Spain and Queen Mary. Around 500 men led by Sir Henry Isley were defeated by around 600 Royalist troops, led by Sir Robert Southwell and Lord Abergavenny, as they marched to join Sir Thomas Wyatt, probably in Blacksole Field just to the north-west of Wrotham in Kent.

York, battles at, 1 November 866 and 21 March 867

A Viking raiding army captured York and held it over the winter before being attacked by the Northumbrians, who failed, losing both their kings in the process.

York, battle of, 923

The Viking King Raegnald captured York, becoming its first Norse ruler.

York, battle of, 28 January 1069

Setback for the Norman Conquest of the north of England.

With the fall of Durham to the English at the beginning of the year, William I realised that he would have to quell the rebellion against his rule himself. Accordingly, he marched to York. Before he reached it, the Norman force in the city was defeated by an English force on 28 January. The surviving Norman garrison was led by William Malet, who then occupied the new castle, which was on the site of the later Clifford's Tower. Relief arrived in the form of King William, who drove the rebels away, killing many. To secure York further he ordered the construction of a second motte and bailey castle.

York, battle of, 21 September 1069

Largest defeat suffered by the Normans in England.

KEY REFERENCE: Bennett, M. *Campaigns of the Norman Conquest* (Osprey Publishing, Oxford, 2001).

After the Norman defeat at York earlier in 1069, William Malet had attempted to stabilise the situation and awaited the arrival of King William. However, once William had left, the English received help from a Viking fleet, who combined with them to proclaim the teenager Edgar as king. Malet was decisively beaten on 21 September, with many of his men killed and himself captured. This was the heaviest defeat suffered by the Normans during the Conquest, even more serious than the defeat at Durham in January 1069. Having taken the city, the Anglo-Danish force took the two small castles as well. William returned to York after dealing with a less serious disturbance in the Shrewsbury area. However, he was delayed by bad weather, taking three weeks to find a crossing over the River Aire. Once William was across, the Danes withdrew to the south bank of the Humber, allowing William to occupy York, from where he carried out the devastating 'Harrying of the North' in 1071. He also bought off the Danes leading to their departure: a necessary act as William lacked an effective fleet to trouble them.

York, siege of, 21 April–15 July 1644

The Siege of York triggered the Battle of Marston Moor, with the loss of both by the Royalists, proving to be the end of any serious ambitions to control the North during the First Civil War.

KEY REFERENCE: Young, P. & Emberton, W. *Sieges of the Great Civil War* (Bell & Hyman, 1978).

Belasyse, the Governor of York, took the majority of his Royalist garrison to Selby in an attempt to catch Lord and Thomas Fairfax in early April. He failed and was defeated, leading to the Royalist Marquis of Newcastle racing south to re-garrison York before the Fairfaxes and their Scottish Covenanting allies could reach the city. He managed to do this, but found himself besieged. The Fairfaxes were on the eastern side, with the Scots under the Earl of Leven to the south-west and west. The encirclement of the city was completed in the first week of June, when the Earl of Manchester arrived with his Army of the Eastern Association, filling in the circle to the north. With this, King Charles I dispatched his nephew Prince Rupert with a large field army, which marched to York's relief via a circuitous route, collecting more men as it went. The Parliamentarians attempted to take the city by digging and placing two mines

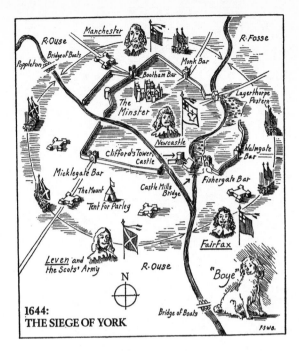

1644:
THE SIEGE OF YORK

Siege of York, 1644.

under Walmgate Bar (the site of a Parliamentarian battery on Lamel Hill to the south-east of this gate by the University can still be seen) and St Mary's Tower, but the latter went off too soon, leading to the storming party being isolated and repulsed. The Parliamentarians and Scots, on learning of the imminent arrival of Rupert's army, drew off to a ridge above Marston Moor to the west of the city, but Rupert had outfoxed them, swinging down and into York from the north on 1 July, relieving the city.

Following the resulting Battle of Marston Moor, the siege was renewed on 4 July. It was clear that no fresh relief would come, and with their enemies poised to assault the city on 11 July, the garrison arranged a parley, surrendering on terms on 15 July.

It is clear that King George VI was not wrong when he claimed that 'the history of York is the history of England', for in this siege and its surrounding events one can see what is a microcosm of the British Civil Wars, as well as the suggestion that what happened in and around York during 1644 was fundamental to the history not just of England, but of the entire British Isles.

LIST OF ILLUSTRATIONS

INTEGRATED ILLUSTRATIONS

56 Battle of Blore Heath, 23 September 1459. Author's collection.

58 Edward Montagu, 2nd Earl of Manchester, was, and is often criticised for being over-cautious to the point of treachery. In 1643 his army captured Bolingbroke Castle after defeating a Royalist attempt to relieve the castle at the Battle of Winceby, which was won by Cromwell and Fairfax. He is depicted in a silver medal he issued as a military reward to his soldiers. Jonathan Reeve.

60 Battle of Boroughbridge, 16 March 1322. Author's collection.

62 Battle of Bosworth, 22 August 1485: probable site (after Foss, 1990). Author's collection.

69 Battle of Braddock Down, 19 January 1643. Author's collection.

74 Siege of Bristol, 1643. P.S.W. Beck.

76 Bristol, 1645. Engraving showing Bristol Castle before it was demolished in 1656. Prince Rupert hoped to use the castle as a final stronghold in 1645, but damage to the wall meant that surrender was inevitable. Jonathan Reeve.

78 Battle of Britain, 10 July–31 October 1940. Author's collection.

89 Carlisle, 1315. Initial letter of Edward II's charter to Carlisle in 1316. The Scots are shown attacking the city with a 'machine for casting stones', while a miner with a pick works at the foot of a wall. Jonathan Reeve.

91 Battle of Chalgrove, 18 June 1643. Author's collection.

92 Drawing from the statue of Sir John Hampden in St Stephen's Hall, Westminster. His nickname, 'the Patriot', explains his lasting popularity. He died as a result of wounds suffered at Chalgrove in 1643. Jonathan Reeve.

94 Battle of Cheriton, 29 March 1644. Author's collection.

99 Chester, 1643–6. Sketch from the 1640s by Randle Holme showing the difficult approach across the Dee bridge. This was one of the factors which made bombardment a better option for the attacking Parliamentarians than storming the town. Jonathan Reeve.

104 Siege coinage like this was common throughout the Civil War. This piece was cut from gold plate and then stamped, being used by Royalists during the 1648 Siege of Colchester. Jonathan Reeve.

111 Battle of Cropredy Bridge, 29 June 1644. Author's collection.

121 Missile weapons such as the sling shown on the left would have been crucial in defence at the Siege of Dover in 1217. The larger figure, the socially superior knight, was crucial in the hand-to-hand fighting which developed once the French breached the defences. Jonathan Reeve.

127 Battle of Edgcote, 26 July 1469. Author's collection.

become the focus of fierce fighting. The motto here translates as 'The Truth Prevails' and was the standard of William Keith, the Earl Marischal of Scotland. A large number of replica standards from the battle are on display at Etal Castle near the battlefield. Tempus Archive.

149 Part of a letter from Thomas Ruthal, Bishop of Durham, to Thomas Wolsey, written on 20 September 1513, including a full account of the Battle of Flodden and the death of King James IV, whose body was found 'having manye wounds and naked'. The first complete paragraph on this page includes an explanation of the advantage of the English bill over the long spear favoured by the Scots. Tempus Archive.

153 Battle of Fornham St Genevieve, 1173. Author's collection.

154 Early medieval ship showing the characteristic pointed prow and stern, although the height is exaggerated here. This is shown with a stern rudder rather than the earlier steering oar. Viking fleets of the late eleventh century would have consisted of ships like these. Hardrada's fleet in 1066 allegedly contained 300 such vessels, which disembarked troops to fight at the battle of Fulford Gate. Jonathan Reeve.

159 Siege of Gloucester, 1643. P.S.W. Beck.

161 Gravesend, 1667. Dutch print of the 1660s showing the first episode of de Ruyter's audacious and successful raid in the Medway, here showing the capture of Sheerness Fort in 1667. Jonathan Reeve.

164 Battle of Halidon Hill, 19 July 1333. Author's collection.

165 Nineteenth-century drawing showing bitter close-quarter fighting at Halidon Hill in 1333, when the Scottish army attacked on foot. Note the accurate preponderance of spears. Jonathan Reeve.

167 Battle of Hastings, 14 October 1066. Author's collection.

168 Hastings, 1066. Scene from the Bayeaux Tapestry showing Norman horse transport with ship's crew. Jonathan Reeve.

169 Hastings, 1066. Page from Simeon of Durham's *History of the Kings of England*, describing the Norman conquest. Simeon wrote this chronicle at the beginning of the twelfth century. Jonathan Reeve.

170 Seal of Battle Abbey. William ordered the abbey to be built on the site of the Battle of Hastings fought in 1066, with the high altar traditionally marking the spot where Harold fell. This remains the strongest evidence for the precise location of the battlefield. Other, also circumstantial evidence suggests the battle may have been fought slightly to the north on Caldbec Hill. Tempus Archive.

172 The death of King Edwin at Hatfield Chase, 633. The victorious Mercians and Welsh would have been better clothed, and chariots had disappeared from use over 500 years before this battle. Jonathan Reeve.

179 Battle of Homildon Hill, 14 September 1402. Author's collection.

223 Battle of Maldon, 10 August 991. Author's collection.

224 Part of a twelfth-century manuscript detailing the payment of danegeld by Aethelred II following the Battle of Maldon in 991. Jonathan Reeve.

224 Archer typical of the Anglo-Saxon period, for example those described in the epic poem *The Battle of Maldon* (991) where 'bows were busy'. Unarmoured and equipped with a short bow around 120cm long, archers rarely formed a decisive element in battles throughout this period. Jonathan Reeve.

224 Reconstruction of a typical Viking long sword showing heavy straight blade, simple guard and decorated pommel. Such swords were relatively high-status weapons compared to the more commonly used spears and javelins. In the epic poem *The Battle of Maldon* (991), the most detailed description of a Viking battle mentions the use of both swords and spears ('darts'). Jonathan Reeve.

226 Armoured foot soldier with a bundle of throwing spears rather than a single longer, stouter, thrusting spear. This soldier is typical of those who fought on both sides of the Civil War of Stephen's reign, for example at the battle of Malmesbury, 1153. Jonathan Reeve.

228 Battle of Marston Moor, 2 July 1644. Author's collection.

229 Sir Thomas Fairfax, commander-in-chief of the New Model Army from 1645 and formerly a thorn in the Royalists' side in Yorkshire, playing a prominent role in the 1643 campaign before commanding the parliamentary horse at Marston Moor in 1644 on the right wing. Of Fairfax, John Milton wrote: 'Fairfax, whose name in armies through Europe sings, filling each mouth with envy or with praise.' Jonathan Reeve.

230 Illustration suggesting that war was not far away in 1642 as the Royalist or Cavalier dog squares up to the Parliamentarian or Roundhead dog. Note that the Royalist dog is portrayed as a poodle belonging to Prince Rupert. This dog, named Boy, was a target for Parliamentarian satire throughout the war, until the poodle's untimely death at Marston Moor in 1644. Jonathan Reeve.

230 Parliamentary standards. Each troop of horse during the Civil Wars would usually carry its own standard. These often reflected the personality and personal tastes of their commander to a greater extent than the more stylised colours of foot companies and regiments. There would have been numerous standards at large-scale actions such as that at Marston Moor in 1644. Jonathan Reeve.

237 Battle of Mortimer's Cross, 2 February 1461. Author's collection.

240 Battle of Myton, 20 September 1319. Author's collection.

241 By the time of the Battle of Myton in 1319, plate armour was becoming a more common sight on the battlefield. This figure has a particularly well-articulated suit of armour, especially in the gauntlets and foot pieces. Tempus Archive.

244 Battle of Nantwich, 25 January 1644. Author's collection.

270   Sculpture showing the massive mid-fifteenth-century gun known as Mons Meg on the left, still to be seen at Edinburgh Castle along with two other, later, artillery pieces (sixteenth-century culverins). Pieces such as the latter pair formed James IV's impressive modern artillery train of seventeen guns for the campaign of 1513 which included the siege of Norham Castle. Tempus Archive.

270   Depiction of a sixteenth-century siege from Raphael Holinshed's *Chronicles of England, Scotlande and Irelande*, published in 1577, showing the use of heavy siege artillery behind gabions. James IV's army had an impressive modern artillery train. Note the use of light pieces and hand-guns by the defenders. The extremely strong castle of Norham by the River Tweed was taken in a similar fashion by the army of James IV of Scotland at the Siege of Norham Castle in 1513. Jonathan Reeve.

270   Naval battle at North Foreland in 1666 between Monk and de Ruyter, from a contemporary Dutch print. Jonathan Reeve.

273   Battle of Northallerton, 22 August 1138. Author's collection.

274   The standard eponymous to the battle known more commonly as the Battle of Northallerton, 1138, from a near contemporary manuscript of the Abbot of Rievaulx, along with a description of the battle. Prior Richard of Hexham described the standard as being made from a ship's mast. Jonathan Reeve.

277   Battle of Northampton, 10 July 1460. Author's collection.

279   The Duke of Marlborough from a Dutch engraving of the early eighteenth century. In 1685 he was still Major General John, Lord Churchill and second in command of King James II's army during Monmouth's rebellion which included the action at Norton St Philip in 1685. Jonathan Reeve.

283   Battle of Otterburn, 19–20 August 1388. Author's collection.

284   This standard was said to have been carried by Archibald Douglas of Cavers at the battle of Otterburn in 1388. However, it has been identified to date from the sixteenth century, and is therefore more contemporary with Flodden. Tempus Archive.

290   Siege of Plymouth, 1643–1645. P.S.W. Beck.

295   General John Lambert, the prime Parliamentarian General in the north of England during the Second Civil War, see Preston, 1648. Jonathan Reeve.

302   Siege of Reading, 15–28 April 1643. P.S.W. Beck.

306   Rochester Castle, 1215. The seal of Rochester shown in around 1300, showing the massive square keep with its forebuilding just to the right. The keep had to be repaired following the successful mining operation under the south-east corner during the siege of 1215. Jonathan Reeve.

308   Battle of Roundway Down, 13 July 1643. Author's collection.

311   Battle of Rowton Heath, 24 September 1645. Author's collection.

370 Battle of Wakefield, 30 December 1460. Author's collection.

377 Battle of Winceby, 11 October 1643. Author's collection.

378 Mounted dragoons of the First Civil War. Mounted dragoons were issued with shorter muskets than foot musketeers, and were mounted on smaller horses than cavalry troopers. Dragoons rarely fired from horseback, preferring to use cover when dismounted. Parliamentarian armies tended to have more dragoons than Royalist armies, and were often deployed as the advance guard, a highly dangerous formation, as at the battle of Winceby, 1643. Jonathan Reeve.

383 Seal of Owain Glyndwr, who campaigned against the forces of King Henry IV at the beginning of the fifteenth century (see Woodbury Hill, 1405). Here he is shown as a heraldic knight on a fully caparisoned warhorse. Jonathan Reeve.

385 Battle of Worcester, 3 September 1651. Author's collection.

386 Oliver Cromwell from a contemporary Dutch engraving, c.1651. Note the decapitated heads bottom left (Charles I) and right. The battle of Worcester in 1651 was one of Cromwell's greatest victories. Jonathan Reeve.

387 Charles II riding out of Worcester after a crushing defeat by the British Commonwealth on 3 September 1651. Jonathan Reeve.

388 Charles II and Jane Lane passing through a troop of Roundheads. Jane Lane acted as Charles' guide during a part of his flight in disguise after the Battle of Worcester in 1651. They are represented here making their way through a troop of Roundheads, who do not recognise the fugitive. Jonathan Reeve.

393 Siege of York, 1644. P.S.W. Beck.

COLOUR PLATES

1   Contemporary woodcut showing the devastation caused by a mine or mortar during the Siege of Colchester, 1648. Tempus Archive.

2   Cropredy Bridge, 1644. This view from Cropredy Bridge towards Hays Bridge (off the picture to the far left) shows the flat-topped hill on which sits the village of Wardington, and demonstrates that any troops in and around that village would be invisible to troops just across Cropredy Bridge. Author's collection.

3   Edgehill, 1642, looking north from the top of Edgehill by the Castle Inn over the village of Radway onto the battlefield. Author's collection.

4   The death and mutilation of Simon de Montfort at the battle of Evesham in 1265. British Library MS Cotton Nero D II, fol. 177r.

5   The firing of an English 'serpentine' from the Piper's Hill position outside Branxton village at Flodden, 1513. The English had five such pieces with them, along with eighteen lighter guns, while the Scots deployed generally heavier siege pieces. Courtesy of Keith Durham.

6   Flodden, 1513. The view from the right-centre of the Scottish position towards the Piper's Hill monument, which is visible in the middle distance. The ridge running to the right of the monument is where the English formed up. Author's collection.

7   Flodden, 1513, looking from the right-centre of the Scottish position towards the village of Branxton, nestling behind the low ridge occupied by the English. Author's collection.

8   Fornham St Genevieve, 1173, showing the tower of the ruined church of Fornham St Genevieve – the only spot from which the church can be seen from public rights of way. Author's collection.

9   Hastings, 1066, Bayeux Tapestry. The Norman cavalry ride up against the English shield wall. By special permission of the City of Bayeux.

10 *Battle of Hastings, 1066* by Frank W. Wilkin (1800?-1842). This painting was originally commissioned for the Great Hall at Battle Abbey and the canvas measures 27ft by 17ft. It was recently discovered under floorboards in a gallery in Hastings. English Heritage.

11 Lansdown, 1643, looking up the hill with the modern road following the line of trees on the left. The Royalists had to attack up this slope towards the waiting Parliamentarians at the top. Author's collection.

12 Lichfield, April 1643, showing the faint remains of a Civil War earthwork in the modern Prince Rupert's Way with the cathedral spire to the left. Author's collection.

13 Lostwithiel, 1644. Shown is Restormel Castle, which was stormed by Royalist troops led by Richard Grenville on 21 August 1644. Author's collection.

14 Lostwithiel, 1644. The prehistoric remains of Castle Dore where Parliamentarian forces made their last stand. Author's collection.

15 Lostwithiel, 1644. The view from the prehistoric fort of Castle Dore towards the advancing Royalists. Author's collection.

16 *Cromwell after Marston Moor* by Ernest Croft. As Cromwell and his weary troopers drew rein after routing Goring's horse on the evening of 2 July 1644, they had played a decisive role in winning Parliament's greatest victory of the war so far. Jonathan Reeve.

17 Mortimer's Cross, 1461, from beside the River Lugg looking towards the Yorkist lines. Note the steep hills in the left background, which would have made an advance from that direction all but impossible. Author's collection.

18 George Cruikshank's depiction of the Peterloo 'massacre' in 1819. Maximum sympathy for the crowd is gained through showing them harmless and helpless under the sabres of the cavalry. Jonathan Reeve.

19 Rochester Castle, 1215, showing the rebuilt circular south-east tower, which was necessary after King John's mining operation during the siege of 1215. Author's collection.

20 Roundway Down, 1643, looking from the rear left of Waller's position, close to the Battlefield Trust's interpretation panel, towards Morgan's Hill. Author's collection.

21 Roundway Down, 1643, looking from the foot of the Down towards Oliver's Castle showing the steep gullies down which some of the Parliamentarian horses tumbled. Author's collection.

22 The second of the Dummer maps of the Battle of Sedgemoor, 1685, showing the nature of the historic environment (e.g. Chedzoy 'island' at the top left-centre) and the detailed dispositions of the troops after the Royalist cavalry were sent across the Upper and Lower Plungeons. The Pepys Library, Magdalene College, Cambridge.

23 Stoke Field, 1487, showing the hill up which Henry VII's army advanced to attack the rebels at the top of the slope. Author's collection.

24 Stratton, 1643, showing one of the deep lanes up which the Royalists advanced to attack. Author's collection.

25 Tewkesbury, 1471. This view shows the surviving part of the Gastons Field, spared from housing after a Public Inquiry. Steve Goodchild.

BLACK AND WHITE PLATES

31 Prince Rupert in the regalia of a knight of the garter. Some of this flamboyance was taken into battle (for example at Aldbourne Chase in 1643), as Rupert's horse swept all before them at the start of the Civil War. Jonathan Reeve.

32 Somewhat fanciful version of Richard III's charge at Bosworth in 1485 with anachronistic weapons, armour and equipment. From Abraham Cooper's *The Battle of Bosworth Field*, 1825. Geoffrey Wheeler.

33 Bosworth, 1485. The view from the top of Ambion Hill showing the position of Richard III's 'battle' as marked by the standard in the foreground, following the Bosworth Battlefield Centre's current interpretation of the battle. Author's collection.

34 Barnet, 1471, showing modern Hadley Common where the centre divisions probably clashed and which in 1471 would have been treeless. Author's collection.

35 Blore Heath, 1459. The Hempmill Brook flows through the gully across the centre of the photograph, which is taken from the Lancastrian right-centre as it advanced down the slope. Author's collection.

36 Blore Heath, 1459, showing the Hempmill Brook looking west. Note the steep slope to the north up which the Lancastrians attempted to attack. Author's collection.

37 Bosworth, 1485. Michael K. Jones' favoured site for the battle taken from the top of a windmill mound with Fenny Drayton in the left middle distance. Author's collection.

38 Braddock Down, 1643. This is part of the site favoured for the battle until publication of Wilton's article – the Parliamentarians would have deployed on the far slope, which would have been open ground if it was then part of the moor, looking west. Author's collection.

39 Cheriton, 1644. The view from the Parliamentarian left towards Cheriton Wood on the skyline, showing the valley between the southern ridge (out of shot to the right) and the 'intermediate' ridge, where much of the fighting took place. D. Rayner.

40 Cheriton, 1644, from the 'intermediate ridge' towards the Parliamentarian-held ridge in the distance, with Cheriton Wood on the left. D. Rayner.

41 Cheriton, 1644, from Hinton Ampner and the likely site of some Parliamentarian artillery towards the southern of the three ridges, with Cheriton Wood to the right. The valley to the front is the site favoured by John Adair for the main fighting. D. Rayner.

42 Clifton Moor, 1745, looking south out of the village. Government troops attacked down the slope towards the spot from where the photograph was taken. Author's collection.

43 The tower of St Mary's-at-the-Walls in Colchester showing the brick rebuilding of the top of the structure, necessary after the 1648 siege. The tower became a target as it served as a gun platform for a Royalist saker. Phil Jones.

44 Evidence of shot holes in timber of the 'Old Siege House' in East Street, Colchester. The Royalists attempted a break-out past this house on 5 July 1648, but were driven back. Phil Jones.

45 Evesham, 1265, looking north from a position just to the west of the houses along Greenhill. Author's collection.

46 Halidon Hill, 1333. The view from the right of the English position looking across to Witches Knowe from where the Scots advanced. The land around the farm on the right of the photograph would no doubt have been boggy ground at the time of the battle, as would the valley off the photograph to the right. Author's collection.

47 Hastings, 1066. The view from the modern terrace walk about half the way up Senlac Hill, looking down to the centre of William's lines. Author's collection.

48 Homildon Hill, 1402. The photograph is taken from where most of the English were formed up, with Homildon (Humbleton) Hill on the left and Harehope Hill to the right. The English archers formed up on the latter, with the protection of the wooded gulley between them and the Scots. Author's collection.

49 Admiral Robert Blake, who was the key English admiral during the first Anglo-Dutch War and achieved a mixed record against the able Admirals van Tromp and de Witt, winning at Kentish Knock in 1652. Tempus Archive.

50 Langport, 1645, looking towards the Parliamentarian positions on Pitney Hill, taken from the Royalist left flank. Note the thick hedges flanking the modern road. Author's collection.

51 Ralph, Lord Hopton, long time friend and, during the First Civil War, sparring partner, of Sir William Waller. Hopton was badly wounded two days after the Battle of Lansdown in 1643 when an ammunition wagon exploded nearby. Tempus Archive.

52 Lewes, 1264, at the top of the Downs above Lewes, showing Burne's 'parade ground' where de Montfort probably formed up his army. Author's collection.

53 Maldon, 991. The view from Northey Island held by the Vikings across the causeway towards the East Saxon position. Author's collection.

54   Marston Moor, 1644, looking from the rear left of the Royalist position towards the slope of Braham Hill on which the Parliamentarians and Scots deployed. The trees on the skyline mark 'Cromwell's Plump'. Author's collection.

55   David Leslie, first Lord Newark, Scottish commander who led the Scottish contingent of horse on the triumphant allied left-wing at the Battle of Marston Moor in 1644. Tempus Archive.

56   Myton, 1319, showing the flat field across which the Scots advanced to meet the English, once the latter had crossed the River Swale. Author's collection.

57   Naseby, 1645. The view from the Cromwell Monument towards Dust Hill, looking across Broadmoor. Much of the infantry fight would have taken place in the area in the foreground. Author's collection.

58   Henry Ireton, Cromwell's son-in-law who commanded the left-wing of Parliamentarian horse at the battle of Naseby, 1645. Tempus Archive.

59   Newark, 1645–46. The view of the Queen's Sconce, constructed by the Royalists as protection for the town. Author's collection.

60   Nibley Green, 1470, showing the steep slope down which Lisle advanced. Author's collection.

61   Imaginative depiction of the Battle of Northallerton in 1138 with the standard at the midst of the English army. Accounts do not mention a large crucifix. Jonathan Reeve.

62   Otterburn, 1388. The view from the edge of the copse with the Percy Cross looking towards the Scottish lines. Author's collection.

63   Solway Moss, 1542, looking from the furthest forward position of the Scots towards the main English line to the right centre. Author's collection.

64   Towton, 1461, looking towards the Yorkist-held ridge in the distance from close by Dacre's Cross. Author's collection.

65   Towton, 1461, looking towards the River Cock showing the steep slopes down which many retreating Lancastrians must have slid and tumbled, before being caught by their pursuers. Author's collection.

66   Towton, 1461. Evocative portrayal of the rout of the Lancastrians at the Battle of Towton in 1461. Many died trying to cross the swollen and close-to-freezing waters of the River Cock. Jonathan Reeve.

67   Wakefield, 1460. The view from the foot of Sandal Castle's mound over the area where the fighting took place. Author's collection.

68   Wakefield, 1460. The chantry chapel outside which the Earl of Rutland was probably killed by Lord Clifford. Author's collection.

69   Winceby, 1643. The view from the line of the 1643 road down which the Royalists advanced towards the ridge in the distance occupied by the Parliamentarian horse. Author's collection.

70 Worcester, 1651. This standard was carried at the Battle of Worcester. It is the Royal Banner of Scotland, which would have been a target for Parliamentarian attacks if it was brought close to the front line. Tempus Archive.

71 Parliamentarian army soldiers were sporadically issued with Bibles. This is the title page of the *Soldiers' Pocket Bible* (1643). Tempus Archive.